THE FIRST VICTORY

THE FIRST VICTORY

THE SECOND WORLD WAR AND THE EAST AFRICA CAMPAIGN

ANDREW STEWART

YALE UNIVERSITY PRESS
NEW HAVEN AND LONDON

Copyright © 2016 Andrew Stewart

All rights reserved. This book may not be reproduced in whole or in part, in any form (beyond that copying permitted by Sections 107 and 108 of the U.S. Copyright Law and except by reviewers for the public press) without written permission from the publishers.

For information about this and other Yale University Press publications, please contact:
U.S. Office: sales.press@yale.edu   yalebooks.com
Europe Office: sales@yaleup.co.uk   yalebooks.co.uk

Typeset in Adobe Garamond Pro by IDSUK (DataConnection) Ltd
Printed in Great Britain by TJ International Ltd, Padstow, Cornwall

Library of Congress Cataloging-in-Publication Data

Names: Stewart, Andrew, 1970- author.
Title: The first victory : the Second World War and the East Africa campaign / Andrew Stewart.
Description: New Haven : Yale University Press, 2016.
Identifiers: LCCN 2016031009 | ISBN 9780300208559 (cloth : alk. paper)
Subjects: LCSH: World War, 1939-1945—Campaigns—Africa, East.
Classification: LCC D766.84 .S74 2016 | DDC 940.54/233—dc23
LC record available at https://lccn.loc.gov/2016031009

A catalogue record for this book is available from the British Library.

10 9 8 7 6 5 4 3 2 1

CONTENTS

	List of Maps and Illustrations	*vi*
	Acknowledgements	*vii*
	Introduction: A Forgotten Campaign	*x*
1	Strategic Miscalculation	1
2	Hoping for the Best	21
3	War Comes to East Africa	48
4	Imperial Defeat: The Surrender of British Somaliland	71
5	Preparing for the Counter-offensive	95
6	The Advance from Kenya	121
7	Second Front: Striking from the Sudan	148
8	Triumph in the Mountains: The Battle of Keren	165
9	A Third Front: The Patriots	191
10	Winning the War, Worrying about the Peace	204
	Conclusion: The British Empire's First Victory	232
	Notes	*249*
	Bibliography	*284*
	Index	*293*

MAPS AND ILLUSTRATIONS

Maps

		page
1	Italian invasion of British Somaliland.	76
2	Defence of the Tug Argan Gap.	80
3	Advance of British and Commonwealth forces from Kenya into Italian Somaliland and Ethiopia.	127
4	Advance of British and Commonwealth forces from the Sudan into Eritrea.	154
5	Battle of Keren (the opening phase).	167
6	Battle of Keren (the final phase).	179
7	Advance of Patriot forces.	196

Illustration credits

4 © The National Archives (INF3/415). 9 *The War Weekly*, April 1941. All other illustrations are courtesy of Ministry of Defence © Crown Copyright (2016). Reproduced under the terms of the Open Government Licence http://www.nationalarchives.gov.uk/doc/open-government-licence/version/3/.

ACKNOWLEDGEMENTS

I WOULD LIKE TO thank the staff of the following archives and libraries for the assistance they provided whilst I was undertaking research for this project: Bodleian Library, Oxford; Borthwick Institute for Archives, University of York; British Library, London; Churchill Archives Centre, Churchill College, Cambridge; Imperial War Museum, London; Kenya National Archives and Documentation Service, Nairobi; Liddell Hart Centre for Military Archives, King's College London; National Archives of Australia, Canberra; National Army Museum, London; South African National Records and Archives Service, Pretoria; Sudan Archive, University of Durham; The National Archives, London; The Royal Fusiliers Archives, London; and, finally, both the King's College London Library and the Joint Services Command and Staff College Library. I am also extremely grateful to the holder of Field Marshal Lord Archibald Wavell's papers who was most generous in allowing access to the relevant documents. Where appropriate, I must thank the trustees or similar of those archives above that have kindly granted access and permission the use of selected brief quotations. The material examined has proven to be of considerable benefit. All reasonable efforts have been made to acknowledge copyright but if there are any omissions these will be corrected at the first opportunity.

ACKNOWLEDGEMENTS

The book's completion has been greatly assisted by the many individuals who have been willing to offer advice or information and I would like to extend my sincere thanks to them all. I am particularly grateful to friends within the Defence Studies Department, King's College London, who have provided their support, most notably Dr Jonathan Hill. Professor Ashley Jackson also generously discussed many of the themes referenced within the text. I am grateful also to my colleagues at the Royal College of Defence Studies who offered huge encouragement and helped me create the time needed to complete the writing. In this regard, I must thank especially the Commandant, Sir Tom Phillips KCMG, and my Senior Directing Staff counterpart James Kidner MVO, without whom it would not have been possible to produce this book. My former students at the Joint Services Command and Staff College who helped shape my initial thinking about the campaign and the Members at the Royal College of Defence Studies who have withstood the writing process must also all be thanked for their patience and good wishes. This book has been written, for the most part, in Oxford and London but sections were also drafted while I was travelling and working in France, Spain, Italy, Canada and the United States.

Andrea Jackson and Luke Vivian-Neal completed research for me in The National Archives. Gustav Betz conducted an initial review of the holdings in the South African archives and Vera Plint carried out copying work in Pretoria. In Nairobi, Humphrey Mathenge copied many relevant files relating to the local political and military wartime situation. Once again, David Steeds has read and commented upon sections of the draft manuscript and I remain indebted to him for the advice and guidance he has offered over nearly twenty-five years which has helped make me a better scholar and writer than would otherwise have been the case. I also welcome the comments made by the anonymous reviewers of the initial book proposal and the first draft version of the manuscript which proved both insightful and of considerable assistance in terms of refining some of the arguments put forward in the text.

ACKNOWLEDGEMENTS

The encouragement and support provided by Heather McCallum and Rachael Lonsdale at Yale University Press throughout the production of this book has been most welcome. I would also like to thank Beth Humphries for copy-editing the text, Martin Brown for drawing up the maps, Samantha Cross for producing the plate section, and Ian Craine for providing the index.

I am extremely fortunate in the support that has been provided by my parents throughout my studies and subsequent academic career. My wife Joanne continues to make enormous sacrifices in terms of the time we are able to spend together and I consider myself particularly fortunate that she remains both understanding and supportive of my work. It is to her that I dedicate this book.

The analysis, opinions and conclusions expressed or implied are those of the author and do not represent the views of the Joint Services Command and Staff College, the Royal College of Defence Studies, the UK Ministry of Defence or any other government agency. Any errors of fact are the responsibility of the author and, if notified, I will make every reasonable effort to correct them.

Oxford, June 2016

INTRODUCTION
A Forgotten Campaign

On 27 November 1941, the mountain fortress of Gondar, the last remaining stronghold of Italy's once apparently great empire in eastern Africa, surrendered following a final attack by British and Commonwealth troops. This assault lasted less than a day but it marked the culmination of a military campaign that had begun nearly eighteen months before and which had witnessed some remarkable acts of leadership, physical endurance and individual bravery. The headlines the following morning in the major British newspapers instead focused on the fighting then going on farther north in the Western Desert, where Operation 'Crusader' was attempting to break the long-running siege of the port of Tobruk. It took two days before the story was published and, whilst it featured on page four of *The Times*, the tabloid *Daily Express* and *Daily Mirror* gave it only small columns on their back pages.[1] The final success won by British and Commonwealth forces in this long and often exhausting campaign received the briefest of mentions. There was, however, an interesting commentary offered by one of the newspaper editors who told his readers:

> Gondar has gone. Or shall we say Gondar has come? The last outpost of Musso's tottering, or rather tottered and tattered, Empire is occupied

INTRODUCTION

by us after two Italian mutinies and one final surrender. That means the end of a six-year Italian attempt to pick a quarrel with us in colonial territories where we tried to deal with gentlemen but found they were jackals. The jackal's [Mussolini's] backyard has now been dug and turned over by the British Army.[2]

Whilst the first part of the statement was correct – this indeed marked the fall of the Italian East African Empire – the rest was far from the case, particularly in terms of the pre-war Anglo-Italian relationship which had not always been the subject of such animosity.[3] This fairly crude wartime propaganda also, surprisingly, entirely overlooked the prominent role that had been played by British and Commonwealth forces in winning the battle; indeed it had been a campaign that depended on contributions of manpower and equipment offered up from around the British Empire. Nonetheless, it was at least a reference to a campaign that had, for all intents and purposes, been forgotten for some months. Following the liberation of the Ethiopian capital of Addis Ababa in April 1941, attention had swiftly turned to the defeats that followed in North Africa, Greece and Crete, not to mention the drama that rapidly developed on the Russian steppe as the newest members of the alliance fighting the Axis powers seemed poised for a catastrophic collapse. In this context an assault on a remote mountain fortress was no longer much of a priority for the newspapers in Fleet Street or the people who read them.

Whilst it was one of the Second World War's most overlooked campaigns at the time and has largely remained so ever since, the fighting that began in early July 1940 in eastern Africa should have featured much more prominently in the crowded literature of the conflict. On one side was an Italian army which included nearly 300,000 European and African troops; on the other, a British-led force just one-quarter its size and made up predominantly of men from across Britain's imperial territories, supported by small French and Belgian contingents. After an initial series of Italian advances, the much smaller of the two forces began a well-organised response the following January; it reached its conclusion just eleven months later in the mountains at Gondar. To get there the victorious coalition carried out one of the entire war's most successful mechanised pursuits, launched assaults on what looked to be impenetrable mountain strongholds and even carried out an audacious amphibious landing. Brilliant logistical planning was required to overcome an often inhospitable and unforgiving terrain which encompassed a huge area extending from the flat, featureless and almost waterless bush of the Northern Frontier District, where Kenya bordered Italian Somaliland, to the rolling bush and hill country of Ethiopia.[4] Added to this were the extremes of weather, from tremendous dry heat through to the humidity of the coastal areas and the cold of the mountains, as well as the threat of the arrival of monsoon rains, all of which meant it was not an area of operations suited to a lengthy military adventure. It was a campaign fought on several fronts and to the north, in the Sudan, whilst the weather was also extreme and the terrain, at times, bordering on impassable, the distances were much shorter and the attacking troops much better equipped.

Despite its tone, the *Daily Express* was not wrong to highlight the abject nature of the Italian defeat, as 50,000 prisoners were captured and 360,000 square miles occupied all at a cost of 500 casualties amongst the British and Commonwealth forces and just 150 men killed. During the course of the fighting there were numerous military curiosities for the British Army and its imperial counterparts, including the last significant cavalry charge made by an opponent, the final sounding of a bugle call to direct the movement of a large body of troops, the first significant mutiny of British infantry troops during the war, and the earliest awards of the Victoria Cross during the Africa campaign. There was also the first loss of territory suffered by the British Empire, with the surrender of British Somaliland, but the campaign also saw the first liberation of occupied land when the small protectorate on the Horn of Africa was later recovered. All of this has been almost entirely overlooked despite, in many respects, providing a perfect episode of the Second World War to study, with its incredible

INTRODUCTION

military engagements and fascinating personalities and human stories which bring alive the nature and character of war.

There are references to the East Africa campaign in the subsequent official histories and longer sections in the individual unit accounts, but the existing bibliography is not a large one. Although an extended narrative was produced by a British Army officer, involving years of preparatory work after the Second World War had ended, no resulting dedicated history was ever written. The work that had been done was heavily edited and later included in the first volume of the more general account detailing the war fought in North Africa and the Mediterranean.[5] An official Italian history was published in 1952 – with a second edition in 1971 – despite there reportedly having been very few official documents left at war's end to provide a factual basis for the writing.[6] A report written in 1970 by the 'Enemy Document Section' of the Cabinet Office in London noted that most high-level documents were believed to have been buried somewhere in Ethiopia and never found.[7] In 1951, some civil administration and police documents had even been observed being sold in the markets of Addis Ababa to be used as cigarette paper. Those that were discovered were transferred to Khartoum, from where they also subsequently disappeared.

In addition to this official work, a small number of military officers and members of the press who were present have produced campaign studies or their recollections of what took place. These accounts effectively convey the often unplanned nature of the fighting and the vastness of the battlespace, but they tend to provide largely narrative descriptions of the fighting they witnessed, with little or no analysis of how this fitted into the wider war.[8] These include, most notably, the recollections of G.L. Steer and Ted Crosskill, both intelligence officers who wrote about the campaign, and the correspondents Kenneth Gandar Dower, also an explorer and aviator, and Carel Birkby, a South African who was embedded with his nation's troops.[9]

There have been very few noteworthy writers who have been prepared to recognise that this campaign actually had a major impact not just on events in Africa but on the entire war's eventual outcome.[10] More recent accounts include limited references at best, and even these are susceptible to error. One distinguished military historian has written about it as having been an 'oddity' and nothing more than 'a footnote to the nineteenth-century scramble for Africa'.[11] Suggesting that there was not really a great deal of activity has been fairly standard; another account was a little more generous but still pointed to the advance from Kenya as having been a 'military promenade with distance, terrain and climate the chief enemies' and not worthy of detailed study.[12] The more recent assessments, aside from being very brief, continue to offer barely any acknowledgement of a 'meaningless' campaign.[13] Those writers who do show an interest tend to focus on how, despite overwhelming odds, the overextended British forces – often ignoring the fact that it had been a British and Commonwealth effort – muddled through to what had actually been a foregone successful ending.[14] There has even been a trend to claim that the decision to fight in East Africa proved detrimental as it distracted Britain from the war being fought elsewhere, specifically in North Africa, where the opportunity was lost to destroy Italian military forces in Libya.

This is a new account based around private papers and documents located in archives scattered around the world, which have been used to supplement the very limited writing that has been done previously. Titled 'First Victory' and not 'First Defeat', it does not dwell extensively on the role played in this campaign by the Italian military and its leaders other than to provide some background for the actions of the British and Commonwealth forces. In addition to the official Italian history, a small number of recent writers have studied the campaign from the other side and these works provide an excellent reference point for those who are interested.[15] It is to be hoped that this book might act as a catalyst for the re-telling of the Italian story extending beyond a narrow one of abject defeat and incompetency. It also does not provide lengthy tactical description of the fighting other than for a few of the most important – or particularly noteworthy – key engagements that warrant some more detailed elucidation. Where there is reference to 'bullets and bombs', this is intended, as much as anything, to give some colour to what was an often unusual and fascinating campaign.

The papers of two individuals have proved pivotal in telling the story in the detail it deserves: one who features actively in the course of events and the other who was not present at the time. Major James Blewitt was a young British Army officer who arrived in Kenya just prior to the start of the British and Commonwealth offensive and who was fortunate to have an important eyewitness role despite his junior rank. The often uncensored letters he sent back to his family provide an invaluable and frank account of the campaign which has not previously been drawn upon. The greatest resource, however, is the huge archive of work produced by Lieutenant-Colonel J.E.B. Barton, an Indian Army officer who was appointed to act as the official narrator. Despite suffering from an illness contracted during the war and knowing that he had not been the first choice for the role, he diligently sought to interview all of the principals who had fought on the winning side and gathered together as many official papers and accounts as he could find.[16] The written documents he prepared were presented only to a small group of British military officers and civil servants who worked after war's end on recording the history of the Second World War, but his findings will now have a bigger audience.

Having carried out such an exhaustive survey and identified and incorporated new sources that remove the previous gaps in the history, resolving the debate about terminology has presented a surprisingly complicated challenge.[17] There was some issue amongst those who were involved at the time as to whether the country should be called 'Ethiopia' or 'Abyssinia' and, in turn, whether it was the 'East African', 'Abyssinian' or even 'Ethiopian and Eritrean' campaign. 'Abyssinia' comes from the Arabic *habesh* meaning confusion, on account of the country's mixed races, and this seemed a fitting description when writing about the battles that had been fought there. Added to this was a post-war argument about the need to ensure that equal credit was given to all who had been involved, with the suggestion that Barton had failed to fully recognise the role played by

INTRODUCTION

some of the British and Commonwealth forces and their commanders. For this reason, and largely at the behest of one senior officer, it was most frequently subsequently referred to as 'the Abyssinian Campaign'.[18] Sometimes the post-war accounts therefore referred to two campaigns, this one and 'the Eritrean Campaign'. This study has chosen 'East Africa' to reflect a more contemporary feel, and to acknowledge that virtually all of the fighting took place in what the United Nations today refers to the as the 'Eastern African' sub-region.[19] It also chooses to use 'Ethiopia' as the country name.

What follows is not merely a story of military adventure and bravery but also one of significant strategic purpose and decisive outcomes. Senior British military and political commanders faced a hard strategic dilemma about how best to manage the limited manpower and resources available to them, but the decisions they ultimately took led to the destruction of Italy's East African Empire. And without the victory at Gondar and the triumphs won before it, there might not actually have been a much more celebrated final battle nearly twelve months later at El Alamein. Looking at it from beginning to end, what emerges is the story of a brilliantly fought campaign which both allowed the British Empire to attain its first significant wartime victory and secured the southern flank for its forces that subsequently battled their way across North Africa.

CHAPTER 1

STRATEGIC MISCALCULATION

On 5 August 1914 the British governor of the East African Protectorate, Sir Henry Belfield, received confirmation from the Colonial Office in London that King George V had signed an executive order and war had been declared late the previous evening. Despite having apparently previously agreed with his German counterpart, Heinrich Schnee, to remain neutral, a special publication was rushed out which carried the governor's proclamations confirming that war had broken out, martial law had been declared across the protectorate and the men of the King's African Rifles (KAR) and the local police were now under conditions of active service against Germany.[1] Emergency measures began at once and the approximately 3,000 military-age white male settlers, both there and in Uganda, were mobilised. The First World War, a conflict fought primarily between the European powers, had reached to the equator and dragged in eastern Africa and the people who lived across the region. This was because, following an agreement reached between Britain and Germany, virtually all of what is today termed 'East Africa' had by the end of the nineteenth century been divided into the two countries' spheres of influence.[2]

What was known as 'the Scramble for Africa' had led to the partitioning of the continent between the European powers.[3] At the Berlin Conference convened in 1884, not only had Britain and Germany agreed to recognise their respective colonial claims, but it had also been made clear to the other powers in attendance that they should make their own territorial interests known. These would then need to be 'backed by the establishment of an effective degree of authority in the areas concerned'.[4] The British eventually secured control of an area mostly to the south of the equator extending from the Indian Ocean in the east to Lake Victoria in the west, still the world's second largest freshwater lake. There was a long-standing interest: HMS *Barracouta* first visited Mombasa in December 1823 as part of a survey expedition and a small presence was maintained there for two years. It was not until more than sixty years later, in 1888, that the level of influence really began to grow. This followed the establishment of the Imperial British East Africa Company, a year before a similar commercial venture farther south and controlled by Cecil Rhodes received its Royal Charter. However, with the company's finances failing, in 1895 a formal East African Protectorate was declared and control passed to London, repeating an earlier political process that had established the neighbouring Ugandan Protectorate. Seven years later the frontiers between the two territories were redrawn for the final time, remaining largely untouched until their eventual independence.[5] There were also two other protectorates established during the period: British Somaliland had been confirmed as such in 1884 and was administered by a commissioner; and six years later the same arrangement was agreed for the islands of Zanzibar and Pemba, about fifteen miles off Africa's eastern coast.

This was a vast imperial expansion: it was calculated that the two larger territories of East Africa and Uganda alone covered an area of about 400,000 square miles, roughly three times the area of the British Isles.[6] With huge African expanses now flying the Union Jack, this was a potentially valuable addition to the Empire, with considerable economic benefits.[7] There was abundant agricultural land – coffee, tea and sisal were initially considered to be the most attractive crops – and it was also relatively simple to raise livestock. Before the First World War there was, however, limited interest from potential settlers in Britain, and most of those who were attracted to the protectorate actually came from South Africa. By 1903 there were only around a hundred European settlers living in or near Nairobi, which was then just a rail depot and four years away from becoming the capital; by 1911 the white population had increased to 3,200 men, women and children.[8] By the start of the First World War it was estimated that in East Africa and Uganda there were several million Africans, nearly 20,000 Asians but fewer than 4,000 Europeans, with only a few hundred of them living west of Lake Victoria, and this led one influential contemporary writer to question why such 'comparative neglect' had been shown by the British people to these new territories.[9] As transport routes improved, and particularly with the additional development of railways which better linked both of the main protectorates to the major Indian Ocean port at Mombasa, in the decades that followed their appeal to both settlers and successive governments in London grew, keen as they were to seize the commercial opportunities that existed. This expansion did not really lift off, however, until after the conclusion not of the first major European war to be fought in the region, but a second.

As the British-administered territories had grown, the same was true of that controlled by Germany. Centred on Tanganyika and Ruanda-Urundi, and covering a vast area encompassing the Great Lakes region, it was also just a little less than 400,000 square miles in size and bordered all the British parts of the colonial map aside from British Somaliland. The proximity of these two European empires meant that in August 1914, as war broke out between them, this part of Africa would become a battleground, albeit with highly dispersed conflicts spreading over vast distances and with much of the fighting being done by locally raised forces. Just three battalions of KAR troops were deployed across the British territories of Central and East Africa at the start of the war. The African troops were referred to as *askaris* and were formed into twenty-one companies, a total of just over 2,300 men, plus a few others who were attached to the respective headquarters. They were led by sixty-two officers who were seconded from regular British regiments for a limited term of service under the Colonial Office, along with a number of NCOs who similarly volunteered. One of those involved described these battalions as 'very efficient units; the officers were mostly adventurous spirits of a sporting turn of mind, who had got tired of regimental soldiering in peace-time, and had turned to service in less civilised parts of the world than they had been used to. They were the very best stamp of British regimental officer.'[10] Only a single battalion was based locally; the 3rd Battalion, KAR had spent most of the period before the war conducting operations against rebellious Somalis in the north, leaving just two companies in position to defend the frontier with German East Africa.[11] There were also large numbers of locally raised but still British-led police who received some basic military training but were not considered to be at the same level as those who had volunteered for military service. With so few men available, areas of the frontier remained unguarded, and not even patrolled. But, at least initially, the Germans were little better prepared.[12]

Despite this, the Committee of Imperial Defence in London – a key body for determining British foreign policy – decided on 5 August, the day after war was declared, that imperial forces would go on the offensive in the region, and orders were given to Indian troops to sail for Mombasa.[13] Following a series of initial attacks against its outposts near Lake Victoria, German colonial forces quickly advanced towards this critical port in what was the war's first invasion of any part of the British Empire.[14] They were held up by a heroic defence fought at Gazi, just twenty-five miles to the south of it, and by the year's end had been expelled from the protectorate. This was followed by a serious reverse, however, as an attempted landing by some of the Indian troops at Tanga, the second port of German East Africa, led to a humiliating defeat.[15] In large part this was down to the superb leadership of the German officer in charge of the defending *Schutztruppe*, the forty-five-year-old Lieutenant-Colonel Paul von Lettow-Vorbeck. Although he had not arrived in Dar es Salaam until January 1914, he was already an extremely experienced officer who had fought previously in the Herero revolt in German South-West Africa. The four

STRATEGIC MISCALCULATION

years he subsequently spent in East Africa confirmed his reputation as a remarkable military commander. Referred to post-war as both 'the lion of Africa' and also 'the uncatchable lizard', he has since become widely respected by those studying more contemporary irregular warfare.[16]

Seen in London as 'the Cinderella of the sideshows', the campaign was barely reported by the British Empire's media during the war's first few years, as events elsewhere dominated the press.[17] This changed in January 1916 when the first South African reinforcements arrived and with the subsequent appointment of Lieutenant-General Jan Smuts as commander-in-chief.[18] He had fought against the British less than twenty years before during the Anglo-Dutch war, but now set about clearing the border region between British and German East Africa and removing any possible threat.[19] Support came from troops from across the Empire but the majority of his forces were drawn from the continent; 250,000 South Africans served during the First World War, a figure which included 20 per cent of the white male population, and Britain's colonies throughout Africa also sent thousands of men to fight.[20] Whilst the German commander's own forces never exceeded 12,000 men, his opponents used more than 300,000 troops in their attempts to defeat him.[21] Despite the now huge size of the forces ranged against him, Lettow-Vorbeck nonetheless continued fighting until November 1918 when he finally received word of the armistice and surrendered. It was two weeks after the war's end in Europe and, having been promoted in the field to the rank of general, he had the unique wartime distinction of having been the only German commander to have successfully invaded British territory. He was never formally defeated.[22]

In the years that followed, the strategic significance of the East African region grew. One factor behind this was that, in addition to its own potential, the region dominated important maritime arterial routes which were essential for the continuing development of the British Empire. Although suppliers had to factor in the transit costs, the Suez Canal – the link between the Indian and Mediterranean oceans, which Britain had seized control of in 1882 – considerably shortened delivery times to and from

European markets.[23] Ships travelling from India, Australia and New Zealand carried vital commodities to Britain: wool, rubber, meat, grain, tin – everything that was needed to keep a commercial entity functioning. At the same time, whilst there remained a British commercial interest in the Kirkuk oilfield in northern Iraq, which by 1931 had been connected by pipelines to the ports of Haifa in Palestine and Tripoli in Syria, the Anglo-Iranian oilfield at the eastern end of the Persian Gulf was still the principal source of British-owned oil. There was only one quick route for this to reach home ports: by 1939 just under one-tenth of all goods arriving in Britain were transiting via the Horn of Africa region to reach Suez and, although there is some debate about just how significant a total this represented at this time, once war broke out and commercial ships had to run the risk of being attacked at sea, access to the shortest route possible would become of critical value.[24] It was believed naval forces operating from Aden and aircraft from the Sudan could provide some protection, but it would likely need more military resources than these. Without this, there could be no guarantee of safeguarding access to the Red Sea and the Canal and Egypt beyond. Some political and military figures in London even warned that the supply chain could potentially become unsustainable, threatening the security of the British Empire.[25] There was, however, still little or no strategic interest in the position in East Africa.

If by necessity India remained vital, the perceived importance of Egypt, the 'essential link in communications', was the other dominating factor in imperial strategic planning.[26] In 1922 the protectorate temporarily established eight years earlier had been formally abolished, but it took another fourteen years for a formal treaty to be signed with the leadership in Cairo. In an era of declining overseas commitments, official policy more generally was described as using treaties and agreements to give up whatever was not vital to imperial interests and to entrench in those places that were deemed essential.[27] The 1936 agreement removed 'certain reservations' that had long existed about Egyptian sovereignty and signalled the end of a military occupation of the country, but with confirmation that security of the Suez Canal would require the continued presence of limited British forces. These were largely confined within a narrow zone surrounding the Canal, and some troops also still remained initially in the capital, although they were to be withdrawn after four years. Permission was also given for the same number of troops to be stationed in Alexandria and for double that length of time. With further agreements to train and equip the Egyptian army and air force and to carry out significant updating of communications and transport networks, this was where Britain intended to maintain its wartime hub.[28] The significant reduction in military expenditure that dominated this period – as was most obviously witnessed by the implementation of the ten-year rule, made permanent in 1928 by the then Chancellor of the Exchequer Winston Churchill and signifying a belief that there was no significant threat of a major war developing – meant that there was little more in the way of defence preparations that could be done.[29]

The scant consideration given to East Africa and its defences was of course symptomatic of a far greater problem. Throughout the inter-war years, very little thought appears to have been given to this issue not just outside the region but also by the various colonial governments who should have taken the initiative yet instead seemed reluctant to act. The political status of the British-administered territories across the region had changed in the years following the First World War's end and protectorates had, for the most part, become colonies: Kenya, Uganda, Nyasaland and Northern Rhodesia, along with one other, the former German territory of Tanganyika, which was administered as a League of Nations mandate. Efforts were therefore made to persuade the governors and ministers sitting in each of these executives to organise at least some basic outline of a balanced military force which could be used if the region found itself threatened with attack.[30] As the security of Europe began to unravel throughout the 1930s, Major-General Sir George Giffard, Inspector General, African Colonial Forces, took the lead, undertaking a number of tours from 1937 onwards to visit the various British outposts and meet with their senior officials.[31] Known amongst his staff as 'Gentleman George', Giffard had first served with the KAR in 1911 and had fought in East Africa throughout the First World War, winning the Distinguished Service Order (DSO) and being mentioned in dispatches five times. Renowned for his organisational skills and quiet but effective leadership, his obituary writer noted that as a result of his work, 'the African Colonial Forces ceased to be merely a "bush whacking" force and became able to fulfil a role within a modern army'.[32] The key challenge he faced was dealing with politicians, and he could never quite persuade his hosts that it was necessary for them to fund the armaments and equipment he proposed in order to build up adequate regional military forces. In fact, so unconvinced were they of the potential risk that existed that even the simple idea of establishing some form of a military reserve struggled to find their support. The authorities in Nairobi were amongst those who were reluctant to accept that there was any real merit in Giffard's proposals.

Although now a formally established colony, Kenya was still in many respects a fairly fragile imperial territory. Its population was distributed in a hugely unequal way and by the time of the 1926 census 12,529 European settlers were living alongside more than 2.5 million Africans.[33] This hardly suggested a strong or established presence. Many of the settlers were described as having come from the 'gentlemanly stratum' and with a military background, hence a popular description of the colony as 'the officers' mess'.[34] Along with the Masai and the Kavirondo, the Kikuyu were the most important local group: one inter-war description referred to them as 'somewhat of a bogey to both former and British and German administrations' but 'warriors [who are] more picturesque than formidable'.[35] Successive governments in London followed the mantra, established in 1923, that in overseas territories such as these they exercised 'a trust on behalf of the African population . . . the object of which may be defined as the protection and advancement of the native races'.[36] Despite subsequent wartime speeches by the British governor which noted that these subjects referred to their monarch as 'Kingie Georgie', as one Kikuyu chief put it, there was growing resentment of 'an island of white settlers surrounded by much larger African and Asiatic population groups'.[37] On the outbreak of the Second World War there had been little change, with a white community of approximately 21,000 people 'administering' nearly 4.5 million Africans.[38]

A further complication came from the peculiarities attached to the way the frontier had been established. From Lake Rudolf (now Lake Turkana) to the Indian Ocean was a distance of 1,200 miles, virtually all of it bush and semi-desert. On the Kenyan side of the frontier there was a desert nearly 300 miles wide, the Northern Frontier District, which was so barren that for their safety Europeans were forbidden from entering it without a permit. There were only the old camel tracks to travel along with three important locations where these converged because of the presence of water: Marsabit, Isiolo and Moyale. A long straight line separated the British colony from the territory to the north, allegedly the result of the young officer in the Royal Engineers who had been tasked with drawing up the correct maps having been unexpectedly told that he had to finish the job quickly. At this stage of his survey, having only reached the El Dima Hills, he concluded that without completing his journey there was nothing he could do but draw a straight line from where he had reached to the shores of Lake Rudolf. The entirely artificial border remains to this day, and is as much of a problem now as it was during the inter-war period, in large part because it failed to take into account the nomadic nature of those who lived along it but moved freely on both sides.[39]

Whilst cross-border tensions were an irritant, the reality was that local defence had not been seen as a priority since 1918 and there was very little sense that any of the senior political figures saw the existence of any threat to security. Before Giffard's intervention, an assessment conducted in late 1927 by the then KAR Inspector General, Colonel H.A. Walker, had considered the possibility of an invasion from neighbouring Ethiopia.[40] Although the report was more interested in technical details about how the various British-led units might operate together, it concluded that it was doubtful that any attacking force could advance far into Kenya. The proposal put forward was that concentrating defences at a key point would probably suffice to defeat any invader, and the report also recommended that the Kenya Defence Force be established. This took place the following year, with compulsory membership for all white males between the ages of eighteen and thirty, but this militia was not particularly well thought of by the settlers and, just eight years later, the decision was taken that it should be disbanded.[41]

Its replacement, the Kenya Regiment, was created on 1 June 1937 to provide what it was hoped might be a better-received alternative. It was at the same time a very visible response to Giffard's efforts. A Defence Force ordinance mandated compulsory training of British subjects of European descent and of youths up to the age of eighteen, and a team of regular army instructors was sent from Britain to help with the training. The intention was to produce a first-class territorial unit, but in reality many settler families continued to prefer that their sons join the KAR reserves; when the war broke out the regiment's white officers and NCOs who were considered suitable were put through additional leadership training courses and posted out of it to take command of various other African units.[42]

The main military forces in the region as war once again approached remained the 3rd Battalion, KAR which was operating in what had become established as its principal recruiting area. This battalion had a listed strength of two machine gun sections and six companies and, whilst most of the men were stationed in Nairobi with the headquarters, constant patrols were still conducted near the northern frontier. As had been the case prior to the First World War, an additional guarantor of security was the local police force, in which there were 115 Europeans and nearly 2,000 Africans who were all armed and attended an annual musketry course. In many respects, Kenya and the wider East Africa region were no better or worse off in terms of their ability to protect themselves than the vast majority of the other territories that made up the British Empire.[43]

STRATEGIC MISCALCULATION

With German power checked by defeat in 1918 and subsequent dismantling by post-war peace treaties, a new competitor was seeking to assert itself across the region – although the story of Italy's involvement ultimately proved to be disastrous.[44] By the time the leadership in Rome decided to join with the rest of the European powers who had already secured control of African territories and the resources they contained, few parts of the continent remained unclaimed. Even so, the decision of successive Italian leaders to pursue a long-running military struggle with a country that was largely inhospitable, commanded no sea routes and had no discernible mineral wealth was perhaps not the best considered. Ethiopia, the final African territory to attract the European powers' attention, could have been annexed by a British military expedition in 1867 but there was no political appetite in London. Two years later the opening of the Suez Canal focused attention on the coastal regions that commanded the Red Sea but still there was no real sign of external interest in the territory.[45] The Bay of Assab was, however, bought that same year by an Italian shipping company and a little over twenty years later a colony had been formally organised in Eritrea with the encouragement of the British, who were looking to counter any potential threat from the Mahdists in neighbouring Sudan.[46] Efforts to expand beyond the coastal area led to the initial conflict between the Italians and the Abyssinian Empire (also referred to as Ethiopia) which had formed from a collection of semi-independent provinces to become a unified kingdom. This led in January 1887 to the defeat of a small Italian garrison and, in response, the authorities in Rome dispatched an expeditionary force to safeguard its holdings in Eritrea.

The succession of Emperor Menelik II to the throne two years later proved a critical step as, faced by a civil war that threatened his precarious hold on power, it was only with Italian military and financial aid that he was able to retain his position as Ethiopian leader. This left him indebted to the government in Rome but, with his crops destroyed by drought, he was unable to pay what he owed and had no choice other than to negotiate the 1889 Wuchale (or Ucciali) Treaty. The emperor ceded the northern province of Ethiopia but a discrepancy in the final document allowed Italy to claim that the remainder of the country now also fell within its control. Menelik's discovery of this, along with a cynical attempt by the authorities in Rome to increase the interest on the debts, led him to denounce the agreement. Seeking to strengthen his military position, he approached the French for equipment, which they supplied. The Italian response was to launch an invasion across the border whilst also supplying arms to the emperor's domestic opponents. Having declared war on his European adversary, Menelik led his forces on 1 March 1896 at what was then referred to as the Battle of Adowa as the Italians suffered a humiliating and catastrophic defeat.[47] Using captured arms and munitions, the emperor next brought the rest of his country – containing two-thirds of the population, mostly Galla – under his control; the methods he employed meant that when the Italians invaded again some decades later, they were much better received in Ethiopia's south than its north. Menelik's consolidation of his power established him as the most powerful leader the Abyssinian Empire had ever seen. For the Italians, Adowa left a 'vindictive memory' that would one day need to be redressed.[48]

Whilst little was done by successive governments in Rome to change the Ethiopian situation, Italy did not entirely give up on its African colonial ambitions and by 1912 had taken over parts of modern Libya. Benito Mussolini came to power ten years later and was 'dominated by his desire to increase the prestige and might of his country'.[49] He had actually opposed the initial attempts to control Libya and described previous efforts to increase Italy's presence in East Africa as jingoistic dreams. Once in power he was faced, however, with two of Italy's perennial problems: rural poverty and overpopulation. The need for expansion was fundamental to Fascist policy and the prestige it would bring was also vital to the continued survival of Mussolini's regime. The conquest of Libya alone could not solve his problems but the fertile Ethiopian highlands might, and at one stage he apparently considered settling somewhere between 5 and 7 million of his subjects in East Africa.[50] As the senior British politician Winston Churchill later put it, there 'seemed no way in which Mussolini could more easily or at less risk and cost consolidate his own power or . . . raise the authority of Italy in Europe than by wiping out the stain of bygone years and adding Abyssinia to the recently built Italian Empire'.[51] What was referred to as the 'Adowa complex', which 'left a deep scar' and 'bitter shame' at being the only white European country to have suffered such a defeat, was certainly a major driver in Mussolini's thinking.[52]

Churchill concluded that to 'proclaim their manhood by avenging Adowa meant almost as much in Italy as the recovery of Alsace-Lorraine in France'; to the leadership in Rome, this appeared an attractive and, more importantly, feasible strategy.[53] Joining Libya with Italian Eritrea would create a significant Italian presence stretching from the Mediterranean coast of North Africa to the Indian Ocean.[54] When Japan marched into Manchuria in 1931 the response from the League of Nations was ineffective and the Italian leader concluded that so long as their commercial interests were safeguarded, its members would do little to interfere with his own plans.[55] Preparations continued until the opportunity to reopen the issue came after a clash between Italian and Ethiopian troops in the disputed Somali–Ethiopian border region.[56] At Wal Wal in December 1934 there was a skirmish involving Italian soldiers and the Ethiopian escort to the British-Ethiopian Boundary Commission, and this appeared to Mussolini to provide an excellent opportunity to implement his plans.[57] Diplomatic arguments dragged on in the attempt to resolve the crisis. So, with no mutually acceptable solution proving possible – in large part because of the onerous terms put forward by the Italians – after a delay of more than ten months their troops once more advanced into Ethiopia.

Despite the technological advantages enjoyed by Mussolini's forces, the defending Ethiopians fought bravely and it was not until 9 May 1936, following the capture of Addis Ababa, which had been almost entirely destroyed by indiscriminate bombing, that Mussolini proclaimed to crowds at home, 'At last Italy has her empire.'[58] By this point the 'civilising' European power had indiscriminately killed as many as 760,000 men, women and children and Emperor Haile Selassie had been forced to flee.

He headed to Geneva and the headquarters of the League of Nations – into which his country had been admitted in 1923, despite some British opposition – in an attempt to persuade its members to intervene. His arguments failed to secure any support, and with no offers of help forthcoming he moved into lonely exile in a large house in the south-west of England. Mussolini, believing that he had achieved the desired increase in prestige and power that both he and the Italian people demanded, formally declared the establishment of the grandly titled Italian East African Empire. This consisted of Eritrea, Italian Somaliland (which had been a protectorate since 1888) and Selassie's former kingdom. Dominated by mountain ranges interspersed with arid deserts, this covered a huge area; at 540,000 square miles, it was nearly five times the size of Italy.

There was, however, an obvious problem insomuch as this newly secured Italian territory was surrounded on all sides: to the north by Anglo-Egyptian Sudan, to the south and west by Kenya and Uganda, and to the east and north-east by British and French Somaliland. It was also isolated from the Mediterranean supply lines as sea routes of communication were controlled by Britain or France. The first Governor-General of Italian East Africa, Marshal Pietro Badoglio, 1st Duke of Addis Ababa, who was appointed on 9 May 1936, did have around 300,000 troops available, spread across four sectors of Eritrea and Ethiopia, to protect the newly won empire. However, only 30 per cent were actually Italian and less than one-third of these were regular soldiers; the rest were *carabinieri* and border guards, who both had a reputation for a sometimes uncertain quality of military expertise. The vast bulk of the military forces were locally raised and, although there were some highly trained fighting units amongst their ranks, most were trained only to a basic level. Mussolini had removed the shame of Adowa but the armed units upon which he depended to maintain the future security of Italian East Africa were optimised for occupation, not for fighting wars against similarly equipped and professionally trained opponents.

Many Ethiopian soldiers remained in the field and refused to surrender, and a resistance movement quickly formed which exposed some of the challenges that could lie ahead for the Italians.[59] Despite the harshest repression and brutal retaliation – such as an indiscriminate three-day massacre of several thousand Amhara in Addis Ababa following an attempt to kill Badoglio's successor, Marshal Rodolfo Graziani – the rebels continued their struggle. Faced by an insurgency for which they should have been better prepared, having previously faced the same in Libya, the military was not adequately equipped or mentally ready.[60] Armour was scarce, with just sixty-three light and medium tanks, and its aircraft, though amongst the best in the region, could only be used infrequently. There were actually 200 fighters and light bombers available and the pilots were well trained and motivated, but the planes were poorly maintained due to shortages of spares. Isolation from Italy would take a considerable toll on military capability with a subsequent lack of fuel, ammunition, spares and other replacements only making problems worse. There was also a small Italian Red Sea flotilla of seven destroyers, seven torpedo boats and eight submarines which was based at Massawa and Assab in Eritrea and Mogadishu in Italian Somaliland. Once again, however, this lacked access to critical equipment and supplies and there were no capital ships, which left the flotilla badly under-gunned in the event of any engagement with either the British or the French navies.[61] By the end of 1939, within Italian East Africa a stalemate had effectively developed. The Italians occupied all of the major towns and the many newly constructed forts that stretched across the territory. Although they avoided unnecessary engagements to reduce their casualties, many places in the highlands and rural areas were controlled by the irregular forces, particularly on the Gojjam plateau.[62]

There was clearly something of a mixed picture in terms of the relative strength of the Italian position. Mussolini now controlled a huge African empire but the stability of its position and the quality and quantity of the forces it depended upon to maintain security were ambiguous. Yet despite the potential frailties that existed, it was nonetheless seen as a 'menace' to Britain's imperial communications and defence system and a threat that could prove critical in the event of a German or Japanese attack.[63] Only in 1934 was the War Office in London finally convinced that the leadership in Rome was intent on conducting military operations in Africa. One military commentator, upon considering the subsequent invasion of Ethiopia, concluded perceptively that it was in many respects a gamble involving enormous stakes with any resulting success proving 'a very expensive luxury'.[64] So weak were British military capabilities across the East Africa region that it was felt there was no choice but to accept Italy's victory as the prelude to a settlement of differences, and in 1938 an Anglo-Italian agreement was signed. For Britain's strategic planners the conclusion remained that, whilst it was hoped Italy might 'remain neutral and may even become a friend', the perceived ease with which her naval and air forces would be able to cut the Red Sea route was a cause for grave concern.[65] The instructions from the government in London, however, were that nothing was to be done which might threaten relations with Rome, and prior to the declaration of war between the two countries in 1940, a strict interpretation was applied in terms of what this meant. From a military perspective the greatest frustrations that arose from this policy were the restrictions it imposed on gathering effective intelligence and countering the hostile propaganda that was being distributed by the Italians. Most significantly, it also prevented the provision of any support to those Ethiopians who continued to fight their occupiers.

This acquiescence to Italy was not the only fatal weakness in pre-war British strategy. Indeed, there was a more significant and fundamental flaw, albeit one that could not reasonably have been anticipated. Anglo-French conversations were held between the two military staffs in London at the end of March 1939, resulting in the announcement that security guarantees would be given to Poland in the face of a continuing increase in bellicose German actions.[66] In terms of East Africa, the two partners agreed that a priority would be to secure the Red Sea route and isolate Italian territories, so as to tighten the pressure and deprive their armed forces of reinforcements and supplies. This meant controlling sea communications in the Gulf of Aden and here the responsibility would clearly fall on the British, who had by far the greater regional resources to carry out this task. On land the aim would initially be to defend British and French territory while also now, at last, seeking to promote an effective and more widespread rebellion in Italian East Africa. Whilst these were seen as the two most achievable objectives, the intention was that, when resources and manpower allowed, an offensive would be started that would advance through Eritrea and into Ethiopia in the direction of the capital. The best base from which to launch this would be French Somaliland, referred to by the British as Jibuti (Djibouti), with its excellent port and rail links which in 1916 had reached Addis Ababa. Ensuring its security was therefore considered to be of great importance. Both militaries also agreed on the strategic importance of Egypt; British forces already in the country, reinforced by troops from Palestine, would be used to hold off any initial attacks. Further reinforcements would, however, be needed, and with the potential closure of the Mediterranean, they would have to travel from Britain via the Cape: this extended journey time meant it would be at least seventy days before they arrived.

Although this was the broad strategic appreciation, at the regional level the primary objective for British and Commonwealth forces in East Africa was to secure the lines of communication with Egypt. For the rest of the area the Chiefs of Staff in London thought defensively. The garrison in the Sudan was too small to defend any significant portion of the border, but it was thought capable of defeating raiding columns, considered to be the most likely form of attack. They believed that, elsewhere, little more than delaying actions were the best that could be achieved as the defending forces fell back in the face of superior numbers. In May, more than twenty senior British and French officers, including representatives from across the region, gathered in Aden for a further meeting to refine and co-ordinate these regional plans.[67] Four committees were formed to discuss naval, military, air and intelligence matters and these merely served to confirm the earlier decisions. It was deemed vital to control the Red Sea for supplies and reinforcements, and French Somaliland as a potential base for operations, although it was now accepted that insufficient forces were available for the latter's defence if the Italians attempted an advance through British Somaliland. Finally, it was agreed that, whilst there were not enough troops to consider instigating any form of advance, with some additional equipment and manpower provided from London and Paris, it might be possible to support a rebellion.

This series of discussions in early 1939 highlighted both the vagaries of the strategic thinking and how little depth there was to the conclusions being reached in London. It also reiterated the comparative lack of interest that continued to exist in regard to East Africa's security, and confirmed that the focus had not moved from farther north. During these discussions an interesting reference was made to the garrison in the Sudan. Like Kenya and the other British regional territories, this remained a largely unknown part of the British Empire. As late as November 1940, a former civil servant in the Sudanese government described in *The Listener* how the Sudan was governed as a 'condominium', what he termed a 'typically British improvisation'.[68] This had developed following the 1898 Anglo-Egyptian expedition and the subsequent Battle of Omdurman which had recovered Khartoum from the Mahdi and his followers and was an established part of Britain's imperial history. This vast territory covered almost exactly a million square miles; except for the narrow Nile valley and tropical forest, the north was bare desert with swamp and heavy bush in the south. In the middle there was scrub and enough rainfall to grow good crops and maintain livestock. What was perhaps most significant from the perspective of the Anglo-French planners was the Sudan's 1,200 miles of shared frontier with Italian East Africa and its resulting potential to become a transit route up the Nile valley and on to Egypt and the Mediterranean. With the scarce resources available to the Allied and military planners, it was this which at this stage gave it something of a priority over Kenya.

There was a final consideration that should have featured in this already complex picture. One other key actor would emerge to take a leading role in subsequent events: the Union of South Africa, a member of the British Empire but a semi-autonomous one with the ability to develop its own potentially different approach to how it viewed the continent's affairs.[69] Explaining the relationship between the two countries prior to the outbreak of the Second World War has often proved complex, as the Union 'occupied a unique position in British imperial strategy and imagination'.[70] The threat of Italian expansion into the Sudan and Egypt, and Italy's potential to take control of the Suez Canal or threaten Kenya, Tanganyika and Uganda, had been of long-standing concern for many leading figures in both London and Pretoria. Prominent amongst these was Jan Smuts who had become one of the two senior political figures in what the British termed a 'dominion' following on from his eventual First World War success. He saw Italy's campaign to conquer Ethiopia as 'but the first step to an African policy which extended far beyond that corner of Africa ... This large African policy is in line with the well-known German aim of a great Empire in Africa, of which Mussolini hopes to have a considerable share.'[71] Later Smuts would clarify his thinking, referring to the threat to 'the young democratic communities' that were being established across Africa, presumably those that had emerged under British leadership. As he put it, 'when the python starts swallowing one or more of them, none of them will be safe', and the fate of Kenya and eastern Africa was therefore of great significance to him.[72] Such were the political tensions that existed in South Africa that it was not certain if it would once again fight alongside Britain; and if it did, the authorities in London could easily find themselves faced with a complicated alliance to try and manage, much as had been the case during the previous war. Just how difficult this would actually prove only became clear later.

In the event of having to fight a war to defend East Africa, there was clearly a good deal of confusion about the strategy to be followed. The thinking of the few politicians in Whitehall interested in the subject, and within the regional governments, was flawed, with the dangers misunderstood or, more often, overlooked and ignored. Successive British governments showed no real sense of recognising that this could be an important wartime hub for raw materials and training. This was symptomatic of a more general lack of foresight regarding how the resources and manpower of the British Empire might best be used in the event of another global conflict. These significant failings were compounded by the failure of senior military officers to make a compelling argument about Italian intentions and the potential challenge these presented. While the Chiefs of Staff in London were right to assume that Mussolini would focus on Egypt, due to the vital importance attached to controlling the Suez Canal, they were wrong to conclude that he would enter the war at the first opportunity. The principals in London also gambled in presuming that East Africa would be a secondary theatre even though operations there could also threaten the flanks of the overall Middle East position. As one of the official historians later recorded, these conclusions were perhaps based more on the weakness of the British forces than on a considered review of Italian intentions.[73] Much more serious than this, however, was the assumption that France would be in a position to co-operate fully; the alternative seems to have been dismissed, presumably because it carried such potentially worrying strategic limitations. Fortunately, when war did come in September 1939, Mussolini chose, at least initially, to wait and see what would happen elsewhere. This gave the political leaders in London a chance to review their thinking and correct the flawed strategy but, in the months that followed, there was little evidence to indicate that the opportunity had been taken or that anything was going to change.

CHAPTER 2

HOPING FOR THE BEST

As the second global conflict of the twentieth century got under way, in some respects the British Empire's position in East Africa remained politically unclear and militarily vulnerable. Since before the First World War there had often seemed to be a lack of conviction from successive governments in London as to the role this region played in their broader strategic thinking. This in turn had left a clear sense that whilst they and the regional authorities were undoubtedly hoping for the best in terms of local defence and security issues, they were failing to make any preparations for the worst. The lack of an appointment of a senior officer to take overall charge of the locally based armed forces had not improved matters and was indicative of how some viewed not just the role but the region. Previously there had been three separate military commands, one each covering Egypt, the Sudan, and Palestine–Trans-Jordan, added to which there was an Inspector General responsible to the Colonial Office for the various territories in eastern Africa as well as the KAR.[1] At the time of the Munich crisis, General Sir Edmund Ironside, who had fallen out of favour and been passed over for appointment as Chief of the Imperial General Staff, was sent to Cairo in readiness to assume the post of General Officer Commanding-in-Chief Middle East. After a few weeks, and with the tensions in Europe dying down again, he was withdrawn to Gibraltar to continue his exile.[2] For a time afterwards it was hoped that he might be available to return in an emergency, but instead he remained at what was actually a highly significant British outpost. This meant that the following year, as the security situation once again deteriorated and the decision was at last taken to appoint somebody to take the role permanently, in June 1939 Lieutenant-General Sir Archibald Wavell was selected instead.

The post was established formally on 2 August and, after some initial hesitancy on his part about whether to accept it or not, with the acting rank of full general the new commander set off for Cairo. The organisational structure which surrounded him was very simple in that he reported directly to the Secretary of State for War and the Chief of the Imperial General Staff, but he had almost complete authority in terms of the planning and conduct of operations. His two most important senior colleagues sitting alongside him, and who he relied upon for collaboration, were Admiral Sir Andrew Cunningham, who represented the Royal Navy, and Air Chief Marshal Sir Arthur Longmore, who acted as the senior air officer. He also had the support of four other generals who were appointed to command his forces spread across the vast region for which he was responsible. There was also one other important figure within his headquarters, who ran it for him: Brigadier Arthur Smith, who had been in Egypt since 1938 and who acted as Wavell's chief of staff.

'Archie' Wavell was born on 5 May 1883 and both his father and grandfather had been professional soldiers. Aged just eighteen, he himself entered the Royal Military College Sandhurst, where he was commissioned into the Black Watch. The experience he gained during the Anglo-Dutch war at the turn of the century and his subsequent staff training left him well prepared for the First World War. He lost his left eye on the Western Front, but his gallantry was rewarded with the Military Cross. Despite the reduced prospects for promotion that followed the war, his previous performance and widely recognised potential meant that, as the next major conflict approached, he was one of the British Army's most senior officers. One of his postings between the wars had been in Palestine where he gained an invaluable knowledge of the Middle East, its people, the terrain and geography, and its history and culture. It was based largely on this experience that Wavell eventually decided to accept the offer made to him in the summer of 1939, as he correctly assessed that it would prove to be a genuinely independent command where he would have a lot of freedom.

Wavell was an individual who was widely respected by his peers not just for his previous military record but for his inspiring leadership skills and resolve.[3] Audacity and forward thinking were his trademarks, along with a sense of daring that saw him taking often significant but calculated risks to achieve victory.[4] He was both a commander who 'always kept his finger upon the pulse despite distance and the many demands upon his time', yet who also gave his subordinate commanders plenty of opportunity to conduct operations without distraction.[5] In the Middle East and eastern Africa this would prove a critical attribute. His tremendous intellect was perhaps his greatest strength, incorporating a knowledge of history, literature, geography and contemporary affairs.[6] According to another of those officers who knew him well, Wavell had an extremely quick and logical brain which he used to solve problems as they emerged, while at the same time thinking in great detail about what might lie ahead. This process required 'a concrete problem to chew', and during periods when Wavell was quiet – when he was described as being 'in one of his dumb moods' – his friends recognised that this meant he was working through one.[7] For some, however, he 'was taciturn to the point of using words as if they cost a guinea each', and, despite his very considerable abilities which made him one of Britain's leading military commanders in the eyes of many of his senior colleagues, as he departed for Egypt he was largely unknown to either the press or the public at home.[8]

Wavell's command area covered Egypt, the Sudan, Palestine, Trans-Jordan and Cyprus, expanding once war was declared to include Aden, Iran and, later, British Somaliland. Over the months that followed he would become the most significant figure involved not just in the fighting that took place in North Africa and the Middle East, but also in the battles which developed during the course of the East Africa campaign. Yet, initially, he had barely any fighting forces to command. In a treaty ratified in December 1936 it had been agreed that there would be no more than 10,000 British troops stationed in Egypt. In addition to these men, at the war's outbreak Wavell had approximately the same number in Palestine, slightly fewer in the Sudan guarding its long frontiers, 8,500 predominantly African troops in Kenya and a further 1,500 in British Somaliland. This represented virtually all of his available manpower, and the outlying territories under his control were left with token forces consisting largely of locally raised volunteers and police. He had been closely connected with pre-war studies on the role of tanks and had an armoured division with him, although this lacked two of its regiments; his artillery units were incomplete and with often antiquated weapons; and his aircraft were equally obsolete: twenty-eight squadrons had to cover more than 4 million square miles. To compensate for his obvious and potentially overwhelming numerical inferiority, Wavell's approach was 'to puzzle and confuse, and to keep the enemy guessing as to where and when they might be attacked'.[9] The standing order issued early on in the war was therefore entirely appropriate: 'make one man appear to be a dozen, make one tank look like a squadron, make a raid look like an advance'.[10]

Despite their weakness, as one contemporary observer later noted, when hostilities began the British and Commonwealth forces actually appeared almost to hem in the enemy, to the extent that this could be done with an opponent consisting of several hundred thousand troops.[11] It was as much a defence based on bluff as anything else and Wavell demonstrated a real talent for playing this particular game. In terms of overall strategy, his main effort remained exactly as the planners had dictated throughout the inter-war period: the defence of Egypt. Faced by a larger and better-equipped force, however, he quickly realised that, while small-scale skirmishes and border clashes were highly effective, he was not in a position initially to think about any large-scale offensive. This would require his forces to be much increased and far better trained and equipped if they were to operate effectively in the demanding desert environment. He had studied the disasters suffered by his predecessors during the last war and had no wish to see any repeat of Kut and Gallipoli, humiliating military losses for the British Empire which had fundamentally stemmed from insufficient preparation and ineffective efforts to keep the forces involved supplied and able to fight.[12] The early policy adopted by the commander in Cairo was therefore aimed at making full use of the region's geographical advantages in tying down Italian forces that might otherwise be used against him.

Wavell also never lost sight of the importance of the Red Sea and saw protecting his crucial communication route as 'the most urgent task of the Services'.[13] To this end, shortly after arriving in Cairo, when it was anticipated that Italy would join the war at the earliest opportunity, he had tried to secure support for an immediate surprise bombing attack on the key port of Massawa on the Eritrean coast.[14] It was to be launched simultaneously from Egypt, the Sudan and Aden using all available bombers, and the general was prepared to accept that, at least temporarily, this would leave him unable to carry out any other attacks against Italian troops in the Western Desert. There was little support from within the Royal Air Force, however, who pointed to the wide range of tasks facing them, the lack of available aircraft and their concerns about any 'spectacular Italian initial success in Egypt'.[15] The Royal Navy was also reluctant to attack particularly if there was no offer of air support, so these plans came to nothing. But the commander had shown that the security of his maritime supply routes held a particular significance for him, and he would return to it later.[16]

In many respects Wavell's real problem at this point was that, although theoretically there was a war to be won, the conflict barely extended beyond northern Europe and there was little real rigour in thinking about activities elsewhere. On 30 August 1939 Middle East Command had received instructions reiterating the earlier position: even with a state of war between Britain and Italy, only defensive measures were to be taken and these should be as non-provocative as possible.[17] As it was, Prince Amedeo of Savoy-Aosta, who two years before had become the third Viceroy of Italian East Africa following on from Badoglio and Graziani, had no desire to challenge this position. Referred to more commonly as the Duke of Aosta – although more popularly sometimes also as 'the Prince of the Sahara' – as a young man he had attended Eton and Oxford University and won a medal for valour in the First World War, fighting on the same side as the British. He had subsequently become 'the most popular member of the [Italian] royal family' and, still only forty years old when war broke out again in Europe, he was firmly opposed to being on Germany's side.[18] A British officer who met with him in March 1938 noted that, aside from his youth, height and athleticism, he appeared 'to think like an Englishman'.[19] Churchill was therefore perhaps rather unfair when he later wrote that at the outbreak of the war the viceroy was 'lacking in ruthlessness and commanding military ability', an assessment which ignored such considerations and also overlooked the significant weaknesses undermining Aosta's position in eastern Africa. Despite the apparent overwhelming advantages in troops and equipment he appeared to hold, Aosta's conclusion was that if there was a fight with Britain and France, his isolation from Italy would leave the territory he governed vulnerable. And his position was made worse by a lack of clear direction from Rome, where Mussolini prevaricated about his overall wartime strategy.[20]

Nor did it help that Aosta's British opposite number had a much clearer vision of how he could proceed despite the handicaps he faced. Within his vast command area Wavell saw victory in East Africa as an essential prerequisite for victory in North Africa and this determined the course of what followed. Rather than view the two areas as separate theatres he considered the first simply as his left flank and the enemy forces there as a threat that had to be removed. It was a visionary approach, recognising the importance of a region that to the vast majority of senior military and political observers who surrounded him was of minimal significance. In his initial detailed notes on potential operations to be conducted against Italian East

Africa, produced in early October 1939, he outlined a range of options for defeating the existing threat to his southern flank.[21] In so doing he was adamant that in addition to local air superiority and properly organised transport and supply routes, there would need to be sufficient numbers of suitably trained troops to cope with the conditions and local climate. His outline plan contained some brief reference to subsidiary operations moving northwards across the Kenyan frontier from Moyale in the direction of Negelli, advancing from the Sudan into Eritrea heading towards the mountains and Keren, and even carrying out a possible landing on the Red Sea coast at Assab. Mention of the last two highlighted Wavell's continuing focus on maritime security as, if the Italian garrison at the obscure fortress could be defeated, the road to Massawa would potentially be opened. It was also clear from this appreciation that the focus for any action would have to be Jibuti or the Sudan with their potentially better communications, and their ports and railways that could maintain supplies for the attacking forces. This had not actually changed from the approach agreed at the discussions earlier in the year, and French Somaliland, with its well-defended base and good lines of communication, was still the key point.

There was, however, an additional possibility for the British to explore. Whilst the size of Aosta's forces broadly remained much the same as they had been since the initial invasion of Ethiopia, the colonial policing role had had a debilitating effect on the Italians' fighting power as they struggled to control a rebellion within their new imperial frontiers.[22] Following the victory in 1936, and the atrocities they had committed against the civilian population during their conquest, the occupied country had become a 'simmering cauldron' where a rebel movement awaited Haile Selassie's return to lead them on to victory.[23] Although the Italians invested considerable manpower and resources in halting the growing insurgency, a visit to the Gojjam plateau three years later by one of the emperor's senior staff along with an agent from the Deuxième Bureau, the French external intelligence agency, confirmed there was still a great deal of anger. A report provided full details of the situation and confirmed that the northern, eastern and southern provinces had been largely pacified but there remained a serious problem for the Italians in western Ethiopia, where large numbers of troops were still being used to maintain internal security.[24] The viceroy had himself admitted as much the previous year during a meeting with a visiting British officer, although the stubborn resistance was being brought under control.[25] Drawing on this and information from other sources, the headquarters in Cairo identified the Gojjam plateau as the focus for British resources, and it was decided that an attempt would be made to 'raise the tribes'.

In February 1933, Wavell had let it be known when lecturing at the Royal United Services Institute in London that he was not averse to using irregular warfare. In his presentation he had declared that a good soldier should be a combination of 'cat burglar, gunman and poacher', a description he defended as being used 'to draw attention to the value of low cunning in war' which, he then believed, was the weak point of the British infantryman.[26] He later wrote a very well received biography of General Allenby and his First World War campaign, and throughout the inter-war period had conducted a correspondence with T.E. Lawrence, who had led the Arab forces in their insurgency against the Turks. During his period in Palestine, the British general had used locally raised unorthodox units, and now, lacking manpower and resources, he concluded there was great merit in encouraging a rebellion.[27] At least initially Wavell had to make his plans in secret as the operations he was considering were in direct contravention of the *Bon Voisinage* or 'good neighbour' agreement which had been signed in April 1938 between the governments in London and Rome. This had referred specifically to the maintenance of friendly relations between the two countries and, at least in theory, it prevented the general from having any contacts with the rebels operating in Ethiopia.[28] Nonetheless he later confirmed in his official dispatch that 'the fomentation of the patriot movement in Abyssinia offered with the resources available the best prospect of making the Italian position impossible and eventually reconquering the country'. It was clear that he invested considerable energies into making this work.[29]

This was because, at least initially, this course of action was the only one that Wavell was able to identify that might really disrupt Italian plans, although there were considerable challenges to overcome. Even during the initial planning discussions it was concluded that the Eritreans and the Somalis would be unlikely to join, and so if it were to be successful it would depend upon those Ethiopians anxious to restore Selassie to his throne and recover their independence from Italian occupation. It was therefore decided that the force would be termed *Arbegnoch*, which translates loosely as 'patriots', a name probably chosen to depict the nobleness of the cause and to give the recruits a sense of being 'freedom fighters'.[30] These men had the classic advantage enjoyed by the insurgent throughout history in that they were familiar with the terrain of the battlefields and could mingle with the local population, allowing them to operate well inside enemy lines. Once the war in Europe began the Chiefs of Staff in London were enthusiastic in their support for the Italians being kept distracted within their own boundaries, and agreed that this was a sound strategy to pursue.[31]

Wavell had adopted an aggressive approach in an attempt to identify potentially decisive advantages, but there remained those within his command and back in London who were still opposed to any thoughts of military action. In October 1939 the Joint Planning Staff in Cairo had been asked to consider what could be gained by attacking the Italians first in order to prevent them from using naval and air bases to target shipping in the Mediterranean and Red Sea.[32] Not only did the response question such a move, it extended to a more general challenge to the view that anything would be gained by going on the offensive in Italian East Africa. This assessment also held that there were no special obligations in terms of restoring independence for the Ethiopians, who were described as 'neither a united nor admirable people'. Instead the recommendation was that the Italians should be kept guessing about possible action against them while another review was conducted with the French about how best to proceed. Similar views were apparently prevalent in the War Office in London, where the firm conclusion was that the enemy's overwhelming military advantage meant the Red Sea could be closed for a time and British and Commonwealth forces would not be able to use it to maintain their positions in Egypt.[33] Were this to happen, alternative overland routes would have to be used even though these could not efficiently handle the volume of supplies that were transported by ship which were needed by the Allied troops. Wavell's concerns about being able to keep his already limited forces adequately equipped were also apparently not universally shared. It seems clear that in both London and Cairo the least regarded of his various commands was East Africa, although this was not an assessment with which he concurred.

Given the apathy that existed, it was important to ensure that the right officer was in charge in wartime Nairobi, but Wavell did not have any say in this selection. Best suited for this role was Giffard but he had been sent back to the War Office for a brief period before being moved on again, temporarily, to become General Officer Commanding in Palestine.[34] His replacement as Inspector General, African Colonial Forces was Major-General Douglas Dickinson, who had been Commandant of the Nigerian Regiment for the previous two years.[35] He was qualified for his role as he had previously gained a good knowledge of African troops and some of the more general issues affecting the region's security. About a week before war was declared it had been decided in London that Dickinson would fly out to Nairobi to carry out an inspection tour, with a brief visit to Cairo to meet with Wavell and a stop in Khartoum for discussions with the British senior commander in the Sudan, Major-General William Platt. He eventually arrived in Kenya on 22 August, establishing himself at Kenton College alongside the headquarters of the KAR's Northern Brigade, the same day as the initial 'Stand By' message had been received warning that war now seemed likely.[36] With selected personnel of the KAR reserves and the Kenya Regiment already beginning to be called up, and having received a telegram on the final day of August confirming his appointment as General Officer Commanding in East Africa, Dickinson's brief war was about to begin.

The new East African commander lacked real support and had little equipment to get his headquarters up and running; at first he had just one regular officer with any experience to lead it and very few trained personnel who could make it function effectively. Fortunately Alec Bishop, despite only recently having been promoted from major to lieutenant-colonel, had accompanied Giffard on all of his tours as his chief staff officer and was a most able assistant. He had remained in this role when Dickinson had taken charge and a great deal of responsibility fell upon him. Aside from seven officers sent from England on 1 September 1939 to provide advice on technical issues, Bishop had to rely upon veterans of the last war then living in Kenya, and even women who were recruited as clerks.[37] There was no shortage of enthusiastic retired military volunteers but many were lacking in staff training or experience and had little current knowledge of military affairs. Nonetheless, in most cases they provided good service until such time as sufficient trained staff officers could be sent from Britain. Sir Donald Mackenzie Kennedy, the Governor of Nyasaland, was appointed as a liaison officer and offered political advice to the military commander. This was an important role, as the colony's civilian affairs rested largely in the hands of a governor-general, appointed by the Colonial Office in Whitehall to represent the interests of the British authorities. Sir Robert Brooke-Popham, who had retired in 1936 as an air chief marshal in the Royal Air Force to take on the role, was still in the post when Dickinson arrived but had already announced his return to military service. Sir Henry Monck-Mason Moore, who had served before the war as Governor of Sierra Leone and had also held senior roles in the Colonial Office, arrived in Kenya a few months later to become the senior British representative and remained in Nairobi for four years before being posted to the same role in Ceylon.

At the time when Dickinson was assuming his new role, Kenya's strategic position was bleak. Thinking was dominated by the Northern Frontier District, and its 600-mile frontier which faced Italian territory. The first decision taken was to evacuate its northernmost portion once war was declared, the conclusion being that the small garrisons there would be quickly lost if any attack followed.[38] Although Italy actually chose not to join with Germany at the outbreak of the Second World War, this important ground was still given up, albeit in error. Evacuations took place from Moyale, Wajir and Mandera and it was two weeks before they were re-occupied, by which point there had been much looting and some local damage to British prestige.[39] More broadly the intention was to use the terrain and hold for as long as possible the general line of the Tana and Uaso Nyiro rivers in an attempt to retain the edge of the Kenyan highlands and the vital water supplies that ran to its north. This would also include trying to prevent an advance through the Lokitaung area around Lake Rudolf. Dickinson's small planning team concluded that, to the east, the absence of roads and the total lack of water between the Juba and Tana rivers made military operations almost impossible. The defending garrison would therefore need to watch closely the approaches towards Garissa and along the Coastal Belt. These initial assessments pointed to this as being where the enemy would most likely advance heading south from Italian Somaliland and down the coast towards Mombasa.[40]

Drawing upon local skills and materiel was a feature of the initial planning stages and remained a constant factor in the conduct of the region's defence. A general paucity of military resources across the British Empire meant that what was available was given to those regions that had been identified by the inter-war reviews as being most important. Eastern Africa was not one of these, and remained a low priority for both men and equipment.[41] In fact, just about the only area in which there was no real concern for Dickinson was rations, which were described as excellent by the troops who arrived as reinforcements; while they were stationed within Kenya's frontiers they enjoyed fresh fruit, vegetables and meat. All of the eastern African colonies were self-sufficient and the exporting of their foodstuffs would later become one of their major contributions to the overall Allied war effort.[42] In terms of everything else it was fairly desperate, with very limited supplies of weapons and small arms ammunition, and authority was given to requisition every vehicle in Kenya which could be of military use. Even with this, the lack of anti-tank guns or anti-tank mines meant that in theory any attacking Italian armour could advance into the colony or any of its neighbours almost unopposed. In response the men of the Kenya and Uganda Railways Workshops devoted much of their energy to producing basic mortars and other weapons. With no trained engineers, work was also carried out by civilians from the Public Works Department to construct defensive lines along the likely route of any Italian advance down the coast, and to prepare bridges for demolition.[43]

The domestic response was impressive but there was still no other choice than to send out urgent appeals for help across the British Empire. General Headquarters India responded quickly and sent large amounts of military clothing, including coats for the cold nights in the Kenyan highlands and web equipment as well as radio sets and even tents.[44] Bishop was meanwhile sent to Southern Rhodesia to ask the government in Salisbury to give whatever assistance they could; even though the pilot of his aircraft got lost on the way – the result of having been forced to use a map of Africa contained in the Philips' School Atlas on a scale of 600 miles to the inch – his mission was a success and it was confirmed that, in addition to aircraft and crew that were already being sent north, the pre-war offers of other manpower and equipment would be made available as quickly as was possible.[45] In the short term, however, Dickinson would have to continue to look closer to home to fill the gaps. Wilson Airways, a small civilian airline named after its owner, Mrs Wilson, and based in Nairobi, was taken over and given military status by being incorporated into the Kenya Regiment.[46] Its light aircraft had previously been used for charter flights but now they carried out coast-watching duties and, due to the shortages of radios and communication equipment, transported important messages. A limited maritime presence was even raised, largely at the behest of a British torpedo officer on HMS *Gloucester*, who addressed a meeting of the Victoria Nyanza Sailing Club shortly before the war broke out and encouraged its members to offer their support.[47] A naval training centre and a Royal Navy Volunteer Supplementary Reserve were subsequently formed at Kampala and stationed at Lake Victoria, 800 miles from the Indian Ocean.[48] Finally, there were the various locally raised coastal defence units who served alongside police and volunteer reserves. These were armed mostly with vintage rifles, or nothing at all, but, between them, they covered the territories of Kenya, Uganda, Tanganyika, Northern Rhodesia and the Nyasaland Protectorate, all of which fell under Dickinson's control.

Much worse even than lack of equipment, the greatest problem facing Wavell's senior officer in Nairobi was the lack of troops available to him. The KAR's main role prior to the outbreak of war was to provide internal security, guarding in particular against raiding bandits attacking across the Kenyan frontier. It was also to form the core of an army in the event of any mobilisation in which the proportion of Africans to British in each of the battalions was about sixteen to one.[49] Dickinson initially only had five of these battalions and one other from the Kenya Regiment although many of the men in the latter were far from fully trained as the war began.[50] They were all short of equipment, lacking transport and guns but, according to one of the British officers serving with them, his African troops were 'best suited to mobile offensive operations in bush country; all their instincts and natural training are in favour of the attack'.[51] There was little hope of reinforcements arriving from overseas as, even before he had arrived in East Africa, the general had been told that 'naval escort difficulties' entailed that, for several months, he would have to be self-sufficient.[52] This meant, for example, that it was only with the arrival of an Indian mountain battery on 11 September 1939 that he gained his first artillery unit.[53]

By the following month the situation had already improved and the headquarters of the 1st East African Infantry Brigade, covering the south of the colony, had been established in Nairobi with the available infantry and artillery split between the capital, and Mombasa and Malindi on the coast. A second brigade was based around Nanyuki in the Kenyan highlands, with companies in Jinja, Wajir and Moyale, which meant there were now six fully equipped battalions.[54] The last of these locations, the headquarters of one of the province's administrative districts, was about five miles beyond the Northern Frontier District's scrub desert where the Boundary Commission of 1908 had established the frontier between British and Ethiopian territory.[55] Before the First World War, the KAR had built a tower and a fort with very thick walls which were considered to be resistant to small arms fire. A company from the 5th Battalion held the position but they were equipped only with four Vickers machine guns, one Bren gun and a number of old training Lewis guns.[56] Its nearest neighbouring unit, another company from the same battalion, was at Wajir ninety miles away. Described as 'the loneliest outpost of the British Empire', Wajir was also a vital source of water and once again had an old fort, this time with white walls, a Union Jack flying within its square keep and a tiny cemetery of graves containing soldiers who had already made the ultimate sacrifice.[57] The wells were forty to fifty feet deep and the water was reasonably pure but, even when boiled, it could still contain sharp crystals of undissolved mica and gypsum. These were the source of great pain for a number of unfortunate troops, and 'Wajir clap' was remembered long after the fighting had finished.[58]

Both of these remote, tiny outposts were in fact critical to Dickinson's thinking as he looked for ways in which he could weaken any future Italian offensive. On his opponent's side of the frontier water was plentiful, but on his own it was confined to this very narrow strip, after which 250 miles of waterless desert to the south acted as a powerful natural barrier. It therefore seemed sensible to use his limited manpower resources in an attempt to defend key strategic points which both dominated local transport and allowed him control of these vital sources of water. At the same time, however, it was always recognised that it would not be possible to hold these forward isolated positions for long, such were the challenges involved in keeping the garrisons adequately supplied. Nonetheless, occupying them was seen as a means of 'showing the flag' both to the local Africans and to the Italians across the border, and Dickinson resolved that the costs were worth bearing, hoping that, if they were lost, the desolate terrain would form a buffer. Given the lack of troops and equipment, the only other strands to Dickinson's strategic vision were the establishment of small mobile columns to harass the Italian units based in southern Ethiopia and, as had been proposed in the various appreciations produced in Cairo and London, to support a locally raised rebellion. Other than this, and with his priority – perhaps understandably – being the preparation of as many defensive positions as possible, the British commander did little to pursue the orders that had been sent to him from London to investigate how he might eventually conduct an advance into Italian East Africa.

Limited as the activity might have been on the British-held side of the frontier, far less was taking place on the other. Along the border between Kenya and Italian Somaliland there was some evidence of trenches being dug and mines being planted but everything was still considered to be 'very quiet and friendly'.[59] Reports from district officers in the north of Kenya in September 1939 consistently referred to the troops on the other side of the frontier as being 'absorbed with their own internal problems' as they continued to battle with the rebels fighting their guerrilla war.[60] These reports also referenced the friendly relations that existed with the Italians, who were at this point taking only 'normal' precautionary measures such as the stopping of leave and the calling up of reserves. To such observers, themselves administrators tasked with the smooth running of colonial territory, it seemed clear that the Italians did not want a war which could only adversely affect their already delayed schedules for completing their imperial ambitions. In many respects such conclusions were correct, as Mussolini never strayed from his initial vision of creating a settlement for surplus population. This had led him to invest money in Italian East Africa at a far greater rate than anything ever attempted by the other European powers as part of their imperial experiences.[61] His entire gold reserve allegedly ended up being spent in this pursuit, where it purchased everything from guns and tanks to mineral water and more than 3,000 miles of sealed roads.[62] High levels of taxation along with the seizing of livestock on what were viewed as unreasonable terms, however, led to the local Ethiopians adopting an increasingly pro-British attitude. Despite this being exactly what the generals in Nairobi, Cairo and London wanted, in October a British officer based on the frontier went so far as to express some sympathy for the European settlers on the other side who were 'at an unfortunate point in their colonial career, when their faults are still obvious and the benefits of their civilization not yet appreciated'.[63]

There was clearly a certain apathy concerning war aims. When Charles 'Fluffy' Fowkes, another officer with a great deal of previous military experience, arrived in Nairobi the following month to take command of a brigade, he found the colony 'completely unprepared for war'.[64] So bad was the situation, he concluded, that the chance of mounting a successful defence in the face of overwhelming Italian forces was 'a forlorn hope'. Dickinson was desperately trying to make best use of whatever he could find but the senior figures in London still appeared to show very little interest in the perilous situation facing him, or even any willingness to accept that it existed. A report produced in late November by the Joint Planning Sub-Committee went so far as to conclude that in Kenya and British Somaliland reasonable risks could continue to be taken.[65] This view was based upon the assessment that although there were up to seven Italian divisions within their East African territories, there was unlikely to be an attack on British or French forces due to the inability to send reinforcements through the Suez Canal. In many respects a reasonable conclusion, it led to the decision that the existing forces would probably be sufficient to mount the defence and that there would no reinforcements. Raising indigenous troops to distract and divert the Italians, and also requesting South African military support, was instead recommended as the best, and indeed only, possible course of action that could be pursued at this stage. The committee also considered Dickinson's idea of creating a Colonial Division drawing entirely on troops from across the continent, but this was rejected, and it was made clear, once again, that he would have to rely upon troops already in Kenya, and, as had previously been agreed, a brigade which would be sent from West Africa. Such was the sense of denial about the perilous nature of the threat facing the British Empire's East African territories that when this far-reaching report did make passing reference to Wavell's concerns about the Red Sea, it took the form of a brief discussion about the potential wider impact of Italy joining the war and not the impact it might have on the region.

Kenya was not, however, the only focus of British and Commonwealth regional activity. For an area that was more than half the size of India, the main defending forces in the Sudan consisted of only three British battalions of regular infantry. There was also the Sudan Defence Force (SDF), which contained a further 5,000 men organised into groups of mounted and regular infantry and motor machine-gun companies, although initially they had no tanks or artillery, which limited their military effectiveness.[66] As was the case in other British-held territories across the region, there were very few sealed roads and during the rainy season from June to early October it was impossible for motor transport to operate in many areas. The only port was Port Sudan and a main rail line ran from it to Atbara, with key branches from there to Khartoum and Kassala on the border with Eritrea. Although this represented a crucial means of movement, both of troops and equipment, the track was a single line and liable to disruption from sandstorms and floods.[67]

Shortly after the outbreak of war in Europe, it was proposed that the size of the available forces in the Sudan be increased by the raising of an extra SDF battalion. The energetic local commander also began preparations for conducting further operations in neighbouring Italian territories.[68] This was William Platt, a professional soldier who had been commissioned from Sandhurst in 1905, joining the Northumberland Fusiliers, after which he had fought on the North-West Frontier of India and was awarded a DSO. He served throughout the First World War, during which he was wounded on four occasions but also repeatedly promoted. After the war he was posted to various home commands, including Ireland, and completed two-year tours in both Egypt and the War Office before being appointed aide-de-camp to the king.⁶⁹ In late 1938 he was promoted to major-general and took up the appointment in Khartoum as the SDF's commandant, a role which carried the Arabic title of *al-qa'id al-'amm*, 'the Leader of the Army', often referred to more simply as 'the Kaid'. According to one of his junior officers, Platt was a 'stick of dynamite in a hot fire when there was a job to be done', and he also, fortunately, proved to be a commander who was not overwhelmed by the size of the opponent facing him.

The Italians had assembled in Eritrea and northern Ethiopia nearly 70,000 men, 300 artillery pieces, 36 tanks and 24 armoured cars. Whilst this included a regular division of white soldiers and a number of Blackshirt militia battalions, most were colonial forces and local troops. The Italian officers commanding these units were renowned for their courage and skilful leadership and worked particularly well in combination with the Eritreans, who were on the whole loyal, intelligent, brave and, except in their fire discipline, good soldiers. The Ethiopians could be much less consistent, at times displaying considerable gallantry and skill and holding up positions or counter-attacking if dislodged, but on other occasions offering little or no resistance and surrendering when the first chance arose. All of the equipment was relatively modern except for the largely obsolete artillery, the value of which was reduced still further by its defective ammunition. Even so it was possible for these guns to be used along with heavy mortars which had a range of 4,000 yards, far greater than anything available to Platt. The Italians were limited, however, in their ability to use their tanks and armoured cars. In the summer of 1940 they still had large stocks of general supplies and materiel, including petrol, but a shortage of tyres meant the mobility of these vehicles was much reduced. This was largely unknown to the British commanders, who focused on defensive preparations and ordered the regular infantry to protect the key locations of Khartoum, Port Sudan and Atbara.⁷⁰ Even with the SDF formed into mobile striking forces which would attempt to slow down any invading columns as they advanced, Platt and Wavell accepted that the frontier towns would have to be evacuated.

This was of course still the period during which Europe was gripped by the 'phoney war' and the lack of any actual fighting produced a stupor in some quarters that extended to the Middle East and Africa. Further staff talks held with the French in early November 1939 only served to highlight the fact that in certain quarters there was no desire to change preparations across the region. The possibility of launching military operations against Italian East Africa was rejected, noting that there were still only 'very small bodies of troops' in Kenya, the use of which was 'quite impracticable' for such purposes.[71] With the manpower position not much better in the Sudan, a possible attack launched from French or British Somaliland was viewed as having 'most undesirable effects on Italian opinion' and the suggestion was dismissed completely. Even the French proposal to establish a joint command for the Red Sea area was rejected as having 'possible repercussions' on Mussolini. The only agreement reached was that the existing headquarters were adequate for the moment and, so long as Allied forces were spread thinly, the talks concluded that it would be a mistake to 'mortgage' them as part of a campaign in eastern Africa. Two months later Wavell wrote to his old friend John Dill, then commanding I Corps in northern France, and revealed that he had still yet to receive notification of any definite policy from London about how he should proceed.[72] He also complained that British prestige remained low in Egypt because the locals felt that 'anyone who let the Italians, whom even they regarded with contempt, outface them, can't really be very formidable'. The failings of pre-war diplomatic policy were being felt and, whilst reserves were slowly being built up 'in the usual solid Anglo-Saxon way', this had begun some months late and he was still short on manpower and very concerned about the lack of aircraft.

The experience of West African Field Force provided an excellent illustration of the existing complications. Although no longer present to lead them, Giffard's pre-war organisation of the forces under his command now appeared to be of considerable value for Dickinson. His predecessor had been able to oversee the establishment of four infantry brigades on both sides of the continent. Whilst the two in West Africa were not quite at full strength – only one battalion in each brigade was fully manned and equipped and the others depended upon the addition of reserves once war broke out – it meant that at least potentially there were some additional forces available beyond the KAR and locally raised troops.[73] The suggestion had been made in London that they might be used in the Sudan, and Dickinson, then in Khartoum on his way to take up his post in Nairobi, had been asked for his views.[74] He challenged the idea, writing to Cairo that the 'West African contingent are first class fighting material but are affected physically if exposed to cold . . . any offensive from Sudan must take them into mountainous country where cold might be too much for them'. He hoped that instead they would be made available primarily for use in Kenya, or in British Somaliland.[75]

Wherever they were to be sent, the original plans had called for the troops to be dispatched within fourteen days of mobilisation, but this soon slipped, in large part because of the lack of available shipping.[76] Some thought had been given throughout the summer to alternative methods of moving the men by road from Nigeria to the Sudan and then on by rail or river steamer and road to Kenya.[77] There was also the potential for transporting all or part of the brigades by air, but as the RAF could spare only six bombers, and the bare minimum number of troops and equipment weighed about six tons, the idea was not pursued.[78] Eventually 'cost and administrative difficulties', not to mention the distances involved, meant that the overland route was also abandoned and it was confirmed that the troops would have to be moved by sea.[79] At the end of December London finally issued a warning that this was likely to begin soon, as the War Office had authorised the sailing of the first contingents towards the end of the following month.[80] In the event this did not happen and all these plans were cancelled without any date being given for when the move might eventually begin. It was not until May that the code-word 'Tempest' was, at last, issued, and Nigerian troops boarded troopships in Lagos the following month.[81] These men would go on to play a significant role subsequently, but it had taken more than nine months to complete something that had been planned for well in advance, and if the Italians had seized the initiative and exploited their opponent's weakness, the eventual outcome of the campaign could have been very different.

During this long delay reinforcements did arrive from elsewhere on the continent. By the end of December 1939, troops from 1st Battalion, North Rhodesian Regiment had been transported along with their equipment in a convoy of 200 trucks which travelled 700 miles from Broken Hill; accompanied by their own mobile workshops to make repairs on the way, they lost only a single truck.[82] For some reason this movement of Commonwealth forces was not reported in London until the following March when it was described as the longest trek of the war.[83] So great was the number of African volunteers that recruiting had been stopped after just a couple of weeks and a second battalion was already fully manned. The newspaper article that revealed the move also confirmed details of the contribution being made by both Rhodesian territories. No.1 Squadron, Southern Rhodesia Air Force had in fact been in Kenya for some months; the first six aircraft, along with thirteen officers and fourteen other ranks, had actually mustered a week before war was declared and set off more or less at once for Nairobi to supplement Mrs Wilson's pilots.[84] After some local training at Isiolo, at the base of the Kenyan highlands, they had then quickly started operations patrolling the north of the colony.

It was their neighbours in the Union of South Africa, however, who would eventually play by far the more important role and a key part in the campaign. Following on from the pre-war uncertainties about what level of involvement could be expected, Smuts had become prime minister in September 1939 in a highly controversial manner and throughout the war he faced an organised domestic opposition that in many cases openly sympathised with Nazi Germany's objectives.[85] The support he could offer, at least initially, was therefore limited and South Africa's leader found himself obliged to maintain a consistently cautious line. To address the chronic lack of pre-war spending, a major programme of military reorganisation was begun but it would take some time for the Union's military to be brought back up to strength. Despite this, within a few months Smuts offered to send a brigade to Kenya; this came as a surprise to those in Whitehall who were already wondering at this stage whether the few military steps that had been authorised for the colony's security were actually necessary.[86] A combination of these doubts and the absence of the spare equipment needed by the South African brigade to bring it up to effective fighting strength led to the offer being tactfully refused. There was also some hesitancy because, at this stage, troops from the Union were restricted to serving at home and only volunteers could be sent north. Planning for a possible future move was, however, welcomed, as was the proposed dispatch of several air squadrons to supplement the Rhodesian pilots and aircraft.

The officials in London who had rejected the offer to send troops failed to appreciate how badly this would be received. Bishop visited Pretoria in January 1940 and met with Smuts, who said he appreciated the reasons behind the decision but was still visibly disappointed.[87] He also made it clear to the British visitor that no further offer would be made and he would have to be asked for help. This did not prevent it being announced the following month that South African forces would be available to assist in 'the defence of British territories in Africa up to Equator including Tanganyika and Kenya'.[88] And at the end of March a voluntary personal declaration, known as the 'Red Oath' because those who took it were issued with orange-scarlet tabs to be worn on the shoulder straps of their uniforms, was taken by nearly the whole of the defence forces. This confirmed they would serve 'anywhere in Africa', but many reportedly crossed out the words 'in Africa'. Over the next few months those who had not taken the oath were removed from military service. Despite the lack of an agreement between the authorities in London and Pretoria, should one be reached, a potential additional reserve of manpower was now available.

Dickinson had meanwhile continued to grapple with the many challenges he faced although he was described by one British visitor who met him just before Christmas as being 'very cheerful' and leading 'a very good family party' in his headquarters.[89] There were now dedicated military units of all types available to him with machine gun battalions, engineers, pioneers, signallers, motor transport, a recce squadron and even the aircraft from the Southern Rhodesia Air Force. Although the numbers remained small, there were also almost two fully trained infantry brigades available to defend this front and he hoped it might be possible not merely to halt any Italian offensive at the edge of the highlands but to launch a limited counter-attack.[90] Whilst his troops were still short of equipment that could halt an advance by Italian armour, much work had been done by the railway workshops to improvise anti-tank mines, mortars and Bren guns, while also turning out water containers and motor ambulances that would, in some ways, be just as important for any eventual advance north. Indeed, Dickinson judged by January 1940 that the military situation he faced had now improved sufficiently for him to consider how he might eventually attack Italian territory.[91]

Although some Whitehall administrative involvement remained, on 3 February Wavell's headquarters took operational control of East Africa, which meant that Dickinson could now be more effectively integrated within the wider regional preparations. The general in Nairobi responded by proposing that, in the event of war breaking out, he should split his forces in order to use them as three mobile columns to harass the Italians, one advancing from Moyale and the others to the east and west of Lake Rudolf. He also intended to use refugees who had crossed into Kenya following the initial Italian invasion four years earlier to capture Kalam in the south-west of Ethiopia while troops from the KAR advanced on Afmadu and Gelib heading on to Kismayu.[92] Both the base at Garissa and the headquarters at Nanyuki, nearly 130 miles from Nairobi, had now been further strengthened and expanded to brigade-level standards. Improvements had been made at both locations to the road and rail links, along with the construction of dispersed shelters for the storage of additional ammunition and other supplies needed to sustain any advance. At Moyale and Wajir the garrisons had been enlarged to battalion strength although the newly arrived men were told that their role was to conduct a heroic final stand and fight to the last round if required. The defences to the west of Lake Rudolf were also reinforced, with troops being sent to guard the important passes at Nepau and the River Moroto.

Despite facing what had seemed a hopeless position back in September, only eight months later the situation appeared to have turned around, with improvised but much-improved equipment and plans for conducting both defensive and offensive operations now in place. In many respects it was a remarkable achievement for Dickinson, who had been faced initially with a huge area to defend, defensive positions which could have been easily outflanked, and very few troops.[93] What he did not know was that his likely opponent had, during this same period of tremendous British and Commonwealth activity, grown more convinced of the need to avoid conflict. In April 1940 Aosta went to Rome to try and convince Mussolini that Italian East Africa was still unready for war. He told the Italian leader that the French and British were 'already equipped and ready for action' and that the local population would 'revolt as soon as they got an inkling of our difficulties'.[94] The viceroy may have been exaggerating, but at least some of his concerns were genuine.[95] The area he governed was geographically far from the Italian mainland, making it increasingly difficult to sustain the theoretically enormous armed forces under his command, an argument he had made throughout the time he had spent in charge in Addis Ababa. This was the weakness that Wavell had identified shortly after his arrival in Cairo and it was shared by the Chiefs of Staff in London. It had in fact become a widely held view, Britain's High Commissioner in Pretoria being told by officials in Whitehall in late April that Italy's fundamental difficulty remained how to maintain its military forces in Ethiopia and the other East African colonies without having command of the sea.[96] As Aosta also seemed to grasp, this meant it was just a matter of time until these grew weaker whilst, at least in theory, the British and French position could only improve so long as the alliance between the two held firm.

With the German attack on France and the Low Countries under way, in May, Badoglio, now Chief of the General Staff and Italy's senior military officer, called a meeting of his fellow Chiefs of Staff in Rome. This was to inform Admiral Domenico Cavagnari, the head of the navy, and General Francesco Pricolo, leading the air force, of the decision that had been taken about how the country would respond to Hitler's aggression.[97] Mussolini had decided it was now time to enter the war in order to secure a share of what he anticipated would be the spoils of the German victory. As one commentator has put it, Mussolini had no real military strategy, only a political one, and every decision he took was designed to ensure he enjoyed the most favourable terms when the war was won.[98] However, Italy would intervene only at such time and in such places as he chose and, whilst he was prepared to order his forces to fight offensively at sea and in the air, on land he had decided they would fight only defensive campaigns.[99] Although the Italians appeared to enjoy a significant advantage in manpower and equipment, the military position was actually increasingly fragile, certainly in Italian East Africa. Italian-held territory was encircled and effectively under siege, but this would only become apparent in the months that followed. While nobody at this time could know what would happen, there might already have been doubts about how the Italian military might perform.

In reality, in both London and Cairo the extent of their opponent's weakness was still entirely unknown. Gaining reliable and accurate intelligence about the intentions of their soon-to-be enemies had proven a difficult task due to the restrictions on military activity during the preceding years. There were no agents in Italian territory who could be trusted, which meant that only the roughest of appreciations could be made of the potential threat.[100] When reports were received in Nairobi that the Italians were reinforcing their side of the border at Moyale, it seemed the inevitable was coming.[101] On 19 May it was reported that general mobilisation had been ordered across Italian East Africa, with considerable troop movements towards French and British Somaliland and in the direction of the Kenyan border.[102] All leave was now reportedly cancelled and travel back to Italy was banned, except by special authority. In response, conscription was introduced in Uganda and Tanganyika and further restrictions were imposed on enemy aliens and other foreigners, but at least some of those reading the reports in Cairo concluded that these were not necessarily indications of a pending offensive.[103] Yet, to the British and Commonwealth officers who had assembled in eastern Africa, the long-anticipated war at last appeared poised to begin.

CHAPTER 3

WAR COMES TO EAST AFRICA

THE MILITARISATION OF East Africa increased dramatically during May and June 1940 as British and Commonwealth forces continued to assemble in anticipation of war breaking out with Italy. The arrivals included the troops from West Africa who eventually reached Mombasa docks as the Italian Air Force flew over, forcing the Nigerians to hurriedly step ashore as the port's recently arrived anti-aircraft guns opened fire against the attacking aircraft.[1] Giffard thought he had managed to persuade the government in London to provide modern equipment for these units but the War Office had proved reluctant to divert funding, and only limited arms and equipment were made available prior to the outbreak of the war.[2] Each battalion had brought with it light machine guns, grenades and mortars and not much else; up until April 1941, few of the officers had revolvers and for the most part, despite being told that the alternative was to carry a rifle, they chose to remain unarmed.[3] Individually, however, the troops were well equipped with slouch hats and specially designed boots, and each man was armed with a .303 rifle, a bayonet and a machete.[4] As fighting infantry units they had just about enough to be able to carry out the role they would be asked to play. With all the troops able to speak and understand what was termed 'good English', they absorbed the junior British officers who were waiting to meet them and fill the gaps that existed within their ranks, and headed north to the frontier.[5] With their arrival, Dickinson was now commanding a force made up of contingents drawn from across the British Empire and he was as prepared as he might reasonably have hoped to be.

For the British general, organising and managing this alliance would be complicated, and trouble could easily lie ahead. At least some of his troops were still subject to orders from their respective colonial governments, which meant there were 'considerable, but varying limitations on the use that might be made of them', most notably the South Africans who were also now arriving in eastern Africa in large part down to Wavell's direct intervention.[6] In mid-March 1940 Wavell travelled to Cape Town for a first meeting with Smuts and, with any confusion about where the troops would be able to serve having been removed, found his host still keen to help. The senior British commander in the Middle East and Africa seized upon this and secured the deployment of a brigade.[7] Wavell was also thinking further ahead and hoped that a limited commitment at this stage might lead to the promise later of more troops to serve beyond the equator as part of operations in the Western Desert.[8] Less than a year later he was complaining about these formations which expected 'to be put into battle straight away and become restive if compelled to wait for equipment or to train for long periods', but for now they were very much appreciated.[9] This was especially true as it became clear that substantial reinforcements would have to be sent to Egypt, where a major invasion from Libya seemed possible.[10] Confirmation followed shortly afterwards that the South Africans would join the forces in East Africa, but they would not start to arrive until the end of June.[11] The German invasion of Holland in May further increased support in the dominion for 'full participation in the war'[12] and even extended to the many Dutch-speaking members of the community. According to Brooke-Popham, now leading a mission to train pilots and aircrew to fight in the Battle of Britain and beyond, even they believed that, 'in spite of all their sins, the British are preferable to the Germans'.[13]

It would take some time for these additional troops to arrive but those Dickinson did have under his command were as well prepared as they could be when William Joyce, or Lord Haw-Haw as he was already known in Britain, broadcast from Berlin the confirmation of what had long been anticipated. As he informed his listeners, 'the world will once again hear the tramp of the dauntless Roman Legions. The flashing eagles have been raised aloft to restore to Italy her historic position in the world.'[14] The leadership in Rome had declared war on Britain and France on 10 June 1940 and, certainly at the outset, there seemed to be a strong belief that the prospects for immediate success were good. On the day of the announcement at least three Italian divisions could almost have walked into British Somaliland from Ethiopia, with only a garrison consisting of one KAR battalion, the Somaliland Camel Corps and a few irregular troops to halt them.[15] Despite the rhetoric of the German propaganda, however, there was little real enthusiasm within the Italian military for such a bold move. As one writer has since confirmed, the official strategy almost entirely remained containing the enemy for as long as possible and assuming that Britain would sue for peace following its inevitable defeat in Egypt.[16] If East Africa was lost during this period it was assumed that Italy would be able to recover this territory and much more. Certainly, when in July Gian Galeazzo Ciano – 2nd Count of Cortellazzo and Buccari, Foreign Minister of Fascist Italy and Mussolini's son-in-law – presented plans to Hitler for how the Middle East would be reorganised following an Axis victory, Egypt, the Sudan and British Somaliland were all highlighted as passing into Italian hands.[17] All Mussolini believed he needed was 'a few thousand dead to justify my presence at the peace table', and so, ignoring the advice of his senior officers, and reassuring them that it would last three months at the most, he declared war.[18]

Whilst he might not have anticipated the dramatic nature of France's military and political collapse, Wavell had considered the impact a belligerent Italy would have on his command. As it now became a reality, it made the direction he had received from London not to take any precautionary action all the more frustrating.[19] He later wrote that a more robust approach 'during the period of waiting instead of our weak-kneed and apologetic attempts at appeasement would certainly not have increased the danger of war and might perhaps have lessened it'.[20] As it was, his preparations were hampered and this appeared to exacerbate the danger that he and his forces now faced as the wartime balance of power was instantly and immeasurably changed, and the failings of pre-war British planning were brought into sharp perspective. Even before the armistice was signed near Compiègne on 22 June 1940, Italy's already strong position in East Africa seemed to be potentially overwhelming. Shortly before the declaration of war, the Italian garrison had a recorded strength of 91,203 military personnel and police and 199,973 colonial troops.[21] Whilst British and Commonwealth numbers later peaked at 254,000, in July 1940 they were a fraction of that figure – in total, just 47,000 men in East Africa, the Sudan and British Somaliland.[22]

Before the war, British military planners had anticipated the huge disparity but accepted it as unavoidable, and assumed that they would at least have an advantage at sea. The collapse of the Anglo-French alliance meant that, having previously outmatched the Italians in every naval category, this was no longer the case. The Royal Navy could now call on just a single aircraft carrier, HMS *Eagle*, five battleships, nine cruisers, twenty-nine destroyers and twelve submarines to protect the whole Mediterranean and Red Sea area.[23] On the day Italy declared war, and though the bulk of the Regia Marina Italiana remained close to its home waters, the Italian Red Sea Flotilla based principally at Massawa still had seven destroyers, a squadron of five torpedo boats and eight submarines. This meant that the routing of every resupply convoy had to be considered carefully, balancing risk of attack against the operational urgency of delivering additional manpower, ammunition and vehicles. Some convoys had no choice but to continue to force their way through the Mediterranean, and the protection Admiral Cunningham was able to offer to these was vital but costly.[24] The better alternative was the far safer, but significantly longer, 13,000 miles from Britain around the Cape of Good Hope, which took between one and two months more travelling time. It was the same case, of course, for Allied vessels making the 6,000-mile journey from Australia and traversing the 2,000 miles from Bombay. With their destination Port Sudan or Mombasa, the ships and the convoys they formed were still exposed to a potential threat from the Italians. More significantly, neutral American ships were now forbidden to transit all of these newly declared combat zones, increasing the strain on the British maritime fleet.[25]

What Wavell and the other senior British political and military leaders still did not know even at this stage was that, despite the great advantages they appeared to enjoy, there was no danger of any significant Italian offensive operations. Despite having complained during his visit to Rome that his command was unprepared for war, Aosta had apparently protested when told by Badoglio of Mussolini's order that he was to adopt a defensive position. He believed that his previous instructions did at least allow him the possibility of bombing British and French naval and air bases and it was certainly the case that in March 1940 the viceroy had proposed to launch offensives against both Jibuti and Kenya.[26] The German consul in Addis Ababa later confirmed that a more aggressive plan had been developed, albeit under his authorship.[27] Allegedly, this called for an immediate invasion of Kenya extending as far as Uganda and with a focus on Mombasa with the intention of capturing, occupying and then retaining it as a fortified base. If this proved impossible the port was to be destroyed and a 'scorched earth' policy adopted as the Italian forces fell back to the mountains in the north of Ethiopia while the air force harassed any pursuing enemy advance. Not only had the leadership in Rome dismissed the plan as 'too ambitious' and 'hazardous', they had assured the German diplomat that their opponents would not be able to cross the deserts of the frontier, and Aosta was instead told to do nothing.[28] It is not clear what Badoglio himself thought about this, but the Chief of the General Staff was considered to be the most able of Italy's soldiers and was certainly the most experienced.[29] Whilst he had previously clashed with the Italian leader over strategy and would later resign from his position as a result of the disastrous military intervention in Greece, at this stage Badoglio would not challenge the direction he received from Mussolini. The same was true of Aosta and his subordinates, who did as they were ordered.

Although this was not the approach he wished to adopt, the viceroy confirmed to General Pietro Gazzera, commanding the 'Southern Sector' around Galla and Sidamo, that his land forces would be used only 'in the improbable event' that the British crossed the Kenyan frontier, and it was made quite clear that no one but Mussolini himself could decide when an attack might begin.[30] Any troop movements conducted before then were intended only for reconnaissance purposes and to alarm the enemy or to better position the men for a counter-attack if this was required. Elsewhere this meant Italian aircraft did not bomb key targets such as Mombasa for fear that Addis Ababa or Mogadishu would be targeted in response. Along the Red Sea, Italian naval forces therefore sat in their ports and coastal defence batteries failed to fire on British shipping so as to avoid the potential for retaliation. A single recorded attempt was made at striking a convoy but this resulted in seven bombers being shot down; Italian Air Force General Giuseppe Santoro wrote that, whilst such losses would normally have been considered insignificant, 'they were too serious for us to sustain in our peculiar circumstances'.[31] Nothing was done to interfere with the reinforcements as they arrived in Kenya and the Sudan to strengthen the local defences; the Italian military was content to simply sit and wait.[32]

The British did, of course, face their own problems at this point in the war. The survivors from Dunkirk had made it home but the vast majority of their equipment was left behind, abandoned on the roads heading to the evacuation ports.[33] British production lines were therefore tasked with working to re-equip the garrison that was assembling to protect the country from German invasion. Even in these most desperate of circumstances, for some the news that Mussolini had now also declared war was still seen as a cause for some cheer. The senior civil servant Sir Alexander Cadogan was not alone when he noted in his diary that he was rather glad as it could now be said 'what we think about these purulent dogs' who he hoped could be given 'an early and hard knock'.[34] Some also felt that Britain owed Ethiopia and its people a debt for not having helped when the country was overrun by the Italians.[35] And for many British officers, they also believed that, despite the much-changed strategic position, this new military opponent was not one that really needed to be feared. Even those commentators who were prepared to accept the existence of some positive attributes within the ranks of the Italian Army concluded that these could not overcome the 'gangster-leadership' and the more general failings of the strategy which had been adopted by the country's senior military officials.[36] Finally, along with critical shortages of resources – coal was commonly mentioned as one example where there was a potentially crippling dependency on German imports – and the problems of supplying its distant and isolated empire, the Italian economy was known to be on the verge of bankruptcy. The conclusion was that Italy was 'a liability and not an asset' for Germany and, once the maritime blockade took hold, the leadership in Berlin would come to question Mussolini's value to the Axis alliance.[37] With France lost, the British Empire was short of friends and stretched on all fronts and any form of potential success would offer some hope. Many thought this could be found in East Africa.

Although the broad Italian strategy was based on avoiding a decisive battle, and with British and Commonwealth commanders still focusing on assembling their forces, at the local level officers on both sides were willing to test their opponent's defences. Where the two bordered one another, skirmishes broke out and offered some early lessons for those involved. Dickinson had correctly guessed that Moyale would be among the first places to see action but for some reason the garrison had been reduced and only a single company of the KAR was in the small fort on the British side of the border with orders to 'Hold on as long as you can and then get back to Buna.'[38] Facing them was an entire enemy brigade of three battalions of colonial infantry supported by artillery.[39] Elderly Caproni bombers attacked on 13 June, also hitting the airfield at nearby Wajir, destroying 5,000 gallons of British aviation fuel and killing four of the defending *askaris*. British-led troops had, however, advanced across the frontier first, a patrol moving out of Moyale earlier on the same day and reaching the Italian Resident's house which they found to be unoccupied. At nearby Dif they encountered only ten defenders and further patrols the following day found rifles, ammunition and equipment, which suggested the enemy had taken to the bush.[40] This first engagement was reported in Britain as evidence of an initial success: it came at the same time as housewives were told new ration books were being distributed and that they now needed to register for margarine.[41] With the announcement that the August Bank Holiday was being cancelled, in comparison it must all have seemed a relatively minor matter in a place unknown to most.

The attack at El Wak, launched by two companies of the KAR on 18 June to capture the Italian side of the frontier, was a much larger affair.[42] Unreliable guides meant any hope of surprise was lost and despite the appearance of the RAF which forced the Italian colonial troops to flee into the bush, the attackers were easily beaten back by 'very wild and inaccurate' fire. However, British officers gained some valuable pointers about the effectiveness of both their own forces and those of the enemy.[43] It was already clear that raids by small groups to gain intelligence appeared to be the favoured form of action. They provided a good opportunity to blood the African troops although the limited attacks had to be well planned; if they were reckless in nature and failed, there was a risk that morale would be undermined. The initial very minor engagements also highlighted the importance of the defending *banda*, formed from Eritreans and Ethiopians, and which were not to be confused with the *shifta*, the groups of wild-haired bandits who roamed the countryside murdering at will. These were generally organised by the Italians into large groups of *bande*, about 1,500 men, which were then split into informal units of 250 each led by two white officers, and whilst they were unwilling to act as infantry in open battle they were used as scouts, a screen for regular troops, and also to harass the enemy rear areas. They put to good use their knowledge of the country, their considerable toughness and mobility, and their limited requirements for food and water to cause some real concerns for the British. By early September 1940 it was estimated that there were as many as 40,000 of them, resulting in warnings that if numbers were to continue growing they could prove 'a potential danger' with their hit-and-run tactics.[44] They also developed, at least initially, a fearsome reputation for murderous deeds amongst the British and Commonwealth troops, with tales of ambushes and sleeping victims dispatched during the night, although such acts were more often the work of the *shifta*.

Back at Moyale, on 28 June the first significant Italian attack of the war in Africa got under way with an assault by 1,000 men which followed a full hour's artillery bombardment. The defending troops from the KAR managed to fight off this assault and were reinforced over the following days to a strength of two companies, although one of their commanders was killed almost the instant he arrived. What the small garrison did not know was that their opponent had also committed a second brigade to the operation and assembled a force of more than 8,000 troops supported by significant amounts of artillery and light tanks.[45] The terrain provided the attackers with a strong advantage with lots of valleys and hillsides and fields of green maize that it had not been possible to clear beforehand, all of which offered good cover. The outcome was inevitable, and on 10 July another concerted attack began using some of the heavy guns which the Italians had now managed to move closer to Lone Tree Ridge, a dominating position to the east of the fort, from where they fired 1,000 shells during the first day.[46] The defenders were quickly surrounded and cut off from their water supplies and, despite some supporting air attacks, the position was increasingly hopeless. Attempts to push reinforcements forward, which reached within 2,000 yards of the besieged troops, failed and the fort was evacuated. It had been a hopelessly mismatched but heroic two-week defence which received considerable acclaim in the British press and led to the Military Cross being awarded to both the British officers serving with the KAR who had overseen the defence and the successful escape.[47]

Over the next few days Italian propaganda referred prominently to the garrison's rout and the capture not just of the Union Jack which had flown on the fort but also guns and ammunition, motor vehicles and rations. When reviewing the situation, Brigadier Fowkes, whose troops had formed the garrison, had not believed more than half the men could be saved. After the order came to withdraw, the British, who had donned black jerseys which could not be seen in the darkness, passed through the enemy lines unheard wearing rubber shoes, the African troops alongside them, barefoot, carrying their rifles and ammunition.[48] After walking for four miles in the moonlight, all but one of the men reached safety at Buna, another isolated post surrounded by miles of bush and with little water. Throughout the fighting just ten men were killed and another thirty-five wounded. The British brigadier later wrote that the loss was strategically insignificant but it had temporarily weakened the morale of the African troops and given a boost to the Italians. He could not understand why this single incident had led to a 'completely unjustified respect' amongst his officers and men for their opponent's fighting prowess, and he thought it inexplicable that the leadership in Rome should refer to it as a victory when it had taken several thousand heavily armed troops to push back a force a fraction of the attackers' size.[49] If the Italian military leaders had been honest with themselves, an analysis of what had really happened should in fact have offered some worrying evidence about the effectiveness of their military forces.

Fowkes considered launching an instant counter-attack the following morning which he believed would be likely to relieve Moyale. He was aware that this could also have presented an opportunity for the Italians to threaten the advance base at Nanyuki and, reluctantly, the decision was therefore taken to halt, and the front quickly became static. Indeed no further action was taken until the end of July when a minor battle took place at Dobel, another of the frontier wells that offered such a vital source of water in the parched desert.[50] Troops from 1st Battalion, Nigerian Regiment captured the position but were then forced to withdraw into a shallow valley overlooked from three sides and were given 'a proper basting'.

They fell back to Wajir 'showing little stomach for the fight' and with their morale in tatters; it was not until the initial stages of the main campaign the following year that they regained their fighting spirit.[51] Despite the British and Commonwealth forces' apparent struggles it was the Italians, however, who were drawing entirely inaccurate assumptions about the outcome of these initial battles – but these would only become clear later.

This was a wartime theatre with two fronts: to the south, running along the Kenyan frontier, as well as to the north, where the declaration of war had been greeted by an equally sparse scattering of British and Commonwealth forces. British strength in the Sudan consisted of an infantry battalion from the West Yorkshire Regiment in Khartoum, along with supporting artillery and service arm detachments, 1st Battalion, Essex Regiment in Atbara, and a battalion of the Worcestershire Regiment split between Gebeit and Port Sudan.[52] The distribution of these troops was entirely in keeping with Platt's appreciation of the previous year. The same was true with the movement of the SDF, which had first been ordered in May to Butana Bridge and then on to Atbara from where its motorised machine-gun companies were meant to delay and harass any Italian advance.[53] In the event of an Italian declaration of war, the initial instruction, however, was that these forces were not to fire on enemy positions across the frontier, and this included a platoon based in the old fort at Gallabat, where it heard the news on the radio that hostilities had commenced.[54] Despite these orders, with twenty minutes to spare before sunset, two Vickers and two Bren guns on a ridge overlooking the Italians opened fire and continued for ten minutes before withdrawing. The men had fired 13,000 rounds of ammunition in that time and, on returning to their base, discovered they had in fact carried out the first attack of the East Africa campaign. On being told there were orders that no action was to be taken, their commanding officer told them to 'write it off to training'.

As was the case on the Kenyan frontier, further skirmishes followed and on the last day of June a more significant Italian attack looked possible in the Karora region until British aircraft bombed enemy troops who were gathering along the border. At Gallabat, which had been temporarily abandoned after this display of firepower, the opportunity to advance and occupy the post was ignored. British-led troops moved back in the following morning and it was not until 4 July that the Italians finally attacked using both European and African troops supported by tanks, aircraft and even motorbikes with mounted machine guns. The still small defending garrison proved no match for the attackers, and was forced once again to withdraw. With the battle won, Italian planes dropped leaflets in Arabic carrying the message that Mussolini was the protector of Islam.[55] A brigade of motorised infantry units supported by armoured cars also crossed the border farther north heading for Kassala, a small border town which held a strategically vital position controlling the potential movement of troops between Eritrea and the Sudan, and even from here on to Egypt and Libya.[56] Its 25,000 inhabitants lived largely in mud dwellings alongside another old fort in the shadow of an enormous granite hill, 'a high rock sticking straight out of the desert', which, added to the heat and dust haze that was common except during the rainy period, made for an unpleasant climate and one of the hottest, dirtiest and windiest towns ever visited by one British civil servant.[57] Flowing alongside the town was the River Gash, which ran past the town from the Eritrean hills for three months of the year at a speed of about four miles an hour 'heavily laden with silt and resembling pale tomato soup on the boil'.[58] This made for some of the best agricultural land in the Sudan and a thriving economic hub, as the cotton which was grown locally was transported by rail from the station just a few miles outside the town. The Italians had drawn upon this same natural resource and dammed the river towards the east at nearby Tessenei to make this the centre of their cotton-growing scheme. They had also continued the main road from Asmara, described as a first-class piece of engineering, so that it ended on their side of the frontier. This allowed for the rapid export of commercial goods and also meant that, if required, potentially overwhelming forces could be moved forward along it towards the Sudanese frontier. Platt knew this but there was little he could do to respond.

Defending Kassala were only two motor machine-gun companies from the Eastern Arab Corps, a mounted infantry company from the Western Arab Corps which had travelled 1,000 miles from Darfur, and the town's small police force.[59] In total there were less than 500 men whilst the Italians had about 8,000 troops assembled in two motorised colonial brigades along with four cavalry regiments, artillery, eighteen tanks and aircraft. Prior to the attack, the town was bombed for twelve hours without pause but the defenders remained in their shelters and did not flee. When this ended, they quickly manned the defences and inflicted serious losses, with several hundred enemy casualties reported, even destroying six of the tanks. Eventually the defending garrison withdrew with the loss of one man killed, three wounded and sixteen missing, some of whom managed to find their way back to their units later. It had once again been an unconvincing Italian victory. The attackers had, however, broken through the frontier's thin defensive screen and could have moved forward to threaten the Sudan with a more general invasion. Although July was the peak of the 1940 rainy season, it had been exceptionally light and movement along the roads and tracks was interrupted far less often than usual. Yet, again, the Italians made no attempt to exploit their advantage, either as a result of a mistaken assessment that it would be too difficult to advance or because they believed the defending forces to be far larger than they actually were. In fact they only pushed on towards Adardeb, close to the important rail line, and another frontier post at Kurmuk which was abandoned later the same day.[60] The British and Commonwealth forces to the north and west were therefore able to quickly reorganise while preparing to harass the anticipated advance towards Khartoum, Atbara or Port Sudan. When this did not come, companies from both the Worcestershire and Essex regiments were sent forward as reinforcements, leading the Italians to retire to Kassala and to establish a garrison of five battalions supported by tanks and artillery. As was the case on the southern front, they now waited.

Having been slow to begin, the opening moves in the East Africa campaign were now largely complete. For the British commanders, the weekly intelligence summary issued on 18 July already offered a much more detailed assessment of the enemy activity than had been available even a few months before.[61] In both the north and the south the Italians had fully demonstrated their overwhelming superiority both in troops and equipment but there was little evidence of this being used in a decisive manner. The report concluded that the attacks had actually been on a minor scale, with Kassala described as a raid and the remainder simply incursions into British-held territory which 'held a nuisance value'. There had been very limited advances and, with no knowledge of the orders that had been given to Aosta and the defensive posture he had been forced to adopt, there was some confusion as to what this might mean. At this stage the conclusion was that the results of armistice negotiations with Vichy France were being awaited and the planners assumed that this would determine what happened next. Nonetheless, the small garrisons of British-led colonial forces, supported by the few regular units that had been sent to the region, had for the large part successfully carried out the plans prepared by Wavell and his senior generals and had managed to keep the frontiers of the British Empire more or less intact.

There was, however, an additional front that the British commander had been considering for some months and which would increasingly come to attract his attention. There were few more unforgiving imperial territories than British Somaliland, an arid plateau covering 68,000 square miles with sandy plains running from the shoreline, in some cases to a distance of sixty miles into the interior. Behind this was a range of hills and mountains 4,000 feet high on average, and rising at times to more than double this height. There was little cultivation and the 1939 population of 320,000, mainly nomadic Somalis, lived for the most part in the interior, where they survived on the livestock they kept, and on the coast in the main population centre of Berbera.[62] This was surrounded by low-lying desert with a little scrub; during the colder months its population reached about 30,000 but during the hot season it could be as little as half this. It was also the chief port for the protectorate although it had an almost complete lack of decent facilities, a failing that had been highlighted repeatedly prior to the war but about which nothing had been done. It did, however, provide good anchorage, with loading and discharging then being carried out by small boats. Described appropriately as a 'mostly thirsty region', the port was entirely lacking in water; this had to be brought in by a nine-mile-long pipe which produced 'a lukewarm, briny fluid'.[63] Between June and August a very hot strong wind called the *Kharif* blew, making it even more difficult to load and unload as it was impossible to work in the heat. It was reportedly said by those who tried to live in Berbera 'that no one could live there for an entire year and be regarded as completely sane thereafter'.[64]

The protectorate had previously been the scene of a long military campaign as Britain fought one of its lesser known imperial wars. The opponent was Mohammed Abdullah Hassan, 'a Moslem religious warlike fanatic' referred to popularly as the 'Mad' Mullah.[65] In the face of continuing raids by his dervishes, which had grown stronger and more sustained over the course of a decade, in April 1910 the garrison had been compelled to withdraw from the interior of the protectorate and seek shelter in three coastal towns which could be more easily defended.[66] Here, in 'one of the disturbed corners of the Empire', the remaining troops clung on throughout the First World War until, ten years and four campaigns later, the insurgency was ended when the now much-diminished dervishes were finally overwhelmed by a combined attack involving local forces, a battalion of the KAR and even some British aircraft.[67] Once again, the climate became the enemy, and Berbera was deemed such an inhospitable town that military commentators believed white officers could only be posted there for a few weeks at a time before they became operationally ineffective.[68]

The peculiar arrangements for administration of the territory made for further complications. Since 1905, following a brief period under the control of the Foreign Office, the Colonial Office had been responsible for British Somaliland.[69] Representing London locally, the senior figure in Berbera was the governor and, in 1939, at the outbreak of the Second

World War, this was Vincent Glenday, only forty-nine years old and in his first appointment at this senior level. He had spent his career in colonial administration, having previously been Provincial Commissioner in Kenya where he had gained a good reputation during many years spent working in the colony.[70] In addition to being governor, Glenday was the nominal commander-in-chief of the locally raised forces, the Somaliland Camel Corps. The Colonial Office paid for and organised all administrative tasks and because there was widespread sympathy for the governor's view that war was unlikely, it was reluctant to commit any of its budget to military activity.[71] Indeed, restrictions were placed on the amount of expenditure made available for defence despite Wavell's concerns about local security.[72] These were based on simple geography, as the Italian occupation of Ethiopia had left British Somaliland entirely surrounded along its 750-mile frontier except for about forty-five miles which bordered French-held Jibuti. This was thought to make the protectorate vulnerable, and a secret plan had been conceived in 1938 to evacuate forces in the event of an attack. Glenday's predecessor, Sir Arthur Lawrence, had bitterly rejected this proposal, writing back to the authorities in London after the signing of the Munich agreement with a reminder that money and lives had already been spent.[73] Whilst he realised that it was 'an insignificant fragment of the vast territories under British administration' and one that could 'scarcely be expected to come prominently into the reckoning', he nonetheless argued that it should still be possible for more to be done.

Lawrence had argued that there were three alternative courses of action available.[74] The first was to make no pretence of conducting a defence and effectively demilitarise the territory. Secondly, it could be abandoned altogether. His preference, not surprisingly, was the final option, which had been suggested to him by Lieutenant-Colonel Arthur Chater, the senior military officer and commander of the Camel Corps. Prior to his secondment he had been a Royal Marine and his only experience of working with British infantrymen was limited to three months during the Gallipoli campaign.[75] Since taking up this role, Chater had gained a huge knowledge of the troops he commanded and, despite limited reinforcements and a small amount of funding, he argued that an adequate defence was still possible. The intention was to hold up an invasion for at least twelve days and allow for reinforcements to be sent from India. Despite the governor's support this proposal was rejected and, in August 1939, the evacuation plan was revised on the basis of two possible situations arising. In the first, and with the French holding their positions in Jibuti, a withdrawal would be conducted towards them to combine the available defending forces. If, however, they had also been driven back, British and Commonwealth troops would withdraw into the hills and await instructions.[76]

In line with the discussions that had been held in Paris and London throughout the year, at this stage all defence preparations were based around joint agreements with the local French commander, Brigadier-General Paul Legentilhomme, who it was also intended would take overall charge in the event of war.[77] Whilst Chater liked his counterpart, 'an exceptionally pleasant man, and I think a very able soldier', he had grave concerns about the plans. With the declaration of war against Germany a number of key positions were manned in anticipation of an Italian attack, which fortunately never came. If it had done, the Camel Corps' military commander wrote later in September, the protectorate would have been thrown 'into a state of panic and disorder, with the result that administrative control of our tribes would probably be lost before a shot had been fired by the enemy'.[78] Chater also now submitted a candid report to the Middle East Command describing local conditions and complaining about the recent confusion and uncertainty.[79] This suggested that, since the Italian invasion of Ethiopia, the Chiefs of Staff had seen British Somaliland as nothing more than 'a tiresome commitment' which they would 'gladly be rid of', an assessment that was probably not far from the truth.[80]

As the months of the phoney war dragged on, Wavell agreed privately that British-led forces should not come under French control until it became necessary for them to withdraw towards Jibuti.[81] This, in effect, gave Chater a free hand in how to mount his defence but with the caveat that he was still also committed to close co-operation with his French counterpart. The British officer now proposed, as a bare minimum, that detachments be left to protect the two largest up-country towns of Burao and Hargeisa even though these would struggle even to resist weak raiding parties; in the event of a meaningful attack their orders were to delay any advance and then withdraw towards the hills. At the same time he was drawn to the vital strategic significance of a semicircle of hills which effectively dominated the main route from the French colony towards Berbera. As there were just six passes these vehicles could use to reach the flat coastal plain beyond, both he and his French counterpart agreed that all of them would have to be held, both to safeguard defence and to provide sufficient room from which to begin any subsequent offensive.

In both London and Paris, however, there was still a great deal of confusion about how any local defence might be conducted, and in December 1939 the British Chiefs of Staff once again changed their collective minds.[82] They now confirmed that there should be a more active policy, issuing orders that British Somaliland was to be defended against an Italian invasion and Berbera was not to be abandoned but held as long as possible.[83] This radical shift in thinking reflected a growing fear that prestige would be lost, both locally and more generally across the British Empire. Wavell had also warned that making no attempt to hold the protectorate in fact ran counter to the agreements about regional defence reached previously with the French and on the basis of which they had constructed strong defences in Jibuti. These comments also touched on some of the problems now facing Legentilhomme who had increasingly found himself at odds with his superiors in Paris about how to proceed. There were tensions within the Anglo-French alliance and these had played a part in the rejection of the French general's requests to fortify the two passes at Jirreh and Dobo. According to his superiors at home, whilst these both may well have fallen within his area of command, they were considered to be too far away from French territory to warrant further work being undertaken.[84]

Military responsibility for the protectorate was only handed to Wavell in January 1940; it was not until ten days before Italy declared war that he was finally also given administrative control. Almost immediately he visited one of his more remote commands and, seizing on the decision by the Chiefs of Staff to make a stand, a series of recommendations was sent back to London later that month which outlined the changes he believed to be necessary to mount a defence.[85] All of Chater's proposals for reinforcements having previously been rejected, at the beginning of 1940 the Somaliland Camel Corps contained just 33 British officers, 22 NCOs and 576 African troops scattered around five different locations, supported by a very small group of police in Berbera.[86] This limited force relied upon a mixture of rifles, machine guns and anti-tank rifles for their firepower, and had 29 cars and trucks, 122 horses and 244 camels for transport.[87] Their weapons included 2,000 .475 calibre Belgian rifles that had been manufactured in Maastricht in the previous century with 1.4 million rounds of ammunition of an uncertain quality.[88] For the most part the men were held in high regard; in fact, an excellent description of the Somalis was provided by one of the British officers serving in the KAR.[89] He found them, individually, to be 'intelligent, handsome and fanatically Moslem. They are also hot-tempered, proud, quick to resent any insult, real or imaginary and have remarkably long memories.' Another writer in *The Listener* referred to them as 'the most interesting . . . and most intelligent tribesmen' he had met during his African travels, but they now faced a daunting challenge.[90]

Wavell now requested that an additional battalion of the KAR be provided to take up forward defensive positions and allow the Somalis to roam more freely conducting patrols of the frontier. It was believed this would strengthen the existing thinly held defences, help improve the 'very shaken confidence' of the local population and allow Chater to also form two mechanised companies drawing upon extra manpower from local recruits who would be used alongside the officers and NCOs who had just arrived from Northern Rhodesia. If morale was to be restored, and for there to be any belief that

Britain intended to mount a proper defence, in addition the commander in Cairo proposed that a second battalion and another artillery battery be made available; but even then, this would still mean that there was no more than an 'absolute minimum' defending force. The defences would also need to be as strong as possible; Wavell told Legentilhomme that the French General Staff had been asked again to fortify the Jirreh and Dobo passes, as the British general recognised that these potential openings were a strategic oversight in the otherwise excellent defensive preparations.[91] Notwithstanding this renewed intervention, it was through these very passes that, eight months later, the Italians launched their main advance.

Despite the improvements, the revised strategy was based almost entirely around deterrence and the hope that the Italians would not see the protectorate as worth making the big effort needed for its capture.[92] Wavell had told his French counterpart that his intelligence branch could find no indication of anything other than a defensive outlook from their potential opponents. This was actually not entirely true, as Wavell had been given a detailed intelligence assessment in early January which considered what form an attack might take.[93] The conclusion was that a speedy advance could be made on British Somaliland, which would be the easiest of the Anglo-French territories to overrun. It was, however, hoped that 'apart from the prestige value of its capture, its occupation would not be of any great military advantage to the Italians', and they would not choose this option as Jibuti remained the most tempting target. With the British planners in Cairo also assuming that, in the worst case, an attack would employ no more than a brigade, the authorities in London accepted the revised plan and by February preparations were being made to send reinforcements, more than 1,100 men in total, including another 46 officers, although they were not due to arrive until mid-May.[94] This was certainly a much better situation than a few months before, but nevertheless the protectorate was still being left vulnerable and exposed.[95]

The inherent weakness was still clear to Chater, who remained uncertain about how he was to proceed; in early March he asked Cairo whether he should train his troops for conducting an active defence or an evacuation. There were no staff in his headquarters and very few officers, and the continuing ambiguity made it 'difficult to keep up interest especially amongst the Rhodesians'.[96] He was also worried about medical facilities as there were only two doctors in the whole territory. More generally, there was considerable confusion: one thing concerning him was the lack of maps, and with no facilities for printing and reproduction these had to come from London.[97] There also remained the questionable support that could be counted on from the civilian departments in Whitehall which continued to exert a strong influence on military policy. The Foreign Office had only agreed to the proposals to send reinforcements provided that the Italians were told of the move and many in the Colonial Office still refused to accept that there was any actual threat from Italy.[98] Although he could see the militarisation that was taking place, Glenday also continued to display a general nervousness about any action that might anger his neighbours and argued for a delay in sending the much-needed reinforcements.[99] This led Chater to complain to Wavell's headquarters that the information the governor received from London was 'in some cases the direct opposite of what he gets from you'.[100] The local military commander had also previously warned that the Colonial Office's control of administration entailed a minimum of three months' waiting for approval of his requests, even for the most urgent items and requirements. This had led him to conclude 'we shall never get anything done', and there remained no indication that the proposed defence was being taken seriously.[101]

As one of Wavell's senior staff officers who visited Berbera in May 1940 put it, whilst the official policy had changed from 'scuttle' to conducting an active defence, Chater had been left to try and implement this action with inadequate resources and questionable support from the civilian authorities.[102] Only when the evacuation from Dunkirk was well under way did Glenday finally appear doubtful about the defending garrison's prospects.[103] As the European women and children and the families of the

KAR troops were evacuated to Mombasa and Bombay, he was reassured that a general military withdrawal towards Berbera would only happen in the face of superior numbers and equipment.[104] He was not told of a revised appreciation, detailing the likely nature of any Italian attack, which estimated that in the region of 40,000 men were poised on the frontiers and likely to launch simultaneous assaults on British Somaliland and Jibuti, supported by tanks and artillery.[105] Events elsewhere were moving quickly and, as the War Cabinet in London considered 'plans to meet a certain eventuality' – what might happen were the French to surrender – there was no more than a brief reference to the specific impact this might have on eastern Africa.[106] It was assumed that if the strategic situation did change this area would be occupied immediately by the Italians, but the British position would not 'materially' be affected by 'a wasting asset' that could not be reinforced other than by air so long as the Suez Canal was held. The Chiefs of Staff therefore recommended that no special action be taken. The following month, with the French armistice signed, the assessment from Cairo was that there remained two possible alternatives for British Somaliland: to try and hold as much territory as possible or to withdraw to a more restricted area around the port while defending the passes that controlled its approach. Legentilhomme had promised to refuse to surrender his troops, fighting on under Wavell's command, but local opinion in Jibuti was weakened by the Royal Navy's attack on French naval vessels at Oran on the Mediterranean coast. Once General Germain arrived on 15 July, having been sent by the new French authority in Vichy to take charge of the colony, the right flank was opened up and the defenders' strength halved.[107]

Wavell wrote to Chater that he was still 'most anxious' to hold the protectorate if it was possible and he believed the second option of trying to retain Berbera carried with it the best potential of avoiding any damaging loss of prestige.[108] However, on one of his final visits to Chater, a member of his senior staff warned him that there could now be a much stronger Italian attack than had ever been anticipated.[109] Chater reckoned this would amount to a force of at least twenty infantry battalions along with heavy and light artillery and tanks advancing either along the coast road via Zeilah or in the direction of the Tug Argan Gap. He therefore pressed for urgent additional support, specifically another battalion of infantry with some light artillery and anti-tank rifles, and the resources to build further defences to protect both of these possible routes. He also noted in this renewed request that if he were given additional rifles he could also raise further units of the Illaloes, the well-thought-of local irregulars who guarded the more remote camel passes and acted as scouts. In response he was told that, other than the reinforcements that had arrived during the previous months, all that could be found immediately were six 20mm anti-aircraft guns captured from an Italian ship, effective only against low-flying aircraft; gunsights and ammunition clips would also first have to be made locally before they could be used. At the same time an updated report by the Chiefs of Staff in London acknowledged that the threat had increased but, other than accepting the potential effect on prestige, it now recommended that there be 'no extensive commitment' to hold the protectorate.[110]

The policy of ambiguity and confusion which had existed since before the war had led to British Somaliland effectively being offered up for occupation. This coincided with the temptation to finally do something: the prospect of taking advantage of the dramatically changed strategic position became too great for the Italian General Staff to ignore. They concluded that an attack against this enemy-held territory and a quick and spectacular success could strengthen the flanks of Italian East Africa and raise the morale of Italian people everywhere. In a territory larger than England and Wales, defended by just one battery of light artillery and fewer than 3,000 British and Commonwealth troops, the scene was set for the first major battle of the East Africa campaign.

CHAPTER 4

IMPERIAL DEFEAT
The Surrender of British Somaliland

At the start of the Second World War, British Somaliland was largely unknown to the average Briton. According to one weekly magazine, it was 'perhaps the least valuable' territory in the British Empire, with its 'burning heat and so parched and barren a ground' making it difficult for Europeans to survive.[1] For an American readership not subjected to War Office censorship there was perhaps an honest conclusion that, with 'no railway, no bank, no hotel', it remained a 'torrid little country'.[2] A lengthy column in *The Times* on the day the war came to this small imperial outpost referred to it as 'rather a Cinderella among British colonies'.[3] The writer was Margery Perham, who had spent her career studying Africa. She concluded that 'man and camel seem to look with equal contempt at the white stranger who visits their ungracious country', which had throughout its history 'been by no means a land of peace'. The long delay in defeating the Mad Mullah's insurgency caused great embarrassment in Whitehall and the territory was left 'with a very bad reputation'. Even with the 'careful nursing' it was given throughout the inter-war period, there remained considerable political and military uncertainty about what policy the authorities in London might pursue.[4] Now it was to be the location of a short but intense burst of military activity.

Wavell had inherited responsibility for the protectorate's security much too late to make any real difference and could not envisage a major fight, but he was committed to making a show of defiance even though faced by a much larger opponent.[5] By mid-May 1940, in addition to the reinforcements which had arrived in Berbera from the 1st Northern Rhodesia Regiment, the Camel Corps had been strengthened by a small number of European officers and NCOs from Southern Rhodesia.[6] To these were added a second batch of troops who followed shortly afterwards, with two Indian Sikh battalions arriving from Aden and another of British-led Nigerians transferred from Kenya by sea. With the increased forces now under his command, and in order to make his discussions with the French authorities in Jibuti easier to conduct, it was recommended that Chater be promoted to brigadier.[7] He himself had requested privately that this be done – that he 'be given a rank in keeping with my responsibilities without delay'. His greatest anxiety was that the recently arrived African troops could not understand who he was and the authority he actually held, and London agreed to the change in rank.[8]

In addition to increasing the size of the garrison, work continued on improving the fixed defences as men from the Camel Corps, supported by Indian builders and Somali labourers, strengthened what were anticipated to be the key positions.[9] The main defensive effort was established at the Tug Argan Gap which dominated the road to Berbera. When Wavell had visited British Somaliland in January he concluded that, whilst this had great potential for halting any Italian advance, there were about four miles of ground to be defended and at least three strongpoints would be needed, set about a mile apart from each other.[10] Another visit was made two months later by a junior officer from the Royal Artillery who viewed at first hand this strategically significant feature, which he measured at about 8,000 yards in length. On his return to Cairo he submitted a detailed appreciation highlighting how the advantages offered by the local terrain could be used to best effect.[11] This also recommended that the smallest possible defending force needed was a full battalion of troops with, potentially, a second in reserve, supported by eight 25-pounder guns split into two groups. With a maximum range of 13,000 yards, these were vital, and it was recommended that ideally they should be situated at the foot of Castle Hill, one of the position's small flat-topped hills, from where there was good visibility over the entire gap. The report noted the need for additional fixed defences to be prepared, but by this stage the lack of available men and money had slowed down work and prospects for anything being finished already looked bleak. The officer's comment at the very end of his report was that 'whatever the type and number of guns employed they are sure to be inadequate for the demands which will be made upon them'. The clear suggestion was that Tug Argan could not be held.

Despite such a pessimistic conclusion, four defended localities were formed and manned by the recently arrived North Rhodesians and a machine gun company of the Camel Corps. Consisting of well-prepared defences with barbed wire and concrete posts, they were dug in on what were named Black Hill, Knobbly Hill, Mill Hill and Observation Hill, with Castle Hill being used as the headquarters. Elsewhere, Indian and Nigerian troops occupied other key positions across the territory, defending routes that offered access either to the coast road or the mountain passes. From an entirely desperate position just a few months before, when the Italian attack eventually began there were in fact a total of 4,507 British and Commonwealth troops scattered across the protectorate, and whilst 75 per cent of these were African infantrymen and Somali irregulars, this was still an eightfold increase on the available strength at the beginning of the year.[12] Although this represented less than 1 per cent of the British and Commonwealth troops then available for active duty across the British Empire, in many respects it was a remarkable outcome, particularly in light of the worsening situation in Europe and the calls for manpower that were being made from elsewhere.[13]

There remained, however, significant deficiencies. Other than a light battery on Knobbly Hill manned by Kenyans, and despite the recommendations that had been made, crucially there were still no significant anti-tank or anti-aircraft guns. This failure to provide adequate firepower, when it was known that the Italians had tanks and armoured cars, undermined any claims that there were plans to conduct a credible defence. Some of the shortages were made up by the homemade mortars that had been produced in the railway workshops of Nairobi, but when they were eventually used, lacking proper dial sites as they did, there was no way of achieving precision when firing.[14] There were other key problems: lack of transport meant that the defenders lacked mobility, despite a strong mobile reserve being thought absolutely critical. The positions were widely separated but the Italians were known to have mules, which would allow them to cross the rough terrain and outflank the defenders. The differences that still existed between the senior political and military figures in Berbera about what strategy to follow only made the situation worse. Whilst preparations had been made at the Sheikh Pass to completely destroy the road and make its repair a very long operation, Glenday continued to refuse to allow explosives to be put in place for fear of unsettling public opinion.[15] He had proved a grave obstacle throughout the year and it was only in July, as the situation dramatically worsened, that the governor finally adopted a new outlook, proposing that he now leave as 'there was not much left for him to do as the military had everything more or less in their hands'.[16] Chater chose to encourage him to stay while also asking Wavell's headquarters what he should do if London's senior political representative did depart.

The lack of clear decision-making was, for once, not mirrored on the Italian side. Despite his previous orders from Rome, Aosta still wanted to launch attacks on Jibuti in order to secure control of the coast and prevent his opponent from using the excellent port to land additional forces. As he assumed that the troops in British Somaliland would interfere, Aosta proposed to march on Berbera at the same time.[17] His plan was once again submitted to Mussolini on 18 June but it was not until early the following month that he was finally given authority to proceed. Aosta had used the intervening period to study how an invasion might be conducted, and the viceroy and his deputy, General Guglielmo Nasi, who had arrived in Italian East Africa the previous May and who was one of Italy's most capable military officers, had produced an accurate estimate of likely enemy forces and an appreciation which outlined the campaign's objectives. On 25 July detailed instructions were issued to his troops by Lieutenant-General Carlo De Simone, who was in command of what would be the main advancing column.[18] He controlled the bulk of Italian fighting power, including the reinforced Harrar Division, with its three colonial brigades comprising eleven infantry battalions supported by plentiful artillery and even some tanks and armoured cars, and a further two Blackshirt battalions. The priority still appeared to be to keep apart the French and British forces and prevent any landings which might lead to a counter-offensive against Harrar. A subsequent British analysis also identified two main objectives, but these were to occupy British Somaliland and to destroy the defending garrison. De Simone had chosen to interpret his main task as being to pass through Hargeisa and Sheikh in order 'to annihilate the enemy and occupy Berbera'.

The timetable for the advance was set and East Africa's period of relative calm was about to come to an end. There were very few aircraft available to the defending garrison, just three Blenheims and a number of antiquated Gladiators, but air reconnaissance on 3 August confirmed that about 400 Italian troops had crossed the border at Biyad. The next morning, a Sunday, additional reports identified De Simone's column moving towards Hargeisa.[19] Along with the road to Odweina further to the south, these were the only practical routes that could be taken to Berbera. Having been held up by the Camel Corps, just after 10 a.m. on 5 August the Italians attacked the protectorate's major inland town with a mixed bombardment from mortars and light and heavy artillery supported by aircraft flying over the position. Three hours later, twelve light tanks advanced in line and, although three were disabled by anti-tank rifles, the decision was taken to withdraw the company of Rhodesians who had blocked the Italians' progress.[20] Moving in three columns but separated by a considerable

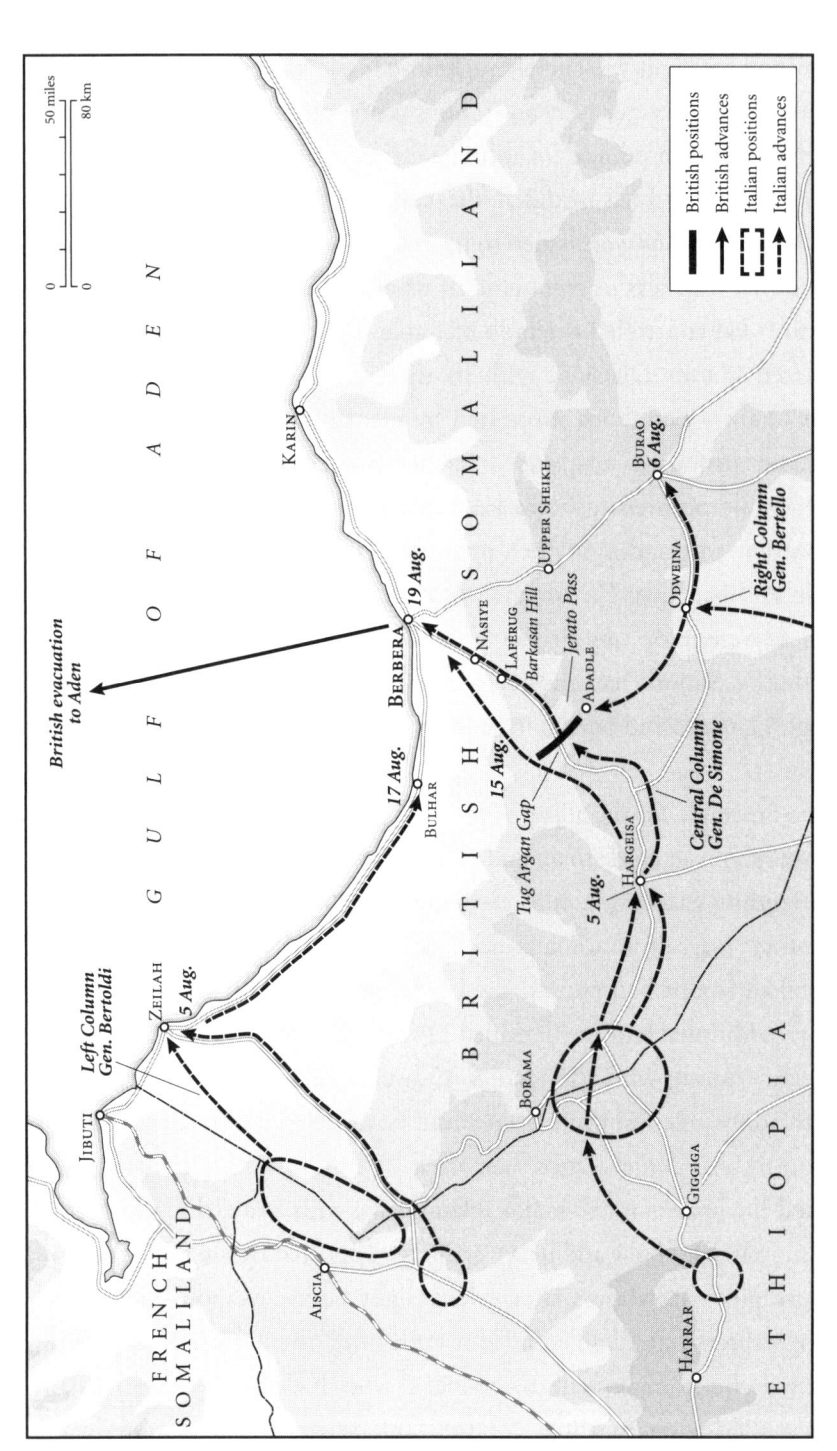

1 Italian invasion of British Somaliland.

distance, Nasi relied upon wireless and aircraft to communicate with De Simone he as manoeuvred into a position to attack Tug Argan from the front. The other two columns tried to mislead their opponent and potentially exploit any weakness as it appeared.[21]

Elsewhere troops led by Lieutenant-General Sisto Bertoldi had occupied the port of Zeilah on the invasion's first day, which removed any possibility of help for the British coming from French Somaliland. The Italian commander failed to exploit the opening presented to him and proceeded cautiously south-east along the coast, managing only to occupy the small village of Bulhar. This was possibly because the local defences had been thought to be much stronger, and thus more able to hold out longer, than was the case. However, had the defenders, operating about 150 miles from Berbera, tried to fight in such an isolated position they would have run the risk of being surrounded and destroyed, and it was sensible that they withdrew. Whilst the opportunity had not been taken to seize this potentially open road to the port, there were now scant defences blocking the advance towards Tug Argan and both sides appeared to recognise, as Wavell had anticipated, that this was the critical point in the coming battle.[22]

Despite British and Commonwealth troops falling back at every point, the initial media reports showed an apparent lack of concern, the suggestion being that the invasion was merely 'a "face-saving" tactic designed to strengthen morale in Italy'.[23] Several referred to it as having been expected for some time, and that the Camel Corps, 'an excellent and capable body of men' with knowledge of the local terrain, was well equipped to use guerrilla tactics and act as a mobile defence that would cause casualties and delays. Great emphasis was also placed on the challenging nature of the terrain, with the Italians forced to conduct long marches over the mountainous Golis ranges, 10,000-feet-high peaks across which mechanised troops could not travel and where British aircraft could easily find targets. There was also the climate: August was the start of the dry season during which a constant burning wind and temperatures in excess of 120°F made conditions almost unbearable. Another cause for optimism were the local nomadic groups who were said to 'both dislike and despise' the Italians and could be counted on to fight for the Empire.[24] These kinds of themes were commonly repeated throughout the campaign's initial days, during which a narrative was developed for the largely ignorant readership in Britain and elsewhere about just how difficult it would be for the attack to succeed. However, this failed to grasp that virtually all of the factors enumerated as slowing down the Italians were also challenges for the garrison. Within only a few days of the fall of Zeilah and Hargeisa there was a subtle change in the media's tone, with references to how much more difficult the defence was due to the collapse of France and the removal of any chance of support from Jibuti.[25] Such reports even accepted that the possible loss of 'the wretched tract' of British Somaliland might have to be considered, and it seemed clear that the British public were being readied for worse to come.

Enemy aircraft had initially flown over Tug Argan late on 6 August, by which point the Italians had already secured local air superiority and the RAF had practically lost the battle.[26] What few aircraft there were had been put in the air immediately following the invasion but there were insufficient fighters to provide any protection, and of the only three bombers one was lost within hours.[27] With no radar and little or no anti-aircraft defence, the decision had been quickly taken to withdraw from the temporary landing strips that had been built at Berbera and fall back on the small permanent base at Aden more than 200 miles from the battle area.[28] Two days later, six Italian aircraft carried out a first raid on the gap, killing an *askari* and three Somali refugees.[29] At the same time reports were received that a small column of tanks and infantry were moving from Hargeisa, and were finding the roadblocks and homemade landmines in front of the hills to be no barrier to their advance. The troops in the forward trenches were consequently withdrawn just after midday on 10 August and pulled back to the main prepared defences. Here they faced an intensive artillery bombardment followed by an advance of troops, both colonials and some of the paramilitary Blackshirts whom the defenders considered to be the equivalent of second-line infantry.[30] The assault continued into the night and, after a brief pause, resumed the next morning shortly after first light as every defended post along the British line was attacked. Although the wire was reached in each case, only one of them fell. Even though by this stage it was clear that the defending forces were handicapped by a lack of adequate provisions, Chater believed that 'my present feeling is that troops will stick it out but [I] do not think we shall be out of the wood for some days yet'.[31]

With the battle under way it was very difficult to provide additional support to the embattled British and Commonwealth forces. A few attacks were launched from Aden by the remaining aircraft, and HMS *Kimberley, Auckland, Carlisle, Ceres* and HMAS *Hobart*, all of which were patrolling the coast, bombarded shore targets.[32] The last of these vessels, a light cruiser under the command of Captain H.L. Howden, Royal Australian Navy, had sailed in October 1939 for the northern Arabian Sea and, from its new base in Aden, its role during the intervening months had been to escort troopships carrying reinforcements to Berbera, and then, as the battle progressed, helping to evacuate refugees. With the invasion now well under way, and in response to an attack by three Italian fighters, the ship's single Walrus seaplane was launched against Zeilah and what was believed to be the newly created Italian military headquarters.[33] The lone aircraft machine-gunned trucks and staff cars and two 112-pound bombs were also dropped within forty yards of the target. When the Walrus returned to the ship it had two bullet holes to show for its efforts but little actual damage had been done; the British media, looking for any positive story at this stage, nonetheless reported it as a great triumph.[34]

Back at Tug Argan itself, one of the war's most gallant defences was being fought. Even according to Glenday, writing a few days later in a letter sent prior to his evacuation, this ranked 'amongst the historic actions of the British Army'[35] – a conclusion which seems to have been widely held. The defenders managed to hold out for three days and nights and only stopped firing when all their ammunition was exhausted.[36] As the various military

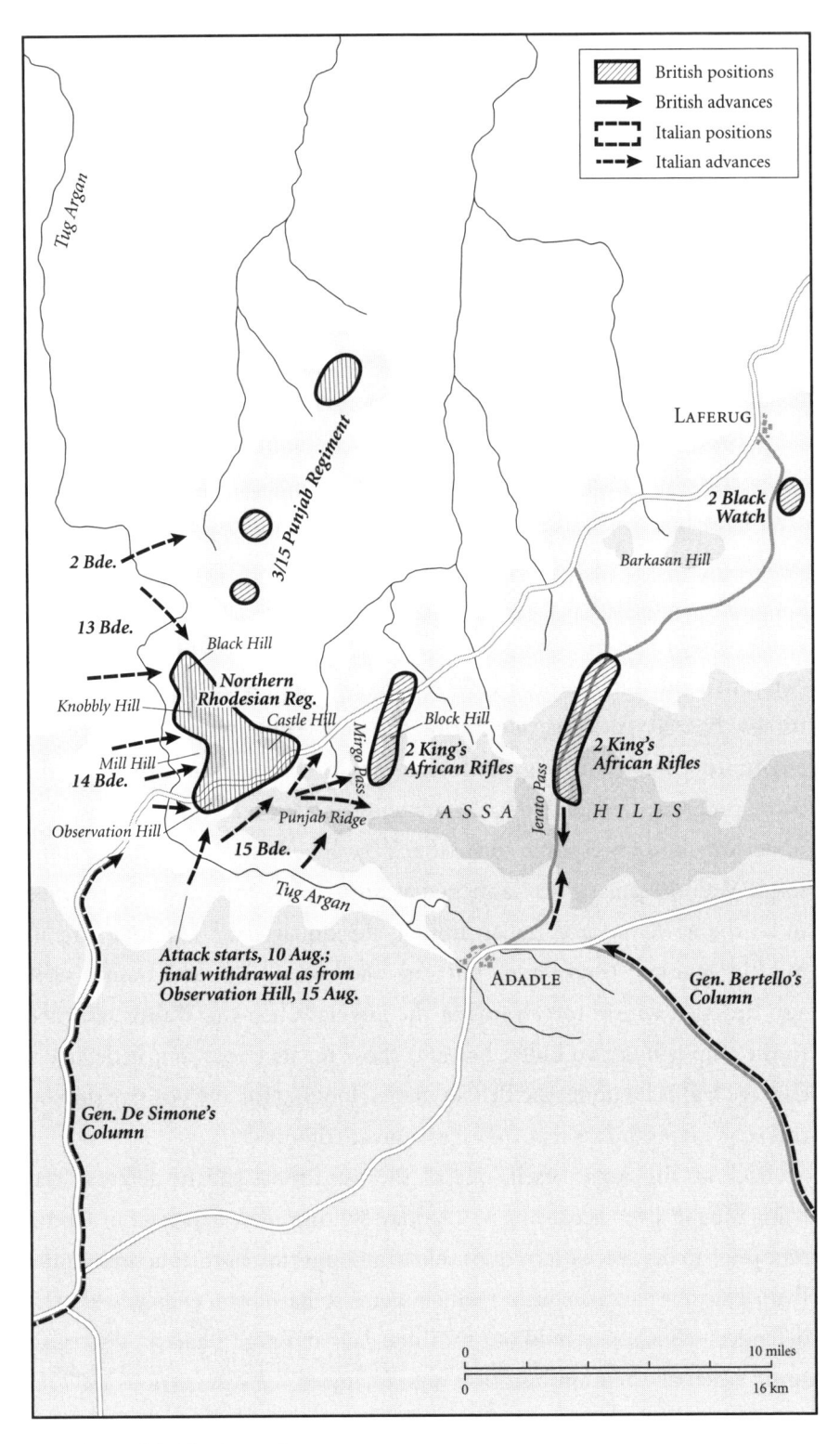

2 Defence of the Tug Argan Gap.

visitors who had made the journey to the protectorate beforehand had warned, it was the lack of artillery that proved decisive: it meant the defenders had little meaningful firepower to halt such a large advancing body. As the Italians neared the gap an urgent cable was received in Cairo pleading for anti-tank guns to be sent by fast ship; while four gunners were immediately flown out, it was more difficult to move equipment, which did not make it in time.[37] When the guns did eventually arrive they were instead sent to the Sudan, later forming an important element of a mobile anti-tank gun troop.[38] The absence of anti-aircraft defences was also considered acute and the headquarters in Cairo issued instructions that the guns helping defend Port Said should be removed and sent at once. This would leave another important element of the imperial network unguarded, and two days later the orders were quietly rescinded.[39] All that did arrive to aid the defenders, driven in on a truck at first light on 10 August, was a three-pounder Hotchkiss gun from HMAS *Hobart* along with three Australian naval volunteers dressed in soldier's uniform to act as its crew.[40] Even this gun, however, had to be dismantled to load rounds, which meant it could only achieve a rate of fire of one shell every five minutes. There were in any case only thirty-two rounds of high explosive and the same of steel shell, hardly a devastating counter to the Italian tanks and aircraft.[41] Although more guns were on the way, it was, however, too little and too late.[42]

Over the days that followed, near-constant attacks by waves of Italian and colonial troops progressively moved closer to the defenders' positions. Mill Hill had been abandoned on 12 August and, eventually, the attackers managed to reach within a few yards of the centre of the entire line. This caused the rest of it to also fall back and, with a counter-attack failing to recover the lost positions, it was only a matter of time before a withdrawal would need to be made. The situation was now reviewed by the local British commander in the knowledge that every man had already fought for seventy-two hours without rest and little ammunition remained. What proved to be the determining factor was the loss of the few available artillery pieces. There had been four guns of the 1st East African Light Battery deployed with the Rhodesians, two on Knobbly Hill and two more on Mill Hill; these either ran out of ammunition or, when the Italians had closed within their minimum range, they could no longer fire, even over open sights.

Observation Hill held out until the evening of 15 August and, even before it fell, the order had been given to pull back towards Berbera. This part of the plan was carried out without any real Italian opposition and the remaining British and Commonwealth troops withdrew in the direction of Knobbly Hill. They left behind Acting Captain Eric Wilson, who had been responsible for directing the fire from the Camel Corps' machine guns on the last of the hills still held by the defenders. Hit by artillery fire on 11 August, which severely injured his right shoulder and left eye, he repaired his weapon and continued to fire on the advancing Italians until his position was finally overrun four days later; by then all of those around him, including his dog, were dead. As the garrison fell back on Berbera his capture went unnoticed, but his actions on Observation Hill were not: he was awarded the first Victoria Cross of the war in Africa, though he was presumed dead. (In fact, Wilson died in 2008, by which point he was the oldest surviving wartime recipient of this medal.) His formal citation, gazetted on 11 October 1940, opened with the words 'For most conspicuous gallantry on active service in Somaliland' and ended 'The enemy finally overran the post at 5pm when Captain Wilson, fighting to the last, was killed'.[43] Wilson's father's comment on hearing the news was that 'he has died, I suppose, as every soldier would wish to die – fighting. It's a great and terrible loss to us, but we know that he did his duty.' The more sensational media wrote of 'Another Rorke's Drift'.[44]

Throughout this period Wavell was away from Cairo, having been summoned back to London by Churchill. The Middle East commander had many admirers but the prime minister, in office for two months and having inherited all of the senior military commanders from his predecessor Neville Chamberlain, did not appear to be one of them.[45] The men had their first disagreement in early June when the general in Cairo had been instructed to send back to Britain from Palestine eight battalions to help man the country's defence against the anticipated German invasion. Wavell was unwilling to reduce his very limited forces and the troops were not sent, a decision which Churchill apparently never forgot.[46] Their differing opinions on how to resource and conduct operations in the Middle East were undoubtedly the principal source of friction, but the military commander's character proved incomprehensible to the politician and Churchill's resulting loss of trust in Wavell encouraged his tendency to become embroiled in operational and tactical details of battle. In late July one well-placed observer in the War Office noted that the prime minister had decided to send for Wavell 'for personal consultation', but it had proved possible to persuade him that removing a senior commander for several weeks when an attack might come at any time was not the best course to follow.[47] Even then Churchill apparently only accepted this delay reluctantly, reversing the decision a few days later and leading to Wavell's 'flying visit'. This was seen by many as an early, very clear indication of Churchill's lack of confidence in his commander and his abilities.

At the same time, and despite the now obvious extent of the Italian military advantage, in London the prime minister and the Middle East Committee were still anxious that the garrison in British Somaliland should hold out.[48] This led to the decision to send a battalion of the Black Watch, which had been kept in Aden as a reserve, to join the four others already there, making, it was argued, a potentially potent force. With only one transport ship available it would, however, take three days for it to be moved and assembled alongside the existing formations. As a further demonstration of this sudden new-found commitment, enquiries were also made as to whether 1st Battalion, Royal Sussex Regiment could be transferred by a fast cruiser, and it was even suggested that medium tanks might be sent, although this idea was quickly amended to the possibility of making some Bren gun carriers available instead.[49] Further discussions also took place about improving the port facilities at Berbera: Wavell had expressed his concern about their poor quality the month before, particularly for maintaining the flow of supplies or, possibly, managing the evacuation of troops. He had warned then about the danger of 'congestion and confusion' but there was no time for this to be remedied.[50] As the fighting around him became increasingly desperate, detailed instructions were now sent from London to the base commandant for the long-term improvements that were to be made.[51] This was a positive step but it had come much too late and pointed to how little understanding there was of the impossible task facing the defenders and the desperate battle that had already begun.

With this heightened interest in London, the headquarters in Cairo was also asked to develop an updated appreciation and proposals for what would be needed to retain control of the protectorate. In Wavell's absence, one of his senior colleagues was quick to offer a view of regional strategy which seemed to run counter to those held by the general. Air Chief Marshal Longmore noted that out of a force of 187 bombers and fighters in Italian East Africa and Eritrea, only 39 were believed to be operating against British Somaliland.[52] He also stated that, whilst the total available to them appeared to represent a significant advantage, the Italians actually faced serious problems in maintaining their forces. Longmore wrote that, at their present rate of consumption, the enemy would have no more than seven months of fuel and faced potentially critical shortages of ammunition, bomb components and aircraft spares. Mindful of both the increasing threat facing Egypt and the successes being achieved by aircraft based in the Sudan in attacking Italian frontier posts and supply bases, Longmore argued that nothing could be spared to help defend the protectorate. All he was prepared to contribute to its defence was sending long-range bombers to attack key objectives in and around Addis Ababa which, he argued, might draw off some of the advancing Italian troops. There was in fact only a remote prospect of this offering any real respite to the defenders in British Somaliland and it highlighted once again the reluctant commitment to its defence which had, since at least 1938, been such a common feature of official policy.

Another decision made in London, which reflected the increased size of the garrison, was to appoint a more senior commander to lead the protectorate's defence. Major-General Reade Godwin-Austen, who inherited the unenviable task, was another professional soldier who had been commissioned from Sandhurst in 1909 into the South Wales Borderers and had fought throughout the First World War in the Middle East, where he received a number of awards for bravery.[53] During the inter-war years he spent periods based back in England but for most of the time he was in Palestine. Wavell thought highly of him, and in August 1940 he had been poised to take command of the 2nd African Division when instead he was ordered to proceed to Berbera as quickly as possible. According to Arthur Smith, when the general was woken in the early hours of the morning to be told that he was to leave Cairo at 6 a.m. he reportedly responded with a booming voice, 'Godwin will be there', before going back to sleep for a few more hours.[54] Prior to setting off to take over his new command he was provided with a single page of instructions with only six points and a brief administrative appendix.[55] The first confirmed he had been appointed to replace Chater, and the next gave him the authority to organise the command as he wanted, with advice that he remain closely in touch with the Senior Naval Officer and Air Officer Commanding in Aden. The strategic advice was brief: he was to prevent any advance beyond the main established defensive position and, whilst the immediate role of his troops was defensive, any opportunities for local offensive operations were not to be overlooked. At the same time he was to prepare for withdrawal and evacuation, although this possibility was to be disclosed to the bare minimum of people.

On reaching the protectorate Godwin-Austen followed his additional instructions to relieve Glenday and also take over civilian administration of the territory alongside his military role. Although he had only just arrived it was already clear what had to be done and on the evening of 14 August he wrote to Cairo to suggest that the position was becoming hopeless.[56] His principal concern was that there was no possibility of concentrating the dispersed forces he still had available which were covering various passes and the routes through them towards the port. Each of the outposts knew it had to hold out for as long as possible, but as there were not enough reserves to provide adequate support the Italians could infiltrate on foot the unmanned openings. As he put it, this meant 'there was no defensive position close in [and] defending Berbera which cannot be outflanked'. The general was also facing difficulties in receiving instructions from Wavell as a shortage of staff and the increased number of messages being sent meant that some were left undeciphered for up to thirty hours.[57] Further hampering him were the limited means of communicating between his units and he had grave doubts about the ability of the African and Indian troops to stand up to concerted Italian artillery fire. This final point was prominent in his calculations as he was concerned about the effect that 'a serious disaster' could have on British and Commonwealth troops elsewhere.[58]

By the following morning it was growing obvious that those men who remained in the forward positions were exhausted and shaken by the continuous bombardment they had experienced for several days.[59] Godwin-Austen assured the headquarters in Cairo that his forces were willing to fight on 'if total sacrifice of forces considered worth it', but at this stage he believed evacuation would allow for about 70 per cent of them to be saved.[60] He therefore decided to fall back on the port and orders were issued to withdraw. General Maitland 'Jumbo' Wilson, deputising for Wavell while he was in London, had received a series of messages from Berbera warning that the situation was critical and this led him to accept the advice and issue the code-word 'Snipe'.[61] As he later wrote, 'I had no hesitation in agreeing to immediate evacuation' as 'we could not afford to waste a single soldier for the heroics of defending to the last man a territory which a year previously was not considered to be worthwhile'.[62] Having indicated that he still had large numbers of men he could pull back to the port, Godwin-Austen was, however, told that it was assumed this final position could then be held for some time. Instructions were also given that, whilst he was not to prejudice the success of the evacuation, he should try and save his heavier equipment.[63] Exactly this type of operation had previously been identified as being fraught with difficulties in a report that had examined the possibility of evacuation the month before the Italian attack began.[64] It noted that it would be impossible to bring ships alongside due to the poor quality of the harbour facilities, and boats would have to take the troops off from the wharf. Using this method and with access to three large naval vessels, one of which would need to be a cruiser, it was calculated that 1,000 men could be moved each day but all 350 vehicles and the bulk of the stores would have to be left behind. This forecast proved entirely accurate and little of the transport was recovered. Parts were removed to disable vehicles but no attempt was made to destroy them as it was feared fires might illuminate the town and allow the Italians to interfere with the escape.[65] At least all of the troops were safely evacuated, the only exception being those of the Camel Corps, most of whom were simply told to return to their homes and await the return of the British.[66] Previously they had been told that in the worst case they were to hold as much territory as they could and harry the occupying Italians, but this plan had apparently now been set aside.[67]

With the withdrawal complete, on the morning of 19 August HMAS *Hobart*'s guns shelled Berbera for two hours and destroyed key structures including government buildings, barracks and storehouses.[68] One of those on board recorded the final scenes: 'as we steamed out we could see the Italian forces in the hollow of distant hills waiting to move in when our guns had finished firing. As we steamed away we watched eagerly to see if there might not be one more man to be saved from the shore before it receded from our sight.'[69] Another witness, a British colonel standing on the same deck, said it reminded him of the Gallipoli evacuation.[70] The warships stayed on for a few more days and kept in touch with stragglers, rescuing those who had not been able to make it back to Berbera.[71] After taking aboard a final group the small convoy set sail for Aden, arriving later the same day. Some of the Indian troops eventually remained there but most of the evacuees headed straight for Kenya and Egypt.[72] The end had been relatively swift, no more than a couple of weeks in total, but the impact of this defeat would rumble on for far longer.

Vice Admiral Sir Geoffrey Blake, Additional Assistant Chief of Naval Staff at the Admiralty in London, was saddened to hear the news of the withdrawal but wrote to the Commander-in-Chief, Mediterranean:

> I don't think, except from the point of view of prestige, that it is going to have any very great effect on the strategical position vis-à-vis Aden, but nevertheless, it seems to me a thing which should not have occurred. It appears to have taken the Military Authorities at home here quite by surprise, and it was only a matter of about 10 days ago that they were talking quite hopefully of the position in the hills being maintained indefinitely until reinforcements arrived at Berbera. Apparently their information must have been rather faulty as they seemed to have no idea of the number of tanks and other armoured vehicles which the Italians appear to have had available to them.[73]

Admiral Sir Andrew Cunningham replied that he also regretted what had happened and that 'the soldiers were caught with their trousers down'.[74] This was a more accurate description than he might have known. Although the need for their evacuation had been recognised as a possible outcome of an Italian attack, the issuing of the actual order had not been anticipated by the British colonial officers who still remained in Berbera, and many of them arrived in Aden with little more than a pair of pyjamas.[75] A post-war review concluded that if the port facilities had been improved as had been recommended, most of the transport could have been saved, but there was an 'insistence on running our Colonies "on the cheap" especially in matters of defence'.[76]

Despite what had happened, Britain's media tried to remain positive. Once the fighting had begun to grow in intensity and the narrative had started to point to the protectorate's possible loss, the argument that this was not that critical an element of the imperial network had begun to play out. One commentator wrote that it was simply of 'scant account' in the overall strategic picture, while others highlighted the idea that the Italians were in fact being deliberately encouraged to wear down their manpower and resources.[77] As late as 12 August it was still being reported that the invading forces had not reached the main defensive positions when the final battle was in fact already poised to begin.[78] In all these accounts Berbera was consistently referred to as being important and it was argued that there was never any intention of surrendering the port.[79] Such statements exposed the initial lack of recognition by the media and the public at large that the situation was so desperate. An editorial in the *Manchester Guardian* three days later argued that there was still an opportunity to inflict a setback on the Italians by mounting a successful defence, and called for more troops to be sent. This also noted that the official statements referred to the situation as 'serious but by no means critical', which was reminiscent of the comments made in France before its final collapse. Even when news arrived that the withdrawal back to Berbera had begun, correspondents on the ground remained optimistic that the British and Commonwealth troops would be able to hold on to the port. One writer for *The Times* described the Italian forces across the region as 'a beleaguered army which must live on its reserves of supplies and whose only hope of survival is that Hitler may pull Mussolini's chestnuts out of the fire by winning the war elsewhere'.[80] Whilst this assessment was, of course, entirely correct, and would later be shown to be exactly what the Italians were also thinking, it was some time before this would become known and did little to help the situation.

Having pursued such a broadly positive outlook, when news of the evacuation was finally made public on 20 August it was perhaps not surprising that many in the British media continued to try to draw out the positives. It was claimed that in addition to the troops and wounded, virtually all the equipment and stores had been safely withdrawn, and prominent reference was constantly made to heavy losses having been suffered by the Italians.[81] Editorials offered a similar analysis, although it was acknowledged that this was 'a blow to our reputation' and 'a distressing setback' that had left 'a most disagreeable taste'.[82] As others wrote, however, although the events were sad, it was not 'tragic'; more 'a sentimental setback'.[83] During the weeks that followed references to a 'distortion of news' and 'a clumsy piece of propaganda' – which had incorrectly suggested the garrison was trying to offer serious resistance – did begin to emerge.[84] This, if anything, had helped to inflate the Italian success. There was also some increasingly critical discussion about the failure to send more men and equipment to British Somaliland once Ethiopia had been occupied in 1936, with claims that 'a handful of British officers could have looked after itself and . . . dealt with the Italians'.[85] Instead, because of neglect and the lack of any general plan for the defence of the British Empire, two territories – the other being the Channel Islands – had now been abandoned in quick succession. The Ministry of Information's daily reports throughout August 1940 also revealed an initial public apathy about events in British Somaliland which was gradually replaced by growing criticism and a sense that 'there is more behind it than meets the eye'.[86] Added to this was mistrust of 'the customary explanation of the military reverse' and the argument that it did not really matter.[87] This was concealed by anxiety over how the Battle of Britain was developing, but reports of the evacuation, although expected, had apparently left many Britons feeling angry, both at the defeat itself and the manner in which it had been reported. As one of those recorded in these reports put it, 'we should have recognised the danger signals: first silence, then inadequate news, then hints that the place wasn't worth defending, then the successful strategic withdrawal'.[88]

Such concerns were not shared, either at the time or subsequently, by a range of senior officials who were centrally involved in events. General Hastings 'Pug' Ismay, now sitting alongside Churchill as one of his senior military advisers, had fought in British Somaliland earlier in the century in the battles against the Mad Mullah. He wrote after the war that in August 1940 it had been 'a foregone conclusion' that the protectorate could not be held. Instead, he argued, the sensible strategy should have been to evacuate

Berbera and send the garrison southwards to the Somaliland plateau from where, using dumps that had been established previously, it would have been possible to harry the Italians.[89] It was also later argued that the defeat had actually forced the Italian forces to become more dispersed, that they had wasted resources to win the battle, and that Aosta had from this point on become fixed on a dubious course of action when alternatives could have yielded better long-term outcomes. According to the official British post-campaign account, a 'little force . . . outnumbered, certainly by ten to one, possibly fifteen to one', had distracted the Italian High Command and delayed them at a time when British and Commonwealth troops elsewhere were still largely unprepared.[90] Few senior politicians, if any, showed obvious signs of alarm too. Lord Halifax referred in his private diary to having lunch with Eden on 7 August and concluding that, although an Italian victory was 'a bore politically', British Somaliland was 'not of much importance militarily'.[91] A week later the protectorate's loss was once again described by him as 'not very important strategically but bad politically'.[92] Even Glenday later concluded that the local Somali population, who had suffered the most, whilst 'disappointed, surprised and puzzled at being left to their enemies without warning after they had been encouraged to resist', remained positive and expected the British would return and drive out the Italians.[93]

The most serious criticism of what had taken place in the Horn of Africa came from Churchill. At first he gave no indication that the outcome did not fit with his wider strategic vision of how the war should develop. Wavell sent a message to Cairo from London on 15 August after his final interview with the prime minister which made no mention of any rancour. This was just before he set off back to Egypt, and he noted that the strategic need for the evacuation had been accepted and there had been 'no recrimination'.[94] All of this changed once a report was received by the War Cabinet containing further details about the action fought at Tug Argan.[95] Churchill now questioned why it had been broken off and whether the attackers had at that stage really enjoyed a 'hopeless superiority', particularly as they had not then pressed home their advantage and continued their advance. Eden was quizzed once again two days later about why the defence of the gap had been 'precipitately discontinued' and why Godwin-Austen referred to heavy losses when the estimate of casualties during the battle was only 33 British, Indian and African officers and men killed with another 220 wounded or missing.[96] The prime minister now pressed for a full report that might enable decisions to be taken about further disciplinary steps. Desperate for a British victory, in his own mind Churchill laid the blame on Wavell's subordinates – and by extension, their commander – who he believed had broken their promise and had not conducted an effective fighting retreat.[97] In his later post-war recollections he pointedly wrote that British Somaliland was the 'only defeat at Italian hands' and failed to make any reference to the political and military constraints that had been imposed upon the various senior British officers in the years prior to the Italian invasion who held any interest in its fall.[98]

The fact that Wavell had chosen to write back to London commenting that 'butchery is not the mark of a good tactician' deepened Churchill's anger. Wavell's explanation for why the protectorate had been evacuated was said to have roused the prime minister to a greater fury than any of his aides and assistants had ever seen. Churchill apparently never forgave this comment, and if his relationship with his commander in Cairo had been uncertain before, it was now fatally weakened; more immediately, it strengthened the misgivings and lack of trust that had been quick to emerge between both men.[99] On 13 August the prime minister had sent a private letter to Eden in which, whilst acknowledging he was 'favourably impressed with General Wavell in many ways', he also wrote that 'I do not feel in him that sense of mental vigour and resolve to overcome obstacles, which is indispensable to successful war'.[100] As he put it, 'I find instead, tame acceptance of a variety of local circumstances in different theatres, which is leading to a lamentable lack of concentration upon the decisive point.' No longer merely meddling in military strategy, he was unashamedly doubting the abilities of one of Britain's leading officers who, Churchill thought, was no better than 'a good average colonel' or a 'good chairman of a Tory association'. Whilst the commander ultimately responsible for the defence of East Africa might not have known it, his position had been damaged irreparably.

Militarily, Wavell had done nothing wrong; indeed, with the disparity between the opposing forces in the protectorate it was remarkable that the defenders were able to hold out as long as they did. The Battle of Britain was, however, in full flow and there was no Churchillian appetite for a defeat that could not be portrayed in heroic tones. The prime minister's vision of strategy may have had moments of genius but it was also often based on acts of heroism and sacrifice, not the logical use of force and the notion that it is sometimes preferable to wait for a better opportunity to secure a decisive victory. Churchill was wrong to condemn Wavell and his subordinates for their entirely reasonable actions, but one of the steps he had taken when he assumed leadership of Britain only a few months before was to appoint himself as the first ever Minister for Defence. It was this title that offered him the conviction that his way was the only way and there would be consequences for those involved in the defeat.

The loss of British Somaliland marked the first redrawing of the British Empire's map since 1931 when a strip of land in the Sudan had been ceded to Italy. Godwin-Austen admitted that he smarted about what had happened and it drove him on during the subsequent campaign to show the Italians 'what being overwhelmed by numbers and superior armament felt like'.[101] Hitler apparently referred to it as 'a hard blow to British prestige', but it was actually more an emotional setback than a military one.[102] As one contemporary writer put it, 'all the British had lost was the privilege of maintaining an expensive garrison in their least valuable colony'.[103] And the outcome could have been much worse. Aosta wrote after his own eventual surrender the following year that the key theme of his plan had been speed and his commanders had been urged to move on as quickly as they could following Berbera's capture.[104] Difficulties in getting supplies forward, particularly food and water, along with some very poor weather and heavy rains which rendered some of the roads impassable, made this difficult to achieve. Having encountered the strong defences around Tug Argan and the additional delay they imposed, Aosta made an attempt to send troops forward by aircraft and a force of 300 volunteers was readied to make a bold attempt to seize the port; but the only landing ground was in British hands and so the plan was abandoned. If it had not been, the haphazard and poorly defended evacuation could easily have been disrupted and some, or even all, of the withdrawing forces captured. Once again, the Italians had failed to exploit the opportunities presented to them and within a matter of months this high point of victory would seem a distant memory.

CHAPTER 5

PREPARING FOR THE COUNTER-OFFENSIVE

There was no doubting that Britain had suffered an embarrassing defeat but, elsewhere, Wavell's vision of a grand strategy had continued to develop as plans to support the rebellion on the Gojjam plateau gathered pace. To bring these to fruition he had appointed Colonel Daniel Sandford to play a leading part. Described as a 'calm, stocky, balding, bespectacled colonel', Sandford was a retired former gunner who had won two DSOs during a distinguished military career, and Wavell had worked with him previously.[1] He had retired to a farm north of Addis Ababa where he lived for fifteen years, during which period he had got to know the country and its people well.[2] At the same time he also became a trusted friend of Haile Selassie and, when the Italians invaded, he went into exile alongside him.[3] Arriving at the headquarters in Cairo in September 1939, he had been given considerable autonomy to come up with a suitable plan for what was intended to be a self-dependent strand in the wider regional military strategy; Wavell made it quite clear that the 'enterprise once launched had to take care of itself while I directed the regular operations against the north and south of the Italian African Empire'.[4] To this end Sandford proposed the establishment of 'Mission 101', which he would also command; he named it after the percussion-type Fuse 101 used widely by the Royal Artillery before and during the war, as it was his intention that his activities would ignite the Ethiopian revolt.[5]

Initially Sandford headed a small group but he later received important support from the likes of Robert Cheeseman, another who had considerable experience of the region. Having been British Consul in the Gojjam for nine years until 1934, Cheeseman was recruited by Sir Stewart Symes, Governor-General of the Sudan, to form an Ethiopian Bureau and act as an adviser both to him and General Platt.[6] He reached Khartoum at the end of March 1940 where he was given the rank of major and appointed to the Kaid's staff as an intelligence officer co-ordinating the various plans involving irregular forces. The next three months were spent reviewing the list of Ethiopian chiefs who were considered potential allies; eleven were selected, who received promises of arms, ammunition and money to help them assemble more men. Cheeseman also oversaw the production of new maps of the region as well as route reports and an updated guidebook which would be issued to those British and Commonwealth officers who were selected to become advisers and help lead the groups once they began fighting.

With Platt having been instructed to give him all possible assistance, Sandford arrived in Khartoum on 17 June 1940. He wanted to cross into Ethiopia at once but the local commanders thought there was little chance at this stage of him or his men making it through Italian lines.[7] This presented the opportunity for a meeting with Selassie who, with Italy now having declared war, had left England in secret, flying to Alexandria, where he paused for a week before travelling on to Khartoum. His arrival had not been expected and, fearful of assassination attempts or Italian bombing raids, 'he was eventually accommodated incognito ... and for several months was referred to as "Mr Smith"'. News of Selassie's arrival was not announced in Britain until early November.[8] It was during this long journey that Sandford's meeting with the emperor took place, at Wadi Halfa in northern Sudan, when the position as it then stood was explained to Selassie.

Also revealed was Wavell's initial intention to mount two operations, one towards Kassala and the other Kismayu, the capture of which would protect his flanks, but Selassie was also assured of the efforts that were being devoted to supporting the rebellion. Insurgent activity was then mostly confined to the Amharic areas and was still strongest in Gojjam, Armacheho and Bagemdir. There were 420 Ethiopian refugees in Jibuti and British Somaliland and 600 more, plus the same number of Eritreans, in Kenya who were prepared to pledge their support to join the struggle. Seven points had been identified near the border where it was intended to store arms, and the plan was for these to be guarded by a special Sudanese unit under the command of Colonel Hugh Boustead.

Using these forces and equipment the plan for Mission 101 was relatively simple.[9] Sandford proposed to start by clearing the border region in the Gojjam to open up routes in and out before exploiting this position to encourage further desertions amongst the enemy ranks in an effort to undermine morale. His force would also attack small frontier posts and camps along with other potentially important targets such as bridges. Only when his position appeared to be established would he target the larger African manned garrisons before threatening those where there were also Italian troops. Upon hearing this, Selassie was apparently disappointed that no air support or anti-aircraft guns were being offered for his men; he seemed to believe a commitment to supply such equipment had been given to him before he left London. During their invasion of Ethiopia, the Italians had used their superiority in airpower to often devastating effect and Selassie was concerned that his men would now once more be exposed. Nonetheless, even without such support, he indicated that he was prepared to accept the proposals he had heard and return home to lead the rebels.

Sandford and a small party of officers and other ranks – according to one account, as few as six men in total – eventually crossed the frontier on 12 August and established themselves in the Wandagaz area, the source of the Blue Nile approximately fifty miles south-east of Dangila.[10] Major

A.W.D. Bentinck, who had been appointed to command the northern section of the mission, followed on 21 September, heading to the Gondar area. Between them they had access to 17,600 rifles and about 10 million rounds of ammunition but there was no artillery and each group had only four mortars with 100 shells. Four hundred Hotchkiss light machine guns and twenty-eight Boys anti-tank rifles were on their way from Cairo but it was not clear when, or even if, these would arrive. What they did have was plenty of counterfeit funds, and an initial budget of 250,000 specially produced Maria Theresa thalers, with twice that amount sent to Khartoum for future use. Minted at a cost of about £25,000, the first batch came from the French Mint before the Royal Mint took over, with production finally being moved to India. (The originals, minted in Austria in 1780, bore the head of the Empress Maria Theresa, and these had been made to look exactly like them.)[11] This currency was crucial for purchasing food and the other supplies the men needed to continue their mission, and it was also used to encourage potential local recruits to offer their support to Selassie and his cause. So vital was the currency that Sandford soon asked for an additional 500,000 thalers to be sent to him each month.[12]

Moves were now under way to signal to Italy that the agreement reached two years earlier had been cancelled, and Selassie was now both considered an ally of Britain and recognised as leading 'the lawful Government of Ethiopia'.[13] As news started to filter through about the worsening situation in British Somaliland, heated discussions in the House of Commons debated the potential value of adopting 'a thoroughly Machiavellian manner' and taking more active steps to highlight the fact that a revolt in Ethiopia was now being fully supported. The September Chiefs of Staff appreciation, which provided a framework for how the wider war would be fought and won and had made such prominent reference to the Italian position in East Africa, also noted that the conditions were right for inciting 'large scale revolution' as this would benefit the wider regional position.[14] It was certainly the case that Badoglio, in his role as Chief of Staff in Rome, was concerned at the beginning of August by reports of

Selassie's arrival in the Sudan, which he believed would 'aggravate' the internal situation.[15] France had been lost, the Battle of Britain was well under way, and there was little else that could be done immediately against Italy other than fight a propaganda war and prepare intrigues.[16]

As these were developing, an opportunity had fleetingly presented itself to the Italians to exploit the advantage they had gained. Despite later claims about their lack of fighting spirit, papers found by intelligence officers after the campaign confirmed that Aosta had developed various ideas about continuing his offensive. Although it is not clear if it was the German plan that allegedly had been given to him before the fighting began, following the occupation of British Somaliland there was certainly an idea to invade Kenya with troops advancing from the south of Ethiopia and Jubaland to join up at Fort Hall just to the north of Nairobi.[17] With the intention that the attacking columns move on the capital next, the Italian viceroy had written on the bottom of the plan, 'Extreme caution must be observed.' His concern may well have been about the inadequacy of his transport and the qualities of the colonial forces available to him; at this stage there were still no more than six battalions of troops defending the British colony. The commander in Eritrea, General Vincenzo Tessitore, had also proposed to Aosta that there should be an advance once war broke out with Britain, but heading towards Khartoum and Atbara.[18] Later, these plans were seen by the colonel who was in charge of intelligence in the Sudan before the war, and he asked the captured Aosta why the attack had not been carried out; Aosta replied that his orders were to co-ordinate his actions, and his strategy depended upon what happened farther north.[19] In September, Marshal Rodolfo Graziani, with an army of 200,000 European and African troops and the best part of the Italian Air Force, had moved forward from Fort Capuzzo in Libya and advanced into Egypt as far as Sidi Barrani. In Addis Ababa, Aosta had concluded he could only risk a move into the Sudan if he was certain that Graziani would be able to complete a link-up with him – and once the attacking Italian forces had been pushed back into Libya, this was clearly not a viable option.

Aosta had in fact retained a generally sound understanding of the wider strategic position that faced him, one which had actually changed little since earlier in the year, even before Mussolini had decided to pursue war with Britain. With his already dwindling stocks of transport and petrol, doing very little appeared the only real option open to him. Some of the more cynical British intelligence officers who reviewed the documents for possible offensives concluded that they were based on a calculation that if everything went badly, any defeats that were suffered 'might at least get rid of their intolerable Duce'.[20] As the author of this assessment added, 'Fascism was a peculiar poison because it eventually made men loathe and despise themselves and wish for their own country's downfall', and there was little evidence that any real attempt was made to secure a decisive victory in East Africa. Following British Somaliland, the advice Aosta received from Badoglio on future operations continued to carry no real sense of urgency.[21] He was instead told that he was now to limit himself to launching an anti-British propaganda campaign and closing up the approaches to the south and west of Italian-held territory. This was because the leadership in Rome believed that the war could end as soon as October, following a successful German invasion of England, which meant there was all the more reason for Mussolini to instruct his forces to maintain an essentially defensive outlook.[22] As a result, other than preparing for possible co-ordination with Graziani, Aosta took no further action.

This reliance on help arriving from the Axis alliance, however fanciful it might have seemed later, was, at this stage, also a cause for some concern for the British and reflected the confusion over the level of assistance that was already being provided. There had been reports in mid-July that a German lorry-borne infantry company had been formed in Asmara which it was concluded could be a group of colonists from northern Italy, Austrians or sailors who had organised themselves into a 'national service' unit.[23] The following month the possibility of parachute troops landing in Tanganyika was raised along with uncertainty about the situation in French Equatorial Africa and the Belgian Congo, which had both recently seen the surrender of their home governments back in Europe.[24] In Cairo, however, mixed conclusions were still being put forward. In the late summer of 1940 Colonel Wilfrid Ebsworth, one of the senior officers from the headquarters, spent eight weeks travelling around Africa and sending back regular reports. From these it was not entirely clear that he recognised there to be any great threat facing East Africa. At the end of his trip he produced an interim appreciation detailing what he had seen and a series of planning recommendations which were both sent to Wavell and Anthony Eden, the Secretary of State for War.[25] Six concerns were listed but only one of them directly related to Kenya: this was the possibility that it might collapse internally, presumably in the face of an Italian attack, although the author seemed less concerned about the actual threat of an invasion succeeding. Ebsworth's interest remained very much the political instability in the Union of South Africa and the threat to the Copperbelt as a result of a local uprising or attacks from Angola.

At the same time in London, where the danger of a German invasion attempt was growing acute, a generally optimistic view of the situation in East Africa still appeared to exist. The focus was on the wider Middle East, as was most obvious in the general appreciation delivered to the War Cabinet in the first week of September by the Chiefs of Staff Committee. This highly significant wartime document examined 'the factors affecting [Britain's] ability to defeat Germany', and aimed 'to make recommendations from the military point of view as to the policy which should govern our war effort and the future conduct of the war'.[26] In this context, Italian fighting power was viewed as much less of a threat than that of its principal ally. As such, an attack on either Italy itself or its African colonies was 'the first important step towards the downfall of Germany', a victory against which would represent 'a strategic success of the first order'. The conclusion, therefore, was that operations against Italy were a priority and should take place as soon as resources allowed. The appreciation also pointed to where this should happen: 'In East Africa the Italian forces are a wasting asset and although they may have temporary successes their situation will be critical after June 1941 even if they exercise strict economy in the expenditure of their limited resources.' The Italian Air Force was seen as being particularly vulnerable; although it was concluded that there were about 200 aircraft in East Africa, 40 or so were being destroyed each month and their replacement was considered to be 'impracticable'. With a more general estimate of just twelve months' ammunition, less than a year's food and only six to seven months of fuel oil, an increase in the scale of attack would threaten this 'precarious' position and force the Italians to use their reserves more quickly. It was this series of recommendations which provided Wavell with the authorisation he needed to move his plans forward.

Orders had in fact already been given the previous month to start strengthening his forces, despite the threat that was then facing the British Isles. A cycle of six-weekly convoys commenced sending reinforcements from Britain, India and Australasia; at their peak, these delivered an average of 1,000 men per day, with a similar tonnage in equipment, vehicles and stores also arriving in theatre. This allowed Wavell to make up the balance of his armoured and infantry units in North Africa while at the same time providing more men and equipment available for the southern part of his vast command. Even with this, in Kenya and the Sudan there were still only nine British battalions, four of Scots, one from the Royal Fusiliers and one each from the Worcestershire, Sussex, Essex and Yorkshire regiments. The remainder of the 'home' troops were from the Royal Artillery, which provided fifteen batteries of guns of various sizes; the Royal Tank Regiment, which sent two squadrons; and a railway construction company from the Royal Engineers.[27] From India there were two famous cavalry units, Skinner's Horse and the Central India Horse, three batteries of mountain guns, sappers, signallers, a number of anti-tank companies and fifteen battalions of infantry. The KAR provided a similar number of infantry; there were also the men of the Kenya Regiment, a reorganised machine gun battalion made up of all the machine-gunners and machine-gun units from the other battalions, along with large numbers of pioneers and support troops. Two armoured car regiments were intended to play an invaluable recce role as were the more lightly armoured vehicles from South Africa which also sent light tanks, twenty-two batteries of guns, a road construction company and nine battalions of infantry. They were joined by the troops from Northern Rhodesia who had been rescued from British Somaliland and Ethiopians who had fled their conquered homeland some years before. Added to this were the South Rhodesians and West Africans, the men from the SDF, the Equatorial Corps and various other exotic-sounding units, some of which were regular and others irregular in nature. This was a truly imperial force made up not just of different armies and air forces but of different races and religions, 'a microcosm of our war effort' as one London magazine described it.[28] Although still significantly outnumbered, Wavell now had a military organisation that was both equipped and trained for offensive operations.

Despite the increasing interest in eastern Africa shown by the Chiefs of Staff in London, however, there remained a serious impediment for the British planners. Drawing upon his own increasingly distant military experiences, Churchill often thought he knew better than the military men around him, and he continued to combine a particularly close interest in Wavell's progress with a mounting level of criticism.[29] Eden had written to the prime minister in late September with a range of topics for discussion; most related to the Middle East and one referred specifically to the alleged 'waste of troops in Kenya'.[30] It was actually an attempt to defend Wavell and, in his letter, Eden detailed the various British and Commonwealth forces available, arguing that the majority of them had been positioned in such a way as to safeguard the defence of the Sudan. This, according to the Secretary of State for War, was something that all three men had been in agreement on as it was viewed as being a greater priority than the defence of Kenya. In a directive sent in August, Churchill had indeed ordered that the defence of the Sudan be put first, arguing that it would always be possible to 'reinforce Kenya faster than Italy can pass troops thither from Abyssinia or Italian Somaliland'.[31] Now Eden reminded Churchill that in the colony, aside from the still limited strength of the infantry garrison, at this point there were only twenty-eight artillery pieces, twelve South African light tanks with untrained crews and another twenty-four guns and forty-four armoured cars due to arrive the following month. This was a recurring discussion over subsequent months as pressure grew on Wavell to go on the offensive.[32] And whilst Churchill remained the most persistent critic, he was not alone in questioning progress: in early October, the Vice Chief of the Imperial General Staff, General Sir Robert Haining, wrote to the Chief of the Imperial General Staff warning that the headquarters in Cairo had become 'over-loaded and rather indifferently organised'.[33] Even Dill, one of Wavell's greatest friends, noted that the deterioration of Italian morale had been widely reported and advised him that it was highly desirable for him 'to hit them wherever and whenever we can'; he hoped the general in Cairo would make the necessary arrangements to carry out operations in East Africa as had originally been intended.[34]

The commander in the Middle East was, however, still prepared to argue the point with Churchill and try to make him better understand the challenges he faced. Wavell's apparent reluctance to commit to offensive action has more often been linked to concerns about the level of training and preparedness of his troops, but it was the overreach of his forces and the ability to sustain any attack, specifically in Egypt but more generally across his entire command, that actually most worried him. He subsequently recalled that Britain's leader 'never realized the necessity for full equipment before committing troops to battle. I remember his arguing that because a comparatively small number of mounted Boers had held up a British division in 1899 or 1900, it was unnecessary for the South African Brigade to have much more equipment than rifles before taking the field in 1940.'[35] As American media reports in October highlighted, the possibility of an Italian thrust to the north also continued to concern Wavell, perhaps more even than the other potential dangers, and his forces were on high alert to prevent 'a gamble to sever the British Empire's jugular'.[36] Yet at the same time, and although recognising that

Aosta's shortages of fuel and other military supplies forced upon him 'very sparing warfare', the military correspondent of *Life* magazine also seemed critical of the failure to launch any attack against the Italians.[37] No one seemed willing to take into account that the greatest problem for Wavell was trying to accurately anticipate the character and nature of Italian military intentions and work out what they were actually doing. In theory his opponents enjoyed a marked advantage but this would progressively decrease. Basic military logic pointed to their superiority being exploited but, at this stage, there was still no clear evidence as to whether the halt following the invasion of British Somaliland was a strategic pause or the culmination of the Italians' efforts.

The increasingly vocal inputs from Pretoria also indicated another delicate consideration for the British commander in Cairo. Leading politicians in London, such as Leo Amery, argued that Smuts should be given greater responsibility for the conduct of the war in Africa, with the caveat that it needed to be made clear that 'his role is purely that of military coordination and does in no way imply political subordination or absorption'.[38] This support helped establish an increasingly prominent role for him, and the subsequent campaign would in fact prove hugely significant for both Smuts and South Africa. The country's official historian later described it as a 'military honeymoon' during which the troops 'were untrained and equipment sketchy but there was plenty of movement and quite a good deal of interest'.[39] It was in many respects more than just this, a more recent account comparing it to a 'dress rehearsal for the struggle which followed further north' and the fighting in the Western Desert.[40] The South African leader had reviewed the first deployment of Union troops beyond the country's borders at a farewell parade on 'Delville Wood Day', when each year the losses suffered during the 1916 battle were remembered.[41] He told the men assembled before him on 14 July 1940 that East Africa formed 'the strategic rampart and defence lines' of their own country and that their role would at some future stage 'open up wider horizons and establish larger interests' for all of them. It was not just the troops which proved so important but also the equipment that was sent north, most of which was produced using domestic resources. In September alone the South African Ford plant assembled 18,349 trucks all of which were destined for the war effort.[42] These were delivered using an overland convoy route with regular fuel dumps and rest camps, which allowed the vehicles to be driven from Pretoria to Broken Hill, a distance of 1,300 miles, and then on another 1,600 miles before arriving at Nairobi.[43]

With this level of materiel and manpower support, it was inevitable that Wavell would have to take into account Smuts' increasingly forceful opinions. A meeting held in Khartoum on 29 October to discuss future strategy brought into sharp perspective just how forceful the South African leader had become. Sitting with both men were Platt and Dickinson and alongside them was Eden, who had travelled out from London as a demonstration of the importance the British government attached to this meeting.[44] Smuts argued that the best strategy was to keep the Italians guessing where an attack might be delivered while preparing to make rapid moves into their territory. At the same time he was adamant that the vital port of Kismayu had to be captured early on if the more general offensive against Italian Somaliland was to succeed. British and Commonwealth forces would concentrate there before launching an advance towards Addis Ababa. Kismayu was also known to be an important supply hub for the Italians and, although the harbour was supposed to be blockaded, reports in November pointed to the number of ships there as having changed.[45] Air photographs and intelligence reports showed movement between Kismayu and Mogadishu but it was not known if this was local traffic or if ships were breaking the blockade. It had been first confirmed two months earlier that supplies were on their way from Japan, the ships subsequently reaching these ports where their cargo, which included lubricating oil, tyres and other spares for motor transport, was offloaded onto dhows under cover of darkness for use by the defending Italian military forces.[46]

There was, however, some disagreement about how best to proceed. Dickinson was more interested in launching an offensive east of Lake

Rudolf and also indicated that he wanted to split the South African forces now under his command and use them only for defensive operations. In so doing he had made a fatal miscalculation as to Smuts' level of authority and the growing relationship that existed between him and his British counterpart.[47] One Whitehall official remarked that the 'personal ties between the two leaders . . . were so strong that there was no thought of contention', while the English prime minister's own private secretary believed that 'Churchill could find no fault in Smuts, who represented so much that he approved'.[48] Churchill's physician went even further, writing after the war that the South African was seen as his most trusted overseas' adviser and one of only two men to whom he ever really listened.[49]

Dickinson's position was further weakened as, despite having achieved some success in developing his military forces, he had also managed to make himself extremely unpopular amongst sections of the local community in Nairobi.[50] In part this was due to his outspoken comments about some of the former members of the Kenya Regiment who had been drafted in to his staff at the outset of the war, but Fowkes, who was well placed to comment, was not alone amongst his subordinates in having little confidence in his general's abilities as a commander.[51] It is not entirely clear who made the actual decision to relieve him of his command but Wavell delivered the news. He appeared to feel some sympathy for Dickinson, although he accepted that he had not been good enough for the job in Kenya and the independent opportunities for command and leadership it required. Nonetheless, Wavell wrote back to Dill asking that his now former subordinate be given another role, arguing that 'he is worth a division, with someone above him close at hand'.[52]

The replacement as commander of British and Commonwealth forces in East Africa was General Sir Alan Cunningham, the brother of one of Wavell's most senior colleagues, Admiral Sir Andrew Cunningham, Commander-in-Chief, Mediterranean Station. Dill had originally intended to send General Francis Nosworthy out to Nairobi from Britain, having watched him throughout the summer command IV Corps, which had been given the critical role of acting as a mobile counter-attack force if the Germans had invaded. Having been offered the post, within twenty-four hours the unfortunate Nosworthy was informed that he required a relatively minor operation and, as this would delay his departure, Cunningham was selected in his place.[53] He was another professional soldier who had been commissioned in 1906 through Woolwich, not Sandhurst, and fought throughout the First World War with the Royal Horse Artillery, being mentioned in dispatches five times and awarded both a Distinguished Service Order and the Military Cross.[54] He was considered one of the two most educated officers in the inter-war British Army – the other being Arthur Percival, who later led the disastrous defence of Singapore – having attended courses at Camberley, Greenwich and the Imperial Defence College. Following the outbreak of the Second World War, he was appointed to command three territorial divisions in turn, the last of which was in Scotland, where he took charge of the 51st (Highland) Division.[55] Prior to Cunningham's arrival in Kenya, the governor, Sir Henry Moore, had been told by Lord Lloyd, Secretary of State for the Colonies, that he was easy to get along with and well thought of by Dill.[56] Within a few weeks it was confirmed to London that Cunningham had been well received and that everybody who met him, including Smuts and South Africa's senior military officer General Pierre van Ryneveld, was 'most favourably impressed'.[57]

The period that followed on the southern front came to be marked by intense activity, with the strengthening and continued preparation of the British and Commonwealth forces for the battle ahead. Moore had also been told in late October that he could anticipate 'a move on – at last' as there was no longer any fear within the British government of annoying Italy.[58] Cunningham unfortunately contracted both malaria and dysentery shortly after his arrival and it took him ten days to recover. This meant a slight extension to the inaction, but by the first week of December he had already gained a good idea of the task facing him and was now well enough to fly to Cairo, where he conferred in person for the first time with his immediate superior.[59]

According to his own post-war account, at this stage Wavell still did not really anticipate anything more than harassing the Italians with whatever forces he had available and, despite the suggestions from London, there was no thought of attempting a large-scale invasion of Italian East Africa.[60] Cunningham had in fact been similarly briefed by Dill before he departed and, as he later wrote, 'his attitude was that I <u>might</u> be able to do something towards Kismayu. But it was quite clear to me that he was doubtful as to its feasibility.'[61] He nonetheless set off determined that if the opportunity presented itself he would 'have a crack', but on arrival in Nairobi found what he concluded were still very limited resources – less than two divisions of trained troops, including the West African units that were not acclimatised and had their training to complete. There were no troop carriers to move these forces, though a locally produced version was being made in the workshops which continued to be so important in equipping the region's military forces. It was also clear that there had been little training in the basic movement of motor transport and there were not nearly enough drivers for the numbers of trucks that would be required to move the men and their supplies around.[62] Despite Dickinson's alleged preparations, Cunningham could find no evidence of planning for how an advance could be conducted and therefore had to start arrangements for the dumping of stores and ammunition and even the – potentially critical – construction of water points.

These omissions highlighted why Wavell had shown his reluctance to commit to an early offensive when pressed by London. During his pre-war lectures on leadership he had made specific reference to the huge importance logistics could have on the willingness of soldiers to fight.[63] Cunningham also recognised the vital need to maintain sufficient supplies for his forces, especially over the long distances that they would need to advance, and, having seen the lack of preparations, he requested a delay. Indeed he went so far as to stress within days of his arrival that no offensive against Kismayu would be possible in February unless there was the 'gravest strategical necessity'. Once again it was the South Africans who took a leading role in helping to overcome the challenge of providing drinking water, and their arrival with water-boring equipment proved crucial.[64] Efforts were made to improve existing supplies such as at Marsabit, where by December 1940 the 1st South African Division was well established, and specialist engineers drilled new wells drawing upon the lake which formed part of the nearby extinct volcano. As one senior South African based in London put it, this location was 'as far north of Capetown as Canada is from the United Kingdom', but it was far less hospitable.[65] An intelligence report written two months earlier confirmed that in this region a little over thirty-two inches of rain fell annually, of which nearly half came between October and December.[66] The engineers helped increase the amount of water available from 6,000 to 52,000 gallons a day; without this work, any attempt at an advance towards Kismayu would have carried enormous risk.

This concern was not overly exaggerated, and weather and the heat were key considerations both during the campaign's planning and operational phases.[67] In the Sudan and Eritrea the rainy season tended to last from April to October but it was erratic and difficult to predict and could peak at any point up to August. On the coast in Italian Somaliland there were dry seasons punctuated by spring and autumn rains, but these tended to be very localised and heavy and could delay motor transport for a day or two, after which no further rain might fall for two or three weeks. With the brief rains came a rapid abundance of camelthorn bushes, the sharp thorns of which cut the men leaving scratches that often became septic. At other times the conditions became more jungle-like than desert, but the elephant grass was generally tinder dry and easily set alight by burning fragments, whether from shells or cartridges, or even discarded cigarettes (although there were not many of these to be had during the campaign). The previous year had seen even less rain, and large numbers of locusts, as a result of which the harvests had largely failed, leading to extreme local food shortages.[68] This all added to the extreme physical challenges facing the British and Commonwealth forces, whether they were operating on the northern or southern fronts of the campaign.

PREPARING FOR THE COUNTER-OFFENSIVE

All this notwithstanding, political pressure for action continued to grow. In a message to Churchill in the first week of November, Smuts once again urged that the focus of initial operations should be on Kismayu. He expanded on his initial argument and warned that its capture would be necessary to allow for movement north into 'the forbidding desert' which lay between the coast and Addis Ababa.[69] He also advised that he had visited Cunningham's headquarters almost immediately following his appointment and found the men's morale to be good, although he worried about the level of inactivity. To show his expanding support for the campaign he also informed his British counterpart that he would be sending another infantry brigade as soon as he had ships to move it, with additional transport for water and supplies. This, he argued, was worth doing as there was serious unrest in parts of Ethiopia and with 'an attack both from the south and north, the Italians may crack in the summer and considerable forces may thus be released for the more important theatre farther north'. This, of course, was exactly the kind of assessment that the British leader wanted to hear and Cunningham was consequently left with only ten days to organise his plans.[70] The first draft of Operation 'Canvas' was being distributed within two weeks of his arrival in Kenya and Kismayu was referenced prominently as a priority to be captured early in any attack. Ideally the general in Nairobi wanted this to take place as early as January 1941 but the shortages of transport meant he feared it could be delayed until May. This led Smuts to intervene once again to say how disappointed he was that offensive operations might now be postponed despite the reinforcements he had provided.[71] Wavell believed that the continuing focus on the port was 'not very satisfactory' but was astute enough to recognise the political imperative.[72] He agreed that no other method could produce quicker results and endorsed the need for rapid action.

Whilst equipment might still have been limited, the British commanders did have a distinct advantage over their opponents as the quality and quantity of available intelligence had increased dramatically, and this greatly aided the planning process. In November 1940 the Italian High Command ciphers had been broken by the analysts working in the Combined Middle East Bureau, the Bletchley Park outstation in Cairo. Wavell could now read all the wireless traffic between Aosta and his senior commanders.[73] Prior to this he and his senior commanders had to rely on RAF aerial photography, information gathered from Italian Air Force ciphers and the results of interrogations of prisoners captured during the campaign's opening encounters. Plans and appreciations were now available and read almost as soon as they were issued, leading it to be described by the official historian as 'the perfect (if rather miniature) example of the cryptographers' war'.[74] Although the source was protected, the intelligence was distributed to all of Wavell's commanders, who were thus afforded every opportunity to surprise the enemy. Crucially, it revealed that the Italians were aware of the British and Commonwealth weakness on their southern flank but the majority of their army and air forces were still being kept in the north against what was perceived to be the main threat from the Sudan.[75]

The reference to the northern front was significant as here the British and Commonwealth forces had just suffered another humiliating reverse. After Kassala and Gallabat had been given up during the first week of July, the Italians had made no attempt to advance beyond these points. Meanwhile the defenders' official policy had been that their remaining small mobile units, if attacked by superior forces, would fight a delaying action rather than abandon their positions.[76] Little else happened and a relative calm prevailed along the 100-mile frontier. It was not until the autumn of 1940, and the arrival of reinforcements from the 5th Indian Division, that Platt was ordered to prepare a minor offensive directed at Gallabat. The objective was 'a pretty little place in wooded country with a mud fort and a customs house' which had become a strongly fortified village surrounded by barbed wire, stone and machine gun posts. Its loss a few months earlier had caused embarrassment back in London,[77] and the object of the operation, according to one of the senior British officers present, was to 'regain the initiative, raise our prestige and lower the

PREPARING FOR THE COUNTER-OFFENSIVE

enemy's morale and, also, to encourage the rebellion'.[78] Along with troops from the SDF, the task was given to the 10th Indian Infantry Brigade, supported by a squadron of eight tanks from the 6th Royal Tank Regiment which had been sent to the Sudan in September when it appeared that the Italians were poised to resume their advance. This Indian unit had only recently been formed and after eleven months spent at home completing basic training it had been sent to the Sudan. Now, just three months later, it was given the responsibility for launching the British Empire's first offensive of the war.

The attack began in the early hours of 6 November and, as the supporting artillery ranged its guns, the area was bombed from the air.[79] The Italians had not realised that the SDF had managed to infiltrate troops and guns up to the edges of their positions and they were completely surprised as the artillery fired 500 shells in the first thirty minutes, after which the supporting tanks were sent forward. Some of the Italians remained well dug in and a number of machine-gunners continued to fire for the next two hours. Colonial troops then launched a counter-attack but nearly half of them were killed and the remainder broke and ran. When the Sudanese and Indian troops occupied the position they found it to be a shambles. They recovered large quantities of supplies and ammunition, Italian money and even some anti-tank rifles, which had been taken from the Black Watch after their evacuation from British Somaliland. The most valuable items were the eighty or so mules, which were quickly incorporated into the SDF's ranks.

It was at this point that the problems began. Gallabat marked the first time Brigadier William Slim, who would later achieve considerable success as the commander of the Fourteenth Army fighting in Burma, had been given overall command at this level. Following the initial success he now went to a forward position with his artillery commander to get a better view of Metemma, which lay beyond him. This was a much more strongly fortified position with a garrison of two African battalions, some artillery, a machine gun battalion from the Savoia Grenadiers and a platoon of light guns. With its commanding position it was clear to the brigadier that the attack could not be continued. The terrain formed natural barriers which would hamper his armour, three light and five cruiser tanks, which he had placed in support of his Indian infantry during the initial advance. Whilst they had played an important role 'firing and inflicting casualties as they went', Slim knew they had already suffered mechanically on the rocky ground that they had crossed.[80] Along with the damage from landmines hidden by the Italians, this had taken a heavy toll on their tracks. Adding to the difficulties, the lorry carrying the fitters and the spare parts to repair the disabled vehicles was bombed, and so, by early evening, only two of the tanks could still be used. There was also an issue with the infantry. Major-General Heath, commanding the Indian division, had insisted on substituting one Indian battalion in each brigade with a British equivalent, one of which was the 1st Essex, which had never trained as part of this formation.[81] The harsh terrain made it difficult for the men, who relieved the original attacking troops that same morning, to dig in, and when Italian aircraft launched a heavy attack soon after, they were exposed to showers of anti-personnel bombs which proved devastating. An hour later another air raid destroyed a number of the artillery pieces, and there was a further attack that afternoon.

Little more happened during the night but at first light another air attack began; it was later discovered that the Italians had hastily collected all the aircraft they could from their bases across Ethiopia. Throughout the day bombers attacked in waves and news was received that as many as three battalions were advancing from Gondar. The British infantry were 'pulverised' and at least some of the men fled from the battlefield. This was one of only four instances in the entire war when officers lost control of their troops, and only twice did this happen in battle: here, and just before the island fortress of Singapore fell to the advancing Japanese.[82] Slim was left with no option other than to order a general evacuation, and the captured supplies that could not be removed were destroyed along with two of the tanks which had still not been repaired.

The British and Commonwealth troops had lost 200 men killed or wounded, but the Italian 27th Colonial Battalion had been largely destroyed, its losses estimated as 600 men killed or wounded.[83] Troops from the SDF continued to conduct active patrols, while Metemma and its defences were largely reduced; Platt could consider this all to be a positive outcome. As he later argued, although it was a tactical failure there had still been strategic success as considerable forces had been assembled without the Italians discovering what was going on, leaving them nervous about what the future might hold.[84] Both sides now seemed prepared to agree that their respective positions were too strong to capture and, at this stage, neither made any further serious attempt to attack the other. Despite the Kaid's optimism, it had, however, been another example of British-led forces failing to secure any form of meaningful military advantage and was a further case for embarrassment.

With this failure in their thoughts, and growing doubts about whether the efforts made to initiate a popular uprising would have any effect, another conference was convened by the senior commanders in early December to once more discuss plans for a general attack.[85] Based on his enhanced intelligence picture, Wavell had designed a three-pronged drive which aimed to contain and divide the large Italian forces at as many points as possible and confront them with overwhelming challenges. It was intended to begin in February with Platt's forces attacking from the Sudan. Operations on the frontier would secure the important railway hub and go some way to recover morale that had been weakened by the action at Gallabat. Concurrently, the irregular forces already operating in Ethiopia were to harass the Italians in the west, allowing Cunningham to move progressively from a defensive to an offensive role. The limiting factor was that, once the flanks had been secured by recapturing Kassala and attacking Kismayu, Wavell feared he would probably have to withdraw as many troops as he could to fight in the Western Desert. This assessment was not changed by confirmation from the War Office that, 'as far as we can see the time has come when risks may be accepted in order to undertake the most energetic operations against the Italians in all quarters'.[86]

There was a further prong to Wavell's strategy: it involved British Somaliland, which had remained central to his thinking. After a brief period during which the defeat's impact had been fully absorbed, some discussion followed within the War Office in London about using Somalis who had been forced to flee, and were now refugees in Aden, to act as small seaborne raiding parties and 'centres of unrest'.[87] In the months that followed, the British government's local representative continued to call for more to be done across the water to agitate against Italian occupation.[88] Eventually steps were taken with the establishment in Aden of Military Mission No. 106, also known as Hamilton's Mission, which was intended to carry out acts of sabotage in the now former protectorate and neighbouring Jibuti.[89] In addition to this a great deal of clandestine work was done by the former Senior Administrative Officer in the Somaliland Government Service, Reginald Smith, who was able on a number of occasions to enter the territory undetected. He used these surreptitious visits to pick up whatever information he could and pass it back both to MI6 and the authorities in Aden.[90]

This activity also helped the commander in Cairo as he crafted an excellent deception story to cover the proposed move of reinforcements from the Western Desert to the Sudan.[91] Operation 'Camilla' was all about making the Italians believe that the troops he was going to send south to support Platt were actually going somewhere else. In the elaborate story Wavell crafted, they were described as being part of a major force which would land in mid-February at various points in the captured territory before pushing on towards the key Italian base at Harrar.[92] Wavell wrote in this highly secret but entirely fictitious document that 'the loss of British Somaliland has always rankled bitterly between my government and myself. I got a rocket from the government and nearly lost my job at the time . . . I have orders to recapture it as soon as resources are available, and am most anxious to remove this blot on my reputation.'[93] It even described Cunningham's advance from Kenya as being intended to draw attention away from the real main effort. The subterfuge was known to only a few specially selected officers in his staff and his two senior generals in Khartoum and Nairobi, and with the language designed to appeal to Aosta, this was then sent to the regional commanders in a form that it was believed could be intercepted by the Italians. The operation's references to the protectorate seem to have been misunderstood, but the suggestion that Cunningham's advance was intended only as a secondary effort was accepted, and this played a key role in how the campaign subsequently developed. When the move from the Sudan began, this even reinforced the Italians' appreciation of the way in which they believed the British actually intended to conduct the attack against them.

With the detailed preparations for the British and Commonwealth forces' offensive now in their final stages, the South African troops at their base in Marsabit were poised to mount their first major military action of war. These were from the 1st South African Infantry Brigade under the command of Brigadier Dan Pienaar, mostly the Royal Natal Carbineers, who were supported by a number of specially adapted Bren gun carriers, described as 'tankettes', as well as the Gold Coast battery of light guns and some Kenyan pioneers.[94] An attack at El Wak on the Italian side of the border post was planned for 16 December, Dingaan's Day, to boost morale and also to allow some practice for brigade-level operations. None of the troops involved had ever fought in a major engagement but this was later judged to have been 'an almost flawless model for a bush-war raid', and was referred to by one of those involved as 'the first Allied victory of the Second World War'.[95]

As the South African troops reached the Italian positions amidst 'a large group of wells of very smelly water in limestone country with thick bush', they charged with bayonets fixed, singing the regiment's Zulu war song, a visual and aural assault that overwhelmed the terrified defenders.[96] Described as 'rather like a Commando raid', it was all over by lunchtime, by which point ninety-nine Italians were dead and another forty-four captured. More than a million rounds of ammunition were destroyed and much equipment recovered, including trucks, cars, machine guns and rifles, and even four camels which were towed back to Marsabit behind an armoured car; congratulating Cunningham on the success, Wavell asked that any of this materiel he did not require be sent to Cairo for onward distribution.[97] The most important items captured, however, were a large quantity of the Italian headquarters' documents; these were used for the breaking of more ciphers and further improved the intelligence advantage.[98] It also meant that the planners in Nairobi had to work 'day and night' sifting through them as the proposed campaign plan was revised.[99]

Despite its success, the raid had, however, highlighted many of the challenges that might lie ahead, with long distances and difficult terrain facing the attackers.[100] In this case the target was 110 miles from the brigade's base and could only be reached along a single badly maintained narrow road. The column of over 1,200 vehicles needed to transport the attackers had to carry not just the men, their weapons, their ammunition and fuel but also enough food and water for five days; with the final section of the approach entirely waterless and the assumption being that the Italians could have contaminated the wells, the latter was critically important. As the attack was carried out in a shade temperature recorded as 105°F, one gallon per day per man was carried in the front line transport, which was enough to last for three days; the troop-carrying vehicles carried enough for another day. The last forty miles of the approach had to be covered in darkness so as not to alert the defending garrison and the infantry and gunners had no choice but to dismount from the convoy and walk the last six of them. Vulnerable to ambush and air attack throughout, if they had been discovered the outcome might have been very different. It should have been clear from this experience that the coming battles would be as much physical trials as contests fought against a defending body of troops.

Despite this, the outcome had been positive, and there was an immediate political dividend as the South Africa press's encouraging references to the attack helped persuade Smuts to offer an additional division to join the fighting farther north. It is hard to say whether Churchill recognised the reason for this offer but he desperately wanted these troops and insisted that it should not be rejected. Wavell in turn argued that at this stage any new troops sent by the dominion would 'be an embarrassment' as it would be difficult to equip them for a fighting role with what was then available to him.[101] He had been warned by Cunningham that the South African battalions under his command were generally understrength and he doubted that they could find the additional trained and equipped manpower.[102] It was left to the senior officer in Cairo to point out to the authorities in London that Smuts was actually still quite restricted by domestic political tensions and the lack of universal popular support for the war that was known to exist in South Africa. This influenced where its forces could be sent and Wavell argued that it would be likely to prevent them from being sent to fight in the Western Desert. Once again Churchill thought differently, insisting that in the time it would take for the units to be prepared and set sail northwards, political approval could be secured in Pretoria for them to be shipped directly to the Middle East. At the same time he expressed his view that, in any case, 'by the end of April the Italian Army in Ethiopia might have submitted or been broken up'.[103] He was ultimately proven correct in both arguments but it was another serious disagreement between him and Wavell. Despite the laudatory comments following the tremendous success of Operation 'Compass', the first large operation carried out in the Western Desert, relations between the two men remained in a parlous state.

Although they had appeared for a time to have a clear advantage, anxiety was growing within the senior ranks of the Italian military. By mid-December 1940 Aosta was writing to Rome to say that he thought an attack from the Sudan was imminent, while another report sent a few weeks later warned that any move against Kismayu would be the opening of a general offensive in the south.[104] These assessments appeared to suggest the Italian commander still believed the offensive from Kenya would be a secondary effort, entirely as Wavell had anticipated, and his deception plans were already proving too sophisticated for his opponents. The British general's strength lay in his agile and innovative mind, his willingness to take risks and to support others to do the same, and his cerebral approach evident in his advice that a commander 'should constantly be considering methods of misleading his opponent, of playing upon his fears and of disturbing his mental balance'.[105] He had several other equally important concurrent campaigns and did not have time to be involved too closely in East Africa, although it is obvious that he did maintain a close overview. To enable Platt and Cunningham's offensive action, Wavell provided clear objectives to his commanders, then stepped back to allow them to get on with the task and was 'the last person to stop anything going ahead'.[106] Even before the attack began, his opponent Aosta appeared to have already been defeated mentally. He confessed to Mussolini that he viewed the local African population as being 'in a state of latent rebellion', urging that plans must be made for the possibility of the collapse of organised defences. He did not believe he could 'save the entire Empire' and his suggestion was that pockets of resistance should instead be established within which the defending troops would be told to resist to the last man.[107] The battle for East Africa was about to begin, and if the British and Commonwealth commanders were hoping for the best, the Italians were now already assuming the worst.

CHAPTER 6

THE ADVANCE FROM KENYA

By late January 1941, preparations on the southern front were nearly complete and Cunningham's forces were poised to advance. Accompanied by his aide, who had recently arrived in Kenya, the general had spent the previous few weeks travelling and had visited almost all of his command area.[1] Major James Blewitt wrote back to his cousin in Britain describing the long air journeys during which they flew over a 'most extraordinary country' and every type of terrain 'from almost tropical vegetation to absolutely dry deserts without a drop of water for miles'.[2] At this point, even before the advance had begun, the British commander suffered a recurrence of his earlier health issues, possibly malaria but described as 'some sort of mild stomach trouble', although he again made a quick recovery. This was not an entirely surprising relapse as he was already juggling the operational stresses of his command and the challenges of leading his multinational forces with political pressures that left him looking 'both ways'.

Cunningham faced a diverse variety of problems. There was, for example, a delicate situation on his personal staff, a scandal described by an American journalist as a case of 'ultra-British correctness [being] suddenly upset by tropic passion', which was centred on the community of white Kenyan settlers who lived in the country's highlands in what was known as Happy

Valley.[3] Cunningham's assistant military secretary, Josslyn Hay, the 22nd Earl of Erroll, was shot dead in Nairobi just before the advance got under way in what was described to Wavell as a *'crime passionelle'*.[4] Whilst the southern front commander thought it 'an unsavoury case', he seemed more upset that he had lost a 'first class' member of his team who 'was clever and quick' and knew everybody, as well as now having to find a replacement at short notice.[5] At the same time he also had to deal with a potentially significant political issue as some of the newly arrived South African officers were quick to agitate that they should only have to serve under their own national commanders. Cunningham discussed these tensions with Smuts, highlighting how they undermined his ability to lead a unified force. This led to the apparent evaporation of the problem but he was also aware that everything done by the South Africans was followed closely by their press correspondents, who scrutinised his actions and emphasised the merits of their countrymen at every opportunity. It was a hugely complicated relationship to manage and there would be trials ahead for those tasked with taking charge of it, both on the East and North Africa battlefields.

If this were not enough, in many respects the greatest issue facing Cunningham was one that faced all Britain's senior military commanders at this stage in the war. With resources stretched, and knowing the importance of the distances that were involved, it was as clear to him as it was to Wavell that campaign success depended entirely upon the degree to which his troops could be kept supplied.[6] When he had arrived in Kenya he found there was 'almost nothing at all – everything was improvised'.[7] Despite the work that had been done by Dickinson, the key problem on the southern front still remained the 300-mile desert they had to cross before reaching the Italian positions and in which, between the rivers Tana and Juba, there was no water at all to be found. He had also discovered that, in addition to the British not having the transport to move both men and water forward, the method of water carriage was poor: it had to be carried in leaky containers that lost much of their load. This shortfall was compounded by an organisational reluctance to accept that the standard

British Army water bottle design was not fit for purpose, particularly for troops operating in a region where the often intense heat meant this simple piece of equipment was vital. Simply put, it spilled more than it held and later, as the advance continued into Italian Somaliland, the Italian version became an important item to acquire. This had been designed to allow for a restricted but continuous flow and, within a short period, most of the British and Commonwealth troops, private or officer, had at least one in their possession.

The lack of water was critical and potentially meant the advance would not be feasible. South African specialists had greatly helped to improve the situation but much more needed to be done. Colonel Brian Robertson played a vital role with his preparations and detailed staff work.[8] Famed for his ingenuity, Robertson would finish the war as a major-general, renowned as one of the best Allied administrators. He deployed Royal Engineer survey teams to locate water and at Hagadera and Galmagalla, both in the desert ahead of the proposed line of advance, brackish but drinkable sources were found.[9] Although to some this was an apparently minor development, in many respects it was one of the key events of the entire campaign. As one later account put it, 'it was said at the time that when Mr Churchill asked General Wavell, "When the hell is Cunningham going to get moving towards Kismayu?" the correct answer would have been, "as soon as Sergeant van de Merwe and his rig strike water at Hagadera"'.[10] This discovery meant that the daily ration of water for the initial stages of the advance could be expanded to a gallon per man and half a gallon per radiator.[11] It was still not a huge amount but much better than had previously been thought possible. Half of the individual ration went to the cooks and a quarter to the water bottle whilst the remaining quarter was used by the men to wash, shave and clean their teeth.[12] They got by, although the smell was noticeable after a few days, which is why some christened themselves 'the upwind boys'. The small increase in water also helped when it came to the troops' food rations as there had also been an apparent lack of thought about what form this might take.[13] Whilst the men from West Africa had access to fresh meat and vegetables, the British and South Africans often only had bully beef and biscuits and the latter, known to the men as 'dog biscuits', could be eaten only if washed down with lots of water.[14] Many of the troops had previously gone hungry, but with the slight increase in the amount of water available, they would at least now have a little more food to digest.

There was another significant logistical problem to be overcome: the amount of fuel that would be needed to keep the advancing troops moving. Robertson shared Cunningham's concerns, noting that men and horses could keep going when food ran short but 'when lorries and tanks run short of petrol, they stop altogether and the force which they compose is at the mercy of its enemy'.[15] This had been a long-standing concern extending back even before September 1939 and the outbreak of the European war. In anticipation of a future conflict, a million gallons of petrol had been stored at Mombasa, but no thought was given to the local climate and the effect it would have.[16] In a pre-war study, the War Office had calculated the amount of tin plate needed to produce solid petrol cans which could be re-used, but it had instead been decided to save money and develop a four-gallon 'flimsy'. This could not cope with the heat of a typical East African day and then the cool of the night, and the men considered themselves fortunate if just one gallon was left after the cans had leaked petrol vapour. Any large dump could be smelled from more than a mile away, and by January 1940 it was reported that 3,000 tons of petrol had already vanished from Mombasa.[17] Apparently simple but important issues such as this had not really been addressed and, when added to the huge distances involved and a shortage both of tankers and drivers, the ability to sustain an advance when an average brigade consumed around 20,000 gallons of fuel a day did not appear guaranteed.[18] The use of the sea for transporting supplies therefore became a key planning consideration for Cunningham and he later acknowledged the role that had been played by the Royal Navy in landing stores. This also served to reinforce the thinking behind Smuts' demands that Kismayu needed to be captured early on in the battle if success was to follow.[19]

The very final steps were now being taken with African colonial troops in the vanguard of the assembled forces.[20] Amongst them was the 3rd Battalion, Nigerian Regiment, under the command of Lieutenant-Colonel H. Marshall, originally of the Royal Lincolnshire Regiment, which was sent to Garissa where it relieved 1st Battalion, KAR. As was the case with all the men of this West African brigade, they were regular soldiers recruited from northern Nigeria and led mostly by regular British officers and NCOs. This particular battalion was the forward unit and had a ten-mile front to defend, which included a bridgehead on the far back of the River Tana where the District Commissioner's house was still occupied by a local administrator.[21] One company was placed in slit trenches guarding the pontoon ferry used for crossing the fast-flowing river, with orders to hold it to the last man and the last round.[22] The remainder of the battalion was two miles to the rear, close to a forward airfield at which the South African Air Force (SAAF) had a squadron of vintage Bristol and Hartebeeste aircraft piloted by Rhodesians. There were also some Natal-born engineers who provided expert advice on how to dig communication trenches and generally help strengthen the temporary base. The only attacks during this period came from Italian aircraft bombing from great altitude and which did little damage. A greater threat was posed by the local wildlife, one patrol having to take shelter in the trees after being surprised and attacked by a troop of elephants.[23] There were giraffe, deer and zebra which avoided the surrounding mines, and one night-time lion which became entangled in the barbed wire and 'roared his disapproval', but pulled free. The real danger at this stage remained the weather as the rainy season produced a sea of mud which made it impossible to move forward. The Nigerians' conclusion, however, was that defending the Tana was 'rather boring' and, along with many of other troops along the southern front, they actually appeared pleased that the advance into Italian Somaliland was about to begin.

After one final regional tour during which he had met with Cunningham in Nairobi, on 2 February Wavell was able to advise Dill that he had given his approval for the attack on Kismayu and this would begin in the middle of the month.[24] Despite having already shared his concerns during the December planning meeting, he took this final opportunity to remind his two senior commanders to make maximum efforts to capture Italian East Africa as quickly as they could. He had already written candidly to his colleague in Nairobi the previous month telling him of the 'continual pressure from home to the effect that operations in your theatre do not look like paying an adequate dividend in the amount of material [sic] and personnel involved', and warning again that 'it is constantly suggested that it would be better to cut them down to pure defence and employ the troops elsewhere'.[25] As he went on, Wavell reminded his superiors in London of the political advantages victory in this theatre offered and that it would 'release a considerable military effort' for operations elsewhere. Cunningham later confirmed that when he met with Wavell immediately prior to the offensive he had been asked if it was possible to begin his attack sooner, but no undue pressure had been placed on him to change his plans.[26] He had been given autonomy of action and Wavell's assurance that 'I think you will be justified in taking considerable tactical risks against these Italians, whose morale cannot be high, and I will certainly support you in any <u>bold</u> offensive you decided is worthwhile'.[27]

A small potential complication arose at this point when a most secret message was intercepted, which suggested that the Italians were actually poised to surrender.[28] Referencing a 'hitherto reliable source', almost certainly a message sent from the Japanese embassy in Berlin to Tokyo, it detailed 'a serious disagreement' that had arisen between the German and Italian High Commands. Due to shortages of war equipment, and 'to save avoidable slaughter', the authorities in Rome were apparently considering seeking terms with the British but the Germans, and the Japanese, wanted them to fight on as long as possible to tie down enemy forces. Reports such as these can only have increased the calls from London for a rapid but decisive effort to be made which might demonstrate to the Italian military that they were right to want to give up the fight and allow desperately

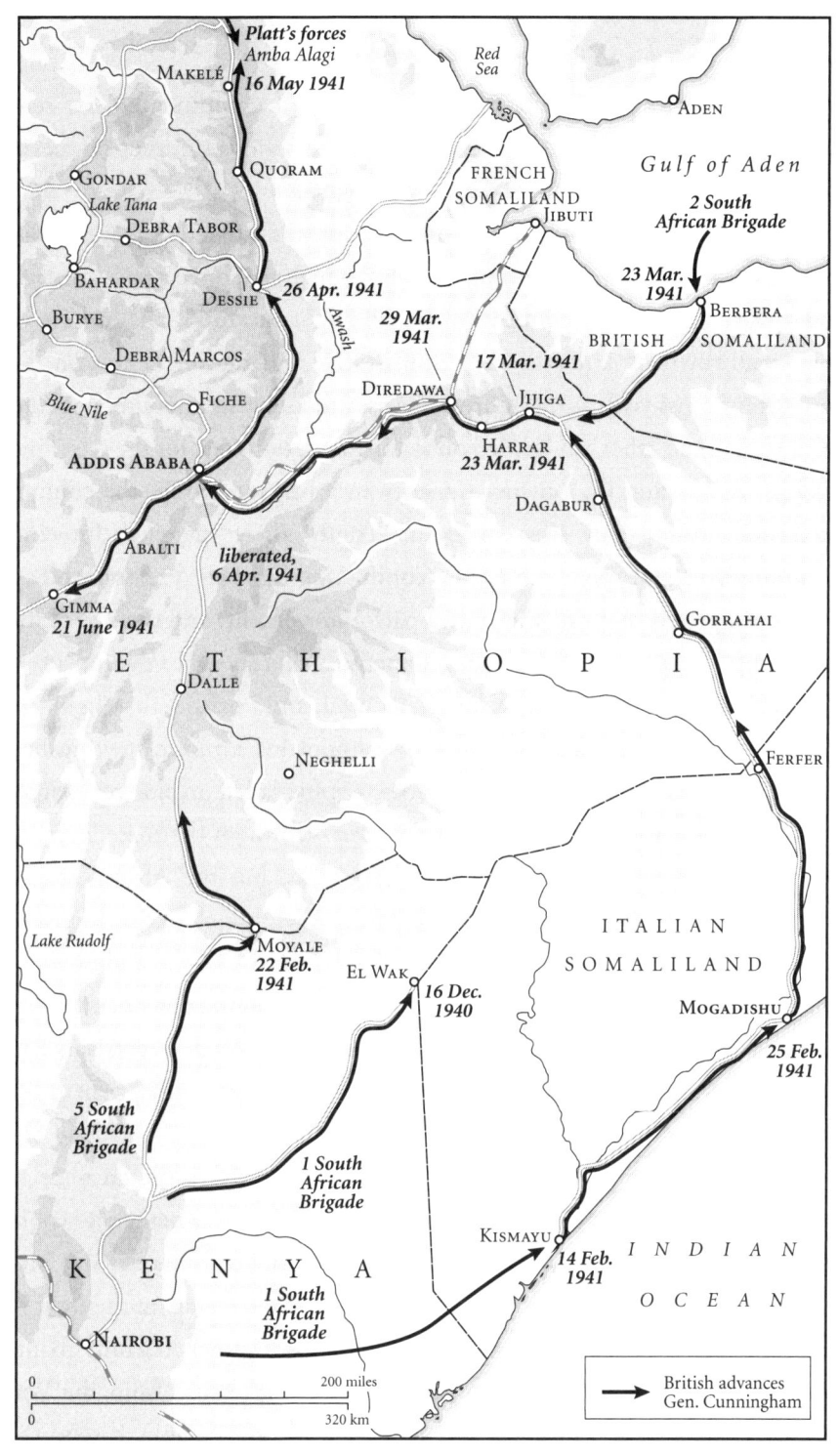

3 Advance of British and Commonwealth forces from Kenya into Italian Somaliland and Ethiopia.

needed British and Commonwealth troops and equipment to be sent further north. Churchill's comments from the previous summer can never have been very far away from Wavell's thoughts.

As it was, shortly afterwards Cunningham was advised that Aosta had now received direct orders from Mussolini which had once again stiffened his resolve to continue, and this meant the fight was on.[29] The capture of the small town of Afmadu, an administrative and trading centre on the important crossroads running from Garissa to Gelib in one direction and Kismayu in the other, was settled on as the first serious test for the attacking troops. Advancing into enemy territory in a brigade group, the column extended more than fifty miles in length as it marched forward. Cunningham had spent some time conducting his own deception piece, which suggested that this was only a patrol movement, and the size of the attacking forces must have come as something of a shock to the Italians.[30] Three battalions from the KAR were used and, before first light on 11 February, and in the absence of any supporting armour, they pushed large numbers of Bangalore torpedoes – pipe-laden explosive charges designed to clear a way through for the men – through the three layers of barbed wire.[31] These failed to create large gaps, but the African troops charged into what turned out to be an empty town, much to the disgust of their commanding officer. Heavily bombed by the SAAF the night before, with nearly eight tons of high explosives dropping on the defenders during the course of an hour-long attack, the demoralised Italian garrison had fled.[32] There were no casualties amongst the attackers other than those already suffering from malaria and dysentery.[33]

It had been an initial success. But just as quickly as the advance to Addis Ababa had begun, uncertainty now arose as to whether it would continue. This small town had fallen easily but the commander in Cairo now had to decide whether he had sufficient forces to carry on the fight in East Africa.[34] Ever since the Italian attack on Greece launched from Albania in October 1940 Wavell had faced considerable pressure from the War Cabinet in London and knew that its policy was to 'be able to send the largest possible land and air forces from Africa to the Balkans'.[35] Now, with the Italian position in the Western Desert appearing to him to be on the verge of complete defeat, Wavell decided that he could afford to take some risk and press on, but once again warned Platt and Cunningham that they might soon have to give up some of their already limited forces.

Unbeknownst to Wavell, the Italian strength in Somaliland had in fact been overestimated prior to the invasion; as it was, they had only a slight advantage, with the best part of two colonial divisions, another brigade of infantry in reserve and various *bande* groups, in total around 20,000 men supported by eighty-four artillery pieces and fifteen armoured cars.[36] The defence was further hampered by De Simone's conviction that the 300 miles of desert would prevent his opponents from carrying out any large movement of forces and limit them to making raids. He had only been given command of the Juba sector in January 1941 and, following a detailed inspection, he found the morale of his men to be very low.[37] When Cunningham's hastily assembled mobile forces launched their surprise attacks, this vulnerability was ruthlessly exposed. To achieve a decisive advantage, the British general had taken great risks and used to best effect his access to intelligence and his belief that the Italians did not really grasp even a basic notion of how deception was used.[38] He consequently sought to make his forces look much stronger than they were and in locations that tied down his opponents. A good example was the 1st South African Brigade which had spent the previous month defending the wide central front but had been moved in secret from Wajir to join the advance, leaving a wide and vulnerable open front. A handful of troops had remained along with a signals unit and sixty dummy tanks that were moved each night and poorly camouflaged during the day so as to be spotted by enemy aircraft. This force was redesignated the 'Fourth Australian Division' and played on Italian fears, convincing the nearest commander at Bardera that he faced a significant opponent when he could in fact have driven straight to Nairobi.[39]

The battle was being fought as much in the mind as anywhere else and De Simone was making huge errors as he tried to anticipate his opponent's plans. He had assumed that once the British-led forces developed their attack they would head for the port of Mogadishu. Cunningham, however, had always assumed that fierce resistance would be met along the natural defensive barrier presented by the River Juba and the capture of Kismayu remained his focus. As he had told his subordinates, they had ten days to achieve this or he would order a withdrawal back to the Tana. What he did not know was that the Italian commander, with Aosta's approval, had at the same time reached the conclusion that the key target – which Smuts had so vigorously argued was central to the entire campaign – could not be held, and orders had been given to evacuate and move the garrison north to defend what was now seen as the vital Juba crossing.[40] The British and Commonwealth forces needed Kismayu to overcome their potentially fatal supply weakness and gain confidence that the advance could be maintained, and the Italians were playing along.

Unaware of the strategic pressures on their commanding generals to conclude the campaign in short order, the advancing troops enthusiastically exploited the initial opening that had been won at Afmadu, moving with a relentless pace. Following an order from their commanding officer, Lieutenant-Colonel 'Tank' Western, the men of the 3rd Battalion, Gold Coast Regiment went into action resplendent with moustaches to hide the fact that the white officers and non-commissioned men were all so young.[41] Despite their youth and lack of experience, the 24th Gold Coast Brigade was able to move sixty miles in a single day across difficult terrain and captured the well-defended positions on the west bank of the Juba at Buro Erillo in what Cunningham described as 'a most courageous and dashing attack'.[42] Nearly 600 feet wide, the river split into two branches with a small island in the middle; both linking bridges had been destroyed and the Italians had created a strongly fortified position guarded by one colonial battalion, a battery of field guns, some armoured cars, tank traps and rifle and machine gun pits.[43]

A delay followed, but by 13 February the defences along the riverbanks had been cleared and patrols of West Africans were searching for a place to cross the river – eventually accomplished at Mabungo – while men from the Royal Engineers provided training for the brigade in how to use paddles.[44] Neighbouring Gobwen and its airfield had been captured by the South Africans at about the same time but the Italians also still held the riverbank opposite in considerable strength and with more good defences. It was three days before their commander, Dan Pienaar, flying overhead in a reconnaissance aircraft, was able to identify a suitable crossing point seven miles upstream at Yonte. The Italians referred to this as the Bulo Merere ford, but the river was five feet deep and crossing it was not easy as the banks were steep and high in places. The South African brigadier nonetheless decided this provided the opportunity he needed and two platoons of his infantry crossed in improvised assault boats. Despite an immediate counter-attack later on the night of 17 February, followed by two more days of sustained fighting and assaults by the Italian 101st Division who were well dug in, the position was held. This allowed a temporary bridge to be constructed and reinforcements, including armoured cars and artillery, to be pushed across the river.[45]

Once their opponent had managed to pass this obstacle, and with their reserves all gone, the defenders quickly lost their resolve.[46] A further dash north followed and a link-up with the Gold Coast troops as the advance headed for the next target, Gelib on the east bank astride the main road north. The limited initial objectives already seemed to have been too cautious in nature. It could also be argued that the battle for the Yonte bridgehead and the successful construction in record time of what was christened 'Union Bridge' was one of the most significant events not only of this campaign but of the entire war fought in Africa. It confirmed to the attackers that within only a few weeks the Italians had been psychologically defeated and precipitated the dynamic advance that was to follow. Cunningham and those closest to him later concluded that this first part of the campaign was all that really mattered, and once a crossing over the river had been secured, in his own words, 'the Italians in front of me broke'.[47]

While the South Africans were fighting to cross the Juba, another success was being completed at what at one stage was considered to be the campaign's principal objective. By the evening of 14 February, just two days later than the schedule originally set by Cunningham, the leading elements of 22nd East African Infantry Brigade had entered Kismayu.[48] They found their opponents had again retreated, leaving behind them a considerable amount of abandoned guns and ammunition along with more than 200,000 gallons of petrol. Kismayu was a dusty little town with litter all over the streets but the residents, many of whom were 'rolling drunk' having looted the wine stores, were pleased to see the men of the KAR who set about checking for booby traps and any remaining Italian forces.[49] There were twenty-five scuttled wrecks in the harbour and the bay was 'an oily swell as a result of the sunken ships and tankers'; with a single jetty and access roads which crumbled within days, prospects did not look great.[50] Whilst some demolitions had been carried out by the retreating Italians, it took only three weeks to make the necessary repairs and the first British freighter was actually moored just five days after the port had been captured.[51] Following De Simone's orders, Kismayu had apparently been evacuated in 'two panic stages', the first following the initial crossing of the frontier and the second when it was heard that additional reinforcements had arrived at Mombasa. This led Aosta, who had visited on 11 February, to give the order to withdraw, which took place in an entirely chaotic fashion.[52]

As this anticlimax to what had been anticipated as being a major battle was drawing to a close, the South African troops who were much farther to the west had continued their advance across the Chalbi desert to outflank the Italian positions in front of them. In the desert – described as a 'vast, flat, white waste of soda and soft lava dust, totally devoid of vegetation and reflecting the scorching sun' – there was a dusty road but it was passable for only three months of each year.[53] The rains had come a month earlier than expected but four days after Kismayu's capture, and following some confusion and heavy fighting in drenching rain and bitter cold, the attackers captured the fortress at Mega – forty miles inside Ethiopia and 7,000 feet up a steep escarpment – taking 1,000 prisoners.[54] Moyale, one of the first locations to have been fought over the previous year, was recovered five days later. Cunningham appeared to be correct in his conclusion that the war in East Africa would not last long.[55] As the pace of the advance increased, the Italians were certainly already showing some signs that pointed to the rapid collapse that would follow.[56]

The approach to Mogadishu was thick with dense bush which was so heavy that vehicles could not push through, and the *askaris* and Nigerians worked in relays with their *pangas* to cut a track.[57] As they arrived at the outskirts shortly before dusk on the evening of 24 February an Italian armoured car, flying a white flag, approached the leading African troops.[58] Inside were well-dressed Italian officers who had come to request that the port be declared an open town. The staff captain for 23rd Nigerian Brigade entered the following morning at dawn and met with the mayor, 'a fat little man looking immaculate in white drill uniform', who accepted all of his orders without question. After the surrender, the senior police officer, who spoke excellent English, took him for a full breakfast. At midday the Union Jack was hoisted over the former Fascist headquarters but only after one of the recently arrived Nigerians climbed the flagpole on top of the building and cut down the Italian flag; some of the Somali crowd cheered but were then forced away by police who were still on the streets.[59] It was found that a prisoner of war cage had already been built and the Scottish NCO from the Southern Rhodesia Regiment who was placed in charge arrived to find the nominal roll and 250 Italians waiting for him.[60] He did not have the most difficult of wartime jobs, although there was at first some disappointment amongst his prisoners that they were not allowed temporary leave and an evening 'sleeping out pass'; breakouts were, nonetheless, rare. The Italians quickly accepted their defeat and 'it wasn't more than a day or so before the shops were open and the policemen back on their little stands directing the traffic, this time however on the left of the road'.[61]

For the victors, a rest camp was quickly established by the sea where they were able to bathe and wash their clothing for the first time since crossing the frontier. The *askaris* could not believe that there was any body of water larger than Lake Victoria, and when they went for a swim in the Indian Ocean many were taken ill after drinking salt water.[62] Fresh vegetables and fruit were also temporarily available to enhance their rations.[63] The men had already advanced 200 miles in two weeks accompanied by a South African water company which, unusually, had white drivers, a reminder that this was considered 'the most vital of all commodities'.[64] These drivers sometimes had to go back 100 miles in a day to fill up and, even with the discovery at Hagadera, it took eight of these companies – equipped with tens of thousands of 44-gallon drums that they had brought, each carrying 250,000 gallons of water – to keep Cunningham's forces moving.[65] Now they could pause and replenish as the press admiringly reported back in Britain that the West Africans had proved that colonial troops possessing 'loyalty, discipline and a high standard of training can stand up to the conditions existing in modern warfare'.[66] The Nigerians were in fact showing themselves to be particularly well suited for fighting Italians, perhaps more so than all the other British and Commonwealth forces.

At this stage there was certainly plenty of evidence to suggest that the doubts and concerns expressed prior to the battle had been misplaced. The advance was undoubtedly going far better than Wavell or Cunningham could have hoped but the successes that were being won led only to further pressure from London to do more. With Kismayu's fall Churchill had returned to his now familiar complaint, urging that Mogadishu be attacked as quickly as possible and complaining to Ismay that with such an easily won victory 'one can see how much enemy resistance in this Kenya theatre was overrated'.[67] This dismissive comment was pointedly first circulated around the Chiefs of Staff Committee and then repeated to Wavell two days later. What the general did not know was that the prime minister had also asked for all of the correspondence from the last four months to refresh his memory of why Cunningham had rejected his 'efforts' to launch an early attack against the port. As Churchill put it in a minute to Ismay, 'it all seems very discreditable to the Kenya Command, who have devoured troops from all directions and on all pretexts, and who have done nothing but patrol warfare and skirmishes, and only screwed up courage to take Kismayu after the rottenness of the Italians became apparent'.[68]

At the same time there was yet another pointed reminder to Wavell and the other generals in his command that everything possible needed to be done to secure a rapid victory. Aside from the situation elsewhere in Africa, there was also the growing concern that Japan had to be deterred and Churchill seemed convinced that the defeat of Italian forces in East Africa could have a considerable positive effect. Whilst there was no suggestion from Dill of 'the slightest doubt' of the plan's soundness, the time factor had become of paramount significance.[69] Three days later the response came that, with no more troops or air forces available, the Middle East commander could not proceed any faster. Ismay was one of the more astute thinkers advising Churchill and he thought it important that discretion should be given to Wavell to reinforce the Eritrean front as, until the opposition there had been defeated, no final victory would be possible.[70] Less than a week later, however, following the capture of Mogadishu, it was confirmed by the War Office that the second South African division would now be moved directly to the Middle East, a 'naughty' decision that was apparently taken without any final discussion with the headquarters in Cairo.[71]

This could have been seen as something of a gamble as there was still a long way to go to the Ethiopian capital. Despite some positive signs that much of the hard work had been done, the junior officers who arrived to replace casualties in the leading units shortly after Mogadishu's capture were told the Italians were likely to stand and fight. Any naturally strong positions available to them between the coast and Addis Ababa were seen as presenting a challenge and Cunningham himself believed that a pause of two to three weeks was inevitable before the advance towards the major Italian base at Harrar could resume.[72] This was based in large part on his knowledge of the still acute shortage of petrol as, whilst everything else that was needed had been found seized in the port, there was no sign of any fuel. The British general offered a reward of £25 – more than £1,000 in current money – to anybody who could show where the petrol had been stored; a Somali revealed the hiding place and large dumps buried in the bush, and 380,000 more gallons were now added to the stocks captured at Kismayu.[73] The advance was being sustained by the ineptitude of the Italians, who seemed unable even to deny their opponent much-needed supplies. With this and the material being landed by the naval convoys at the recently captured ports, Cunningham was able to reverse his earlier assessment and set loose his 'mobile' capability: not just armoured cars and trucks but also road-making machinery, water-boring equipment and water-carrying vehicles. As the lead forces moved out of Mogadishu they managed to advance on average sixty-five miles per day, a rate that was far beyond the enemy's ability to resist.[74] Following the initial breakthrough and breakout, the southern front was now poised to witness one of the war's great exploitation and pursuit phases.

This was led by the 11th African Division reinforced by the 1st South African Brigade Group and 22nd East African Infantry Brigade. According to one of the British intelligence officers seconded to the KAR, once the Juba had been crossed Cunningham's strategy was one of 'genial simplicity'.[75] With this formation he made sharp jabs on the left flank while the 12th African Division made a terrific right swing heading in the direction of Addis Ababa. Describing 'one of the most thrilling and triumphant campaigns ever attempted by British arms', the renowned British war correspondent Alan Moorehead confirmed to his readers that 'Most of the preconceived ideas of colonial warfare went west in Abyssinia . . . As the guns breasted each rise they blasted the enemy out of the valley below and charged after them. It was untechnical and unprecedented, and it knocked the Italians into bewildered surrender.'[76] The leading forces had advanced the 200 miles from Kismayu in just three days but then took the same period of time to catch up and generate the largest force possible to exploit this initial advantage. At the front was a reinforced brigade which, having left Mogadishu, motored north covering 740 miles despite there being no supplies of any kind to be found locally and with everything, including water, still having to be carried. The rains dictated the route that was taken and the Strada Imperiale was chosen over the Strada Royale as, although longer, it was less subject to the bad weather. It was also a well-maintained road that allowed for a rapid rate of progress to be made with no need to stop.

The Nigerians continued to demonstrate a particular talent for this form of warfare despite the fact that they had been given virtually no training in mobile warfare, and before their arrival in East Africa 'the only methods of advance they knew were the slow, weary bush treks where everything was head loaded'.[77] With the speed that was being maintained, however, there remained some potential risk as it was only possible to keep the two forward companies of a battalion adequately supplied. The remainder of the men were anything up to 100 miles behind these leading troops while the rest of the brigade was separated by the same distance again as the advance was strung along the road and potentially vulnerable to counter-attack.[78] This never came, and it took only seventeen days to reach Jijiga where it had been assumed that a stand would be made by the Italian forces. Climbing to over 10,000 feet, the advancing troops found 'a filthy little spot, full of flies and only one house [in which] the sanitation didn't work', which had been abandoned without a fight.[79] To reach it the men had travelled through a dust bowl in which the extremely fine sand could at times be more than a foot deep; this and the other challenges of the heat, poor diet and relentless nature of the advance meant that by its end at least one South African unit had lost 50 per cent of its drivers who in some cases 'had sores on their backs the size of tennis balls'.[80]

Cunningham already knew his supply problems were about to resolved entirely as a result of his being able to open another front with a typically daring operation.[81] The reconquest of British Somaliland, lost in such an unfortunate fashion the previous summer, had a significant part to play in the overall outcome of the entire campaign. Having written about it in his

'Camilla' deception plan, Wavell genuinely believed in the importance of recovering Berbera as, despite the port's limitations which he had himself witnessed, with some quick improvements it would help open up a much shorter supply line for the southern advance.[82] With a devastating turning manoeuvre to open up his opponent's flank, its recapture would have a huge propaganda impact throughout the British Empire. Whether he had believed the initial ruse or not, even Aosta had concluded by mid-February that the British would now be looking to conduct landings to recover their lost territory.[83] Described in the official report as a 'lash-up' that used whatever local resources and facilities happened to be available in Aden, the plan called for the port to be seized, allowing an army supply base to be established which could sustain up to 15,000 troops.[84] To achieve this, 3,000 men, mostly from two Punjab regiments, would be transported with their equipment across the Gulf of Aden, a distance of about 140 miles, by a small landing force of eight Royal Navy ships with additional transports carrying their vehicles and heavy equipment.[85] Supported by naval bombardment provided by the three largest available surface vessels HMS *Glasgow* (which carried the flag for the senior officer Captain H. Hickling who was in command of what was termed Force D), *Kingston* and *Kandahar*, this small invasion force was then to land on open beaches inside the reefs to the east and west of Berbera and, having secured the bridgehead, it would push on to recover the remainder of the protectorate.[86]

Prior to its launch there were very real doubts about several aspects of the proposed operation, not least relating to lack of knowledge about the gaps in the reefs and even the difficulties attached to locating them in the dark when there were no visible features and the town was unlit. Such was the importance attached to the attack that it was decided to accept the risks involved and, after the issuing of an initial operation instruction, the expedition set off just a week later. The 'Aden Striking Force' assembled in the early hours the next day, on 16 March, at a point ten miles north of Berbera and 1,000 yards from the shore, and here it waited while small parties headed out to search for landing spots.[87] Interrogations of prisoners had indicated that as many as seven battalions of troops were acting as a garrison but some were known to have been withdrawn, along with all the armoured vehicles. There was in fact a detailed Italian plan for conducting a fighting withdrawal in the direction of Gocti before linking up with forces from Harrar.[88] A number of heavy guns and machine gun posts had been placed to cover the beaches on either side of the port, but when the landings began very few offered any fire.[89] With the opening bombardment most of the locally raised troops – as many as 1,500 men – along with their Italian officers and NCOs fled from the port in the direction of Hargeisa, and only limited fire was directed against the boats that, just before 5 a.m., started to ferry the Indians to the shore.[90] What little real fighting there was took place to the east of the port where a diversionary landing had been made and this attracted a more forceful response from the sixty men who were guarding this area. Amongst the attackers, casualties were limited to one African soldier killed and one British officer slightly wounded, and by 10 a.m. the town had been captured. The signal 'The British flag again flies over Berbera' was sent back to London; unfortunately nobody had thought to bring a Union Jack with them, but one was borrowed from a local Somali.

Much of the success was credited to the level of preparation and training that had taken place from January onwards when it had first been proposed that a landing of troops might well prove desirable. In the few weeks that followed, shipping was converted for troop-carrying purposes while ramps were added to lighters to allow armoured cars to be driven off them. Further innovation, prominently referenced in the subsequent reports written about Operation 'Appearance', involved using some of these vessels as floating piers to make the offloading of vehicles much easier, an idea that may well have inspired the Mulberry harbours used during the D-Day landings in Normandy.[91] The RAF also played an important role, carrying out numerous air photography and reconnaissance missions to identify possible landing places on the beaches, the Italian defences and the state of potential local landing strips.[92] For the three nights before the attack, the major Italian airbase at Diredawa was bombed repeatedly and throughout the day of the invasion and the four days that followed a continuous fighter patrol was established over the port. With the defenders having fled or surrendered, a camp was quickly built at Berbera for the Italians captured here and elsewhere by Cunningham's advance, and this was eventually able to hold 5,000 men. The general himself visited on 21 March to congratulate those who had taken part in the invasion and to discuss how to get the port up and running.[93] The following day a brigade of South African troops arrived in the bay who were to play an important role in the subsequent advance.[94] As for De Simone, he was left to lament that more had not been done to hold British Somaliland, but the order to withdraw had once again come direct from Rome, where Mussolini increasingly seemed intent on giving up his empire without much of a struggle.[95] Back in London the leader writer of *The Economist* approvingly noted that the occupation had lasted only seven months.[96]

The main attacking force had now reached the final phase of its already remarkable advance as on 21 March it fought an extraordinary battle to capture the important Marda Pass beyond which was the Italian base at Harrar.[97] A few years earlier, during the Italian invasion of their country, this position had been held for three months by Ethiopian troops but it now fell within twenty-four hours. It was a bright and clear day under a cloudless sky as the first battalion of the Nigerian infantry attacked at around midday across open ground supported by a troop of armoured cars from the Kenya Regiment and some South African field guns that fired more than a thousand rounds of shells as they duelled with Italian guns hidden from view on the other side of the pass.[98] No attempt was made at concealment as the leading company used the main road, advancing along a broad front followed by the armoured cars and heading in the direction of Camel Saddle Hill which was believed to be clear of defending troops.[99] There was supposed to have been a primitive portable wireless system available to co-ordinate the attack but the company commander had little faith in it and instead took his bugler into battle at his side. As the Italian artillery and mortars in the foothills ahead of them opened fire, compass bearings were taken and counter-battery fire began as the bugler sounded the 'Retire'. It was later agreed that this was probably the last time during the war that this form of communication was used to manoeuvre a large unit of British and Commonwealth forces. The subsequent follow-up attack was conducted that same night and the position was occupied fully by first light. The Italians withdrew, abandoning more than forty machine guns and considerable amounts of ammunition and other equipment before blowing up the road behind them, although even this was done badly and there was only a six-hour delay before the advance resumed. The attackers had lost a total of thirty-two officers and men, including seven men who could not be rescued from the hillside and were said to have died from exposure during the bitterly cold night.[100] Cunningham never could understand why the Italians gave up this position so easily; it was just the latest in a series of decisions by his opponents which made no military or strategic sense to him.[101]

Capturing the Marda Pass marked the end of the open mobile phase of the southern advance and the beginning of the fight for the mountains. With the terrain becoming increasingly difficult to cross at speed, the prospects for the defenders should have improved greatly as both the Babile Gap and the Bisidimo Pass again offered significant advantages to them. The first of these was described as 'a narrow defile leading down to a river, with high, rocky features on either side' and what 'appeared to be an almost solid wall of rock running from north to south'.[102] Italian troops did put up some heavier resistance here during which several firefights developed before they were broken up by accurate artillery fire from the South African guns. One junior British officer calculated that 40 per cent of the shells fired at his men were duds whilst the enemy's heavy mortars, which had a much greater range than those of the British and Commonwealth forces, were also used too badly to have any real effect.[103] This in fact proved to be the last major engagement of the advance on this front. The pursuit which had begun at Mogadishu had been too quick for the Italians to counter and they were forced to continue their retreat to Harrar and the now inevitable conclusion. This was one of their most significant military bases and had been prominent in Cunningham's thinking; held by three full brigades it had, once again, been expected to provide a very tough challenge but it was declared an open town even before the advancing forces arrived. Diredawa, another important administrative centre, and with a large Italian civilian population, was also simply abandoned by its garrison. Pursuit had turned into a rout.

There was no chance that the initiative would be surrendered as the British-led forces continued to apply constant pressure on the retiring troops who were heading to the natural barrier of the Awash, one of the largest rivers in the whole of Ethiopia, some 150 miles away. This was the last possible line of defence and provided yet another formidable position, a deep gorge which almost cut a trench in front of the country's central plateau that lay beyond. Cunningham was not alone in thinking the Italians could have formed positions here that would hold indefinitely and American media correspondents accompanying the advance speculated that 'the road to Addis Ababa may be the scene of a series of battles'.[104] But whatever fighting spirit the Italians might once have had was long since gone; the defending troops were entirely broken and their commanders were worrying more about the route along which they could fall back than anything else.[105] As they continued the chase, and nearing exhaustion, South African armoured cars took the lead and, when they ran out of petrol, were passed by the 22nd East African Infantry Brigade. They reached the riverbanks before the machine-gunners from the Savoia Grenadiers, supported by the Blackshirt militia and colonial troops, had the chance to make good their defences, and troops from the KAR, supported by the guns of the 22nd Indian Mountain Battery, forced a crossing at dawn on 3 April which led to the defenders being outflanked. The battle for the village just west of the gorge lasted until the next morning, when most of the Italians withdrew. In the meantime, during the night six armoured cars were dragged across the 200-feet-deep gorge, using block and tackle and the strength of 200 *askaris* to manhandle them across. Another improvised bridge was quickly built across the river, one of seventy that were constructed by the engineers during the advance but the last one that would be needed on this stretch of road. The Italian commanders had calculated that destroying the road and rail bridges at the Awash would halt the advance by two days, just enough time to evacuate the capital, and all the other crossing points along the remaining 140 miles were left intact, so the road to Addis Ababa was wide open.[106]

The southern front advance had achieved an incredible success – far beyond what anybody, even Wavell, had anticipated might be possible – and the statistics were nothing short of exceptional. During a remarkable fifty-three days, this one arm of what was turning into a two-pronged pincer advanced more than 1,700 miles from the Kenyan frontier to the Ethiopian capital, occupying some 360,000 square miles and capturing more than 50,000 prisoners, all for the loss of 135 men killed, 310 wounded and another 59 missing.[107] At the time it was described as a military record and, as Cunningham's obituary later noted, it was carried out at 'a pace seldom surpassed in history'.[108] The eventual scale of Operation 'Canvas' was huge: to put it in a European context, had Cunningham's headquarters been in Cherbourg, his three fronts would have been centred on Marseilles, Madrid and Milan.[109] Wavell himself calculated that it was the equivalent of conducting operations in Inverness while based in London but having a railway line that extended only as far as Newcastle.[110] That this did not present an insurmountable problem only served to highlight that the main difference between his troops and those facing them was that the British and Commonwealth force 'was mobile and dashing while [the Italians] were sluggish and unenterprising'.[111] Indeed, as another contemporary account noted, in contrast it had taken 'Marshal Badoglio seven months to advance 425 miles in 1936 against the brave but sadly ill-equipped Abyssinian forces'.[112]

Despite the terrific pace of the advance and the other challenges he had to face, Cunningham remained throughout in 'terrific form', according to his aide, and had stood up extremely well to 'what must have been a terrific strain'.[113] As his forces captured territory there was never a place that he had not visited within twelve hours; he was in the second aircraft to land in Mogadishu and entered Gelib while his troops were still fighting in the outskirts. He had a narrow escape flying into Jijiga in one of three South African Junkers 52 aircraft which landed and taxied to a halt but were then attacked by three Italian fighters.[114] The planes were machine-gunned but nobody was hit and the damage was minimal as, by this stage, the attackers only had a few rounds of incendiary ammunition remaining.[115] It could have been far worse if they had been loaded with more of these and if the attack had come five minutes earlier when the aircraft were coming in to land.[116] The Italians probably did not know they had missed a chance to kill almost the entire British headquarters staff. They returned the next day and bombed the airstrip again, this time with more incendiary rounds as a single resupply aircraft had arrived overnight from Benghazi. Without the element of surprise, and faced by South African fighters, including two of the Hurricanes, they inflicted further damage on the ground, including to one of the transport aircraft, but for the loss of two attackers.

The greatest problems Cunningham faced were those which he had anticipated from the outset: the constant difficulties in organising supply and transport, and, once the scale of the potential opportunity for success became clear, urging his forces to maintain their phenomenal pace. When the general had been at the Imperial Defence College a few years before, as part of the studies examining any possible future war involving the British Empire, a campaign against the Italians in East Africa had been considered. The conclusion his syndicate had reached was that an advance from the south was quite impossible so he was 'very pleased that he had got there first when it was never dreamt of by anyone that he had the slightest chance'.[117] Blewitt had witnessed it all at first hand and was not alone in his conclusion that the Italians had simply assumed it would not be possible to advance as quickly as the British and Commonwealth forces had done. This outcome he put down 'largely to the general's own personal

1 On the left, General Archibald Wavell, the British commander of forces in the Middle East, meets with the South African leader Jan Smuts during his March 1940 visit to Cape Town.

2 The governor of Kenya, Sir Henry Moore, takes the salute as South African troops begin to arrive in the colony. Standing to his right is Major-General Douglas Dickinson, the senior British military officer in the region, and on his left is the South African commander Brigadier Dan Pienaar.

3 Wavell meets with Major-General William Platt, his commander in the Sudan, to discuss strategy.

4 A propaganda picture showing Acting Captain Eric Wilson manning his machine gun at Tug Argan during the heroic defence.

5 The British fort at Moyale, a good example of the defences available to the British and Commonwealth forces.

6 Following Dickinson's dismissal, Major-General Alan Cunningham was appointed as his replacement to lead the advance from Kenya.

7 Troops of the Gold Coast Brigade marching through Kismayu on 14 February following the capture of this key strategic port.

8 During the advance made by the Patriots, the Ethiopian emperor, Haile Selassie, receives advice from Colonel Daniel Sandford (to his right) and Lieutenant-Colonel Orde Wingate (to his left).

9 A contemporary popular magazine rendition of the recapture of Berbera in March 1941 as part of Operation 'Appearance'.

10 The Union Jack flies over Government House in Berbera following the success of Operation 'Appearance'.

11 Pack mules and Bren carriers in a forward area in front of Keren.

12 Indian troops resting at a signal point in a fort overlooking Mount Sanchil.

13 Indian troops marching into Asmara on 1 April 1941.

14 Troops from the Transvaal Scottish march through Addis Ababa.

15 The emperor is driven into Addis Ababa with Cunningham accompanying him in his official car.

16 Italian troops marching down from Fort Toselli after the surrender of the garrison at Amba Alagi.

17 The viceroy of Italian East Africa, the Duke of Aosta (second from left), leaves his mountain fortress following his surrender. Behind him, in the centre of the picture, is Major-General Mosley Mayne.

18 The Patriots on the march – entering Debra Tor in July 1941.

19 The enemy positions as seen from inside the fort at the Wolchefit Pass.

20 The Union Jack flies over the ancient Portuguese castle at Gondar at the end of the final battle of the British and Commonwealth campaign in East Africa.

driving power'.[118] In another letter his aide once again referred to the role Cunningham had played and 'his foresight and readiness to take risks which had made the campaign the complete success that it had been'. He did, however, also refer to those moments when his commander had wondered what might happen if the decisions he was making had been mistaken. Fortunately this did not prevent him from urging those around him ever onwards, whether it was the fighting forces as they continued the advance or those tasked with keeping the flow of supplies moving alongside them.

Just as the British general had believed it was the decisive moment, De Simone also recognised that after the failure of his defence of the Juba he had not been able to form another coherent front or mount an effective defence. He was interviewed following his capture and revealed that although wireless interception had provided him with a good deal of knowledge about British plans, he could not capitalise on the advantage to achieve any real success on the battlefield.[119] The Italian had clearly been worried from the beginning that his flanks would be turned by his opponent pushing on from Bardera towards Mogadishu. This was his reason for ordering the garrison there to hold out for as long as possible and its failure to do so was described as a critical reason for why the entire position was lost. As Kismayu was abandoned to avoid its being cut off, the troops moved to strengthen Gelib but were pursued all the way and De Simone himself was machine-gunned by a British aircraft while travelling in his staff car. His task was not helped when Aosta took his best troops, the 101st Division, who had offered the stiff initial resistance at the Juba, for the defence of Addis Ababa. De Simone claimed that he had still intended to halt at Modun but as he drove there his staff car was once again attacked from the air, whilst shelling from the Royal Navy was so effective that it destroyed his mobile headquarters and even his own personal tent. With all of his senior commanders having fled by this stage and most of his remaining men having disappeared into the bush there was little he could do to halt the advance of his opponent.[120] As he concluded, 'in many cases the senior officers were lacking in ability and . . . he had not much faith in them'; his best men, he felt, were the *bande*.[121] He had also considered the position at Harrar to be particularly strong but the resistance mounted there was another great disappointment. Troops who had displayed 'definite dash and courage' only a few months before during the invasion of British Somaliland now 'disappeared like "fluff in the breeze"'; of the 20,000 men originally under his command, only 2,000 remained, leaving him still with twenty-two batteries of guns but almost no infantry.[122]

It was certainly true that, aside from a few of the initial battles, throughout the advance from Kenya the Italians seemed prepared to withdraw very readily. The more obvious examples were at Mega, where the South Africans could very easily have been forced back, and also at Afmadu, where a lone Italian left behind told those who found him 'you only have to make a noise like an armoured car and you will be in Mogadishu in a fortnight'.[123] This was, in large part, a result of their main operational weakness which, according to one assessment by a senior British military officer, was their leadership. The staff officers were only considered moderate in terms of their abilities, whilst with only a few exceptions higher commanders lacked enterprise, vigour and determination. As a result, there rarely seemed to be any thought given to launching counter-attacks even though the Italian company commanders would often put in effective and well-directed local actions. Neither were their intelligence services thought particularly good, although, as De Simone had confirmed, wireless interception was excellent, as was the field telephone system he used which meant his ability to communicate instructions was often much better than that enjoyed by Cunningham.

The daily summary of enemy intercepts produced on 3 March for the British and Commonwealth commanders included reference to a commentary on Italian radio about the losses that had been suffered. During this it was said that 'the Empire is a stronghold which can be surrounded or even partially dismantled, but as a whole it can resist any attack'; this, it was concluded, was clear evidence that the Italian people were being prepared for defeat.[124] Even at this stage the prospect of Germany intervening to save the day apparently remained a commonly held belief and the best hope for the rapidly shrinking defending garrison. This outlook, along with a 'Maginot mentality', was believed to account, at least in part, for why neither the regular Italian forces nor their locally raised troops had seemed particularly keen on offering any resistance during the fighting on the southern front.[125] By late March their strategy was assessed by their British opponents as being one of holding onto a foothold, which seemed to be in Eritrea, where the defence that had been fought until then appeared to have been comparatively better. In the south they had already lost the war.

CHAPTER 7

SECOND FRONT
Striking from the Sudan

THE OPENING SHOTS of the East African offensive actually began on the northern front. The advance by British and Commonwealth troops that started from the Sudanese border saw some of the heaviest fighting and the most resolute defence conducted by the Italians, not just in this campaign but in any of the entire war. In many respects it was what Wavell had anticipated from his earliest strategic reviews: that the Red Sea would prove an attractive draw to his opponents, who would place many of their best units in Eritrea and northern Ethiopia. As part of his wider plan, he had given Platt – who had been promoted to lieutenant-general on 7 January 1941 – the twofold objective of securing the security of the Sudan and removing the threat to the maritime supply routes which were vital to his operations both in East Africa and also in the Western Desert. Once the safety of the Red Sea was guaranteed, the United States could once again permit their merchant ships to use this route, which meant that more of the hard-pressed British shipping would be available for use elsewhere.[1] It also meant that at least one point of access to the Suez Canal could be guaranteed for the convoys being sent to him from around the British Empire.

In his headquarters in Khartoum, Platt continued to believe that Kassala, where the battles had been fought the year before, remained the key target for his forces. The original appreciation made in the summer of 1940 had apparently concluded it would be impossible for a force of any great size to advance in the direction of Asmara from the small frontier town. This was due to difficulties of supply and even just the handling of those units which had been assembled on this front.[2] Once again terrain and weather were also vital considerations. As the Kaid's forces completed their preparations, many of the troops were camped near the River Atbara in which it was possible for them to bathe. From here, however, it was thirty-seven miles to the next water feature, the River Gash, described as 'a seasonal stream', with no water at all to be found in between. At the time of the advance the Gash was actually a dry and sandy bed and the men had to dig seven feet to find any form of liquid. As for the ground they were covering, one of the officers described it as 'an immense dusty plain in which grow an endless number of stunted, dark, thorny and evil smelling trees' which had three-inch thorns that could puncture the tyres on the trucks.[3]

Facing Platt was Luigi Frusci, a sixty-two-year-old veteran of the Spanish Civil War who had three full divisions and three independent brigades under his command, and with additional reserves he could call upon from northern Ethiopia. Consequently his forces outnumbered those of his opponent by more than two to one, once again a significant, even potentially decisive, advantage, particularly when combined with the excellent defensive positions presented to him by the terrain. It was much hillier in the north and the Italian equipment, including mule transport which was essential for mountain warfare, was also of a generally higher quality. The British and Commonwealth forces were, however, better prepared and equipped for a campaign based on manoeuvre and Frusci was worried about the challenge of defending an area that he believed favoured mechanised columns.[4] Platt was initially unaware of this, or that in June 1940 the SS *Umbria* had been detained as it tried to force its way through the Red Sea, including amongst the munitions and military equipment it was bringing from Italy a consignment of anti-tank guns. Their loss meant that the Italian troops had practically no ability to stop British tanks if any were sent to fight on this front.[5] Frusci did have some armour of his own but it was no match for what his opponent could produce and he generally doubted whether he had sufficient capabilities to stop the British. Added to his more general concerns about the stocks of ammunition and petrol available, his anxiety about the demoralising effect on his troops if they were forced to fall back did not bode well for the battle ahead.

The Italian Air Force, the Regia Aeronautica, also offered him little support as by this stage in the campaign it was easily dominated by its opponents.[6] In late January 1941, the ageing fleet of British aircraft was augmented by newer Gladiators, Blenheim bombers and Hurricanes. They were employed most effectively as their landing strips were positioned as close as possible to the forward edge of the advancing troops. This meant they could stay longer in the air, providing cover for the ground forces and, as Platt later wrote, their impact on the subsequent fighting was considerable: whilst the Italians had at first machine-gunned and bombed the advancing columns, 'thanks to the efforts of [our British] airmen, their appearances and their effectiveness gradually diminished'.[7] The general even went so far as to conclude that 'this was a prime factor enabling greater distances to be covered', and, although it was not clear at the time, it was this success in the air which went a long way to hampering the chances of a successful Italian defence.[8]

Despite the much larger size of his ground forces, in a number of critical areas Frusci was actually at a disadvantage. As was the case for De Simone, he was not helped by having to rely upon intelligence of dubious quality and, as a result, he tended to overestimate his opponent's strength. Platt did much the same as Cunningham in the south, exploiting this advantage ruthlessly, often in tandem with a better use of deception, to undermine the apparent Italian superiority in manpower and equipment. With his limited military strength Platt had actively sought to deceive the Italians about the size of the forces facing them; post-war accounts that highlighted the 'extraordinary incompetence of the Italian intelligence services', and the degree to which they were taken in, were entirely accurate.[9] There were numerous examples such as at Aqiq, an anchorage on the Red Sea south of Port Sudan, where repairs were made to the jetty and landing grounds and dummy camps were laid out in an effort to make the Italians think that a major attack would come from this direction.[10] Another was the attempted commando raid in early January 1941 carried out in the Gallabat region, approximately 200 miles south of Kassala. This was intended to distract the Italians forcing them to send more reinforcements to Metemma where the battle had been fought two months before. Relying on an incompetent local guide, after a long night march up the Atbara the men got lost in the darkness but eventually managed to make their way back home; this nonetheless left the Italian garrison nervous about their opponent's intentions.[11]

Platt's establishment of a dedicated mobile column to continually harass and raid their positions proved the most successful method of confusing the Italians.[12] Referred to as Gazelle Force, this had been formed in October 1940 around Skinner's Horse to which was added a machine gun regiment from the SDF and other supporting units, including even some light artillery.[13] Wavell ordered that maximum disruption be caused in order to intimidate the Italians and fix their defensive positions, and this unit proved hugely successful at making it appear that a much larger force was operating along the frontier. They were under orders from their commanding officer, Colonel Frank Messervy, to 'Terrify the enemy. Make his life absolute hell!' As Messervy said, 'I want it to be that they are afraid to move by day or sleep by night, so that they think more of protecting themselves than probing for our weak points. They must become completely defensively minded.'[14] Described as 'a charming, efficient, very brave and determined commander', before the war Messervy had been an Indian Army cavalry officer and a very good polo player.[15] Another of his colleagues noted his 'great dash and verve' and his 'always itching to get where the fighting was fiercest', and it was certainly the case that this small force achieved a much greater effect than could have reasonably been anticipated.[16] With a headquarters staff divided more or less equally between Indian Army and SDF personnel, although there was lots of 'horse talk', the unit was entirely mechanised with armoured cars and trucks. As a result it was known as the 'tin cavalry' but, even with limited numbers, it proved too much for the Italians.[17] Throughout November and into December Platt's troops lay 'in wait like a cat watching a mouse' whilst everything was done to undermine the enemy's morale and harass the Italians, who believed they were facing five heavily armed divisions.[18]

A good intelligence network on the ground also helped as it recorded the movements of enemy troops in and around Kassala. By this point British signals intercept stations were positioned in various locations in eastern Africa and Wavell and his generals in the field were provided with near real-time decrypts of Italian messages. These outlined the enemy's strength and identified where the troops were and how their commanders intended to use them. Such was the advantage this provided that the Deputy Director of Military Intelligence in Cairo believed there was no equivalent in any other wartime theatre.[19] Gazelle Force even had its own attached air reconnaissance which provided invaluable support, photographing the enemy frontier posts and carrying out occasional bombing attacks on them.[20] This Rhodesian squadron also took Messervy into the skies to observe the terrain over which he and his men would be operating – visibility which offered huge advantages later as they played a prominent role in the rapid advance into Italian territory. This ability to view what was happening along the frontier meant the senior British commanders could monitor what was believed to be one of the most vulnerable points for attack and which, if it was in Italian hands, could have led to a potentially dangerous northward advance.

It was as much concern about this threat as anything else that had led Wavell to order that, when the opportunity presented itself, his main attacking forces should regain complete control of the border region. With his flanks protected, the aim would then be for the British and Commonwealth forces to press on towards the Red Sea port of Massawa, a distance from the frontier of approximately 230 miles. Wavell had made available two divisions from the Indian Army to lead the advance on this front and the first of these, the 5th Indian Division, reached the Sudan in September 1940 having been moved in a convoy of nearly forty ships. Although attacked by Italian aircraft as it neared Port Sudan, nothing was lost and this fully equipped and trained body became Platt's main resource of manpower throughout the months that followed. Perhaps the key decision of the whole East Africa campaign, however, was Wavell's subsequent move of the 4th Indian Division from the Western Desert, albeit only for a few months, to operate alongside them. This division had been involved in the decisive victory won at Sidi Barrani in December and could potentially have been used in North Africa to help with the pursuit of the retreating Italian forces.[21] The commander in Cairo concluded that securing his maritime supply routes was too important an objective to ignore and ordered the division's temporary move south, which was a bold move.

The lead elements from the 7th Indian Infantry Brigade arrived in the Sudan on the last day of that same month.[22] They were accompanied by a battery of six-inch howitzers and a squadron of Matilda tanks from 4th Royal Tank Regiment. At the time, nobody could have guessed the level of concern Frusci had about facing British armour: he was subsequently proved to be entirely right to fear the impact of the enemy's tanks and these played a huge role once the advance got under way. Thanks to Wavell, Platt also benefited from having, at this stage of the war, two of the best divisional commanders. In charge of the 4th Indian Division was another gunner, Major-General Noel Beresford-Peirse, 'an extrovert, plain-spoken, orthodox soldier' who had already established something of a reputation for himself as 'a dashing commander' during the fighting in the Western Desert.[23] In charge of its sister unit was Major-General Lewis Heath, known universally as 'Piggy', and 'his qualities of dash and drive, [and] his humane and sympathetic disposition made him a popular commander' both throughout the division and beyond.[24]

The attack had originally been scheduled to begin on 8 February 1941 by which point, it was believed, the two Indian divisions would both be available along with their supporting armour. It called for an advance to

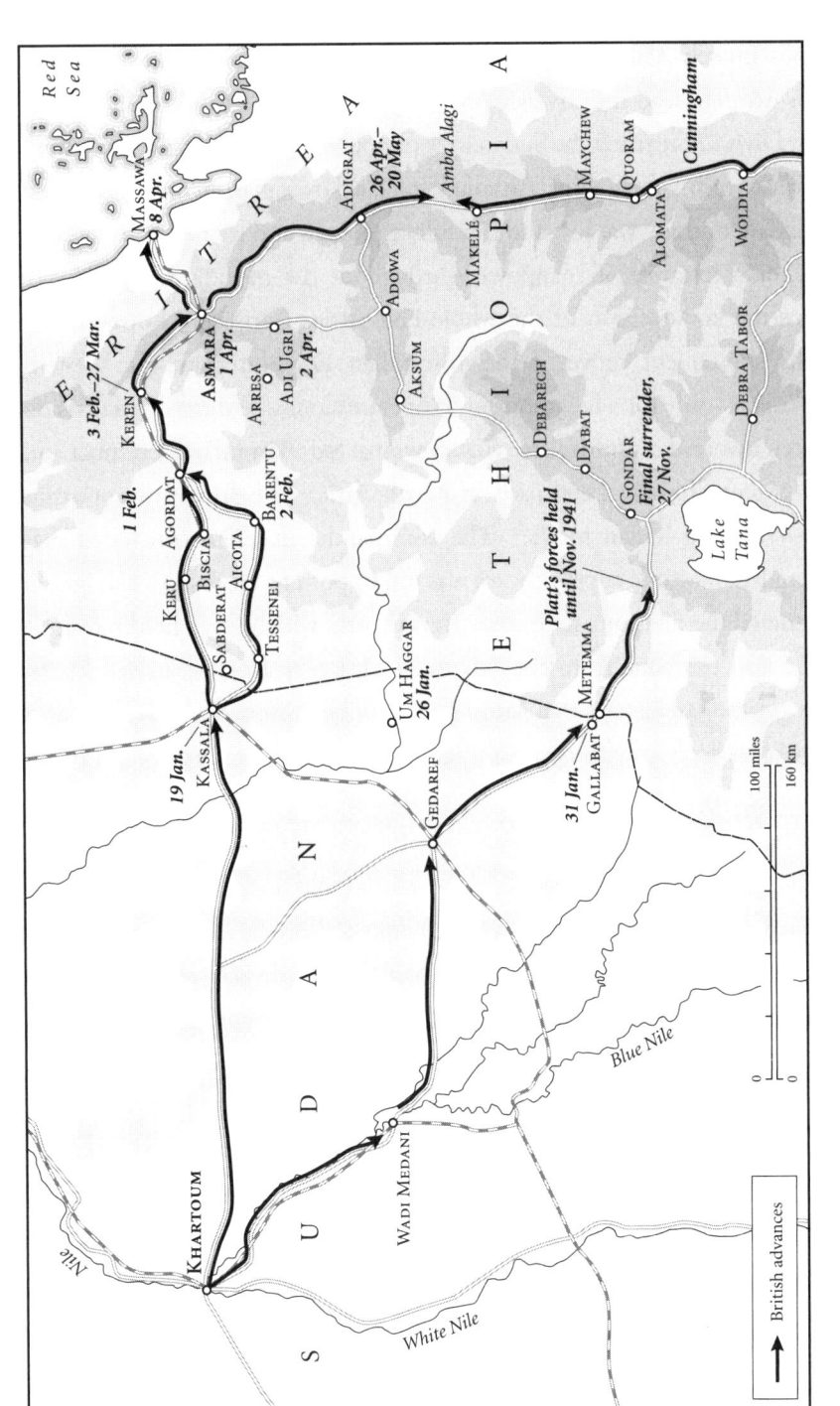

4 Advance of British and Commonwealth forces from the Sudan into Eritrea.

Kassala, leaving two brigades for defence against any possible Italian flanking move, before eventually heading in the direction of the Italian garrison at Gondar and on to the Red Sea. The immediate key objective was Agordat, 2,000 feet up on the Eritrean plateau and where the well-surfaced Italian road began which travelled all the way to the coast. Prior to the offensive beginning, there were still the best part of two colonial divisions facing Platt's forces and nothing to suggest the Italians would not put up a strong defence. British intelligence reports noted that enemy morale was low but as the enemy had 'good rations, a strong defensive position to hold and little air activity against them' it was assessed that they could still potentially hold out indefinitely.[25] Perhaps the most significant contribution provided by Wavell's intelligence advantage came at this point with the discovery that the Italians were actually already withdrawing from their frontier positions. Plans were now hastily revised and it was confirmed that the advance could begin nearly three weeks earlier than planned, on 18 January, even though elements of the 4th Indian Division were not yet ready. Although he had only recently arrived, Beresford-Peirse nonetheless seemed to fully understand Platt's intentions and what the plan entailed and he was prepared to accept a much greater level of risk than his opponents.[26] As the advance subsequently developed, he in fact took considerable risks extending his lines of communication to a sometimes dangerous length as he quickly concluded that the initiative lay with the British and Commonwealth forces.[27]

In only a few months Messervy had 'made a name for hunting Italians' and, as Platt's Indian divisions swept east from the Sudan into northern Ethiopia, they were preceded by Gazelle Force, now reinforced by an infantry battalion.[28] It was still focusing on distracting the Italian defenders, but more generally it provided flank protection. It also offered protection for the sappers who were clearing tracks through the minefields for the advancing troops. Across the whole border sector more than 1,200 prisoners were eventually taken, including 30 officers, but when Kassala was reached it was found to be largely deserted.[29] To get to Agordat there were two routes the advancing troops could take: the northern one, a poor and narrow road passable only in dry weather, went through Sabderat and Keru and this was taken by two brigades of the 4th Indian Division; to the south there was a much better but less direct road passing through Tessenei and Barentu and this was assigned to the 5th Indian Division. Although each division had only two of its three normal brigades, both made rapid advances along the parallel roads. On the southern road little opposition was encountered and Tessenei was occupied without any fighting. The bridge over the Gash was found to have been mined, and although many mines had been set off by stray camels the attackers were still forced into the sandy bed of the river, which was crossed with some difficulty. Even so, the pace of the advance proved too much for the defenders, who were left with no choice but to fight disorganised rearguard actions and escape with whatever equipment they could.

After the huge recent defeats suffered in the Western Desert, mounting some form of protracted defence now increasingly seemed the best prospect for the Italian and colonial troops scattered across Africa. For the isolated garrisons this meant a withdrawal from their exposed forward positions in Eritrea to where the rocky foothills of the mountain ranges began at Aicota and Keru.[30] The British-led troops followed but, as the lead company advanced towards the first of these points, it began to run into some delays. In addition to the liberally strewn landmines there were three- and four-pronged metal spikes which had been designed to puncture tyres and these slowed down the advance.[31] Slim commanded one of the leading brigades and, despite the difficulties he had experienced during the battle at Gallabat, one of those who met him at the time referred to 'a fighting soldier, clearly well aware, well briefed and fully conscious of the nature of the problem ahead'.[32] As another observer put it, 'he gave every impression of being a chap who was determined to do the job and he clearly in his approach invited full cooperation'. Unfortunately this latest battle was to prove no better an experience for the brigadier than before. On 21 January, when he was being driven on the Aicota road with an escort from the Highland Light

Infantry, his truck was attacked by two Italian planes and he was hit by shrapnel in four places, including his backside.[33] Slim had to be evacuated to a hospital back in Khartoum, removing him from the battle and the campaign, a somewhat ignominious start to the war for an officer who would go on to become one of Britain's most distinguished generals.[34]

Whilst there was no significant opposition in Aicota, it was entirely different at Keru where an enemy brigade held a strong position and made a concerted effort to fight.[35] Troops from both attacking divisions had to work together in what was later described as 'a brilliant stroke', as men from the 4th Indian Division advanced towards the town while colleagues from the other – Slim's 10th Indian Infantry Brigade – defeated an Italian rearguard, allowing them to surround the remainder of the garrison. This rapid move north enveloped the Italians, forcing the surrender of 800 men and several guns. Fought on the same day as Slim had been injured, this action also included the last cavalry charge faced by British troops during this or any other war. There are various accounts of what happened, but a force of between 60 and 250 Eritreans from the Italian Colonial Cavalry, led by a lone Italian officer mounted on a white charger, targeted Gazelle's artillery, leading to a desperate action involving the guns of D and F Troops of the 144th Field Regiment (Surrey and Sussex Yeomanry). They were defended by the command post staff, armed only with a few rifles and revolvers, which allowed the gunners to turn as quickly as they could before opening fire over open sights.[36] This was later described by one of those who witnessed what happened:

> About two miles away to our left flank we heard peculiar noises and saw a lot of dust. The noises and dust came near. Suddenly we saw a mass of mounted men, galloping towards us at a great pace. It was a very very brave cavalry charge commanded by a baron on a white horse. They very nearly caught us completely napping. Two Brens and one machine gun started firing as well as rifle fire. Then of course a moment later considerably more. But they got to within 30 yards of us, firing wildly from the saddle. The gunners wheeled round their guns through

180 degrees and fired point-blank; shells slid along the ground without exploding, others pierced the horses' chests. The carnage was quite frightful and I think most of us felt sorrier for the horses than the Italians. But it was an outstandingly brave attempt which very nearly had complete success.[37]

By the time the Eritreans wheeled and headed for safety they left twenty-five of their number dead and sixteen wounded but their charge had come close to halting the advance.[38] Had they been able to do so, even for a short period, the offensive could easily have been slowed and the outcome of the campaign proven entirely different.

As it was, by 25 January Platt's forces had already managed to cut communications between Agordat and Barentu and, as the two divisions once more returned to different axes of attack, reinforcements arrived over the next three days, including the British tanks which were being used for the first time. They now moved on to tackle both of these important positions, each of which had excellent natural defences. Dominating the approach road, Agordat was surrounded by rough bare slopes which extended up to Mount Cochen, a massive hill feature, and the isolated rocky Fort Laquetat. Realising it could weaken his entire defensive position, Frusci had recognised the danger of losing this town and moved his best troops to bolster the garrison: the 2nd Colonial Brigade, which had an unbroken tradition of victory since its formation nearly fifty years earlier. This meant that there were now fourteen battalions supported by seventy-two guns and twenty-four tanks, a formidable force in a well-prepared position. Initial attempts were made by Gazelle to once again outflank the position, first from the south and then later from the north, as part of efforts to convince the Italian garrison that much larger forces had been moved to face them. Once again, they were taken in by this deception.

Brigadier Reginald Savory's men had fought in the Western Desert and led the attack at Sidi Barrani; aside from the action at Gallabat this had been the first time during the war that troops from the British Empire had gone on the offensive. Along with the rest of the 4th Indian Division, they had then been transported south but Savory's experiences during the battle for Mount Cochen now left him apprehensive. There was a suggestion that, after the success they had enjoyed previously, the morale of his Indian troops was extremely high but, perhaps, this had led them to underestimate the fight the Italians might put up. Of much greater concern, it was the first battle of the campaign where the troops were organised on a mechanised basis with the infantry being moved by trucks and then debussing to fight the battles. This was because it was impossible for wheeled transport to move too far forward and, with no horses, mules or camels, all the supplies had to be physically moved down the main Barentu road; at least one company in each battalion was forced to carry water, food and ammunition. Some units were consequently left understrength and unable to do much beyond holding their positions, and all the troops suffered severely from thirst.[39] This physical exertion severely affected their fighting ability and the men from the 3rd Battalion, 14th Punjab Regiment were eventually forced to withdraw in some disarray, exhausted. Savory concluded that as the advance continued it would take nearly half a battalion delivering the supplies to allow the other half to keep fighting. Along with the other senior British officers, he greatly worried about the difficulties that might lie ahead.[40]

Nonetheless a decisive victory was secured at Agordat and the key proved to be the intervention of British armour. As the Italian tanks were drawn out into the open by Indian and British infantry they were attacked by four of the Matildas, which left most of the opposition flaming wrecks. Frusci's concerns about the inadequacy of his equipment proved well-founded and the only weapons available to the defenders against this potent threat were Boys anti-tank rifles that had been captured in British Somaliland, but even these had no effect.[41] It had been a stern defence with repeated attacks and counter-attacks but the introduction of the tanks proved decisive and the battalions facing them fled in confusion. According to the British regimental history, so great was the impact that 'no more Italian armour appeared for the rest of the campaign'.[42] At the same time the 11th Indian Infantry

Brigade was able to capture the crest and advance along the heights to secure the position. After three days of hard fighting, on 31 January other troops from the 4th Indian Division had also managed to outflank the town and these cut off the road to the east when they captured the four fortified hills which sat astride it.[43] This left the remaining garrison exposed and, although the bulk of the defenders were able to withdraw towards Keren, the town fell the following day, leaving the attackers to collect more than 1,500 prisoners and a number of captured guns.

Instructions having been issued that all Italian civilians were now to fight side by side with the defending garrisons, elsewhere a combination of fire and manoeuvre by the 5th Indian Division pushed the Italian forces back towards Barentu, which was attacked next.[44] With its aerodrome, Swedish Mission Hospital and, twenty-eight miles away, the Guala goldmine, this was another naturally strong position with skilfully prepared defences, including a very well-sited fort, a strong garrison of 8,000 infantry and thirty-two artillery pieces.[45] As had been the case at Agordat, at first all the signs pointed to a potentially effective defence and the British and Commonwealth forces faced heavy resistance as they approached.[46] The Italians had blocked the main road in two places by blasting away huge portions of the rock face and it took painstaking work by Indian engineers, sometimes under heavy fire, to clear the way. Three defensive lines had also been well prepared, one behind the other, which, although not particularly extensive, allowed for some organisation of troops and guns.

When the attack began on 31 January, the 1st Battalion, Worcestershire Regiment, part of the 29th Infantry Brigade, were amongst the leading troops and had their first real experience of fighting as they captured the ridges to the west.[47] They fought in extreme heat and, as well as the thirst, were also battling the thorn bushes, which cut and tore clothing and skin, and the dry soil which crumbled under their boots. Two of the defensive lines were quickly cleared but the Italians had kept precise coordinates of these positions and mortared and machine-gunned their opponents, who were forced back. So effective was this response that the Indian troops who were part of the attack had to withdraw entirely, but what the defenders had failed to do was to secure their flanks and a machine gun company from the SDF discovered a track that allowed them to approach from the east. As this opening was exploited, and with news reaching the defending garrison that Agordat had fallen, the town was evacuated on the night of 1/2 February and the garrison withdrew rapidly using any vehicle they could find. Once again, large numbers of prisoners and all of their artillery were captured. Such was the speed of the Italian flight that when the Indians of 3rd Battalion, 2nd Punjab Regiment and men from the Worcestershire Regiment entered, they found field kitchens containing hot food that had just been prepared. During the first two weeks of the advance the lead battalions had covered 130 miles and already fought four actions, each of which had ultimately resulted in an overwhelming victory. British and Commonwealth forces had taken 6,000 prisoners, and captured or destroyed 80 guns, 26 tanks and 400 trucks, but there was still a large number of untested Italian and colonial troops remaining on the road to the Red Sea.

In the brief pause at Agordat that followed during clean-up and salvage operations, a message to the garrison from Aosta was found, urging all ranks to fight to the last. Although this had not happened there was plenty of evidence of just how well equipped the Italian forces still appeared to be, and more than 300 rifles and thousands of rounds of ammunition and grenades were sent back to the brigade headquarters.[48] The men from the Royal Fusiliers who had taken part in the attack were, however, allowed to keep the Chianti, brandy, mineral water, sugar and tinned tomatoes they found, which made an excellent change from their normal diet of tea, biscuits and bully beef. At Barentu the post-battle phase was not so organised and the town was systematically looted, first by the Italian troops, then by the local population but finally by the British, a rare example of ill-discipline which lasted for the best part of twenty-four hours.[49] The civilians who were caught looting were flogged on the spot but nothing could be done about the British offenders because they included some of the junior officers, so news of what had happened was suppressed.

In some respects Frusci had displayed a good deal of military logic in withdrawing from the often exposed forward positions he had held on the Sudanese frontier. He had fought a series of delaying actions, some better than others, as he moved his troops towards the high Ethiopian plateau which extended broadly all the way to the distant mountain fortress at Gondar. He was also doing so in the knowledge that he was falling back on what was one of the best natural defensive positions available to any commander throughout the entire Second World War. The main road from Agordat climbed through a gradually narrowing gorge with hills and mountains on either side, rising several thousand feet before it reached Keren, where the Italians had the best chance of halting the northern thrust. The town had no great fortifications but was protected by eleven peaks which dominated the only route of advance and afforded the Italians excellent observation of the flat, waterless plains below. To the north-west of the single road winding through the mountain pass were Brig's Peak (the highest, at 5,890 feet) and Mount Sanchil (5,860 feet), both of which were covered with boulders and scrub and razor-edged ridges. These were particularly difficult obstacles as artillery could not fire on the rear-facing slopes where the defending forces gathered and from where they were able to easily launch attacks against any troops who attempted to gain the summit. Another important feature in front of these was Cameron Ridge (5,245 feet), which would need to be taken first prior to any assault on the other two features. To the left of them was Mount Samanna, which was not quite as much of a challenge, but behind this and approximately midway between it and Brig's was Mount Amba. Here the Italians had created excellent artillery positions and used the ideal terrain to conceal reserves from which numerous counter-attacks would later be launched. To the east of the approach road was Fort Dologorodoc and the equally commanding features of Mount Zeban (5,630 feet) and Mount Falestoh (5,770 feet). Along with Mount Zefale, known as 'Sphinx', and Mount Becana, all of these combined to make the prospect of a successful attack extremely difficult.

The defenders had certainly used their time well to prepare the defence both by strengthening natural positions and taking steps to slow the progress of the advancing troops, meaning the attackers spent a great deal of time clearing obstacles. Gazelle Force had been delayed by the demolition work carried out on the Ponte Mussolini, a large bridge twelve miles east of Agordat on the Keren road, where the access road was heavily mined and damage to the structure meant that advancing vehicles could not cross. The brave and resilient engineers took only eight hours to complete repairs and showed just how crucial they were in helping keep the attack moving forward. It was during the initial move from Gallabat that Second-Lieutenant Premindra Singh Bhagat, an engineer in the 5th Indian Division, won the war's first Victoria Cross to be awarded to the Indian Army.[50] He had lifted over a hundred mines and his personal carrier had been twice destroyed in the process. Forty miles to the east of Agordat the retreating Italian troops reached the Dongolaas Gorge and just a few miles from its entrance further demolitions destroyed several hundred yards of cliffside roads. One of the main routes was also found to be blocked by 300 vehicles with artillery and machine guns all of which had been abandoned during the retreat. According to an eyewitness, 'the guns stood ranged wheel to wheel across the valley, like a picture of a battle of a hundred years ago in an old Christmas coloured supplement'.[51] As maintaining their tempo was so important to ensure his enemy had no time to regroup, Platt later wondered if, without these delays, his troops might have got to their main objective before the Italians could have properly organised their defences.[52] Wavell had certainly hoped that it might have been possible to capitalise on the initial success and had even hoped that Asmara could be taken within a couple of days, but this did not happen.[53]

Despite the frustrations they had encountered, the pursuit nonetheless reached Keren, with Gazelle Force amongst the first to arrive. By this stage Platt's army was very much a multinational force, numbering about 13,000 troops, with fifteen Indian battalions, three English and two Scottish, added to which there were even a small number of Free French and Belgian troops.[54] Forming a broad semicircle, the defences they encountered had been constructed on what was referred to as 'interior lines', which meant that any area that was attacked by the British and Commonwealth forces could be easily reinforced by the Italians. Platt's plan called for one of his two Indian divisions to clear these, allowing the other to exploit the opening and take the town which lay beyond. With only the single road and no space to move, the standard tactic of outflanking manoeuvres using mobile forces was not possible here; indeed with the advancing columns unable to bypass the fixed defences, the battle that developed quickly became an entirely attritional one. In order to defeat the Italians it would be necessary for the attackers to find a way to dominate the high ground and then concentrate overwhelming fire support, a throwback to the kind of strategy that had been employed in many of the battles of the First World War.

Making this even more difficult, the lack of pack transport, which had previously been identified as a serious concern, meant that until the gorge was reached supplies could only be brought forward by using the main road as there were no practical alternative routes. For several miles it was exposed to Italian artillery fire which meant the troops faced considerable danger even before they reached the battlefield. Once there, the mountain conditions placed a tremendous strain on the attackers and it demanded enormous effort, ingenuity and bravery to overwhelm the defences. Savory's troops, along with the rest of the 4th Indian Division, had 'chased the enemy from Gallabat to Keren' but one of the commanders who led the 11th Indian Infantry Brigade in from the north described what followed as 'six weeks of hard slogging' before the Italians were finally worn down.[55] Its combination of outstanding terrain and key strategic position meant it was in Keren that Frusci gathered his most capable forces and most of his remaining firepower. This represented the last stand as defeat at this apparently impenetrable fortress would mean that there was little to prevent a continuation of the swift advance by the British and Commonwealth forces and final victory. Both sides were set on fighting a decisive encounter which would, in large part, determine the outcome of the entire campaign.

CHAPTER 8

TRIUMPH IN THE MOUNTAINS
The Battle of Keren

Cunningham had enjoyed huge success on the southern front and initially Platt had also advanced from the Sudan with ease. Wavell sensed that the Italians were in increasing disarray. He ordered the British and Commonwealth troops to now quickly push on towards Asmara but to reach it they would first have to pass through Keren. This town was important to both the Italian and British and Commonwealth forces as road and rail routes through it afforded access to Asmara, the capital of Eritrea some forty-five miles to the east, and to Massawa, the main port in the southern Red Sea. To capture it, Platt's two Indian divisions would have to confront the best Italian troops remaining in East Africa. It was estimated in late February that in the whole of Eritrea there were still more than 14,000 Europeans and 44,000 colonials, approximately two-thirds of whom were now concentrated at this key position.[1] The Italians had actually assembled slightly fewer, forty-two battalions or approximately 31,000 men, including elements from the Bersaglieri, Alpini and Savoia Grenadiers, but these were the best they could muster. To begin with, they also outgunned their opponents with 144 artillery pieces, twenty more than the British had, and with better transport to move them around.[2] Some of the guns were of an ancient vintage but they were ideal for mountain warfare because the shells could be fired almost vertically over the steep hills to reach the enemy positions below, something the British 25-pounders were not able to match with their flat trajectory.[3] Even the Italian mortars outranged the British versions and could also be moved more easily by their mules. With such a potentially decisive advantage in firepower the defending garrison appeared poised, at least at the outset, to dominate this battlefield.[4]

Perhaps most significantly, facing the attacking forces was an accomplished Italian commander who was highly motivated and prepared for a fight. General Nicolangelo Carnimeo had been an army officer for more than thirty years and viewed each of the peaks that made up the Keren defences as an opportunity to halt the British and Commonwealth troops. His confident outlook helped bolster the garrison's morale and there is no doubt that the men he led throughout the battle were well disciplined and a much more formidable opponent than any of the units being encountered by Cunningham's forces on the southern front.[5] This extended to the Italian colonial troops; as had been seen elsewhere, they were generally reliable but needed strong leadership, and this was now provided by Carnimeo. The Eritreans were particularly inspired by him, at least initially, to stand fast and help defend this position.[6] The Italian general also proved adept at organising the defenders to exploit the natural advantages offered by the terrain. His forces dominated the key high ground and exploited this to the fullest extent.[7] Fortifications were added and trenches and intercommunicating trails prepared which allowed reinforcements to be quickly moved to any threatened position.[8] Although there is little evidence of any clear strategic vision besides the attrition of the enemy, the resulting tenacious Italian defence nearly proved decisive as Wavell came very close to calling a halt to the entire campaign.[9]

The battle, which lasted for nearly two months, can be divided into three phases. The opening involved just a single Indian infantry brigade that had led the advance from Agordat. This was Savory's 11th Indian Infantry Brigade which consisted of battalions from the Camerons and the

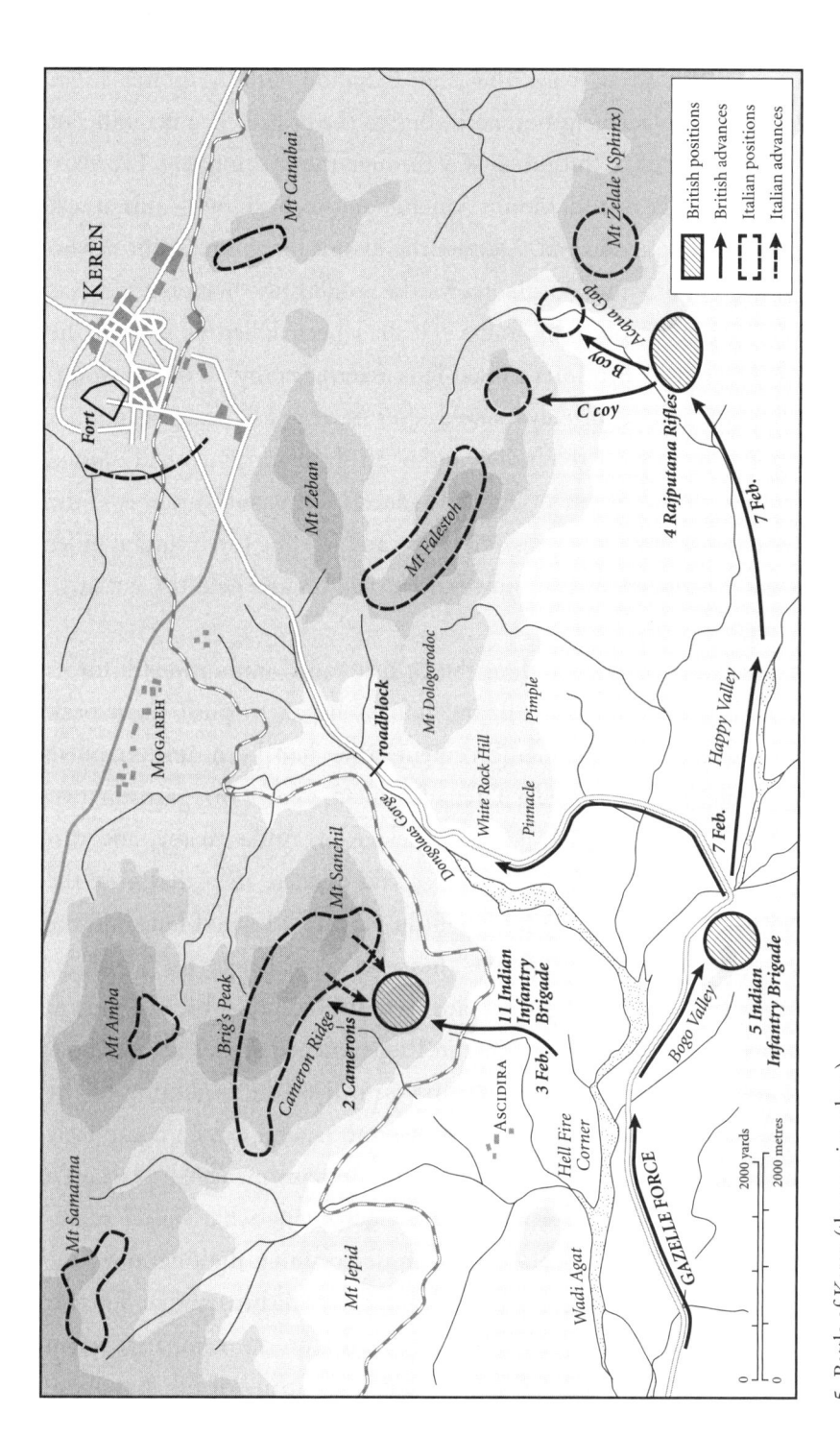

5 Battle of Keren (the opening phase).

Rajputana Rifles along with the 2nd Battalion, 5th Mahratta Light Infantry, a late replacement but, according to the brigadier, 'a magnificent lot'.[10] They had tried to force their way through the position on 3 February to capture Brig's Peak and Mount Sanchil, and to begin with this attack looked as if it might succeed. Despite the loss of the gunner officer who was supposed to provide coordinates for the artillery, the first objective was captured within twenty-four hours. He had been killed as soon as he reached the crest of Brigadier's Peak, later referred to by all of the troops as Brig's Peak and reportedly named after Savory. His loss meant that throughout their assault the Indian and Scottish infantrymen had limited support from the heavy guns.[11] Artillery rounds consequently flew over the top of the Italian positions, missing them, and landing often several miles to the rear. The attackers had, however, pushed on and held the initiative at this stage.

Fortunes now changed and, as the British and Commonwealth forces headed towards Mount Sanchil, the Italians began to push them back using the recently arrived reinforcements they had been able to move up. A regiment of the Savoia Grenadiers had joined the garrison two days before, having been rushed on trucks from Addis Ababa, and this made all the difference. One writer has said of these men that only the German parachute division that fought in North Africa and Italy and the Japanese troops in Burma proved more of a challenge to British or Commonwealth troops.[12] The Indians were slowly forced back, although they managed to hold on to Cameron Ridge, named after 2nd Battalion, The Camerons who had been the first onto it at the beginning of the initial battle. This was just in front of Mount Sanchil, which completely dominated the ridge, and the Scots and the Indians managed to retain a tenuous hold here for the next six weeks, occupying what would subsequently prove to be a critical position in determining the final outcome of the battle.[13] It was during this early fighting, on 8 February, that Subadar Richpal Ram won the second Victoria Cross of the campaign when acting as second-in-command of the leading company of 6th Battalion,

Rajputana Rifles. He led a bayonet charge to seize a position, which he then held against six enemy counter-attacks before finally being forced to withdraw.[14] There was no shortage of gallantry on each side but Platt's concerns about the delays his advance had encountered were already proving correct.

The fighting continued without a break and the next move involved an attempted flanking manoeuvre further east against the Acqua Col which it was hoped could avoid the main Italian defences.[15] Men from 5th Indian Infantry Brigade now joined the assault as Beresford-Peirse committed the best part of two brigades in an attempt to find a route through the defences to the east of the gorge and press forward from Cameron Ridge. These efforts unfortunately failed: one reason was a lack of machine guns, which meant that the attackers were unable to put down sufficiently heavy suppressing fire against the Italian positions. Had this been available the outcome might well have been different; as it was, the defenders were able to wait for the artillery barrage to finish, emerge from their cover and shower grenades onto the climbing infantry below. On the night of 10 February another attempt was made and once again the attack might have succeeded if it had been possible to get enough troops and supplies forward to help hold the positions that were captured on and around Brig's Peak. The attacking troops, however, ran out of ammunition and with no means of resupply they had to fall back. It had been another story of great bravery but, with some of Platt's attacking units sustaining losses of twenty-five soldiers killed per day, and to no apparent significant advantage, the general concluded it was 'a rate we could not afford'.[16] A pause was urgently needed and, whilst Platt refused a suggestion to withdraw to a better defensive position, orders were given to halt and hold what ground had been captured while fresh supplies and reinforcements were brought forward. At the same time some of the men, including the Worcestershire infantry who had been rushed up to support that attack, were now withdrawn back to Tessenei, where they trained for mountain warfare and the battle ahead.[17]

The Italians had already put up a much stiffer fight at Keren than had been anticipated and it would require some real thought from the British commanders about how best now to proceed.[18] As it proved impossible to find a way around the defences, the conclusion was that a frontal attack involving both divisions appeared to offer the only prospect of success. Lengthy preparations followed throughout the next month as the men consolidated their positions while the lengthy resupply line was shortened. For the remainder of February and into March, the troops also cleared wells and dug boreholes to improve access to water, and improved the existing mountain tracks at the same time as trying to create new ones. The railway that ran from Agordat to the gorge was refurbished in order to increase the amount of supplies it could carry forward, but huge amounts of manpower were still required for the final leg of the journey as there were no pack animals and motor transport could progress only to the edge of the Italian artillery's range. As Savory had anticipated, approximately one-quarter of each battalion continued to act as porters, carrying everything on their shoulders up the extremely steep slopes to their forward positions. Water in two-gallon tins, rations in sacks, ammunition, barbed wire, first aid equipment and anything else needed to conduct the battle were carried several miles in hot, dusty and difficult conditions. These supplies were then dotted around the hillsides in dumps as the British and Indian troops made ready to attack.

In the middle of March two Cypriot mule companies finally arrived and provided some relief but they were insufficient in number to allow the men to shift their focus away from bringing up supplies. There were also times now when stampeding mules, terrified by the gunfire around them, were themselves a danger to the men moving along the narrow mountain tracks.[19] So bad did the situation become that the rear elements of the battalions were stripped of any available personnel, including those who usually worked in transport or clerical roles. This had to be done to ensure there remained enough troops to retain the key ground that had been won right at the beginning of the battle. Throughout this period two battalions sat on Cameron Ridge halfway up the hill as well as on the extension that ran to its west which was sometimes called Mahratta Ridge. Every morning and evening the Italians fired mortar and artillery rounds at these positions but the men held on in desperate conditions. Despite their best efforts to keep the battle-space around them as tidy as possible, they 'got used to the heavy, sweetish, carrion smell of the dead since it was never out of our nose and lungs', and the millions of flies that gathered around the bodies of hundreds of men and mules which it was impossible at this point to bury.[20]

This was a particularly arduous and difficult period for the British and Commonwealth troops; one brigade major who was present throughout the campaign and fought throughout the entire war later wrote that he knew of no worse battle either in the Middle East or in the Far East.[21] Another of those involved described it as 'really a hell especially from the physical point of view. In the nine months I served in western Europe as the commander of my company I assure you that I have never encountered such unendurable and exhausting days like those of Keren.'[22] Even men who later took part in the assault on the Italian monastery fortress of Monte Cassino in Italy described this battle in Eritrea as having been more arduous.[23] Aside from the generally exhausting nature of making all the preparations, life was made more difficult by the stark nature of the terrain which was almost entirely barren and interspersed with the same hard scrub as had been encountered elsewhere. The soil around the boulders crumbled easily, dislodging the smaller rocks, and the steepness of the big climbs to reach the summits meant that the task for the attackers appeared almost impossible.[24] Added to this was the lack of cover or shade; one of the commanders who was present later noted that thirst and the resulting exhaustion were major factors in the initial failures to dislodge the Italian defenders.[25] The rations were not much better and, as their counterparts on the southern front had found, the biscuits were too hard to eat and merely aggravated the thirst. The preferred alternatives were packets of spearmints and chocolate, often in an almost liquid state, which were far more pleasant, especially with the luxury of a mug of hot tea. Physically, this battle was a shattering experience for the British and Commonwealth forces and unlike anything that had been encountered during the war.

The attacking forces also had no option but to conduct their stockpiling of supplies in full view of the enemy, as they were restricted to the single approach road they had followed from Agordat and Barentu and no alternative could be found.[26] The Italians, commanding the high ground, were able to observe the events taking place below them and the British commanders were astounded that they did not take better advantage of a position which appeared to offer such an enormous benefit to them. Other than the regular artillery fire and some raiding aimed at Cameron Ridge, little else happened during this consolidation phase and it was only deserters who penetrated British-held lines.[27] Frusci's decision to pull his forces back towards Keren had considerable merit but he failed to do far more to harass his opponent, who was clearly set on mounting an attack against him. Carnimeo was restricted in terms of what his orders allowed him to do and, whilst there was some pressure applied against his opponent, there was no sign of any real offensive intentions.[28] Certainly, during the early part of the build-up, the attacking forces would have been extremely vulnerable to a concerted counter-attack but the Italians preferred to wait. In many respects this proved to be the most critical of their many military mistakes as, by allowing the British commanders to concentrate their forces in front of them, they effectively sealed their fate, not just at Keren but for the campaign as a whole.

For the two Indian divisions, they used this opportunity to train together as it was the first time they had fought alongside one another during the war. For ten days they conducted intensive mountain warfare training and shared information on enemy methods and the difficulties of the terrain, which proved to be of crucial benefit later. With little actual fighting taking place, propaganda also became a focus of activity for the besieging forces. Captain George Steer, Chief of Offensive Propaganda, produced everything from leaflets and loudspeaker 'battle' broadcasts to a local weekly

Ethiopian-language newspaper.[29] A South African who had been educated in Britain, he had been a journalist with *The Times* and had covered the Italian invasion of Ethiopia, the Spanish Civil War and the Russo-Finnish conflict before arriving back in Africa in 1940 as a young officer in the British Army. He had a close family connection to Haile Selassie and, as he was skilled in psychological warfare, he played an important part in the battle.[30] His aim was to weaken morale and his efforts proved so successful that widespread desertion followed, especially amongst the Ethiopian and Somali irregular troops fighting with the Italians; such were the numbers involved that the death penalty was abandoned for this offence. Instead, weapons were removed at night and the colonial troops barricaded into their defensive positions.[31] Afterwards, 6,000 deserters were recorded as having surrendered or escaped before the battle's final stages, nearly one-fifth of the overall garrison. The use of communications would have benefited from some greater thought; these remained fairly poor throughout the battle and there was still a great reliance on signal flags and lamps to send messages across the area held by the British and Commonwealth troops.[32] Each brigade had just one wireless set, and these did not function very well despite telephone cables having been spread across all the hills.

With General Erwin Rommel and his Afrika Korps making an increasingly decisive impact following their arrival in the Western Desert, and the mounting requirements of the Greek campaign, by mid-March pressure was growing on Wavell's generals to withdraw units from both the Sudan and East Africa to send north.[33] The commander in Cairo once again had to make the decision about what level of overall risk he was prepared to accept but, despite the worsening situation facing him, he remained committed to the strategy devised the previous year. At Keren the combined divisional attack, designed to resemble 'the snapping of a pair of pincers', was allowed to proceed and began on 15 March, the Ides of March, one of the hottest days recorded in the entire campaign.[34] Following another sultry morning, temperatures rose on this sticky day to reach 118°F in the shade, which added to the men's fatigue.[35] Thunder and a sandstorm rolled in later in the day to add to the misery.[36] Yet, prior to the assault beginning, blankets had been rolled and stacked and greatcoats issued to provide some protection against the cold that would face the men as they climbed higher up into the mountains, where the temperature dropped quickly once night fell. Before the start there was a final check of the equipment that would be carried, and a fortifying ration of rum was issued to those who wanted it. With all the preparations completed, a massive artillery bombardment was launched at 7 a.m. and 'an unbelievable concentration of shellfire' marked the opening of what was to be the biggest battle of the East Africa campaign.[37] One British pilot witnessed the initial artillery barrage, which 'was so great that it all became a white mass of smoke, it was a white mass of cloud, the cloud formed, it was right along the top'.[38] Below him he could see the British and Commonwealth troops, overlooked most of the time by the Italian positions as 'they literally clawed their way to the top'. Brig's Peak had been captured – and then lost – six weeks before by a single rifle company, but now almost two full divisions supported by the largest number of artillery pieces yet used against the enemy in Africa were deployed in an attempt to capture it and the positions beyond.

Men from 2nd Battalion, West Yorkshire Regiment were involved in the initial assault directly the artillery fire had ended, following on from the Sikhs of the 3rd Battalion, 5th Mahrattas who were the leading element. The attackers were heading for Dologorodoc, which they approached from the west, but they were checked in the afternoon and had to spend hours sheltering in stifling heat as a new plan was developed.[39] During this time the British infantrymen fought off furious counter-attacks, 'shouting their forthright battle cry', and it was only once darkness fell that they were able to continue. Passing through the Indian positions, they headed towards the final objective.[40] This was the fort just below the hill's summit which was surrounded entirely by a concrete trench. The axis of the attack was so steep that hands as well as feet were needed to make the climb, and the troops up at the front discovered that metal shields were useful against the small Italian grenades, known as 'red bombs', that were thrown at them.[41] When their turn came, the Indians charged up the final stretch of the hill with loud cries which could be heard far back in the brigade headquarters; once they had managed to pass beyond the range of the hand grenades, they pressed home their advantage.[42] One discovery that had been made was that not only were the enemy's bayonets rarely sharpened, they were also shorter than the combined length of a British rifle and bayonet. As one of those present put it, those Italians who were captured alive had to consider themselves fortunate as 'sepoys, with their blood up' had little time for an opponent who refused to hand over his gun.[43] The Italians' reluctance to part with their weapons was due to their desperation to hold onto the principal means of defending themselves both against the Patriots, whose presence was becoming known amongst the garrison, and against their own increasingly mutinous colonial troops. It took the intervention of British officers to explain these fears to their men, after which prisoners were once again sent back down the hills.

It had taken more than two hours to climb just under 700 feet but the defenders had been driven from the summit and the two prominent features referred to as 'Pinnacle' and 'Pimple' had been captured. Initial media reports were even more optimistic, with it being claimed that both the fort and Brig's Peak had also been seized.[44] But the success had come at a considerable cost: within the ranks of the attacking forces, there had been more than 1,000 killed or injured during the first twenty-four hours.[45] All of the immediately available British and Commonwealth reserves had been used and, believing that a counter-attack might succeed, the senior British officers prepared to lead a charge with rifles in hand. The north of the road had been largely secured but, as further reinforcements from the 29th Indian Infantry Brigade were brought up to just in front of the fort, the attackers were halted. The position was completely overlooked on three sides and exposed to extensive artillery, mortar and small arms fire, and for many of the men caught in the open, conditions grew progressively worse. British and Indian troops remained here for the next ten days under scorching sun and shivering without blankets at night. As they ran out of ammunition and food and it became more difficult even to walk back down the hills, such was the amount of fire from the high ground, they became increasingly dependent on resupply by air drops which landed on the rocks surrounding them.[46] The Scottish troops of the Highland Light Infantry, who were out in the open for an extended period, held on supplied by the RAF with their mail, army iron rations and whisky, and, according to one of the pilots, 'seemed quite happy with that'.[47] They broke through during the final attacks but at a roll call after the battle only twenty-seven men responded; the regiment suffered a worse casualty count than even the Camerons who lost eight officers and 250 other ranks throughout their time at Keren. An Indian battalion, the 3rd Battalion, 1st Punjab Regiment, which had fought at Agordat and then during the first two phases of the battle, was another to suffer huge casualties and, with more than 300 men killed or wounded, including one of the company commanders, it eventually had to be withdrawn.[48] The Italian defenders were certainly offering a staunch defence and, after eight determined counter-attacks which left bodies strewn over the slopes, even the reports from the British and American journalists embedded in Platt's headquarters showed for the first time some grudging respect and an acknowledgement of the enemy's fighting spirit.[49] As for the commander of the northern advance, he later argued that this intensity had actually been to his advantage as 'the Italians fought their side of the battle on the false principle that every acre was sacred and must be regained at any cost'.[50] In the process they exhausted themselves and helped bring about their eventual defeat.

Efforts continued to be made to capture Brig's Peak and Mount Sanchil but a further attack on 17 March once again proved unsuccessful and led to an almost complete withdrawal back to Cameron Ridge. Despite what the troops had to endure, their success in capturing and holding the fort at Dologorodoc was probably the key action, as this changed the course of the battle. Whatever happened, so long as this was held it gave them a position they could consolidate and from which they could eventually move forward.

The gains had been slow and incremental but the defenders were being worn down. For now, however, the plan reverted to the use of intensive artillery shelling, including some additional medium guns which Wavell had sent up, and letting the Italians exhaust themselves with their increasingly desperate counter-attacks. Conditions for the British and Commonwealth forces nonetheless remained very difficult. For example, the two companies of Royal Fusiliers, who were part of the force that had attacked Mount Sanchil, were given breakfast prior to moving forward but then received nothing for the next thirty-six hours other than the rations they carried. The war diary noted 'the hard work of climbing, the lack of shade and the heat of the sun reflecting off the rocks [making] the troops more thirsty than they could ever have imagined in time of peace', and now twelve tins of water, some bully beef and biscuits and an orange for each man were carried up to them.[51] Another account referred also to the worsening smell of a battlefield that had seen many weeks' worth of action, as well as the flies and the lack of water, and the large numbers of men who had to be evacuated with dysentery.[52] Virtually all of those involved in the battle for Keren were also suffering from desert sores by the end, and hardly anyone emerged without some form of injury or illness.

Whilst the extremely high level of losses Platt was suffering were clearly a key factor, the change in his plan was made in the knowledge that he now had complete control of the air. Reports after the battle referred to 'the perfect co-operation of the two fighting arms' and described how well the air and land components worked together.[53] Without this, and with the increasingly grim situation facing the men on the ground, the stronghold could not have been taken at an acceptable cost.[54] Air Commodore Leonard Slatter, Air Officer Commanding No. 203 Group, had prioritised the support of Platt's force above all other tasks, ensuring that there were aircraft always available, despite his superiors in Cairo still believing this to be a waste of resources.[55] The Hurricanes of No.1 Squadron, SAAF were also under his control and he used them to attack targets in both northern Ethiopia and Eritrea so that 'air superiority and comparative comfort for the army were snatched from the Italians; they never recovered either'.[56] This allowed the tempo of British ground operations to increase as the restriction of travelling only at night could be discarded, and the obsolescent bombers could be used. The pilots prepared for these missions by conducting detailed joint briefings, including discussions over large sand models of the mountain positions.[57] For the final main attack, the RAF conducted a four-day preparatory bombardment, which allowed the troops on the ground to advance with minimum casualties; by the end of it more than 120 tons of bombs had been dropped on the targets.[58] The constant hours spent on operations left them exhausted by their efforts; an American observer with the South Africans commented that towards the end they were 'worn out, run down and sick with fever, dysentery, [and] veld sores ... [but] they never gave up and their offensive spirit was matchless'.[59] Keren actually marked the end of the Regia Aeronautica as an effective fighting force: the British, Rhodesian and South African pilots destroyed it in the air and on the ground, so that by 22 March, from a high point of 325 fighter and bomber aircraft, there remained only 37 aircraft of all types.[60]

Platt had also gained another advantage as he knew that his 7th Indian Brigade Group was in position to attack the enemy's last defences to the north-east of the main battle. Troops under the command of Brigadier Rawdon Briggs had been advancing southwards from Karora to cut off the road to Asmara and leave the Italians isolated. The aim of what was called Briggs Force was to create a diversion from the main attack coming from the west by advancing on Massawa from the north. Within its ranks there was a Foreign Legion battalion and another from the Free French Brigade d'Orient, men from Chad and Senegal, under the command of Colonel Ralph Monclar who had fought previously in the Norwegian campaign.[61] Briggs Force had landed on 10 February at Marsa Taclai, a small anchorage on the Red Sea coast, and from here it quickly pushed on south. The roads were non-existent and movement was virtually impossible while the intense heat and lack of water made it an extremely inhospitable

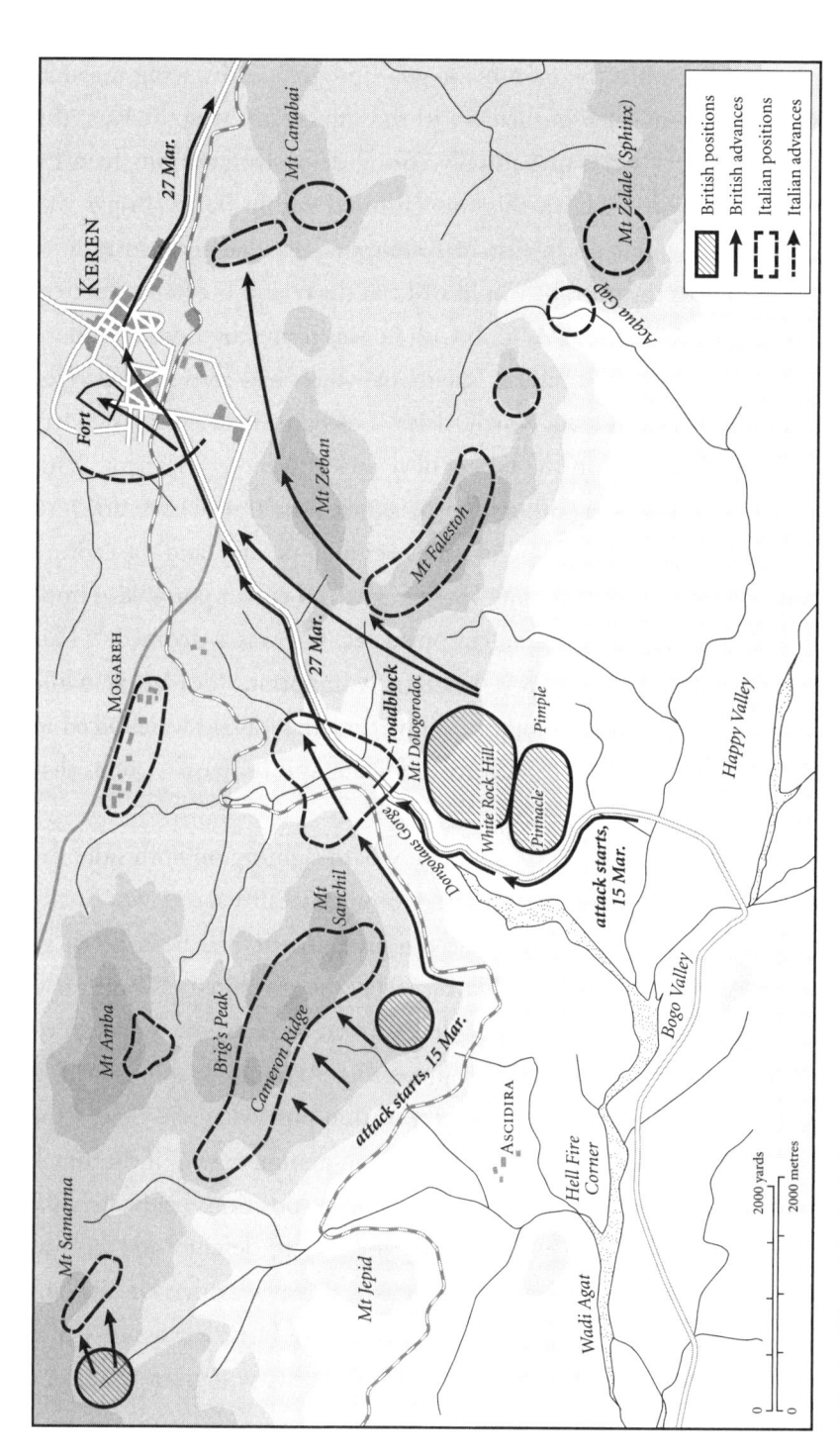

6 Battle of Keren (the final phase).

area of operations, but the men made good progress. Advancing through Karora and Elghena they pushed on to the important Mescelit Pass, the first in yet another series of naturally strong defensive positions held by the Italians, and on 1 March this was captured within hours. Briggs was now just fifteen miles north-east of Keren and decided that, instead of marching towards the port, he would strike at the rear of the Italian fortress to support the main attack. At Cub Cub he was joined by British artillery and a company from the Sussex Regiment which had arrived as part of Wavell's move of troops from North Africa. The battle here again lasted less than a day and resulted in the taking of nearly 500 more prisoners. With most of the supplies being brought in by camels, the troops were down to a maximum of only half a gallon of water per man per day, and the capture of a range of items, including tins of asparagus and even a portable gramophone with a good supply of Italian opera records, was welcomed.[62] This flank march along the coast proved extremely important for Platt as, while it continued to make rapid progress, all the time the Italians were forced to move troops to try and halt the British, French and Indians – troops that were desperately needed elsewhere.[63]

Back at Keren, after twelve days of very hard fighting on both sides the final breakthrough by the British and Commonwealth forces was finally achieved, although not before some serious thought had been given to halting the battle. Throughout March 1941, the pressure on Wavell had been growing to an almost impossible level and he had now flown down from Cairo to review the situation in person. Arriving at the airfield at Agordat he was driven to a forward observation post where he viewed the terrain.[64] As the events of the recent weeks had demonstrated, if the attack were not continued to a successful conclusion the positions below the hills held by his forces would not be suited for a long defence and he was thinking about pulling the men back. His real fear was that the Italians might be tempted into a major counter-offensive but Platt assured him that one last effort would succeed, and the authority was given to make a final attempt.[65]

Even now, and with all of the improvements that had been made and the work undertaken, for the last offensive one-third of the British and Commonwealth forces still had to be used for carrying supplies up and casualties back down the mountain.[66] Nonetheless, the final assault was conducted with great determination and courage. In the early morning of 25 March Platt's men launched a co-ordinated attack which included troops from 10th Indian Infantry Brigade who had been able to infiltrate Mount Sanchil from an unexpected position, a railway tunnel at its south-east corner. Despite everything that had happened in the previous six weeks, and the hugely impressive defence they had conducted, this move took the Italians by surprise and proved to be critical as, despite continuing their counter-attacks, they were unable to regain their lost ground.

Once an opening presented itself, part of the plan called for a force consisting of the Matilda tanks (which had been present throughout the battle), along with around 100 personnel carriers which had been collected from the two Indian divisions, to break through and push on to Fort Keren. In order for this to take place, the roadblock which barred the way was first cleared during thirty-two hours of hard labour involving explosives, picks and shovels, allowing a track to be made. At first light on 27 March, three troops of tanks approached the obstacle, but it was discovered that the carriers could not ascend the steep gradient.[67] The British armour drove on up through the gorge, one of those involved later recalling 'an unforgettable sight and stench of dead, unburied, and bloated bodies' that littered the road, and found Keren to be deserted.[68] With the Italians' defensive position broken by the capture of Mount Sanchil, and facing a threat to their potential escape route, a complete withdrawal had been ordered on the night of 26/27 March. With no opposition, two troops of the ranks moved off quickly down the Asmara road while the third stuck to the original plan: to destroy the Italian artillery that had been identified in advance by the RAF.[69] This being done, the vehicles took a while to catch up with the others, but by mid-afternoon they were all pursuing the retreating Italians who were struggling in a complete state of disorganisation and who 'looked like a crowd dispersing from a football match'.[70] By the end of the day more than 4,000 prisoners and a large number of guns had been captured either in the town or on the hills surrounding it, and many more followed during the pursuit.[71] When the final Keren battle was done, other than those troops already in the few remaining key garrisons, there were now fewer than three Italian battalions and a few batteries of guns between the British and Commonwealth forces and the sea.

After the battle Wavell is reported to have said that 'the road into Eritrea was opened, and the end of Italian power and influence in East Africa brought within sight'.[72] The real target of the Red Sea remained, however, and, despite their exhaustion, the men had no thought of any further delay. The advance resumed, led by the 5th Indian Division, but almost immediately they were presented with another, potentially even better, natural defensive position at Ad Teclesan. This was another place that the Italians had improved with road demolitions and the preparation of additional fortifications. The battle that followed never quite received the attention it should have in the post-war accounts, largely because of what had just happened at Keren, but it was still another hard encounter. Some of the former defenders of Keren, including the remaining Savoia Grenadiers, were joined by three more battalions and supporting artillery that had been rushed up from Addis Ababa and Gondar. The advancing Indian troops were restricted to a single road and only had a limited amount of artillery as equipment was passing slowly through the Keren Gorge, but, on 31 March, they broke the enemy's centre. As no opposition remained to challenge the RAF's aircraft they had been able to bomb and machine-gun the enemy's defensive posts at will. Faced with these attacks the initially heavy opposition soon faded away, and the garrison surrendered en masse to the West Yorkshires supported by Punjabi infantrymen and sappers.[73] This rapid collapse demonstrated that the same was happening here as on the southern front; the Italians had become reluctant to carry on with the fight, and were increasingly conscious of the road to the sea behind them and the possibility of escape it offered.[74] Messervy, who had taken command of the 9th Indian Infantry Brigade and who was at the front of the march, believed that at some point 'we had to fight it out' and he was actually glad that it happened at Keren and not at Ad Teclesan which, he concluded, was potentially the stronger of the two positions.[75]

The imperative was still to maintain the momentum. Next was Asmara which, aside from being the capital of Eritrea, was also the administrative centre for the Italian army with a major airfield and plentiful barracks for the troops. At an altitude of about 6,500 feet and cool in the evenings, it had been turned into a pleasant health resort with gardens, boulevards, shops and even a cinema; as the principal centre for leave for Italian military personnel, it was the home of the famous nightclub La Croce del Sud with its cabaret and local hostesses. The city, with its 20,000 European civilians, was not well suited for a major battle, however, and the local administrative authorities were acutely conscious of the large numbers of white women and children there. This concern, added to growing fears of what might happen if there was an uprising by the African troops, encouraged a willingness to co-operate with the advancing troops. On 1 April Asmara fell without any resistance, the Bishop of Asmara along with the Chief of Police and the senior government officials having negotiated the surrender during a conference in a large Italian bus that had been driven two miles to meet the leading British troops. As the advancing forces entered they found that a mutiny of colonial troops had taken place the night before and there had been widespread looting despite the presence of thousands of fully armed Italians.[76] The mutineers were rounded up and separated from their ammunition and guns before being shepherded into large compounds that were used as POW cages. As Platt was anxious to push on and had few troops to spare, the Italian police were allowed to remain on duty and guard them. Although they kept their guns along with a few rounds of ammunition, they had orders not to use them for fear that a massacre might follow.[77] It took some time before the police and Italian troops were also eventually disarmed in batches and also put into custody.[78]

Capturing Asmara represented one more step towards the Red Sea and it also provided excellent intelligence on the defences that lay ahead at Massawa. Documents discovered in one of the official buildings included information marked clearly on maps showing the locations of the artillery guarding the approaches and the anti-tank guns, most of which had been removed from ships in the harbour.[79] It also brought with it access to a number of locomotives and a good deal of rolling stock which was found intact at the city's railway station. This was the location for the Italian military forces' main workshops and was where most of the transport equipment was held in reserve. The Italian civilians operating the trains were offered, and readily accepted, the same terms under which they had previously been employed, only now with British supervision. By 8 April the line running back to Agordat had been cleared and up to three trains a day were able to move along it, releasing a large amount of motor transport for other duties.[80] By the end of the month the line to Massawa was also reopened and became the principal means for sending troops and other equipment for embarkation to Egypt.

With all of Platt's forces concentrating on their final objective, the final battle of the campaign was now poised to begin, not much more than ten weeks after the invasion from the Sudan had got under way. After the earlier victories, the advancing 7th Indian Infantry Brigade had moved on to the 7,000-foot Mount Engiahat which was eventually captured just as news was received that Keren had also fallen. The brigade was once more directed back towards its original objective and ordered to link up with the 10th Indian Infantry Brigade, and it played a central role in Massawa's subsequent capture.[81] Situated in a shallow plain and surrounded on three sides by low hills, the port was actually built on low coral reefs and linked to the mainland by a long causeway, the seaward end of which formed one side of the large harbour. The daytime temperature was more than thirty degrees higher than in Asmara but this was a pleasant change for troops who had been exposed to cold breezes and frequent thunderstorms in the uplands which were nearly 7,000 feet higher. About four miles west of the harbour both the road and railway passed through a bottleneck that presented another ideal defensive opportunity and it was here that the Italian positions started. On a pronounced range of hills three forts had been built with barbed wire and trenches placed across the whole area, added to which there were extensive minefields. Approaching from the north, a ridge ran parallel to the road with a prominent feature on its eastern end known as Signal Hill, part of a semicircle of broken hills and sandy valleys that ran away to the coast. As had been the case at Keren, the defenders had constructed many concrete battery positions in which they had mounted seventy-four guns of various calibres on prepared gun emplacements. It appeared to be another formidable position.

Although the Italian garrison was believed to consist largely of second-class troops and included many of the stragglers from the previous battles, there remained approximately 10,000 men sheltering behind the extensive defences, but their food and fuel supplies were exhausted. They were, however, in touch with Rome and receiving directions from Mussolini which complicated the efforts that were being made to negotiate the surrender by telephone from Asmara. Rear-Admiral Mario Bonetti was overall commander of the forces that had either retreated there following the earlier battles or had spent several months waiting while the battle developed around them.[82] Platt was hoping to prevent the scuttling of the naval vessels in the harbour but the senior Italian officer refused to accept the terms even though he was warned that any destruction of the port's facilities could cause most harm to those civilians who would need it for future supplies.[83] As it was, many ships in the harbour were scuttled, and five destroyers put to sea intending first to attack Port Sudan and then flee; these were engaged and sunk by a combination of naval gunfire from surface vessels and attacks by Swordfish aircraft from HMS *Eagle*.[84]

Seven days after Asmara's capture, and with a second demand to surrender having been refused, at 4 a.m. on 8 April three brigades largely of Indian troops attacked the port's perimeter. These were now supported by plentiful artillery and a number of light tanks which still remained operational.

There was also an abundance of airpower as HMS *Formidable* launched its squadrons of Albacores against targets in the port, believing the Italians to be particularly terrified of the threat of air or sea bombardment.[85] Operating alongside the Fleet Air Arm was the Free French's Lorraine Squadron which was based at Khartoum and equipped with British Blenheims.[86] As the troops approached the defence along the main road, there were frequent roadblocks, many of which took some time to clear, but no serious resistance. One brigade made good progress, and one of the others was briefly held up, but by 5 a.m., just an hour after the attack had begun, the Highland Light Infantry had captured Signal Hill, allowing the tanks to push forward. As had been the case from the start of the advance from the Sudanese frontier, the armour continued to be one of the most obvious differences between the two sides as, when progress appeared to be held up, it was able to clear any obstacles ahead. Now they drove on to occupy Fort Victor Emanuele, the last position between the troops and the town.

It had been agreed that Briggs and the tanks would enter Massawa first in recognition of the critical role they had played.[87] This was to take place at 2 p.m., but Monclar apparently could not restrain his impatience and entered the port about an hour before at the head of a platoon, accompanied by an Italian policeman and followed by a group of war correspondents who quickly pushed past him and were the first to reach the naval barracks.[88] The main battle had taken place between five and ten miles outside the town and there were very few visible signs of the fighting other than the results of the air attacks and the smouldering ammunition dumps on the north-western outskirts destroyed by the Italians themselves. As had been feared, the inner harbour and the wharves had been put out of action, with sunken naval vessels strewn across the water. Two hours later, troops from 7th Indian Infantry Brigade finally entered the port and just twenty minutes after them came Heath, who had been leading the attack himself, in a small mechanised column which made for the headquarters. With the French commander already heading back out of the port, the general passed him as he was driven to the nineteenth-century domed palazzo that had been built for the Ottoman governor, where he accepted the formal Italian surrender. Approximately 10,000 prisoners were taken during the battle, including 465 officers, among them Major-General Vincenzo Tessitore, the acting commander for the whole of Eritrea, and over 7,000 other ranks.[89] Bonetti was 'found sitting rather moodily in a deck-chair at the side of the harbour. He had tried to break his sword across his knee but it only bent, so he threw it in the water.'[90] The mangled object was later recovered and became a war trophy that was hung in Platt's headquarters in Khartoum. Its previous owner, and the four Italian generals who had surrendered with him, were transferred to Asmara that same day, Heath escorting them personally, where they were granted permission to spend a final night with their wives and families.[91] Even the large steamer Bonetti had sunk at the entrance to the harbour subsequently drifted from its intended position, allowing passage in and out, an entirely fitting epitaph to the rear admiral's entirely ineffective attempt to defend the port.[92]

The war in the north had been won, and won decisively. Platt's forces had lost approximately twenty-five men killed and fifty wounded during the assault on Massawa, its fall marking the culmination of the northern advance during which more than 40,000 Italians had been captured along with 260 guns and artillery pieces. For the defenders still remaining in Italian East Africa there were now no longer any tanks, armoured cars or aircraft available to them as they had all been captured or destroyed.[93] The last significant enemy forces were in the neighbourhood of Amba Alagi, 200 miles to the south of Asmara, and at Gondar where there were 20,000 men although they were entirely surrounded by irregular forces. As Wavell had gambled, with this final victory Italian and German surface raiders and submarines had lost their naval base in the Red Sea. On 11 April President Franklin D. Roosevelt announced in Washington, DC, that both it and the Gulf of Aden were no longer considered combat zones.[94] American shipping was therefore now free to carry supplies to anywhere along eastern Africa's coast and beyond, to the British and Commonwealth forces who were fighting an increasingly challenging series of battles in the Western Desert.[95]

The attack on the Keren position had been the pivotal point in the East Africa campaign as it delivered the decisive blow to the Italians and allowed Platt the opportunity to accomplish what Wavell had asked him to do, securing the Sudanese border and then clearing the Italians from the coast beyond.[96] Fought against 30,000 Italians, including many elite troops trained in mountain warfare, it took fifty-three days before the white flag was seen flying from Mount Sanchil.[97] The Italians conducted one of the best defences of the war, using their equipment well, defending their positions with great skill and showing considerable courage. Platt had worried about how effective the Italian defensive operations had been in slowing his initial advance, and Heath later praised the Italians, noting that they often showed great ingenuity in constructing cleverly concealed cement reinforced positions.[98] The repeated and increasingly frenzied attempt to recover Fort Dologorodoc should have been enough to convince any observers of the Italians' courage and resolve. In the process, they suffered great losses: during the eight weeks of the battle more than 3,000 men were killed and 4,500 wounded.[99] Amongst the casualties was Brigadier-General Orlando Lorenzini, respected by both sides as an inspiring leader, and the loss of this influential officer on 17 March certainly weakened Carnimeo's forces.[100] The garrison commander was also hampered by Frusci's indecisive interventions, with his wavering as to whether Keren was his principal defensive position and his belief that the main attack would come from the north, which meant he refused to move reserves forward during the final stages.[101] Added to this were the relentless ground attacks, the incessant aerial bombing and the eventual impact of the British and Commonwealth artillery and tanks, the psychological effect of the heavy casualties they suffered and the news of defeats elsewhere, as well as the generally intolerable conditions on the battlefield.[102] In light of all of this, it was an extremely impressive performance but one that, ultimately, could not stop the inevitable.

Unable to break through the Italian defences, the British and Commonwealth forces had had to conduct frontal attacks and at great cost.

TRIUMPH IN THE MOUNTAINS

The final engagements were extremely hard, with bitter hand-to-hand fighting and – although the sources vary, sometimes wildly, in their totals – it can be ascertained that around 400 men died and a further 3,000 were wounded, almost one in two of them front-line troops.[103] A junior officer who climbed Mount Sanchil the day after the battle had ended wrote:

> Dead lay everywhere and parties were working flat out to bring away the bodies for proper burial. In the enemy position itself, efforts had been made to bury our dead, but with little success, as it was impossible to dig in the rocky ground. A head protruded from under a pile of stones while feet emerged from the other end. The stench and flies were nauseating.[104]

A senior British officer who had been present throughout described Keren as a 'Soldiers' Battle', in which relatively junior troops employed 'brilliant improvisation and initiative' to defeat a well-equipped and motivated opponent in prepared defensive positions.[105] Wavell was so impressed by the British success that when he was later ennobled he chose as one of his additional titles 'Viscount of Keren in Eritrea'.[106] He knew that Platt's success had also been felt many hundreds of miles away on the southern front as Italian reserves and equipment were moved from there northwards towards the Keren battlefield. In so doing they undoubtedly made Cunningham's task a little easier, and had helped determine the outcome of the campaign.[107]

At least one of the post-war writers to have studied Keren has concluded that it could 'claim to be considered as one of the truly decisive battles of the world'.[108] This assessment was based upon the lack of equipment available at this stage of the war to the attacking troops and the difficulties they faced in mounting the offensives. Another review reached the same conclusion but based upon wider strategic considerations in the sense that the victory had not only precipitated the collapse of the Italian East African Empire but had also allowed neutral American shipping once again to transport equipment to Egypt.[109]

As one of the brigadiers who had fought at Keren concluded, 'the enemy had fought well and bravely, but our men had fought better and had been infinitely better directed', and the victory received considerable acclaim as a high point of the war to date.[110] In a subsequent House of Lords debate, one of the government speakers argued that the success at Keren stood out for special praise, noting that 'alpine climbing at a snail's pace and then to assault at the summit again and again demands great physical strain and determination'.[111] He described it as 'a task of supreme difficulty' and a 'formidable job' and, rather forgetting the contribution that had been made by English and Scottish soldiers, doubted whether any troops in the world could have completed it as successfully as the Indian units. The press in Britain also made prominent references to experienced Indian Army officers' descriptions of the terrain around Keren as being worse than anything that could be found on the North-West Frontier.[112]

After this defeat the remaining Italian forces were weary and discouraged and for the first time even Eritrean soldiers, who had previously been the most loyal colonial troops, deserted in large numbers.[113] There still remained important strategic objectives to be secured, but thoughts could begin to turn to how the campaign might end.

CHAPTER 9

A THIRD FRONT
The Patriots

While Cunningham's forces had enjoyed a relentlessly paced advance from the south and Platt's divisions had fought and won their decisive action in the mountains, the final element of Wavell's grand plan had also played its part. Providing support for the rebellion in Ethiopia had involved a much lower level of activity and the results were nowhere near as significant as some later claimed, but credit was still due. What this did was to open up a third front in the war for Italian East Africa as mobile attacks on isolated posts and ambushes along the main routes helped to create 'a deep sense of insecurity in the minds of Italian forces'.[1] The defending troops came to fear the possibility of being captured by the irregular forces that increasingly swarmed around them and their real value lay in this psychological distraction. In sponsoring the use of these forces Wavell demonstrated once again his formidable understanding of warfare and the degree to which the greatest weapon was not always bullets and bombs but something a little more sophisticated.

Having entered Ethiopia in the late summer of 1940 Sandford had continued his planning and preparations to expand operations. In this he was subsequently supported by a young Royal Artillery officer who had served on Wavell's intelligence staff in Palestine and clearly made an impression on him.[2] Major Orde Wingate quickly forged a key role for himself and eventually acted as an adviser to Haile Selassie while also leading insurgent forces into battle against the Italians.[3] Indeed, he proved particularly effective in this latter role at the head of his men who he called 'Gideon Force' – a name he chose based upon his biblical knowledge since he intended them 'to smite the enemy hip and thigh'.[4] As one of those who served under him in Burma later wrote, 'his genius will be a topic as long as military history is studied'; he described Wingate as an 'unusual man, gifted as a tactician, whose life was based on the belief that anything is possible if the effort is sufficient; one whom we all respected, disliked, but were prepared to serve, [and who] still casts a strange influence over thoughtful historians who study the profession of arms'.[5] Another contemporary pronounced him 'a dynamic leader and a magnetic personality' but noted that he was also needlessly offensive to his juniors as well as to more senior officers, 'and his showmanship was carried to rather silly extremes'.[6] Wilfred Thesiger, who had been born in Addis Ababa and had a close personal attachment to Ethiopia, served under Wingate, and whilst he recognised there was something inspiring about him he also struggled to work with a man who was 'ruthless and uncompromising, an Old Testament figure; brutal, arrogant and assertive'.[7] Such observations, and much worse, were commonly shared at the time, and Wingate was fortunate at this stage of his career that he had the patronage of Wavell to protect him.

Wingate arrived in Khartoum in October and quickly set to work. Whereas Sandford's approach had been based more around mentoring and a slow build-up of the insurgency, Wavell had decided that a more active basis was now to be adopted. With Platt's agreement, Wingate started preparing the Ethiopian refugees already in the Sudan for battle. He established Operational Centres for this, each being commanded by a British officer supported by five sergeants, and these small training teams took responsibility for 200 new recruits. Eventually there were ten of these centres led by men who 'disliked the formal side of regimental life, or were merely bored with garrison duty and in search of adventure' – men such as

'Billy' Maclean, Basil Ringrose and Bill Allen, former journalists, hunters, bushmen and adventurers who would all go on to have distinguished wartime careers carrying out irregular warfare.[8] These men lived and fought alongside the Patriots in a difficult environment and shared in all their sacrifices. Wingate's involvement brought about instant results and, aside from the revised training schedule, he helped ensure that more supplies and arms were made available to his expanding forces. When they eventually crossed back into Ethiopia each man carried an American rifle and 200 rounds of ammunition, and plentiful supplies of three-inch mortars were also distributed amongst the various groups.[9] To transport them they had 15,000 camels; although these were traditionally suited to carrying baggage, the troops were trained to ride them, allowing for more rapid movement over the harsh terrain, though only fifty-four animals survived the campaign.[10]

As part of his preparations, in November Wingate flew to meet with Sandford who had continued his harassing operations despite there being 'a heavy price on his head' as the Italians conducted sweeps searching for him and his small group of insurgents.[11] This hazardous flight to Gojjam was piloted by a volunteer, Flight Lieutenant Reginald Collis, who was subsequently awarded the Distinguished Flying Cross, and the plane landed on a roughly cleared bush strip at the Mission 101 camp.[12] The pilot described his passenger's appearance as being 'like a missionary with a big hat', remarking later that he had never seen anybody who looked less like a British Army major. All Wingate carried with him was some money 'for bribery and corruption' along with 'an alarm clock and half a loaf of bread with a big slice of cheese on the top and an onion sitting on top of it'.[13] Returning safely to Khartoum having discussed their plans, the following month Wingate presented his proposed strategy to Wavell and the senior staff. The general confirmed that he still supported the idea of a rebellion but he was worried that there was no sign of massed desertions amongst Italy's African troops, and questioned what effect could be achieved by the Patriots.[14] He believed that they needed the stimulus of British and Commonwealth forces first winning a few battles before they would commit to serious activity, and it seemed clear to him that any major revolt would have to follow rather than precede victories gained by regular British forces. Wingate's response was to propose that his insurgents should spearhead the operation from inside Ethiopia as, with Sandford's approval, it had been agreed to establish an advance base from which arms, ammunition and manpower could be distributed, allowing the various small groups to operate effectively.[15]

Once again Wavell was at odds with the leadership in London who wanted the revolt to begin in advance of the British offensive, hoping that Selassie's early return to the country would confuse and disorientate the Italians. Platt, however, agreed with his commander in Cairo and was concerned that if this action were premature it could potentially have negative results, as he knew that the emperor was not yet supported by all of the Ethiopian chiefs.[16] There were great internal rivalries within the country and objections to Italian rule varied significantly between the different leaders. The Kaid later acknowledged that whilst the Patriot forces were 'capable of great endurance for a sufficient prize and fanatical in their gallantry', at the time he had, at least initially, advised Wavell against this aspect of his strategy and wanted, at a minimum, for the attacks to be co-ordinated.[17] As Platt later confirmed in one of the post-war lectures he gave at the Staff College at Camberley, he had believed that the 'Ethiopian pot of revolt should be encouraged to simmer, and fed for simmering, but should not be allowed to boil until the might of the British Army and Air Power was ready in sufficient strength to strike in support'. Ultimately, Selassie was able to cross the border only because of Churchill's direct intervention; as he later wrote to the emperor, 'Your Majesty was the first of the lawful sovereigns to be driven from his throne and country by the Fascist-Nazi criminals, and you are now the first to return in triumph.'[18] It was Platt, however, who won the battle in terms of the exact timing of this action, and it was only after his main force had already begun its attack that the Patriots moved across the frontier in any numbers.

To co-ordinate his strategy, Wingate relied upon a small number of men for support. One was Major Tony Simonds whom he had first met in

Palestine. He had been commissioned into the Royal Berkshire Regiment in 1931 and five years later was serving on Wavell's intelligence staff when he was selected for a key wartime role. By the autumn of 1940 Simonds had joined Wingate in Khartoum and, crossing the frontier on Boxing Day, he attempted to establish a route for motor transport and to make contact with Sandford.[19] This did not go well and he was forced to abandon his four trucks and continue on foot, but by the first day of January 1941 he had made contact with and taken command of No.1 Operations Centre, which was marching into Ethiopia from Roseires. Eighteen days later this group established contact with Sandford and, as the colonel was leaving to link up with Selassie to act as his personal adviser, Simonds took charge of Mission 101. Over the following four weeks he secured control of all the insurgent activities in this area, capturing Engibara on 20 February. Wingate arrived the following day and assumed command, with Simonds being given a separate role operating independently on the left wing where his leadership was noted for its ingenuity and bluff. With an ultimate objective of Dessie, his more northerly thrust towards Lake Tana was known as Begemder Force, named after the province in which it did most of its work, and his experiences were typical of the small group of British and Commonwealth men who fought as part of the successful insurgent campaign.

As for the emperor, he had crossed the Dinder River the day after Platt's forces, raising the Ethiopian flag on 20 January at the small village of Um Idla, about 250 miles from Khartoum, with his son Crown Prince Asfa Wossen standing beside him.[20] With Sandford and Wingate now with him, as he began his advance small numbers of insurgents joined him and this expanding force moved on to the Gojjam plateau in the direction of its capital Debra Marcos. Progress was slow but steady, although Selassie was frequently frustrated by the rate of the advance, as Wingate, who had been given a temporary promotion to lieutenant-colonel on taking command, was looking to pursue an Italian force ten times his size. Having been harried for weeks, the enemy finally turned to face him on 6 March and fought on the banks of the River Bir at Burye. According to one account,

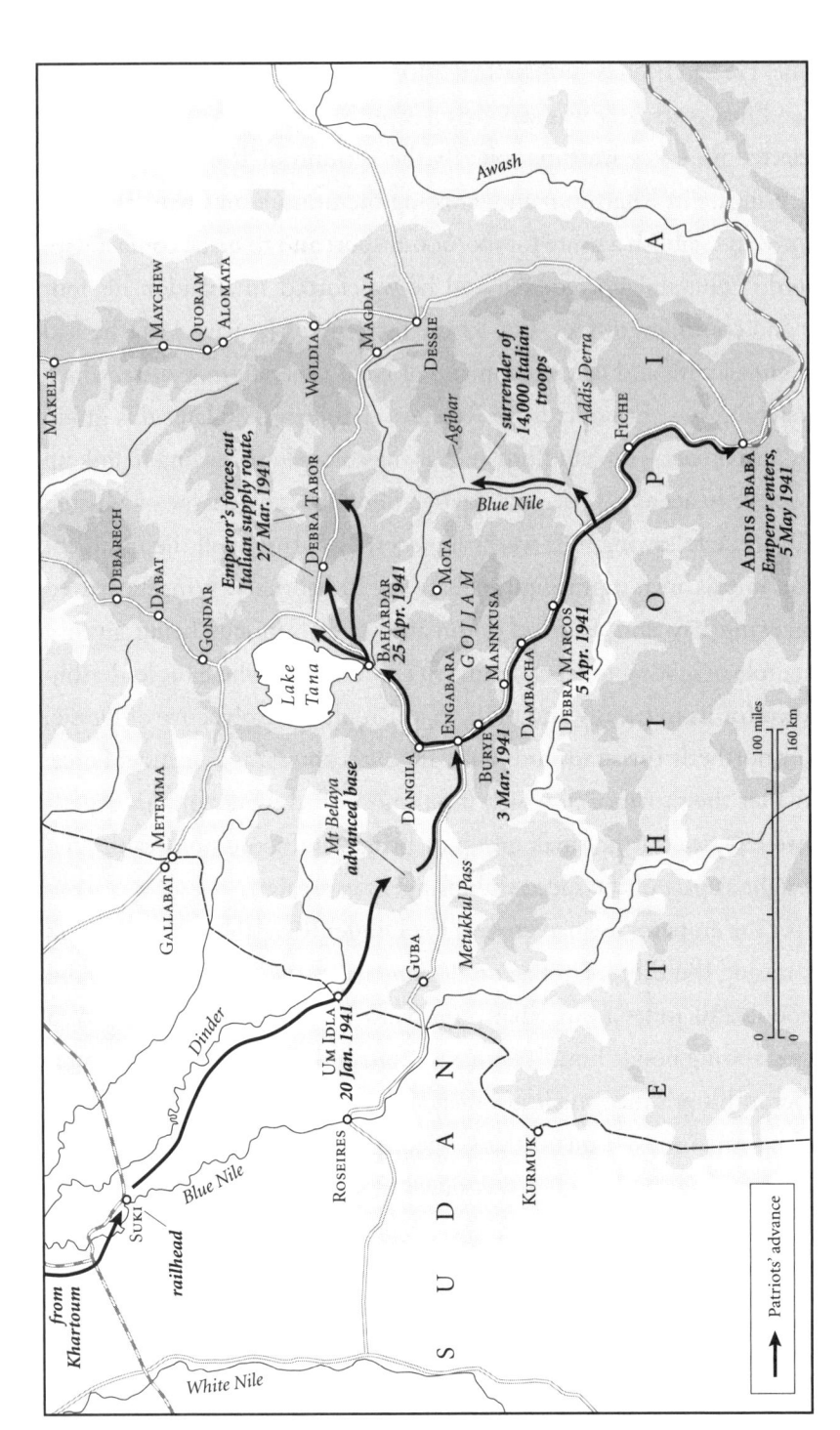

7 Advance of Patriot forces.

this was the first time since the Battle of Maychew nearly five years before that an Ethiopian unit commanded by the emperor had engaged with Italian forces.[21] After a series of skirmishes, and despite the loss of a quarter of his already small force, Wingate was eventually able to celebrate his first major victory – won by just 450 men with four mortars and a few anti-tank rifles who defeated 5,000 men fighting with supporting artillery and cavalry. A last concerted effort to push Gideon Force back followed. Ras Hailu, one of the local leaders opposed to Selassie, had raised an army of several thousand men and joined the Italians. General Nasi ordered his regular forces, in conjunction with these Ethiopian irregulars, to retake Burye and cut off the Patriots' escape route. Wingate chose not to withdraw but instead fight on, and his largely Sudanese battalion proved to be a skilled and aggressive body of men against an often disorganised opponent. Ras Hailu's forces, which were completely lacking in discipline, proved no match and deserted the Italians, who were left with little alternative other than to abandon the attack.[22]

The unfortunate Italian commander in the field, Colonel Leopoldo Natale, now changed his plans and, instead of making a further stand as had been ordered, fell back towards the east.[23] The unconventional tactics of Gideon Force supported by an active propaganda unit made him believe that they were being attacked by a much larger opponent. Wingate later wrote that he 'laid down as an essential point for propaganda that it should follow the lines of David versus Goliath, the strength of the unarmed man versus the man-at-arms'.[24] In reality he had fewer than 300 men but they pursued their enemy all the way across the Gojjam. In the capital, the Italians had concentrated their remaining troops from across the area, as many as 12,000 of them including mountain artillery and some aircraft, along with their own colonial and irregular forces. Even so, Nasi ordered the city to be abandoned and Selassie entered five days later, on 6 April; this was the first regional capital he had liberated in person and, having established his authority, it was here he waited, reluctantly, only 100 miles from Addis Ababa, as events developed around him.[25] From this point onwards more and more Ethiopians joined the emperor, and they were increasingly prepared to risk themselves in attacking the Italians. The final major battle fought at Agibar on 17/18 May is perhaps the best example of how this small, irregular but professionally handled force dominated the Italians. Wingate later described the surrender scene when altogether 14,000 men under the command of Colonel Saverio Maraventano, who had replaced the unfortunate Natale but who was no more successful, 'marched in order of battle, while to receive them stood thirty-six Sudanese . . . [they continued] over the edge of the valley where they found myself with Ras Kassa and a few patriots'.[26]

The Italians seemed paralysed by the rebellion. In February 1941 Aosta had himself concluded that the British would be looking to make best use of the insurgency in the Gojjam but it still appeared to have struck at least some of his troops with an almost devastating psychological blow.[27] From the earliest days of their occupation there had been a strong and understandable commitment to protect the large European civilian population but this had become a dominating concern that hampered the possibility of conducting a more aggressive response to Wingate's forces. When this was added to the direction from Rome to adopt a broadly defensive posture, it helped to critically undermine the morale of the troops and eroded their willingness to fight. So bad did this become that Italian units sought out British forces when defeat seemed imminent as there was a huge fear of retribution from the vengeful Patriots.

This was not misplaced. Following the fall of Addis Ababa there was some suggestion that the insurgents were getting out of hand; as one senior officer who witnessed them in action concluded, 'they were all over the place, no more under control than wasps in wall-fruit'.[28] Another of those who met them on the battlefield recalled their commander as being 'a very haughty man with a blue cape on [and] nice white bush hat' but with 'no control whatsoever' over his irregular 'natives'.[29] This observer witnessed the legs being cut off Italians to get at their boots and the women being murdered, and his unit intervened to try and restore some order. Wingate may not have had much control but he was, however, ideally suited to the task of spreading revolt in favour of a dethroned emperor for whom he held considerable respect; he was 'a man with the singular objective to defeat the Italians and secure the freedom of Ethiopia'.[30] His force never exceeded 20 officers, 50 NCOs and 1,600 troops, half from the SDF and the remainder only partly trained Ethiopians, but they battled hard against superior Italian forces and grew in stature and confidence as the campaign progressed.[31]

Whilst it makes for a fascinating story, arguments remain about the overall military contribution the insurgency actually made, and there are various assessments of just how many Italian troops were diverted from elsewhere. The official War Office publication pointedly made a distinction between Mission 101 and Gideon Force when it claimed that the former tied down the equivalent of fifty-six battalions of Italian and colonial troops who were deployed in an attempt to counter the uprising.[32] Once the fighting had begun, another account referred to four Italian brigades' worth of Aosta's combat power being drawn away from Platt's forces as they began their northern advance.[33] It was certainly true that during the decisive battle for Keren an entire regiment of the elite Savoia Grenadiers were left in Addis Ababa solely in the event of a Patriot attack on the capital. Not only were they unable to join the defenders in the mountains where they might easily have delayed, or even helped push back, the British and Indian troops, but they also played no part in the fighting that followed and the advance towards the Red Sea.[34] The official history perhaps best sums up the role played by Wingate and the men who followed him when it concluded the value could not 'be precisely assessed, but there is no doubt that it was considerable and that it reached its climax at exactly the right moment'.[35] It was also probably true to claim that, although the British and Commonwealth forces 'might have prevailed eventually, it would have taken more time to achieve'.[36] Wavell's main biographer, however, concluded that, whilst the Patriots had contributed to the campaign's success, it was because of their having fixed large numbers of Italian forces in northern Ethiopia that otherwise would probably have gone to assist the troops fighting in Eritrea. Having examined the general's extensive papers to reach this assessment, it was not exactly an enthusiastic endorsement of their role.[37]

This question of effectiveness is certainly difficult to answer. Although the Italians were vastly superior in numbers, Platt later remarked that 'there was another weapon in [his] armoury [so long as it was] used in the right way and at the right time, "Insurrection" by native inhabitants in Italian East Africa'.[38] In the post-war lectures he delivered to a largely military audience, he recalled that the 'more [the Patriots] roamed and the more they stung, the less often the Italians left their defences – they put up more wire instead'.[39] Yet, only a few years before, after the campaign had ended, he held a different view about unorthodox forces and their value – his comment was that 'the curse of this war is Lawrence in the last' – and had a fractious relationship with Wingate, reportedly saying he disliked him 'more than the devil himself'.[40] The general later concluded that the Patriots as a whole 'did just about as much as I expected they would and no more', something of a cryptic comment and, coming from an individual who was closely involved with their initial development, not exactly a wholehearted endorsement.[41]

Much the same degree of ambiguity is evident from Cunningham, who had fully supported Wavell's proposals for irregular warfare when they were first presented to him but faced significant local challenges in achieving any real success. The people living in southern Ethiopia were happier with Italian rule than their central and northern counterparts and, in the main, better off, leading to a lack of motivation to assist in any uprising. To overcome this, the Brocklehurst Mission was sent out by the War Office in December 1940 but, with no prior consultation with Wavell or his headquarters, it proved to be a disaster. This late addition to Sandford's and Wingate's efforts was poorly received by Selassie, who had heard about it through his sources in London. The emperor distrusted its purpose as it proposed to operate outside of his area of operations and provide assistance to groups within the country that did not necessarily support him.[42] The two principals, Henry Brocklehurst and Esme Erskine, were both former military officers who had spent the inter-war years in the Colonial Service and knew the region well. Although Wavell liked the former, the latter held some strong views about the future of Ethiopia and the role of the Galla and he antagonised the general in Cairo who, in his own words, 'took a strong dislike to him' and saw him as 'an intriguer'.[43] Wavell therefore made it clear that the 'F.O. gaffe' (which was how he later privately referred to the Mission) could carry out work in Italian Somaliland but was not to be allowed to operate in Ethiopia. Eventually he had Erskine recalled back to Britain.[44]

This experience is unlikely to have impressed him but Cunningham later confided that he also believed Wingate had actually made very little difference to the outcome of the overall campaign and had exaggerated the contribution made by the Patriots.[45] Wingate, who became leader of the Chindits, was killed in a plane crash in Burma in March 1944, and through the years that followed his wartime experiences, including the relatively brief period he spent in Ethiopia, he subsequently received a great deal of flattering coverage.[46] Unfortunately, many of the details of what had actually taken place in Africa were overlooked in favour of more doubtful versions that focused on his eccentric character and the apparently daring exploits he had carried out while commanding his irregular forces.[47] This meant that the background to the British policy, as well as how Wavell had helped to promote the insurgency and the role that had been played by Sandford, were not always entirely accurately portrayed. The southern front commander was particularly angered by some of these accounts and 'the somewhat distorted picture' that was allowed to develop of the rest of the British effort.[48]

Cunningham was another of the regular senior British officers who had endured a progressively difficult relationship with the leader of Gideon Force. In post-war recollections, he was happy to point out that much of the insurgent activity had taken place after Addis Ababa had already been occupied. He had received very little support during the advance from the

Kenyan frontier and, on at least two occasions, Wingate chose to ignore or interpret in a particular way direct orders he had been given by the general. His failure to respect the chain of command certainly created friction and animosity between both Cunningham and Platt which lasted throughout the campaign and beyond.[49] The two more senior officers did not appreciate the antics of their often arrogant and acerbic subordinate who failed to recognise their authority and proved highly effective at both attracting the media's interest and exploiting the support he appeared to enjoy back in Cairo.

In his post-war dispatch, Wavell described the operations which cleared the Gojjam as 'a very remarkable achievement', which he put down to the 'energy and initiative' shown by both Sandford and Wingate.[50] There were undoubtedly positive effects but these operations acted more as a psychological threat. A Gold Coast Regiment officer recorded that the Patriots' fire discipline was non-existent and they often advanced firing their rifles into the air, presumably because they assumed the noise was sufficient to make the Italians run.[51] Considering its actual level of military impact, it was reasonable to argue that Gideon Force was not that decisive although it did distract the Italian higher commanders and prevent them from focussing exclusively on the more conventional moves made by Platt and Cunningham. This alone, however, was worthy of some credit; of all of the British forces fighting on the various fronts Wingate's was the smallest, and the risks that he and his men faced were high: certainly on at least one occasion his forces were close to being overwhelmed by the Italians and a more organised opponent might easily have hunted him down.

At the same time, many of the ideas attributed to him had reportedly been put in place long before he ever reached Khartoum.[52] Slim had first met Wingate in Ethiopia and told a post-war official historian that, whilst 'his strategic ideas were to be admired and cultivated . . . his tactics on the other hand were often unsound'.[53] There were also doubts about the Patriots' reliability; as Platt put it, their 'acceptance of proposals for battle was no guarantee of their appearance and participation'.[54] Finally, to achieve even this, the level of financial support they required was massive and huge amounts were spent maintaining this sometimes questionable form of support. Operating near Wolchefit and the Gondar region, Ringrose later confirmed that he alone had spent over £1 million keeping his forces in the field.[55] Nonetheless, at a time when there were limits on what could be provided in terms of manpower and equipment, Gideon Force appears to have been viewed as a potentially cheap force multiplier.

From a purely military perspective, the main role played by the Patriots was to conduct mopping-up operations throughout much of the country as the northern and southern advances secured the key objectives that had been given to them by Wavell at the campaign's start.[56] The insurgency made for an excellent distraction, as had been intended when it was initially proposed and at a time when a military campaign lacking in resources was looking for innovative ways to get at the enemy. As for Wingate, following his death Churchill told the House of Commons during a debate on the war situation that he had 'paid a soldier's debt' and to this he added the famous line, 'There was a man of genius who might well have become a man of destiny.'[57] Despite such praise, the suggestion that Wingate had been a military figure similar in stature to Lawrence came under sustained attack, one commentator referring to them as 'chalk and cheese'.[58] His wartime role remains a subject of intense scrutiny and debate to this day, but despite the entirely valid criticisms made of Wingate, he did make a contribution to the final outcome of the East Africa campaign. It was, however, nowhere near as significant as he, and some of his post-war supporters, apparently believed. Their main contribution actually followed on from the initial stages of the British and Commonwealth advance, by which point Wavell's key strategic objectives had already been almost entirely secured by the troops fighting under the command of Platt and Cunningham. The generals' post-war disdain of an abrasive and apparently egotistical character was not, therefore, without some merit, particularly as the focus on Gideon Force detracted from the recognition of the campaign that they had led and were now about to win.

CHAPTER 10

WINNING THE WAR, WORRYING ABOUT THE PEACE

WITH THE ITALIANS having lost the Red Sea, two main objectives remained for Wavell's commanders. From the south Cunningham's rapid march had left him poised outside Addis Ababa and its capture would complete the main part of the plan that had been given to him, leaving only the hinterland beyond to be brought under control. As for Platt, he had also done everything that had been asked of him and was now looking to link up with his counterpart, which would complete the devastating pincer movement and destroy any remaining enemy forces in the process.

The numbers of available troops to accomplish this, however, were diminishing. Only a few months before, the commander in Cairo had made the bold decision to strengthen his forces in East Africa, believing that continuous pressure could lead to victory in the summer or autumn of that year. He had remained resolute despite the Greek expedition which had robbed him of forces and the reversal of fortunes suffered in the Western Desert.[1] Wavell had told Platt, 'I want every aeroplane, every gun, every vehicle and every fighting formation I can get hold of but I am not going to take a single one from you until you have finished your attack here. Then, directly you are through Keren, I expect you to offer everything you possibly can.'[2] He always remained acutely sensitive to the almost symbiotic relationship between the two theatres, and when, in April, Rommel threatened as victory in East Africa drew close, he was quick to order the changes. In the first instance this meant the 4th Indian Division was recalled back to Egypt, leaving its sister division and the South Africans as the main British and Commonwealth force. With the pressure from London growing ever more acute, this was just the start.

Ethiopia, 900 miles long and 750 miles wide, was larger than the combined area of Italy and France, and some of Cunningham's units, having first also crossed Italian Somaliland, had travelled almost its entire length.[3] These troops who had advanced from the Kenyan frontier now had one last major objective to capture. At 8,700 feet above sea level, Addis Ababa was 'a capital in the clouds' where, according to one of the war correspondents writing in typically expansive tones, 'the altitude makes your heart race and your pulse throb' and the mountain air left everybody 'with a false hangover, an unfulfilled feeling of an ebullience never quite achieved'.[4] It had been founded in 1897 by Menelik II after he had camped on the Entoto Hills and liked them so much he decided to make it his permanent base.[5] Originally there was a forest of cedar trees on the hills but these were used as building material and fuel, so the Ethiopian leader imported from Australia blue gum eucalyptus trees: it was from them that Addis Ababa, which translates as 'The New Flower', got its name. Orders were given for these trees not to be destroyed, and in the years that followed they thrived in the hot and moist climate. The conquering Italians added to the existing city buildings a large airstrip, a railway station and even a racecourse and, much as Mussolini had hoped, the white settler population grew quickly to 40,000. The Royal Palace had been built for Selassie by a German firm a few years before the Italian invasion and was not damaged in the fighting.[6] Used by successive Italian leaders, it was here that Aosta now waited for the inevitable.

Having crossed the Awash, the 22nd East African Infantry Brigade had passed through the South Africans on 1 April to continue the advance as the leading element of 12th African Division.[7] The viceroy of Italian East Africa had contacted Rome the following day and asked for permission to open discussions with Wavell about the capital's surrender.[8] As one magazine in London put it at the time, 'Honour requires no more from the Duke than he has done.'[9] Mussolini agreed, and within twenty-four hours Aosta had left the city, heading north to join Frusci and leaving General Renzo Mambrini, Inspector-General of the Police, to take charge and make preparations for the city's occupation. Four days later, a young major, Fausto de Fabritus, accompanied by an armoured vehicle and thirty Blackshirts and police motorcycle outriders, was sent to meet with the advancing troops near the Garibaldi Pass. This envoy carried an urgent request that British forces now occupy Addis Ababa as quickly as possible to protect civilian life and property. The recently appointed Italian commander feared possible retribution from the local Ethiopian population and had issued an order on 4 April instructing all women and children, if they heard a ten-minute siren blast, to take shelter in one of a dozen security zones that had been established. These were in hotels and other large buildings which had been surrounded with troops and barbed wire for their protection.

At this very late stage orders were received from Nairobi for the South Africans to move up to lead the advance and enter the city first. It was apparently done at Smuts' personal request as he hoped to use the victory and the role played by his men to strengthen domestic support for the war. There was some discussion, however, amongst the more senior British officers who had been involved in the advance as to why the brigade of West African troops that had led it so well was now to be prevented from securing its final objective.[10] Fowkes, leading at the head of the column, gave orders that every vehicle should have its tanks filled with petrol so that none would remain in the column's accompanying fuel tankers, and he could truthfully say to division headquarters that there were no reserves to hand over.[11] He was apparently determined to get to Addis Ababa first, so much so that when he received formal confirmation telling him to let his Commonwealth partners through he replied, 'your message not understood', and his own troops pushed on. He also gave orders to the rear party that no one was to be allowed to pass up the column; this was intended to prevent a written message being delivered by motorcycle dispatch rider.[12] This resulted in an aircraft being sent: it flew over and just ten miles from the capital, at Akaki, the order was dropped in front of the brigadier's car, leaving him no choice but to comply. Relations between him and his South African counterpart Pienaar did not suffer as a result of this decision and their joint motto remained 'Straight and hard at the enemy and keep right on going'; subsequent accounts which referred to a 'curious, unexplained episode' failed to acknowledge the Machiavellian intervention that Smuts had made.[13]

Although the 1st South African Brigade was to pass through and have the honour of the ceremonial entry, they were preceded by an official party. The two brigadiers and their staff along with Brigadier Gerald Smallwood, who was commanding the Nigerians, and the divisional commander Major-General Harry Wetherall, were the first into Addis Ababa, having driven into the city on the morning of 6 April in a small, lightly armed convoy. About six miles from its outskirts they found a huge welcome banner strung across the road and an Italian family with two small girls throwing flowers at the vehicles as they went past.[14] Other than them they saw little else of the general European population apart from a few groups of Greeks waving blue and white flags, until the final four miles when the route was lined on both sides by hundreds of armed policemen. Aosta had actually left behind 5,000 armed police and two complete battalions of the paramilitary Blackshirts, ostensibly to protect the civilian population, but, once again, some of these later ended up being pressed into guarding their fellow countrymen who were now prisoners of war.[15] Arriving at the emperor's palace, the 'Little Ghebbi', which the media correspondents had reached an hour before, the Union Jack was hoisted in front of the viceroy's now former residence.[16] (At the first attempt it was upside down but this was soon corrected.)

At the airport there were 1,200 fully armed troops, under the command of a general, waiting to surrender. On 3 April it had been attacked by the

SAAF, who had destroyed the final thirty-two Italian aircraft and any remaining threat of a challenge from the air that could have halted the advancing forces. When a company from 6th Battalion, KAR arrived, they took the men prisoner simply by ordering them to parade. The offices and messes were found to be luxuriously equipped and furnished and the men had excellent meals that night.[17] At 8 p.m. orders were received that they were to be gone by 5 a.m. the following morning so that the South African troops could be filmed entering the capital.

Churchill sent the message to Wavell: 'Will you convey to General Cunningham the thanks and appreciation of His Majesty's Government for the vigorous, daring and highly successful operations which he has conducted in command of his ardent, well trained well organised army.'[18] The commander of the southern advance was not present at the surrender as he wanted any accompanying publicity to go to the troops who had been responsible for the victory. It was not clear if he was aware of Smuts' latest intervention or if his absence was a deliberate response. He actually spent the day at his headquarters in Harrar where he would also have heard the news that the Germans had invaded Yugoslavia and Greece that same morning and were continuing to make advances in Cyrenaica.[19] This dramatic worsening of the Allied position completely overshadowed the incredible success that had been won in East Africa.

Cunningham visited Addis Ababa for the first time on 7 April, landing at the airfield just twenty-four hours after troops had entered the city.[20] His aide accompanied him and found it to be entirely as he expected, 'perfectly filthy and not at all attractive'. They visited the viceroy's former official residence which was already fully staffed by the division and, after weeks of bully beef, were provided with an excellent lunch at Little Ghebbi with steak, fresh vegetables and dessert accompanied by pre-lunch cocktails followed by two types of wine. Although they returned to Nairobi that same day, the two men were soon back again as there was already an 'immense' number of political and administrative details that needed to be resolved. For this second visit they were accommodated in Aosta's private house, which was still fully furnished and staffed, leading Blewitt to comment, 'as the Italians are still good waiters, whatever they are as fighters we should be comfortable'. He also later offered some more vivid impressions of the liberated city:

> ... a mixture of squalor and filth like so many of these Italian colonial towns. The wops were in the process of building a number of quite imposing buildings but none of these were finished and the wops as far as I could make out lived all muddled up with the natives in the same sort of little shack which didn't look as though a pig should be allowed to live in them. The natives themselves are filthy but rather picturesque.[21]

Clear from this description is that there was at least one British officer who was not entirely convinced about what the victors had actually accomplished.

Despite not having been at the front of the procession that had entered Addis Ababa, the 1st Battalion, Nigerian Regiment were selected as the garrison battalion and one company was billeted in the Royal Palace with another put up next to the former Italian officers' brothel.[22] Whilst the commanding major noted how little trouble there was between the Italians and Ethiopians, other accounts referred to continuous night-time shooting in the old town.[23] However, this was between Ethiopians and Somalis and the British lost no time in 'clearing this up'.[24] The plan had been that the Italian troops would be employed to provide security for the European women and children who had been left in the city, but the restraint shown towards them by the newly liberated Ethiopians and the nervousness of the military, and the shooting incidents that this caused, led to a disarmament programme being 'pushed on with all speed'.[25] With no sign of any other outbreaks of fighting and it still unclear how many Italian troops remained in the field, Cunningham believed that the campaign was now to become one of sending out 'cleaning up parties'. As for himself, he thought he would soon be sent elsewhere as there were more important jobs in the Middle East.[26] It would be a couple of months before this happened, though, and until then responsibility for the majority of the decisions would lie with him.

To Platt, having returned to Khartoum and his pre-war headquarters, the final operations were of little direct interest. While the Ethiopian capital was being liberated, rapid advances were, however, also being made from the north to link up the British and Commonwealth forces. Two companies of Sudanese troops supported by a mechanised cavalry regiment pursued the retreating Italians down the Via Imperiale in the direction of Addis Ababa which was 700 miles distant.[27] Arriving at Adi Ugri on 2 April they found a prison camp which had been used for the 187 men captured in British Somaliland; amongst those released was Eric Wilson, who was in excellent health, and who had already been told that he was believed to have been killed in action and had been awarded the Victoria Cross. Continuing to move forward in a single rapid column, the next day both Agidrat and Adowa were rolled over. As the armoured cars entered the first of these they found buses drawn up in the main street and two battalions of heavily armed Italian troops preparing to board.[28] Simply driving in front of them was enough to induce their surrender and the prisoners were marched into an open space in the middle of the town where they laid down 1,500 rifles and many machine guns. The conquering force was counted as seventy SDF other ranks, highlighting how much of their opponent's fighting spirit had disappeared. The 29th Indian Infantry Brigade was following behind as this southward march reached Amba Alagi, which had to be captured to open up the road north and to allow its use by troops being withdrawn to join the fighting elsewhere in the Middle East. It had also been the site where in 1892 an Italian officer, Major Toselli, and a force of 3,000 men were surrounded and eventually massacred; hence it was referred to by the Italians as the 'Toselli Pass'. A very large battle had also been fought there during the more recent Italian invasion when the defending Ethiopian troops had held out for nine months before finally succumbing to poison gas. It was now to be the scene of the last major battle of the campaign.

It was an even better defensive position than Keren: twice the height, at 11,200 feet, the last 300 feet of which took the form of a pyramid crowned with a small chapel. It was described by one of those who saw it as being 'very like a star-fish', radiating a series of spokes and ridges running off in various directions.[29] As had been the case at Keren, it was surrounded by several other hills also in excess of 10,000 feet, making it ideally situated to conduct a long defence. The garrison had carried out a great deal of work to strengthen it, adding another fort along with the usual assortment of dugouts, shelters and covering gun emplacements. A subsequent inspection of the captured position confirmed its impressive nature: it had around forty artillery pieces and a battery of naval anti-aircraft guns including some of the latest types, all of which had been well dug into the rock, along with ample ammunition and stores kept in galleries.[30] What the defenders did not have was any supporting airpower; as had been the case ever since the RAF and SAAF had gained control of the air, this was a critical weakness. The greatest challenge for the Italians, however, was that, with a front of nearly ten miles to defend, the position actually required a much larger garrison than had been assembled.[31] The defenders consisted of the last three remaining regular battalions from the Savoia Grenadiers along with a few other odd detachments of troops, making a total of around 9,000 men. Even so, there were initially eight Italians for every one of the attacking force, and, as one account concluded, if 'such an unrealistic scheme at the Staff College [had been proposed], one would immediately [have] been sent down to the bottom of the class'.[32]

Some weeks after the battle Cunningham flew up over Amba Alagi. Later his aide wrote that it was 'the most terrific stronghold. We flew round it and saw the holes in the side of the mountain side where the Wops hid during the short battle. It looks as though nothing could have taken it even after years of siege, and only Wops could have given it up after such a short fight.'[33] Aside, once again, from its tone, this was a far from accurate, or indeed fair, assessment but it certainly appeared to have been an even more difficult objective than Keren. The mountain could only be attacked in two ways, and both from the front: either along steep slopes which were dominated by machine gun and artillery fire or by advancing from the high ground where there were ridges protected by barbed wire and further gun positions.[34] The British commander, Major-General Mosley Mayne, who had previously led the 9th Indian Infantry Brigade before taking over the divisional command from Heath, had wanted to commit his entire division to the attack but had been forced to leave four battalions behind in Asmara and Massawa for 'internal security'.[35] Some reinforcements were sent forward and these included troops who had been involved in the pursuit from Keren along with additional guns and the men of 51 (Middle East) Commando. The latter were described by a war correspondent in his account of the campaign as 'one of those units of shock troops, which were a secret at the time'.[36] Armed with American tommy guns and knuckle-dusters, what was most remarkable about the unit was that, though it included British officers, it was largely made up of Jews and Arabs from Palestine who fought alongside one another as well as various refugees who had escaped from Nazi Germany. Even with these additions, Mayne later wrote that he would have liked more men and aircraft for what he thought would be 'a very stubbornly defended' position and he concluded that he would need to build up his strength further before launching any attack.[37]

When his men reached the forward outposts approximately five miles north of Amba Alagi, they halted, and the first fortnight was spent repeating the process that had taken place at Keren: preparing dumps of ammunition and supplies. Even during this initial preparation phase, the division was still using 20,000 gallons of petrol a day, and in the three weeks prior to the launch of the final attack a total of 1,120 tons of ammunition and artillery rounds was also fired.[38] With transport again at a premium, around 800 donkeys were collected from the surrounding countryside to keep the troops who were massing in the foothills below the main feature supplied, though a typical round trip took ten hours.[39] A further difficulty was the lack of maps; the best available was on a small scale and finished a mile or two short of the position. This meant that, at the same time as assembling the forces, considerable attention was also being given to working out lines of advance, all without attracting the enemy's attention. Mayne developed a methodical plan which kept the Italians constantly uncertain where the next attack would come from, and while his troops and guns were safely moved forward, their casualties mounted and morale fell.

This was another battle that was fought largely on ridges and slopes and so, once again, a variety of names were used by the attackers to refer to these features, amongst the most significant of which were Sandy Ridge, Castle Hill, Khaki Hill, Whale Back and the Pyramid. The first of these was actually the start position for the eventual battle but it required a six- to eight-hour climb to reach it, while the last of them, again typical of the terrain the attackers faced, consisted of a belt of sheer rocky cliffs that looked impossible to assault, especially under fire. Yet, when it was ultimately attacked by the Sikhs, the speed at which they climbed took the enemy almost completely by surprise. To distract the defenders the British general had also decided to create a diversion on the left flank: Fletcher Force, which was similar to the now disbanded Gazelle Force, and again centred around Skinner's Horse. This was supported by the commandos, Sudanese machine-gunners and Sikh infantrymen, and after some initial success and in advance of the main attack, on 3 May it was sent south-east towards the Falaga Pass, forcing the Italians to reinforce their troops in that area. Another move the following day, to the west of the main road leading to Amba Alagi, created further doubt as to which direction the main attack would come from. This also captured a number of important local features, which helped confine the Italians here to a much-restricted area which was susceptible to artillery bombardment. The barrage that followed lasted for several days, but, as at Keren, there were once again considerable challenges for the gunners because of the steepness of the terrain.[40] This made it extremely difficult to achieve any degree of accuracy, while very rapid changes in wind and temperature caused further problems. Even so, the defences were slowly worn down, and after six days the Italians on the dominating peak, known as Tongue, surrendered.[41]

With the men on both sides finding themselves battered by rain and icy winds, it was not just the relentless assault that undermined morale.[42] The hilltops were very cold, and continuous heavy rain showers added to the discomfort; during the siege the weather deteriorated further, with dense mists, heavy thunderstorms and cold temperatures making conditions more trying. According to one of those involved, if the Italians had been able to hold out for another two weeks, the attackers would have had to withdraw to Asmara and wait for the end of the rainy season.[43] Once again the incessant tempo of attack combined with a lack of tangible defensive spirit and some good fortune to allow the capture of a key position that should never have been lost, but which surrendered after a short battle. With the Falaga Pass captured, the attackers continued their advance towards Amba Alagi and the South Africans now made a decisive contribution.

After leaving Addis Ababa, Pienaar's men had been moving north clearing the road to the ports of Massawa and Port Sudan so that the troops could be embarked for Egypt.[44] In the process they forced their way through the Combolcia Pass and besieged and captured Dessie on 22 April, taking more than 8,000 prisoners and huge amounts of equipment and supplies.[45] Described by South African writers as 'the battle that counted' and the 'longest and toughest of all those fought by Cunningham's forces', despite the grandiose nature of such claims this six-day engagement certainly proved the now considerable fighting capabilities of the attackers.[46] Orders followed to provide support to Mayne and the South Africans established themselves on the far side of Amba Alagi and turned their guns on the Italian positions from the rear.[47] On 12 May their assault began which effectively closed the circle, meaning that the artillery bombardment could now have the fullest effect. The defenders knew that they could no longer link up with their colleagues at Gondar as the only possible route for retreat had been cut. With the Patriots increasingly controlling territory around them, there was no chance of escape. The capture of the position referred to as Triangle by a mixed Indian and South African attack three days later pushed the Italians back farther still and, as one British officer put it, 'with the multitude now herded together there, and the rotting dead bodies, existence was becoming rather insanitary even for our foes'.[48] What is often termed 'the friction of war' worsened the situation: a burst from an artillery shell hit a fuel dump and the leaking oil contaminated the only source of drinking water.[49] It was perhaps this more than anything else which finally forced the Italian decision to surrender.[50]

Plans for a final assault were nearly complete when, at 7 a.m. on 16 May, envoys arrived at Mayne's headquarters asking for an armistice and an opportunity to evacuate casualties. They also proposed that the garrison be allowed to keep their arms and retain their positions until the war's end, but this was rejected out of hand.[51] The general sent back verbal terms that would allow Aosta to 'surrender with honour', agreeing that his forces could march off the hill a few miles from the battlefield to hand over their arms and equipment. In return the Italians provided complete details of the mines and booby traps they had prepared and agreed not to sabotage or destroy any of the equipment or other reserves that remained. The armistice began six hours later, at which point the garrison almost immediately began moving around freely, giving away their positions to the observers below.[52] Early the following morning a white flag was seen to be raised in the Toselli Pass and another envoy, General Volpini, a close personal friend of Aosta, was sent down by him. He was attacked on the way by locals from the surrounding villages and killed. This led Mayne, who was appalled generally by much of the behaviour he had seen from the irregular forces scattered around the battlefield, to order that a delegation be sent up the mountain to continue the discussions.[53]

At 11 a.m. on 19 May the remaining garrison of about 5,000 men, including five other generals, marched past Mayne and his brigadiers before moving down the hill to hand in their arms and be evacuated. Various detachments from the 5th Indian Division presented arms as they passed and the pipe band of the Transvaal Scottish piped them past the saluting base. According to one eyewitness 'they were a sorry sight, overloaded with kit and unable to keep up their places or step'. The native wives joined in the procession led by a small Eritrean soldier with a saucepan slung around his neck, and one Italian officer who appeared to have forgotten his trousers.[54] Despite having fought one another for several months, there was apparently little animosity between the European soldiers. This was evident from the observations made by one of those watching British officers that the Italians 'were very friendly and pleased with themselves as they felt they had put up a fine show, although outnumbering us by three to one, and they entertained our officers to dinner in the evening'.[55] The following morning, Aosta, accompanied only by three officers of his personal staff, surrendered to Mayne with a guard of honour provided by men from the Worcestershire Regiment.[56] Although these were not the last Italian troops to capitulate, this defeat effectively marked the end of the major fighting in East Africa.[57] After pausing briefly at a little cemetery in which were buried some of the Italian officers who had died in the battle, the now former viceroy was shortly afterwards handed on to Platt at the divisional headquarters and from there escorted to Adi Ugri where he spent the next three weeks living with his staff in the Duke of Ancona's house.[58] He was next moved to Kenya, where he unexpectedly died of tuberculosis the following March and, with Platt in attendance, was buried with full honours at the military cemetery in Nairobi.[59]

As the final Italian stronghold in the north was being subdued, Cunningham's strategy, following his occupation of Addis Ababa, was driven by Wavell's direction to secure the main routes out of the capital leading to ports or rail routes that could be used to move men and equipment north to Egypt.[60] The role played by Pienaar's brigade in clearing the road to Asmara was part of this, but at the same time the British general also set about isolating those remaining Italian troops who had not yet surrendered.[61] His aide had written home in late April to say that they were fighting rather well in the mountains; he attributed this to the German success in Greece and North Africa having 'put [guts] into them'.[62] He also thought this sustained the Italians' belief that their allies were going to intervene in East Africa to save them and it would be only a couple of weeks before they were back in charge.[63] Although Blewitt was not normally very favourable in his assessment of their fighting qualities, he also reluctantly recognised that the Italians had learnt throughout the course of the campaign. This meant they had retired to the outlying districts 'in order to be of nuisance value', and it was clear to him, and presumably those around him, that the fighting would continue. Indeed, as they took advantage of the change in the weather there was the first hint of doubt as to whether the campaign might drag on into mid-May with a race 'between us and the rains' as the back roads deteriorated and the rate of the advance slowed.[64] It would in fact require most of Cunningham's two remaining divisions and the rest of the year to secure the final surrender.

When Aosta had moved his headquarters to Amba Alagi for his final battle, the remainder of the Italians who were able to withdraw from Addis Ababa either joined him in the strongholds to the north, between the capital and Eritrea, or headed for the southern province of Galla-Sidamo. With the headquarters of the Supreme Command having been moved to Gimma, this was the left flank of what was termed the Lakes district and within it there were still seven Italian divisions and 40,000 troops of varying qualities. As Cunningham's forces had advanced along two roads – one from the capital and the other from Soddu – heading for their new objectives, the West African troops were tasked with destroying or capturing those remaining forces west of the River Omo.[65] The swift river, which was about six feet deep and flowed along terrific gorges up to 100 yards wide, was compared to 'the Thames at Maidenhead in flood' and its eventual crossing only proved possible in large part because the Italians did not think it could be done.[66] They had relied upon a ferry and a cable to transport men and equipment across and in flood after the rains the river was extremely hazardous. There was, however, a sharp bend and a relatively shallow area with some calmer water and it was here that the infantry of the KAR and the Nigerian Regiment eventually managed to cross after 'titanic and often heroic efforts'.[67] Later, on seeing the Italian defences on the opposite bank, Cunningham concluded that it could have been held 'if manned by a company of machine gunners with guts'; his assessment was not improved when it was discovered that the Italian artillery had not started firing until much later in the battle because their observer had been captured asleep.[68]

This brief phase of the campaign was perhaps rather grandly later described as the Battle of the Lakes; during it, 'division after division of the Italian army' surrendered 'to a few armoured cars and infantry'.[69] By this stage of the campaign there was even some suggestion from Wavell that it might be best to leave the enemy forces that still remained in southern Ethiopia as to fight them would result in 'a fresh commitment in the way of prisoners of war and civilians to protect'.[70] When Gimma was eventually reached on 21 June, 8,000 Italians surrendered; as Blewitt later wrote, 'the place was lousey with Wops both prisoners and civilians', who were giving themselves up wherever they could.[71] Among those captured were a colonel and two staff officers who came down from the town to see what was going on and wandered straight into an enemy patrol, a reminder of the 'despicable fighting qualities of the Wops', but half were women and children. Although he had done the opposite on every other occasion, Cunningham now refused to divert his fighting forces to guarantee their security, in an attempt to force the final Italian forces to surrender. One of the retreating Italian divisions subsequently found itself surrounded by lightly armed Patriot forces and sent an appeal to be saved, leading to the capture of 1,100 men along with some armoured cars and even tanks.[72] Accompanying the West Africans was a small contingent of Belgian troops, one of the more curious groups fighting on the British side. They reportedly had never adapted their technique to fighting in Africa nor did they appreciate the degree to which the Italians were fearful of any threats to their rear.[73] A typical attack consisted of them advancing along the main road until they met the enemy positions, then being fired upon by the defending forces and made to retire.[74] They were, however, able to claim 'the glory of having finished the campaign' when, on 3 July, General Gazzera, the toughest Italian commander Cunningham had encountered, finally capitulated. There were at this point five weak battalions remaining; he had begun with seven divisions, and the Belgians were the only enemy troops he could find to take his surrender.[75] It was an abject end.

With the fighting nearly over, in the middle of June Cunningham's headquarters had returned to Nairobi as there was no longer any need for him to be forward.[76] The focus had already turned to various post-conflict matters, the first of which related directly to Kenya where there had been growing tension in recent months.[77] The military successes further north had initially been well received amongst the local African population, particularly because of the prominent role played by the KAR, although there were some concerns that once the war was over the authorities would seize land and give it to British soldiers as a reward. By mid-April the situation had changed: enemy broadcasts in Swahili referred to heavy losses at Keren, Mogadishu and Kismayu were said to have been recaptured already, and the retreats were explained as a trap to lure in the British. In every case it was stressed that the Germans would soon complete their victory in Europe and the Italian losses therefore did not matter: all that had been lost would be recovered, and more. These threats led to reports of an increase in defeatist views and fear of what the future might hold.[78] Not until the arrival of prisoners, sent back to the colony from the battlefields in Italian East Africa, along with the removal of blackout restrictions, was this seen by many as proof of the victory that had been won by British and Commonwealth forces and any doubts were dispelled.[79] But by June, Moore was writing to London to report that with the end of Italian resistance in sight, and with Kenya likely ceasing to be an operational area, the white civilian population not in uniform, particularly the farmers, were inclined 'to feel a sense of frustration'.[80] The governor proposed that more be done back in Britain to help and suggested that the purchase of more Kenyan produce would encourage a sense that the colony was contributing fully to the wider war effort. This correspondence between the leadership in Nairobi and the Colonial Office in Whitehall seemed much more concerned with local political issues and prospects for the future than anything else. Already it seemed that the military campaign was a distant memory even though it was not yet over.

This was a relatively minor concern for Cunningham as he began to grapple with the biggest issue facing him: what would happen next in Ethiopia at the political more than the military level. Prior to his return home Selassie had tried repeatedly to conclude a treaty with the British to re-establish formal relations, but with no real success. There was, however, widespread interest in his plight in Britain, both in the media and the House of Commons. During an August 1940 Westminster debate one parliamentarian had urged Churchill to tell 'the Abyssinian people that we want them to be free, that we will help them to be free, and that we ask them to fight for their freedom and for the world'; the rhetoric had not resulted in any firm commitment to support the emperor's position.[81] This became clear on 4 February 1941 when Eden stood before the same chamber and welcomed the reappearance of an independent state with Selassie restored to the throne.[82] Whilst the Foreign Minister also stated that there were no territorial ambitions, an important caveat was added insomuch as it was expected there would be consultation with the authorities in London.[83] As it was also stipulated that any future Ethiopian military operations would need guidance and control, this left doubts amongst Selassie's followers as to whether the British government could be trusted.[84]

These doubts were not misplaced. While British and Commonwealth troops were still marching, there were some within the War Cabinet who were opposed to restoring the emperor if it meant giving him back the whole of his country. The argument was that it was an entirely artificial creation formed following the Italian defeat at Adowa, and that it did not respect the rights of those living within its borders. A leading opponent was Leo Amery, who campaigned 'against restoring Amhara tyranny' and proposed that whilst Selassie be given back his tribal kingdom, the Galla regions could be left to the Italians or brought under an enlarged British Somaliland.[85] Smuts also continued to favour some measure of post-war international control for the country although, as yet, there remained no direct suggestion that Pretoria wished to be involved.[86] Whilst he was willing to agree that there should be some supervision, Eden was, however, committed to restoring 'the integrity and independence of Ethiopia'.[87] In the first instance, this meant that a Military Administration was established, a British Military Mission to Ethiopia, with Major-General Philip Mitchell, referred to in Nairobi as 'the big political man', appointed as Wavell's Chief Political Officer.[88] This, along with the accurate but also rather cynical statements from the likes of Amery, only added to tensions amongst Selassie's followers as to Britain's true intentions.[89]

The adoption of an approach that seemed at times almost antagonistic ran counter to the argument that had first been put forward as to why the Patriots would be prepared to fight. It also helped strengthen increasing doubts amongst the emperor's supporters about his intended future role.[90] Although it was later insisted that Selassie's leadership had never been in question, it was actually some time before there was a general acceptance that only he could hold together the proposed uprising and lead the country. Cunningham was aware of the tensions that had developed and he worried about the 'fractious Selassie' and the potential for trouble.[91] He had maintained good relations with the emperor throughout his advance and kept him fully informed of how operations were progressing while also providing clear directions as to the role he wished his Patriot forces to fulfil.[92] Following the liberation of Addis Ababa, the British commander had, however, chosen deliberately to keep Selassie away from the capital until he could improve the local security situation.[93] This had created some further tensions as the emperor was anxious to assert his authority and regain control of his throne in the face of challenges directed at him from some senior Ethiopian figures.

It was the Defence Committee in London which actually took the decision that he should be allowed to enter the capital as soon as possible, although after he had first been reminded of the terms announced earlier in the year.[94] Churchill remained adamant that the emperor be restored to power, his concern being that 'political circles' – presumably other exiled governments and allies who had sought refuge in London – had always assumed Selassie would be returned to power as soon as possible and not to do so now ran the risk of British motives and aims being questioned. The prime minister's support did, however, come with the assumption that, in governing his country, Ethiopia's restored leader would 'no doubt tak[e] advice from us', and any future assistance could be limited to food and money without the need to leave any large garrison of military forces.[95] It was this in combination that resulted in Selassie being able to return to his capital on 5 May, exactly five years after the conquering Italians had seized it from him. As the first monarch to be toppled from his throne by one of the Axis powers became the first to be restored, the great stone eagle that had been placed on top of his palace by the first Italian viceroy was destroyed by his excited supporters.[96]

In Nairobi, Sir Henry Moore also appeared to have doubts about what the future would hold. Relations between herdsmen and villagers who lived on either side of the frontier between Kenya and Ethiopia had always been volatile, with long-standing disputes. Moore wrote back to London in May to warn that there could only be 'peace on the borders' if the outstanding issues relating to grazing and waterholes were resolved.[97] The governor urged that now was the time to settle these with Selassie, before he became 'more intractable' and while he was still dependent on British military support. The following month Cunningham returned to Addis Ababa where he was awarded the Star of Solomon, which only the emperor himself and George VI had previously received. A discussion followed during which his aide speculated that the general had reminded his host 'he had got to do what he was told'.[98] Blewitt had continued to be particularly forthright in his criticisms of the relationship with Ethiopia and, almost immediately following the capture of Addis Ababa, he had worried about 'a Gilbert and Sullivan position which would be funny were it not for the amount of stuff which it still keeps tied up in this place'.[99] He continued privately to share his dislike for the emperor who, he believed, was set on making things very difficult, writing that it was 'a tragedy handing the country back to him and the popular idea that the public have at home that we are restoring a popular and democratic ruler to the country from which he had been kicked out by the wily and brutal Italian is quite definitely wrong'.[100] Evan Wavell had shared similar feelings back in May when he had mused on the idea of using the threat of withdrawing financial support and troops as a means of exerting pressure on Selassie.[101] By the middle of July, Cunningham confessed that he was looking forward to being out of a job which was becoming more and more political. He also did not agree with the policy being carried out in Ethiopia, 'which comes from our Dictator himself and therefore which has to be carried out at any rate at the moment' – this was presumably a reference to Churchill who remained adamant that Selassie's position was to be guaranteed.[102]

The immediate issue became exactly as Amery had suggested would be the case: the Galla looked to Britain to provide protection but at the same time managed to arm themselves with thousands of Italian rifles and large quantities of ammunition and other supplies. The fear amongst the local British military was that this would be used at some future stage if they were 'required to submit themselves again to the Amhara' and there was a potential for civil war.[103] This would remain a long-term concern although there were different interpretations of what it meant for Britain. In October Amery wrote once again to Eden highlighting his fears about what would happen if the emperor was not given sufficient recognition and could not therefore exercise authority or keep control.[104] According to Lady Mary Barton, whose husband had been the British Minister in Addis Ababa at the time of the Italian invasion, whilst Selassie was 'often very difficult and inclined to be truculent', she believed he needed support from somebody who understood him and whom he trusted. This was not in her opinion Sandford, who had remained one of the emperor's most trusted counsellors following his return to the capital. She thought he was excellent as a farmer and guerrilla leader but was not the right man to act as a political adviser. Eden dismissed these concerns, but he did confide that he also had misgivings about how things were shaping up in the country.[105] Churchill nonetheless continued to provide reassurance to Selassie but it was only in December that a draft agreement was signed between him and Mitchell that was acceptable to both sides.[106] Confirmed on the last day of January 1942, this limited direct British control within Ethiopia to certain Reserved Areas, including the vital railway link to the frontier with Jibuti, but even with this the 12th African Division remained in the country until April of the following year ensuring that tensions also remained.[107]

A further complication for Cunningham was that his unprecedented success had led to a requirement not merely to administer vast swathes of conquered territory but also to provide security for the large Italian civilian population.[108] Even before his advance had begun he worried about what might happen in Ethiopia where he feared many civilians could be murdered, leading to 'shrieks to us to get them out of trouble'.[109] Despite the atrocities committed by the Italians during their occupation and the local hatred of them, there was in fact no serious breakdown in order.[110] The advancing troops had often found themselves pressed into an impromptu peace-keeping role and this had, for the most part, been sufficient to prevent trouble breaking out. According to his aide the general quickly formed the view that the Ethiopians had 'behaved extraordinarily well on the whole' and there had only been 'a few massacres of stray Wops'.[111] The same was true in the capital, where as many as 35,000 Italians were still living and most of the key municipal activities remained in their hands.[112] The British intention had been for these civilians to be repatriated, which had been calculated as taking the best of a year to complete, but it soon became clear that there was no great rush to move this forward.[113] It was later agreed that 500 technicians would remain until suitable replacements from elsewhere could be found, but in early November 1941 the War Cabinet reiterated the decision that all Italians were to be evacuated from Ethiopia. This was something that Selassie and a majority of his newly liberated people had initially demanded, but the local authorities in Addis Ababa decided at the last moment to retain a large number of their former occupiers.[114] In many cases they even went so far as to hide them, and generally make every effort to prevent their deportation. The truth was that many of the Italians made an essential contribution and were prepared to stay and help with the country's future development. Even the authorities in London quickly came to share a similar view; by November 1942 fewer than 30,000 Italians had been repatriated or moved elsewhere in the region.

Cunningham was finding himself tied down by often highly complex civil/military issues but there were also questions still to be resolved about the French position. It had been possible to put these to one side while the fighting continued but, both locally and back in London, pressure was now growing for decisions to be taken. Relations had been complicated ever since December 1940 when the Free French forces of General Charles de Gaulle had drawn up a scheme to capture Jibuti.[115] Unfortunately this plan for a brigade attack, Operation 'Marie', was not fully shared with senior British officials until a very late stage and it was abandoned only when it seemed clear that there would be no rapid surrender. Although Churchill once again favoured military action, Wavell, Dill, Eden and even the Free French commander in the Middle East concluded that the best strategy was to negotiate with the authorities in Jibuti about allowing the use of the port in exchange for the blockade, which had begun the previous year, being partially relaxed. Over the months that followed there was little progress in reaching an agreement, and throughout the summer confusion remained about how to proceed. Hopes that the Vichy leadership was on the point of surrender came to nothing, but there were also insufficient forces available to launch an attack against strong defences, and the knowledge that the Vichy French troops had made preparations to destroy the port rather than see it surrendered intact.[116] During a late June visit to inspect some of the Senegalese troops at the customs post of Douanle, Cunningham observed a Free French aircraft dropping pamphlets over the town and being fired upon. This led his aide to comment that 'it makes one realise what a difficult time the French are going to have after the war whichever side wins'.[117] As it was, tensions continued until November 1942 when, following Operation 'Torch' and the Allied landings in North Africa, a large section of the garrison finally deserted and fled to British Somaliland. The following month, the acting governor signed an agreement in which he at last agreed to side with the Free French, thus removing the final potential threat facing the British Commonwealth in East Africa.

With this range of political challenges distracting him, a major military development during the summer appeared almost to slip by Cunningham and everybody else in the region. On 8 June Wavell advised London that six brigades would be the maximum force required to garrison the British administered and occupied Italian territories in eastern Africa. With the priority still remaining the moving of troops north, the War Office tentatively accepted this proposal although it insisted that the troops must be colonial, from the SDF and the East and West African divisions. This agreement proved to be the final contribution made to the campaign by the senior military officer in Cairo as, less than two weeks later, following the failure of Operation 'Battleaxe', Churchill removed Wavell from his role. Ismay, who knew him well, was one of the many who felt some sympathy and he later concluded that Wavell had 'shown strategic genius of the highest order' as he tried to conduct 'five campaigns at once and the same time, much as a juggler keeps five balls in the air at once'.[118] This did not stop him from endorsing the prime minister's decision and dismissing the 'groundless' accusations that Wavell had been made a scapegoat for the reverses that had taken place in the Western Desert and Mediterranean. His wartime military assistant was recorded at the time as saying that his general's transfer had come as a great blow to him and was, he thought, the result of Churchill's resentment of his popular success; Rommel was reported to have rated him as 'the most redoubtable' of the opponents he faced.[119] There was, however, some recognition that the defeats might have been 'a subsidiary cause' but he made no reference to the argument which had begun the previous August about British Somaliland or the impact of the subsequent tensions that developed about how the East Africa campaign was being fought.[120] Whatever the exact cause, Wavell's new posting to take charge in India, then seen as a non-fighting command, was considered to be 'very humiliating'. When the news was received at the headquarters in Nairobi there was some shock, but it had also been heard that his replacement, General Claude Auchinleck, was 'a first class man and the war simply carried on'.[121]

The situation in East Africa also seemed generally to have been largely forgotten, albeit not for the troops who were still involved. The German attack on Russia in June 1941 had seen the coalition fighting the Axis powers grow in size but it looked as if this would be short-lived. In Africa, Wavell had gone and so in turn had Cunningham who, in August, left with his reputation hugely enhanced to take up a senior role in Cairo in General Headquarters Middle East Forces. According to *Punch* magazine, along with his brother he had become one part of 'Cunningham Brothers, Removal Contractors by Land and Sea', and Auchinleck had selected him to now head north and take the fight to Rommel and his Afrika Korps.[122] In Ethiopia, fighting (or more accurately, surrendering) continued, following the conquest of Galla-Sidamo and, in addition to the small groups of stragglers across the region, a further 3,000 prisoners were captured at Dendi at the end of June and 2,900 more at Amba Gorgias at the end of September.[123] Wetherall was in temporary charge of the British and Commonwealth forces and there were still significant numbers of enemy troops to be rounded up in a conquered territory of more than half a million square miles. For the final operations his forces were much reduced, with the South Africans having left for Egypt after the fall of Amba Alagi. The majority of the West African troops had also gone, the Nigerians having left in August and the Gold Coast brigade following them in October. The greatest challenge the new commander faced, however, was maintaining law and order in a country awash with weapons as more than 20,000 rifles and 20 million rounds of ammunition had been sent by the British authorities to support the Patriots. The Italians had also issued their own arms and equipment in the hope that they would be used by those Ethiopians who were opposed to Selassie's return to support their defence. Added to this, many thousands more were found on deserted battlefields and in hidden reserve dumps. With the military campaign not yet concluded this was clearly a heavily armed country in which there were significant political tensions.

Against this volatile background, the final battle of a campaign that had started the previous June with minor border raids was another complicated set-piece mountain attack on the last Italian outpost. 'Fluffy' Fowkes had been wounded four times during the last war and awarded the Military Cross and bar, serving afterwards in various roles and locations including Russia and China, in the process of which he gained a diverse range of military experience.[124] He had been one of the original brigade commanders appointed in 1939 and during this campaign he had probably seen more fighting than anybody. It was therefore perhaps fitting that he should be given the final task of capturing Gondar on the Ethiopian plateau. The town was situated at a height of about 6,800 feet but surrounded by other peaks to the north-east and south-east which rose to more than twice its size as the terrain fell away rapidly to the south towards the depression which contained Lake Tana. There was also a series of steep-sided valleys with numerous streams and plentiful supplies of water. Approaching from Asmara in the north, there was a good road which went through the Wolchefit Pass, an earth track with uncertain bridges which offered a route from Dessie, and another rougher route from Gedaref with no bridges. The Italian forces were hemmed in but in a strong defensive position and it would need a progression of attacks to force them out. The Italian commander was the experienced and capable Nasi, Vice-Governor of and victor in British Somaliland, and he had placed strong detachments which allowed him to effectively control the three main approaches.

In many ways, Gondar provided a perfect image of how the entire Italian East African Empire had functioned. Interrogations by the British of captured prisoners revealed there was still good morale and they knew little or nothing about the forces massing against them. One of the first correspondents to arrive after the battle described it as 'a full-grown city with three-story [sic] office buildings and many villas and large, deep air-raid shelters now scarred by the siege'.[125] A postal service still operated, with letters typed on cloth and sewn into the clothing of some of the Africans who lived there and smuggled them out. These were also intercepted and from them it was established that there were between 100 and 200 civilians still in the town, including ten or eleven white women and a small number of children; an additional four white women worked in the brothel. Unlike at Massawa there was no radio link with the outside and only five planes had arrived from Italy in the preceding five months having taken a route via Benghazi to the Yemen and then on to French Somaliland. They carried money, medical supplies and ammunition, and took back with them air force pilots, young children and serious medical cases.[126] Although the cheese factory continued to operate, food was scarce, but it was still possible to produce alcohol and shops continued to function despite the damage caused by the bombing from British and South African aircraft.[127] High up in the mountains the war had seemed to be far distant, but it had now come much closer.

In preparing for the assault some of the more remote Italian posts were cleared, but resistance continued elsewhere and troops from the KAR still faced often stiff fighting. With the weather intervening to make transport difficult, it was something of a relief when, and totally unexpectedly, the defending garrison at neighbouring Wolchefit surrendered despite their own exceptionally strong position. This was put down to a combination of the pressure that was created by unopposed air attacks and a fear of what would happen if the Patriot forces entered the town. It meant that the route was clear for the advance towards Gondar itself and, although the attackers continued to take a number of casualties from mines and booby traps, plans were hastily revised to allow for a speedier move. As the troops from the 26th East African Brigade moved closer, they found that the road had been comprehensively destroyed and it was so steep at one point that the men trying to make repairs had to be let down on ropes. The advance was therefore made either on foot or using mules and donkeys which had been commandeered from the local inhabitants, but there were no saddles and the African troops did not have any experience of using pack transport. Although Fowkes had concluded that it was impossible to move a large force and achieve any measure of surprise, what he did not know was that the Italians refused to believe regular forces could cross such country. They were now to be proven wrong: moving forward on 25 November along a single track, the troops, along with 150 donkeys and mules for each battalion, were able to carry between them to the assembly area enough food, ammunition, communications equipment and medical supplies to operate for four days. Efforts were made to camouflage this approach using branches and nets and this, along with the glare of the morning sun which was directly in the eyes of the Italian defenders, allowed for a force of about 5,000 men to be readied for an attack.

The final military action of the campaign fought in East Africa began at 5.30 a.m. on 27 November as artillery opened fire on the main Dalflecha Ridge which, along with the plateau at Maldiba, was the principal target of the attack. The defending troops had at least a three-to-one advantage and were dug into positions they had been preparing for up to seven months. As a result, the fighting was heavy, but only for the initial stage throughout the morning, and the ridge was captured by lunchtime. When the commanding officer, Brigadier William Dimoline, moved forward along the route of this initial advance shortly afterwards it took him nearly an hour of climbing, often crawling on his hands and knees. Exhausted by the exertion, he marvelled at the job his men had done by getting up there in the face of stiff Italian opposition and with mines and booby traps strewn across the battlefield. As the troops paused, British aircraft were now used in a bombardment that lasted more than two hours, after which the advance resumed. The second objective fell shortly afterwards as, at 4 p.m., word was received that Nasi had sent an envoy from the plateau requesting terms and Italian ammunition dumps were soon being destroyed. By the day's end the town was captured and 23,000 prisoners were taken. Guards had to be placed everywhere both to protect Italian personnel, such as those working at the electricity plant, from the local Ethiopians and the Patriots, and to stop other key sites being wrecked. The divisional commander warned that any looters were to be shot on the spot but this did not stop the violence immediately.[128] Some of the surrounding garrisons did not get the order to surrender until the following day and it took several more days to restore order in and around Gondar before the battle could finally be considered to have come to an end.

Churchill sent a secret and personal message to Fowkes to congratulate him on this final victory, which appeared 'to have been brilliantly conceived and brilliantly executed'.[129] Whilst the only British troops involved in the final assault were from 1st Battalion, The Argyll and Sutherland Highlanders, casualties for British and Commonwealth troops throughout November were the highest for any one month since the campaign had started. A total of 369 men had been killed or wounded, a clear indication of just how tough this final but largely forgotten stage of operations had been.[130] According to one of the attacking soldiers, the Italians fought better at Gondar than anywhere else, something that was put down almost entirely to Nasi's leadership skills and personality.[131] When the battlefield was cleared, a number of positions manned by African troops were found to have fought to the last man and even the last round. In a fitting final touch, the Union Jack hoisted over the final Italian outpost to surrender was the one that had flown in Addis Ababa, sent to a British officer in the 22nd East African Brigade, Major Michael Biggs, by his wife with the instruction that he should 'hoist it over somewhere for me'.[132] He had dutifully carried it throughout the campaign and, with nobody apparently having remembered to pack an official flag, it was used to mark both the entry into the Italian-held capital and at the surrender of their final outpost when it was raised above the castle that had been built by the Portuguese in the sixteenth century.

On 15 December the East African Force was abolished and replaced by East African Command, now once again directly under War Office control as opposed to the commander in Cairo. Platt had arrived ten days before to take over this new role giving him responsibility for a huge area from Eritrea in the north to the River Zambezi in the south. This final act also carried with it confirmation that the British Empire had decisively won its first campaign victory of what would prove to be a very long war.

CONCLUSION
The British Empire's First Victory

THE CAMPAIGN IN East Africa was a great success both for the British and Commonwealth forces who fought there and the commanders who led them. A massive pincer movement through Italian Somaliland and Ethiopia converged with another that had advanced through Eritrea and ended with a final series of assaults against a remote Italian mountain fortress. With a speed and comprehensiveness that was not foreseen in the original plan, an eventually significant victory came about gradually through the development of events and the overwhelming of a confused and progressively shattered opponent.[1] This was the unanimous view of the small number of published eyewitness accounts where it was described as 'a military masterpiece of its time', whilst another conclusion stated with confidence that the campaign would 'go down in military history as a classic'.[2] It was not simply a case of writers striving for hyperbole but a genuine series of assessments that this was seen as having been a triumph of the first order.

Blewitt, Cunningham's ever-present military aide who recorded how the battle had been conducted, described the entry of the troops into Addis Ababa as completing 'probably the fastest and longest advance in the history of the British army', an assessment with which others much more experienced than he in the conduct of war agreed.[3] According to one former senior military officer speaking in the House of Lords in late May 1941, the strategic significance of the campaign was in fact much greater than most people understood.[4] Lord Birdwood, who had been a soldier since the war fought against the Boers in South Africa, believed that had the Duke of Aosta's army remained intact and able to take the offensive, Germany would have had the freedom to attack and capture not only Egypt but possibly also Syria, completing the encirclement of Turkey. One of his equally experienced colleagues believed it could not 'be surpassed in the annals of the British Army'.[5] Yet for Wavell, who remained modest throughout, it was no more than 'an improvisation after the British fashion rather than a set piece in the German manner'.[6] This may have been how it was conceived but the outcome was devastating for the Axis, and Italy in particular.

The post-battle Westminster review paid special reference to its having been a wonderful story 'of planning and organisation and endurance and valour', and also highlighted the need for everyone to 'be inspired by the thought that the men taking part in it came from all parts of our Empire, motivated by the same high ideals'.[7] At this stage in the war there were Commonwealth troops in Britain, but they were committed to a largely static role, waiting for an invader that it was hoped would not come.[8] In East Africa it was entirely different: here an exotic and potent range of forces were demonstrating the power available to an empire still trying to come to terms with the defeats of the summer of 1940 which had highlighted the apparently preeminent power of the German blitzkrieg. Platt's force consisted of two Indian divisions, which included in their ranks both members of the SDF and English infantry battalions.[9] Cunningham's force was even more multinational, with South Africans, regiments from Kenya and British Somaliland, Indians, Ugandans and Ethiopian irregulars who fought alongside Rhodesians, Nigerians, Gold Coasters, Belgians, French and even a handful of Australian sailors.[10] It was an international coalition in the truest sense and, in many respects, a rehearsal for the next, much larger and final military imperial campaign which was fought to an ultimately successful conclusion in North

Africa. With the end of the pre-war 'special relationship' with France – albeit an often confused and uncertain one that ended in defeat and increasing bitterness – and with the United States destined to fill this vacant position but still hesitant about the merits of involvement in what appeared to many of its citizens a distant war, Britain's Empire filled the void.

Within this complex mix, the role that was played by the South Africans needs to be particularly acknowledged. They undeniably played a significant role in the campaign. Militarily, their deployment brought with it a level of equipment that would otherwise not have been available and it certainly impressed the troops who fought alongside them. The mechanisation that had hitherto been unavailable enabled a surprisingly modern war to be fought in which speed and tempo could be used to overwhelm an already doubtful opponent and exploit openings as they presented themselves. As a Rhodesian officer concluded, it was the trucks that had 'made possible the procession to Addis Ababa' and he later highlighted how their armoured cars had taken full advantage of the excellent roads built by the Italians but which subsequently contributed to their defeat.[11] The availability of mechanised transport also allowed for regular supplies of ammunition and, perhaps of greater significance for morale, water and food. A veteran of the First World War campaign, his unit was the first to enter Kismayu, Mogadishu and Addis Ababa. In three years and three months spent fighting in the first war, he reckoned he had walked more than 10,000 miles; the South African transport meant that in his second war, this was reduced to no more than 300 miles. The arrival of aircraft also had a major impact as the troops on the ground grew in confidence once they had air cover to provide support. Interestingly, according to the Rhodesian observer, the vital contribution actually came from the artillery, which broke the Italian will to fight.

Perhaps of greater significance, despite some of the concerns that had existed in London and elsewhere, no immediate political cost resulted from this demonstration of South African largesse. During the summer of 1941 Cunningham met various senior political figures in Nairobi who had

CONCLUSION

travelled north to see him and there was some speculation about the role they might wish to take in Kenya's future. They were not then involved in its administration but it was suggested by the general's aide that they ought to be: Smuts was widely known to have ideas about a united Africa and Blewitt concluded that if an offer of some greater involvement was not made 'the time will come when they take it whether the local people like it or not'.[12] No demands came, however, and, buoyed by its successful participation, the South African military continued marching north and onwards to the Western Desert where eventually two divisions took part in the action there as part of the British Empire's war to control the Mediterranean.[13] In its first campaign of the war it had lost only 73 men killed and had 197 other battle-related casualties, with an additional 79 members of the SAAF also lost and 5 reported missing. It had been a good war. As for the South African leader, he remained close to his friend Churchill throughout the wartime years and was lauded across the British Empire as one of its greatest figures.

A complex campaign which presented considerable technical and logistic challenges, the East Africa war required exceptional military leadership – and this is what was provided. Virtually all of those involved, perhaps aside from the irascible Wingate who had an often impossibly high opinion of his contribution, recognised that much of the credit for the final victory lay with Wavell, who 'kept his finger on the pulse'.[14] The chronic lack of available resources gave him no option but to move forces to where they were most required in anticipation of the likely enemy threat. It also meant that there could be few thoughts of conducting an early offensive; initial British strategy was aimed almost entirely at tying down Italian forces that might otherwise be used against Egypt. Key to this defensive approach Wavell adopted was the geographical advantage enjoyed by the British, which allowed for the isolation of Italian East Africa both from the other Italian colonies in North Africa and from their home base. By these means, the British commander believed, his opponent would be cut off and eventually run out of petrol and essential supplies.

The Red Sea lines of communication became critical and, consequently, he viewed victory in East Africa as an essential prerequisite for securing victory elsewhere. It meant that, when he considered his entire command, Italian East Africa was viewed as a threat to his flank which needed to be removed if he were to have any hope of winning in North Africa. Despite this assessment, as late as October 1940 the commander in Cairo estimated that he had sufficient troops in the Sudan and Kenya only for defensive purposes and to potentially conduct minor attacks aimed at the frontier posts; yet, six months later, he had virtually defeated his opponent.

Certainly, Wavell's compelling leadership style and the skilful manner in which he moved forces around this vast theatre were decisive elements in the British and Commonwealth success. Wavell's willingness to do this has been described as 'inspired strategic juggling which by its timing and finesse was to suggest to the Italians that the same British soldiers were defeating them in simultaneous battles a thousand miles apart'.[15] The manner in which he deployed his forces during Operation 'Compass' was both bold and inspired and he persisted in managing his command as a whole rather than as a series of isolated theatres.[16] For one commentator who fought in East Africa, this decision required 'imagination, faith and a plenitude of moral courage'; as it was, it proved a successful gambit and could well rank alongside 'major military decisions which have set the course of history'.[17] Keeping with the idea of the East Africa campaign being an early example of a modern battle, the official history was correct to claim that it was the only 'completely successful [joint] campaign during the Second World War before 1943', recognising the significant role played by land, air and naval forces.[18] This was no more than a reflection of the conclusion that had been put forward in Westminster debates following the capture of Addis Ababa, when it was said that the achievement would 'probably come to be regarded as the first brilliant example of the use, in co-operation, of all three arms'.[19]

Despite such accolades, the victory never quite received the acclaim it deserved, due largely to events that followed elsewhere – most notably relating to the catastrophic defeats in Greece and Crete along with the later failures in the Western Desert – but Wavell had demonstrated his significant military acumen and intellect. Before the war he had given three lectures on generalship to a small, largely military audience at Cambridge University. Largely overlooked at the time, in these he had offered a wide-ranging explanation of his approach to soldiering, particularly the essentials he thought were needed for a senior officer. A good general, he told the audience:

> must know how to get his men their rations and every other kind of store needed for war. He must have imagination to originate plans, practical sense and energy to carry them through. He must be observant, untiring, shrewd, kindly and cruel; simple and crafty, a watchman and a robber; lavish and miserly; generous and stingy, rash and conservative. He should also[,] as a matter of course, know his tactics; for a disorderly mob is no more an army than a heap of building stone is a house.[20]

Wavell had followed these principles at all times throughout the battles fought in East Africa and had proved himself to be one of the leading military commanders of his age.

His guidance was decisive in terms of the campaign's success, but the same could not be said of the immediate impact it had on his career. Like all British military operations throughout the war following Churchill's appointment as prime minister in 1940, the planning and conduct of military operations in this region were liable to his interventions and whims, and from very early on he demanded that some form of offensive action be taken. He grumbled constantly about the size of the forces that had been kept in Kenya and it often appeared that he hoped Wavell's calls for action 'would waste away if ignored and blockaded'.[21] Writing after the war about the subsequent operations and the comprehensive success they secured, he still chose to argue that the 'results showed how unduly the commanders on the spot had magnified the difficulties and how right we were at home to press them to speedy action'.[22] Even though it was nine years after the events had occurred, Churchill's recollections offered a clear and withering indictment of the apparent lack of confidence he had at the time in his generals' abilities to effectively translate tactical victories into strategic success. Cunningham complained to the official historian that such claims were 'quite untrue', and there were others prepared to say the same, but the former prime minister's semi-official account had a huge, global readership and it did clearly 'give the impression that Archie Wavell and I were unwilling horses requiring to be kicked over the fence by the Churchillian Spur before we would advance'.[23]

Driving Britain's wartime leader in the writing of this narrative was the unfortunate impression he had formed of Wavell in August 1940 as a somewhat taciturn individual who was reticent and prone to overstating the difficulties he faced. The military commander was intuitive enough to realise that their first meeting had not gone well and prophetically commented shortly afterwards, 'I do not think Winston quite knew what to make of me and whether I was fit to command or not.'[24] More than a decade after Wavell's death, his biographer John Connell wrote to Ismay, who had been on good terms with both Wavell and Churchill, to ask him about the campaign in East Africa. In this correspondence Connell argued that, back in 1940, the prime minister had 'tended to look at small scale maps, and ignore the size and the difficulty of the country'.[25] The two men agreed that Churchill had not understood the vast nature of the region and 'his contempt of the fighting qualities of the Italian Army' had clouded his views.[26] Such was his loyalty, however, that even twenty years later Ismay still would not challenge the decisions that had been taken at the time.

Within this brief exchange of information the events that had taken place in British Somaliland were overlooked. The protectorate's loss exemplified the tensions that existed in the relationship between Wavell and Churchill and it was undoubtedly poisoned by what happened. Britain's wartime leader entirely failed to acknowledge the political constraints that had been imposed on planning, the small size of the garrison and the only

CONCLUSION

limited firepower that had been made available to aid its defence.[27] In draft notes prepared for his post-war history, it was stated that the pre-war policy had been 'to evacuate Somaliland, which was regarded as an uncomfortable commitment in a theatre of minor strategic importance', but, largely at Dill's urging, in December 1939 this had been changed to mounting a defence.[28] Desperate for a British victory in the summer of 1940, the politician subsequently blamed his general and his subordinate commanders for the defeat, despite there being a series of factors over which they had had little or no control. Wavell's own dispatch put the blame on successive governments which had, through their inaction, contributed to what had happened. The original draft of this document was submitted in October 1940 and it was clear then that its tone and 'frank criticism' could only add to existing tensions.[29] As it was, the dispatch, along with all the others produced during the war, was retained until after its end. When it was finally published the War Office still took the unusual step of including an introduction which attempted to offer some defence of the policies that had been followed, although it did also acknowledge that political constraints had played a pivotal role in the defeat.[30] There was, of course, no reference to the acrimonious exchange of telegrams about 'a big butcher's bill' and it 'not necessarily [being] evidence of good tactics'.[31] One of the prime minister's wartime advisers was very much of the view that Wavell's defence of the low casualty numbers suffered in Somaliland was never forgiven by Churchill, who 'raged, but could think of nothing to say in return'.[32] He could, however, remember the exchange and take the necessary steps the following year to exact retribution.

Wavell had better fortune in the relationships he enjoyed with the men who worked for him. Although he did not select either of his two principal subordinates, Cunningham and Platt, they nonetheless formed a highly effective working relationship and the influence this had on securing the campaign's final outcome cannot be underestimated. As *The Times* put it, he 'had had two competent and determined commanders who took to this quick-moving warfare as ducks to water'.[33] Wavell himself put the victory down mainly to the boldness and skill in execution of his generals, the quality of their subordinates and 'the dash and endurance of the troops', privately noting that it was 'fully justified in the end'.[34] He set the targets and provided the resources but then gave them considerable discretion in deciding how they went about fighting the campaign.[35] In terms of who was better, having read Wavell's account *The Times*'s military correspondent concluded that 'No comparisons are called for. Let both divide the crown, with their subordinate commanders and troops, who served them so well.'[36] This was not the only such accolade: writers in Britain at the time constantly referred to the fighting qualities of these two generals and their 'dash, stamina and enthusiasm'.[37]

Cunningham was the more charismatic of the two operational-level commanders. One leading historian has described how 'in eight weeks he seemed to have marched half across Africa; his speed and dash delighted the British public'.[38] The general later wrote that the Italians had relied upon the extremely difficult terrain to protect them and it was the shock of finding that his forces could cross country they considered impassable which fatally weakened their morale and any willingness to continue the fight.[39] As he noted, prior to the war the opinion on all sides had been that an advance across the deserts along the frontier between Kenya and Ethiopia was 'a military impossibility', yet he thought differently. He also appeared to have confidence in his subordinates and apparently did not meet his two divisional commanders from early February to the middle of May but let them get on with the battle, providing support and encouragement as it was needed.[40] The rapid exploitation of the successful engagement on the River Juba offered an early demonstration of Cunningham's agility and offensive spirit and the subsequent advance showed that in this war a small, well-led force, with a strong, aggressive spirit and the will to win, could overcome a numerically superior enemy.[41] He was also modest in recognising the extent of what he had achieved, later describing the campaign's success to Wavell as down to 'a bit of luck, two first class commanders, and troops with their tails right up'.[42]

CONCLUSION

Cunningham's reward would come with a call from Auchinleck to travel north to take charge of the newly forming Eighth Army, although this proved to be a bitter one as he was relieved of command just days after the start of Operation 'Crusader', its first battle.[43] On Cunningham's return to England on medical grounds, Churchill, who had in any case initially preferred somebody else for the role, ruled that he was not to be put in charge of troops again. Brooke believed he had been badly treated and found him a role as Commandant at the Staff College, although one of his peers believed that he had 'hardly the intellectual qualities needed to stimulate the ideas of our future staff officers'. In the opinion of a post-war writer working on the South African official histories, this was far from the case, and 'if anything Cunningham was too alert; as Napoleon would say he "saw too many things at once"'.[44] After his spell in purdah, which also included a period as the senior officer in Northern Ireland, Cunningham finished the war as GOC Eastern Command and in November 1945 it was announced that he was being sent abroad as High Commissioner and Commander-in-Chief Palestine and Trans-Jordan.[45] Churchill was gone but even so the victor of East Africa still had his critics; Field Marshal Bernard Montgomery wrote personally to the then Secretary of State for the Colonies questioning the decision, describing Cunningham as somebody who 'inspires no confidence' and suggesting there must be better alternatives.[46] This proved not to be the case, and his performance was well received. He lived until the age of ninety-five, which made him the last surviving senior officer to have fought in Africa. This was fitting for the commander who had largely overseen the British Commonwealth's first victory in this vital strategic theatre.

As for Platt, he summed up his achievements in a lecture he delivered in 1951 at the Staff College in Camberley, during which he told his audience that, ten years before, 'the soldiers and airmen of all races and creeds who fought from the Sudan and East Africa can fairly claim to have been the bright light in a dark year, and to have laid the foundation not only for victory in Africa but in the world'.[47] He went on to say that good pilots and technically superior fighters (once South African Hurricanes had arrived), in combination with a much superior tank and the fighting spirit of his troops, had provided a critical advantage.[48] Platt's northern column also had a shorter distance to cover, 450 miles from Kassala to Amba Alagi, and, although this was completed in four months, it did include the siege at Keren. Platt's troops managed to take positions from the Italians in the north which they had had every intention of holding, and this led them increasingly to withdraw forces from the south in order to concentrate their defences and retain their grip on the vital Eritrea. In turn, Cunningham liked to make the point in private that the victory in the mountains could not have been achieved without the rapid advance by the men under his command as it was this which actually helped draw away Italian forces from further north. However this was viewed, what was clear was that the two operations were 'complementary', so had to be viewed together. The two senior officers in fact seemed to enjoy a good working relationship throughout the campaign.[49]

The end of the fighting would eventually result in Platt's appointment to take charge of the new East Africa Command. This covered Ethiopia, Italian Somaliland, British Somaliland, Uganda, Kenya, Tanganyika, Northern Rhodesia, Madagascar and other assorted Indian Ocean islands, an area comparable to that which Wavell had overseen. Other than undertaking the capture of Diego Suarez and Madagascar and an 'invasion scare' during the summer of 1942 when it was feared Japan might launch a raid on the east African coast, this proved to be a largely administrative posting. Perhaps the most important role was the training and preparation of the African forces that were sent out to fight in Burma, and in this Platt proved extremely effective.[50] The former Kaid also lived a long life and after he died at ninety years of age his lengthy obituary referred prominently to him as having been the 'victor of Keren'.[51] It also offered an anecdote he apparently liked to tell of how he had responded modestly to congratulations from King George VI following the victory in Eritrea, referring to the engagements his troops had fought as 'bows and arrows' compared to the battles in the Western Desert. The men who had fought there knew that the experience had actually been far more difficult than that.

CONCLUSION

For the Italians the campaign was nothing short of a disaster. As one of the official histories summarised the outcome: 'The Empire which Italy took seven months to gain was lost in four . . . [and] resulted in the complete destruction of an Italian army of 300,000 men.'[52] The question was asked both at the time and subsequently as to why they had done so badly in the land battles. Despite its being a largely barren desert, the capture of British Somaliland in August 1940 should have acted as a catalyst in seizing the initiative, as the Italians had gained an additional 450 miles of coast with a harbour to be developed at Berbera and the opportunity to build airbases that would have allowed them to target Aden. Instead it marked a disappointing high point as they subsequently dug in and waited for an attack which six months later obligingly came. Whilst they often fought bravely at the tactical level, poor decisions, inactivity and incompetence at the operational and strategic level lost them the engagements that they did fight.[53] One contemporary assessment offered by a junior Indian officer identified four critical areas in which the Italians had failed. These were: poor morale; superior British training, determination and initiative amongst junior officers, NCOs and the ordinary ranks; successful use of the bayonet; and a lack of Italian confidence in their cause.[54] To these could perhaps be added the degree to which they were unprepared for the war they would have to fight, with a legacy of fighting irregular warfare and poorly equipped opponents during their previous regional campaigns. Accordingly they had no real answer to fast advancing columns and well-trained and highly motivated professional troops, and did not understand armoured warfare. Theoretically, Ethiopia was an easy country to defend against invasion, given the near impossibility of movement except on the very few primitive roads, the almost total lack of communications and the great distances involved. Ultimately it was shown that these severe restrictions applied equally to the defenders as to any invading force. The British and Commonwealth troops, however, proved far more adept at overcoming the resulting logistical challenges, showing themselves time and again to be able to move over poor terrain at great speed and keep their opponent uncertain of their strategy.

From his position as an intelligence officer, George Young concluded that the mystery of the Italian collapse was not a particularly profound one:

> The generals were rather old perhaps but well versed in the history and lessons of war. There was nothing wrong with their actual ability to handle masses of men according to a plan. They were well up in the science of what is now called logistics. But they did not want the war, they had made up their minds that war would mean the loss of their Empire, if they did have a war then Mussolini and his German friends could do the fighting. They proposed to content themselves with putting prepared plans into effect.[55]

These were to conduct an essentially static defence and, if they were defeated, to withdraw with the minimum loss while waiting for Rommel to defeat the British in the Western Desert and push them out of Africa. In July 1941, faced with now inevitable defeat, Mussolini ordered his forces to continue their resistance, tying down as many British soldiers as possible and preventing reinforcements being sent north. Even this revised strategy did not work. Their military forces often gave the appearance of simply not wanting a war for which they believed they were hopelessly unprepared.[56] The fact was that Italy was not organised for the battle ahead; the country's leader had told his commanders to prepare for war in 1942 at the earliest, so when it came two years ahead of schedule his forces were not ready.[57] Aosta was left to operate under orders from Rome to conduct an entirely defensive campaign and, whether he agreed with these or not, it meant that the men he commanded for the most part lacked offensive spirit. Indeed, it could be said that as a result of Mussolini's failings, in Italian East Africa strategic paralysis set in at almost every level and the land battle was lost almost before it had begun.

If their fighting on land was often of a very poor quality, the other major failure was the decision not to attempt any offensive action in the Red Sea. Italian naval strategy was also flawed from the outset as it allocated very

CONCLUSION

limited resources to the area – only seven fleet destroyers, two escort destroyers, eight submarines and five motor torpedo boats. Although at the time Italy had more cruisers than the combined British and French Mediterranean fleets, it chose not to operate any of them south of Suez. The retention of 108 submarines in Italian home ports was another curious oversight at a time when nothing could have made a more effective contribution to what appeared to be their main effort; the invasion of Egypt could only have benefited from a strong and active regional naval presence. At the same time the strategic effect that even a small submarine force operating from Massawa could have had on British shipping bringing supplies and troops to support the advance from Kenya was apparently lost on the Italians. Even so, the United States took the decision to declare this a war zone and out of bounds to their shipping. This was an additional burden on British merchant tonnage, with the Mediterranean supply routes already closed, but the Italians did not exploit the potential advantage.[58] With resources so thinly spread, offensive action by even the relatively small Red Sea forces could have entirely closed the route to Allied shipping and severely affected Wavell's strategic planning. The impact would have been devastating: Britain would have been isolated from one-twelfth of its oil supply while forces in Egypt would have been left dependent on desert tracks through neutral Iraq to Palestine, or from Mombasa via rail to southern Sudan and then an 1,800-mile journey to Cairo using river steamers and railways.[59] However, Italian naval forces sat in their ports without venturing to interfere with British shipping and in so doing ensured that the 'immense strategic asset of [Massawa], astride a vital sea route, had been neglected'.[60]

Deliberately encouraged by the British media, the military performance during the campaign, coming after the disasters that had already been suffered during Operation 'Compass', helped create an image of Italian incompetence. The public's general perception of the quality of its forces was made clear in mid-July 1941 in an anecdote repeated in *The Times*. By this stage Italian troops had assumed responsibility for the garrisoning of the conquered Greeks but they were widely treated with scorn by the populace, who said of them: 'This year the German army is to clean up Europe, in 1942 the German army will occupy Asia; in 1943 the German army will occupy the Americas; in 1944 the glorious Italian army will occupy Malta.'[61] It was very difficult to find anybody who was willing to say a positive word. One of those speaking in the House of Lords review that followed the capture of Addis Ababa did make some attempt, highlighting the defence of Keren where the Italians and their locally raised troops 'fought stubbornly and bravely in a series of counter attacks, all the time suffering heavy casualties'. Another of those present was prepared to give 'great credit' to them for their fighting qualities and remarked that on the retreats from Dessie and at Keren they had demonstrated some ability.[62] This brief speech noted that, 'although we might not have a very good opinion of the fighting qualities of the Italian forces, we must all of us realise what extraordinarily clever, astute and resourceful engineers and miners they are, especially in work connected with fortifications and demolition'. There was also praise for Aosta, who 'made a terrific effort to save the honour of his country so tarnished by the Dictator who calls the tune in Italy'.[63] With no real sense at this stage of just how close the battle for Keren had actually been, this was the extent of the appreciation that was offered.

Cunningham's military aide believed the offensive would not have been possible if the opponents had been German; and the Germans, he speculated, held the same opinion.[64] For the young Major Blewitt the war remained 'us against the Bosch [sic]' and he was actually quite correct in questioning the unity of the Axis alliance.[65] The German consul in Addis Ababa was interviewed by a South African intelligence officer in April 1941 as he moved through British Somaliland on the way to being evacuated back home.[66] Dr Strohm was described as 'Hitler's personal "man on the spot"' for Central and North Africa, who had been sent to the region by the authorities in Berlin to survey the post-war potential for immigration and settlement and the exploitation of the local economy by a victorious Nazi state. Strohm began a series of observations about what he had witnessed over the recent months by stating 'bluntly that "the Italians, although a

CONCLUSION

great cultural people, were the world's worst and most timid fighters'". He went on to put the defeat down to 'a lack of guts' and the inadequacies of their training and equipment. Following on from the initial defeats they had suffered, he believed that it was the ferocity of 'white troops on the native mind', the effective use of propaganda and the impact of British and Commonwealth armour which had combined so that 'once the "rot" had started it had a "snowball" effect and could not be checked'.

For the British Empire as a whole the victory was a huge morale boost as it struggled to fight on alone in the war against the previously dominant Axis. For Mussolini, defeat did more than cost him an empire: it also deprived him of a force of 300,000 men, 325 aircraft and 23 ships and submarines. The strategy Wavell employed, one born entirely of necessity, was certainly a triumph of improvisation, offensive spirit and, above all, the imaginative use of limited resources.[67] Whilst it has never been confirmed precisely who said it, one contemporary description of the campaign apparently involved a revision of the Churchillian flourish to 'Never have so many been defeated by so few.'[68] Once again this seemed to imply that there had been little in the way of a real challenge for the British and Commonwealth forces when this was not the case. Lord Croft, speaking in his conclusion to the House of Lords, accurately identified why there had not been a much greater response to such a tremendous victory.[69] As he put it, 'if our eyes had not been fixed on other great events our countrymen would have been full of pride and enthusiasm – as I am sure they are – at the success of these remarkable achievements'. Another of those present referenced in his review the actions at Kassala, Agordat, Massawa and Asmara, Mogadishu, Bardia, Gorai, Gojjam and Gondar, 'a string of names ... that will convey very little to most people'.[70] Yet, writing about the British Army and the Second World War more than forty years later, David Fraser, by this point a retired general and pre-eminent military historian, argued that, when compared to the outcome in the Western Desert, the successful campaign in East Africa 'was no less sensational in its results and more lasting in its consequences'.[71] It is just that it has remained largely forgotten, superseded by later victories that gained much more fame in British memory. The fact that the entry into Addis Ababa took place on the same day as the beginning of the German attacks that would ultimately lead to the disaster in Greece and Crete provides a clue as to why this might have been the case. It also helps to explain why the heroics of the British and Commonwealth forces that fought and won so decisively in East Africa remain largely overlooked in the vast narrative of the Second World War.

NOTES

Introduction: A Forgotten Campaign

1. 'Surrender Of Gondar', *The Times* (London), 29 November 1941; 'Gondar Victor is Only 46', *Daily Express* (London), 29 November 1941; '46, He Ends an African Empire', *Daily Mirror* (London), 29 November 1941.
2. 'Opinion – Going in Gondar', *Daily Express* (London), 29 November 1941.
3. 'King's Crisis', *Time*, 24 April 1939.
4. 'Notes on Operations in East Africa 11th February 1941–3rd July 1941' (Army Staff College), n.d., p. 1, JSCSC.
5. Major-General I.S.O. Playfair et al., *The Mediterranean and Middle East: Vol. I, The Early Successes against Italy (to May 1941)* [History of the Second World War: United Kingdom Military Series] (London: HMSO, 1954).
6. *La Guerra in Africa Orientale: Giugno 1940–Novembre 1941* (Roma: Ministero della difesa, Stato maggiore dell'esercito, Ufficio storico, 1952).
7. Brian Melland, 'The Campaign in East Africa', December 1970, CAB146/374, TNA.
8. Possibly the best known account remains Michael Glover, *An Improvised War: The Ethiopian Campaign, 1940–41* (New York: Hippocrene, 1987). Glover had served in the British Army during the war and wrote several military-themed books before his death in 1990.
9. *The Abyssinian Campaigns: The Official Story of the Conquest of Italian East Africa* (London: HMSO, 1942); W.E. Crosskill, *The Two Thousand Mile War* (London: Robert Hale, 1980); Kenneth Gandar Dower, *Abyssinian Patchwork* (London: Frederick Muller, 1949); Carel Birkby, *It's a Long Way to Addis* (London: Frederick Muller, 1942).
10. Gerhard L. Weinberg, *A World at Arms: A Global History of World War II* (Cambridge: Cambridge University Press, 1994), p. 211.
11. John Keegan, *The Second World War* (London: Hutchinson, 1989), p. 324.
12. John Terraine, *The Right of the Line: The Royal Air Force in the European War 1939–1945* (Suffolk: St Edmundsbury Press, 1985), p. 323.
13. Max Hastings, *Finest Years: Churchill as Warlord, 1940–1945* (London: Harper Press, 2009), p. 118; Andrew Roberts, *The Storm of War: A New History of the Second World War* (London: Penguin, 2010), p. 121; Williamson Murray, 'British Military Effectiveness in the Second World War', in Allan R. Millett and Williamson Murray (eds), *Military Effectiveness – Vol. III, The Second World War* (Cambridge: Cambridge University Press, 2010), p. 102.

14. James J. Sadkovich, 'Understanding Defeat: Reappraising Italy's Role in World War II', *Journal of Contemporary History* (Vol. 24, No. 1, Jan. 1989), p. 38.
15. For example Giorgio Rochat, *Le guerre italiane 1935–1943: Dall'impero d'Etiopia alla disfatta* (Torino: Einaudi, 2005) and Andrea Molinari, *La conquista dell'Impero: La guerra in Africa Orientale, 1935–1941* (Bresso: Hobby and Work Publishing, 2007).
16. Colonel Harry Latham to Philip Allen, 10 November 1943, CAB103/178, TNA.
17. It is not uncommon to see notes in books written previously on this subject making reference to the use of language within the text. Amharic, the Ethiopian language, is also Semitic and written in Ethiopic script and there are different ways of translating it into English. For the purposes of this study it became most obvious in terms of geographic locations and, reviewing the archival material, it is clear that there was often a struggle to agree upon a uniform usage, with variations to be found even in the same document. Without being able to offer a definitive answer to the competing claims, this book has instead sought to adopt a consistent approach which may, or may not, be considered entirely correct by all readers.
18. 'The East African Campaign – Compiled by the Indian Historical Section', comments by Lieutenant-Colonel J.E.B. Barton, 12 November 1954, J.E.B. Barton Papers, 7203–33–2, NAM.
19. 'Composition of macro geographical (continental) regions, geographical sub-regions, and selected economic and other groupings', *United Nations Statistics Division*, 31 October 2013, http://millenniumindicators.un.org/unsd/methods/m49/m49regin.htm [accessed 10 April 2016].

1: Strategic Miscalculation

1. 'The Special Official Gazette of the East Africa Protectorate' (Vol. XVI, No. 374, 5 Aug. 1914), pp. 823–826; Robert M. Maxon, *Struggle for Kenya: The Loss and Reassertion of Imperial Initiative, 1912–1923* (London: Associated University Presses, 1993), p. 79.
2. John Lonsdale, 'East Africa', in Judith Brown and Wm Roger Louis (eds), *The Oxford History of the British Empire: Vol. IV, The Twentieth Century* (Oxford: Oxford University Press, 1999), pp. 532–534; Nazifa Rashid, 'British Colonialism in East Africa During the Nineteenth Century', *IOSR Journal of Humanities and Social Science (IOSR–JHSS)* (Vol. 19, Issue 3, Mar. 2014), pp. 8–11; 'First World War – A Global View', TNA, www.nationalarchives.gov.uk/first-world-war/a-global-view/ [accessed 20 October 2015].
3. Roland Oliver and Anthony Atmore, *Africa Since 1800* (Cambridge: Cambridge University Press [Fifth Edition], 1994), p. 100.
4. Ibid., p. 107.
5. *Kenya Colony and Protectorate, 1936* (London: HMSO, 1937), pp. 3–4.
6. In addition, further to the south there were more British territories. In 1899, the British South Africa Company had received a royal charter to administer the territory which later became known as Northern Rhodesia, and twelve years later North Western and North Eastern Rhodesia were united under a single administration. This territory also shared a 150-mile north-east border with German East Africa and a shorter southern border with German South West Africa. Southern Rhodesia had become a British possession in 1888 and the British South Africa Company was set up to run the territory as a commercial venture. Ten years later the British High Commission for South Africa was given responsibility for its overall supervision. Nyasaland became another British Protectorate in 1893 and administrative control passed to the Colonial Office in 1904, after which it was governed as a Crown Colony.
7. Brigadier-General C.P. Fendall, *The East African Field Force 1915–1919* (London: H.F. and G. Witherby, 1921), pp. 15–22.

8. *Kenya Colony and Protectorate*, p. 4; Claude Lützelschwab, 'Colonial Settler Economies in Africa', *XIVth International Economic History Congress*, Helsinki, 21–25 August 2006, p. 4.
9. Sir Charles Eliot, *The East Africa Protectorate* (London: Edward Arnold, 1905), p. 303.
10. Fendall, *The East African Force*, p. 23.
11. Ross Anderson, *The Forgotten War 1914–18: The East African Campaign* (Stroud: Tempus Publishing, 2007), pp. 21–22; Lieutenant-Colonel Charles Hordern [from a draft by Major Henry FitzMaurice Stacke], *History of the Great War, Military Operations: East Africa, Vol. I, August 1914–September 1916* (London: Historical Section of the Committee of Imperial Defence, 1941).
12. Lieutenant-Colonel H. Moyse-Bartlett, *The King's African Rifles: A Study in the Military History of East and Central Africa, 1890–1945* (Aldershot: Gale and Polden, 1956), pp. 259–261.
13. Hordern, *History of the Great War*, pp. 18–30.
14. Edward Paice, *Tip and Run: The Untold Tragedy of the Great War in Africa* (London: Weidenfeld and Nicolson, 2007), pp. 29–30.
15. Anderson, *The Forgotten War 1914–18*, pp. 51–55; Moyse-Bartlett, *The King's African Rifles*, pp. 275–279.
16. Dan Whitaker, 'The Uncatchable Lizard', *History Today* (February 2013), pp. 29–35; William Weir, *Guerrilla Warfare: Irregular Warfare in the Twentieth Century* (Mechanicsburg, PA: Stackpole Books, 2008), pp. 46–58.
17. Major-General S.H. Sheppard, 'The East African Campaign, 1914–1916', *The Journal of the Royal United Service Institution* (Vol. 87, Issue 545, 1942), p. 71; Moyse-Bartlett, *The King's African Rifles*, pp. 259–415.
18. These included Francis Brett Young, *Marching on Tanga: With General Smuts in East Africa* (New York: E.P. Dutton, 1917) and several popular post-war accounts such as Fendall, *The East African Force, 1915–1919* and Christopher J. Thornhill, *Taking Tanganyika: Experiences of an Intelligence Officers, 1914–1918* (London: Stanley Paul & Co., 1937).
19. Ross Anderson, 'J.C. Smuts and J.L. van Deventer: South African Commanders-in-Chief of a British Expeditionary Force', *Scientia Militaria – South African Journal of Military Studies* (Vol. 31, No. 2, 2003), pp. 117–141.
20. Ian van der Waag, 'The Union Defence Force Between the Two World Wars, 1919–1939', *Scientia Militaria – South African Journal of Military Studies* (Vol. 30, No. 2, 2000), p. 184.
21. General Paul von Lettow-Vorbeck, *My Reminiscences of East Africa: The Campaign for German East Africa in World War One* (London: Hurst and Blackett, 1920), p. 325.
22. Bill Nasson, 'Africa', in Jay Winter (ed.), *The Cambridge History of the First World War: Vol. I, Global War* (Cambridge: Cambridge University Press, 2014), pp. 439–440.
23. Simon Ball, 'The Mediterranean and North Africa, 1940–1944', in John Ferris and Evan Mawdsley (eds), *The Cambridge History of the Second World War: Vol. I, Fighting the War* (Cambridge: Cambridge University Press, 2015), pp. 359–362.
24. Kevin Burley, *British Shipping and Australia 1920–1939* (Cambridge: Cambridge University Press, 1968), pp. 73–75; David Abulafia, *The Great Sea: A Human History of the Mediterranean* (Oxford: Oxford University Press, 2011), pp. 604–605; Correlli Barnett, *The Collapse of British Power* (London: Eyre Methuen, 1972), p. 9.
25. See, for example, 'Defence Loans Bill', House of Commons Debate, 27 February 1939, *Hansard*, Vol. 344, cc 927–1043.
26. 'Future Size of Our Regular Army – Memorandum by the Secretary of State for War', C.P.200 (23), 17 April 1923, pp. 1–14, CAB24/159, TNA.
27. George Kirk, *The Middle East in the War* [Survey of International Affairs 1939–1946] (London: Oxford University Press, 1952), p. 19.
28. Playfair et al., *The Mediterranean and Middle East: Vol. I*, pp. 5–6.
29. 'Meeting of the Cabinet' (Basis of Estimates), Cabinet 39(28), 18 July 1928, CAB23/58, TNA; Barnett, *The Collapse of British Power*, pp. 237–572.

30. Major-General W.H.A. Bishop to Barton, 3 November 1949, CAB106/910, TNA.
31. 'Obituary: Sir George Giffard', *The Times* (London), 19 November 1964; ibid., 'I.L.W. writes', 21 November 1964; ibid., 'C.R.A.S. writes', 26 November 1964.
32. Ibid., 'I.L.W. writes', 21 November 1964.
33. Colonel G.M. Orr (Retd.), 'The Future of Defence in Eastern Africa', *The Journal of the Royal United Service Institution* (Vol. 74, Issue 495, 1929), pp. 606–607.
34. Lützelschwab, 'Colonial Settler Economies in Africa', pp. 4–5.
35. Major Sir Humphrey Leggett, 'The British East African Territories and their Strategical Implications', *Journal of the Royal African Society* (Vol. 39, No. 156, July 1940), p. 203; Orr, 'The Future of Defence in Eastern Africa', p. 610.
36. Barnett, *The Collapse of British Power*, p. 125.
37. Ralph J. Bunche, 'The Land Equation in Kenya Colony: (As Seen by a Kikuyu Chief)', *The Journal of Negro History* (Vol. 24, No. 1, Jan. 1939), p. 34.
38. Ibid.
39. Bishop to Barton, 27 February 1950, CAB106/911, TNA. The officer in question was Charles Gwynn who, as a major-general, was later commandant of the Staff College at Camberley.
40. 'Memorandum by the Inspector General, The King's African Rifles on Defence of East Africa', 8 January 1928, CO820/3/10, TNA.
41. Christine Stephanie Nicholls, *Red Strangers: The White Tribe of Kenya* (London: Timewell Press, 2005), p. 215.
42. Bishop to Barton, 27 February 1950, CAB106/911, TNA.
43. Andrew Stewart, *Empire Lost: Britain, the Dominions and the Second World War* (London: Continuum, 2008), pp. 15–25.
44. Glover, *An Improvised War*, pp. 3–16.
45. Ibid., p. 3.
46. J.S., 'The Rise and Fall of the Italian African Empire', 21 January 1943, CAB106/404, TNA; 'Ethiopia: From Solomon to Haile Selassie', *The Listener*, 13 February 1941.
47. Glover, *An Improvised War*, p. 9.
48. G.M. Gathorne-Hardy, *A Short History of International Affairs 1920–1939* (London: Oxford University Press, 1950), p. 403.
49. Angelo Del Boca [trans. P.D. Cummins], *The Ethiopian War 1935–1941* (Chicago: University of Chicago Press, 1969), p. 12.
50. Major G.P. Wallace, 'Abyssinia', 17 October 1941, DO35/1001, TNA.
51. Winston S. Churchill, *The Second World War: Vol. I, The Gathering Storm* (London: Cassell & Co., 1948), p. 149.
52. Del Boca, *The Ethiopian War 1935–41*, p. 6; Lieutenant-Colonel A.C. Arnold, 'The Italo-Abyssinian Campaign, 1935–36', *The Journal of the Royal United Service Institution* (Vol. LXXXII, No. 525, 1937), pp. 71–75.
53. Churchill, *The Gathering Storm*, p. 149.
54. Robert Mallett, *Mussolini and the Origins of the Second World War, 1933–1940* (Basingstoke: Palgrave Macmillan, 2003), p. 9.
55. A.J. Barker, *The Civilizing Mission* (London: Cassell & Co., 1968), p. 64.
56. Ibid., pp. 62–63.
57. Richard Carrier, 'Blindness and Contingencies: Italian Failure in Ethiopia (1936–1940)', in Richard G. Davis (ed.), *The U.S. Army and Irregular Warfare* (Selected Papers from the 2007 Conference of Army Historians), pp. 107–110; Lieutenant-Colonel H. de Watteville, 'Italy and Abyssinia', *The Army Quarterly* (Vol. XXXI, No. 2, Jan. 1936), pp. 206–207.
58. Del Boca, *The Ethiopian War 1935–41*, p. 205; David Clay Large, 'Mussolini's "Civilising Mission"', *Military History Quarterly* (Vol. 5, No. 2, Winter 1993), pp. 44–53.
59. John Gooch, 'Re-conquest and Suppression: Fascist Italy's Pacification of Libya and Ethiopia, 1922–39', *The Journal of Strategic Studies* (Vol. 28, No. 6, 2005), p. 1022.

60. G.L. Steer, *Sealed and Delivered: A Book on the Abyssinian Campaign* (London: Faber and Faber, 2009), pp. vii–viii.
61. Lieutenant Commander Francesco Marino (Italian Navy), *Military Operations in the Italian East Africa, 1935–1941: Conquest and Defeat*, Master of Military Studies Paper, United States Marine Corps Command and Staff College, 2008, pp. 24–31.
62. Steer, *Sealed and Delivered*, pp. vi–ix.
63. James J. Sadkovich, 'Understanding Defeat: Reappraising Italy's Role in World War II', in Nick Smart (ed.), *The Second World War* (Aldershot: Ashgate Publishing, 2006), p. 379.
64. De Watteville, 'Italy and Abyssinia', p. 217.
65. Martin Gilbert, *The Churchill War Papers: At the Admiralty, Vol.I – September 1939–May 1940* (London: William Heineman, 1993), p. 402; 'Foreword to East African Campaign', n.d., CAB106/919, TNA.
66. Playfair et al., *The Mediterranean and Middle East: Vol. I*, pp. 23–26.
67. 'Report on a Conference held at Aden from 30th May to 3rd June 1939', WO201/248, TNA.
68. Sir Angus Gillan, 'The Importance of the Sudan', *The Listener*, 28 November 1940. He went on to explain how 'the various local tribesmen were good fighters, the Berberines from the north, the Arabs in the central zone and the Fuzzy Wuzzy to their east who wandered the Red Sea hills. These were practically all Moslems, Arabic speaking and semi-civilised. South of the latitude of 12 degrees was the area from which the Sudan took its name, the land of the blacks, tribes who were much more diverse, pagan, with different languages and less civilised in their customs.'
69. Andrew Stewart, 'The British Government and the 1938–1939 South African Neutrality Crisis', *English Historical Review* (Vol. CXXIII, No. 503, Aug. 2008), pp. 947–972.
70. Shula Marks, 'Southern Africa', in J.M. Brown and W.M. Roger Louis (eds), *The Oxford History of the British Empire: Vol. IV, The Twentieth Century* (Oxford: Oxford University Press, 1999), p. 545.
71. Eric Rosenthal, *The Fall of Italian East Africa* (London: Hutchinson, 1941), p. 8.
72. Ibid., p. 31.
73. N.H. Gibbs, *Grand Strategy: Vol. I – Rearmament Policy* [History of the Second World War – United Kingdom Military Series] (London: Her Majesty's Stationery Office, 1976), p. 665.

2: Hoping for the Best

1. Playfair et al., *The Mediterranean and Middle East: Vol. I*, pp. 31–32. In peacetime this officer was Inspector General of the Royal West African Frontier Force; it was only in war that he was to command the troops in East Africa.
2. Brian Bond, 'Ironside', in John Keegan (ed.), *Churchill's Generals* (London: Cassell & Co., 1991), p. 20; 'Life Goes Calling on Britain's General Ironside at Gibraltar', *Life*, 31 July 1939.
3. 'Obituary: Field Marshal Lord Wavell', *The Times* (London), 25 May 1950; Ian Beckett, 'Wavell', in Keegan (ed.), *Churchill's Generals*, pp. 70–88; Nick Smart, *Biographical Dictionary of British Generals of the Second World War* (Barnsley: Pen and Sword, 2005), pp. 324–326.
4. Robert Woollcombe, *The Campaigns of Wavell 1939–1943* (London: Cassell & Co., 1959), p. 1.
5. Heath to Barton, 24 August 1946, CAB106/905, TNA.
6. Crosskill, *The Two Thousand Mile War*, p. 79.
7. Comments by Major-General R.J. Collins, 24 August 1945, CAB106/904, TNA.
8. Major H.A. De Weerd, *Great Soldiers of the Second World War* (London: Robert Hale, 1946), p. 53.

9. Adrian Fort, *Archibald Wavell: The Life and Times of an Imperial Servant* (London: Jonathan Cape, 2009), pp. 176–177.
10. Alan Moorehead, *African Trilogy* (London: Hamish Hamilton, 1944), p. 22.
11. Denise Richards, *Royal Air Force 1939–1945, Vol. I* (London: HMSO, 1974), p. 249.
12. William Jackson, *The North African Campaign 1940–43* (London: Batsford, 1975), p. 24.
13. Wavell to Mitchell, 5 August 1939, WO201/246, TNA.
14. Wavell to Gort, 10 August 1940, WO201/248, TNA.
15. Headquarters, Royal Air Force, Middle East to Wavell, 12 August 1940, WO201/246, TNA.
16. Ibid., A.H.Q. Aden to H.Q.M.E. (r) A.S.O. Khartoum, 1 September 1939.
17. Playfair et al., *The Mediterranean and Middle East: Vol. I*, p. 41.
18. 'The Fox and the Prince', *Toronto Daily Star*, 13 February 1941; 'Aosta on Alag?', *Time*, 2 June 1941.
19. 'Report on the visit of Lt-Col. A.R. Chater DSO, Officer Commanding, Somaliland Camel Corps to Italian Somaliland and Ethiopia – March 1938', n.d., WO201/247, TNA.
20. Winston S. Churchill, *The Second World War: Vol. III, The Grand Alliance* (London: Cassell & Co., 1950), p. 82.
21. 'Notes on Operations against Italian East Africa by G.O.C. in C. M.E.', 3 October 1939, WO201/246, TNA.
22. Playfair et al., *The Mediterranean and Middle East: Vol. I*, pp. 93, 165.
23. 'Abyssinia on the Verge of Revolt', *The War Illustrated*, 31 January 1941; Barton (with handwritten notes by Fabin), 'Note on Rise of Patriot Movement', 11 July 1945, CAB106/904, TNA.
24. Christine Sandford, *Ethiopia Under Haile Selassie* (London: Dent, 1946), pp. 94, 104; Christine Sandford, *The Lion of Judah Hath Prevailed* (London; J.M. Dent & Sons, 1955), pp. 85–86; Steer, *Sealed and Delivered*, pp. 8–9.
25. 'Report on the visit of Lt-Col. A.R. Chater DSO . . .', n.d., WO201/247, TNA.
26. A.P. Wavell, 'The Training of the Army for War', *RUSI Journal* (Vol. 78, Issue 510, 1933), p. 258.
27. Playfair et al., *The Mediterranean and Middle East: Vol. I*, p. 182.
28. 'Britain and Italy', *The Times* (London), 18 April 1938.
29. Wavell, 'Operations in East Africa, November 1940–July 1941', p. 3528.
30. Aregawi Berhe, 'Revisiting Resistance in Italian-occupied Ethiopia: The Patriots Movement (1936–1941) and the Redefinition of Post War Ethiopia', in J. Abbink, M.D. Brujin and K. Walraven (eds), *Rethinking Resistance: Revolt and Violence in African History* (Netherlands; Koninklije, 2003), p. 90.
31. M.O.1 (Records), 'East Africa – The Sudan – Somaliland, September 1939 – January 1943', n.d., WO106/2337B, TNA.
32. Ibid., 'For Consideration by Joint Planning Staff – Operations against Italy in Libya and I.E.A.', 13 October 1939.
33. Ibid., 'Extract from letter from Major-General Dewing', 17 October 1939.
34. Smart, *Biographical Dictionary of British Generals of the Second World War*, pp. 117–118. He soon returned in June 1940 to head the newly created West Africa Command where he did a remarkable job, but he remains 'probably the least known of all British generals who held high command in the Second World War'.
35. He was another officer who received only brief mention in post-war accounts as a result of his early death in 1949, which left him unable to contribute to these histories; 'Obituary: Major-General D.P. Dickinson', *The Times* (London), 12 January 1949.
36. Provincial Commissioner, Nyanza, 'History of the War – Nyanza Province, First 3 Months', 9 March 1940, History of the War – PC/NZA/2/3/61, KNADS; Bishop to Barton, 27 February 1950, CAB106/911, TNA. Another account notes that he was initially assigned a small hut at Egerton School without a clerk or even a typewriter.

37. Bishop to Barton, 3 November 1949, CAB106/910, TNA; Major-General D.P. Dickinson, 'East Africa Forces Report', 31 December 1939, p. 4, WO106/2335, TNA.
38. Bishop to Barton, 27 February 1950, CAB106/911, TNA.
39. 'History of the War – Summary of the more important events, decisions etc. during September, October and November 1939 in the Northern Frontier District', R.G. Turnbull (Officer-in-Charge, N.F.D), 26 January 1940, PC/NFD4/1/11, KNADS; Charles Chevenix Trench, *Men Who Ruled Kenya: The Kenya Administration, 1892–1963* (London: The Radcliffe Press, 1993), pp. 152–153.
40. Bishop to Barton, 3 November 1949, CAB106/910, TNA.
41. David Killingray and Richard Rathbone (eds), *Africa and the Second World War* (Basingstoke: Macmillan Press, 1986), p. 26.
42. 'Draft Notes on Administrative Aspect – Additions resulting from Brigadier Martin's notes', n.d., CAB106/910, TNA.
43. Bishop to Barton, 3 November 1949, CAB106/910, TNA.
44. 'Draft Notes on Administrative Aspect . . . ', CAB106/910, TNA.
45. Major-General Sir Alec Bishop, 'Look Back with Pleasure, Vol. 1', n.d., p. 60, LHCMA. Bishop only remained in Kenya until March 1940, when he inadvertently trod on one of the homemade anti-tank mines and was lucky only to suffer a serious foot injury, but the result was that he was next posted to London, where he served in the War Cabinet Secretariat.
46. Bishop to Barton, 27 February 1950, CAB106/911, TNA; Bishop, 'Look Back with Pleasure, Vol. 1', p. 60, LHCMA.
47. 'Obituary: Fallen Officers', *The Times* (London), 20 July 1940. The brief obituary did not offer any further details of his death other than that he was 'killed in action'.
48. 'East African Defence', *Cape Argus* (Cape Town), 2 November 1939.
49. Captain R.E.R. Smallwood, 'Developing the KAR', *The Army Quarterly* (Vol. XLIX, No. 2, Jan. 1945), p. 215.
50. M.O.1 (Records), 'East Africa . . .', n.d., WO106/2337B, TNA.
51. Ibid., p. 214.
52. Troopers to Kaid, Khartoum, 18 August 1939, WO201/248, TNA.
53. Dickinson, 'East Africa Forces Report', 31 December 1939, p. 8, WO106/2335, TNA.
54. 'Force Headquarters, Intelligence Summary No.5 – Disposition of Troops', 25 October 1939, Military Intelligence Report and Survey 1938–1939, DC/LDW/2/18/4, KNADS.
55. It had been the only place along the whole border where the British had a foothold in the Abyssinian highlands, the result of the Greek trader who had previously established a post there always having flown the Union Jack to impress the locals; 'The Role of British Forces in Africa', Lieutenant-Colonel Thomas Leahy (2nd Battalion, King's African Rifles), Box 10, No. 163, MSS.Afr.s.1715, ODRP.
56. W.D. Draffan and T.C.C. Lewin, *A War Journal of the Fifth (Kenya) Battalion* (Uckfield, East Sussex: The Naval and Military Press, 2007), pp. 7–9.
57. J.F. Macdonald, *Lion with Tusk Guardant* (Salisbury: The Rhodesian Printing and Publishing Co., 1945), p. 60.
58. The wells were reputed to have been drilled through the limestone by a race of giants when the world began; John Pitt, ''Adui Mbele (Enemy in Front) – Some Recollections of a Platoon Commander in the East African Campaign (1940–1941) and on Brigade Staff in Madagascar (1942–43)', p. 17, John Pitt Papers, 89/1/1, IWM.
59. 'Force Headquarters Intelligence Summary No. 3 – Disposition of Troops', 20 September 1939, Military Intelligence Report and Survey 1938–1939, DC/LDW/2/18/4, KNADS.
60. 'History of the War, N.F.D., Period 1st December 1939 to 28th February 1940', Gerald Reece (Officer-in-Charge, N.F.D.), PC/NFD4/1/11, KNADS.
61. Glover, *An Improvised War*, p. 15.

62. Del Boca, *The Ethiopian War 1935–1941*, p. 4.
63. 'Force Headquarters Intelligence Summary No.5 – Disposition of Troops', 25 October 1939, Kenyan Archives, Military Intelligence Report and Survey 1938–1939, DC/LDW/2/18/4, KNADS.
64. 'Chapter "H" – Comments by Major-General G.C. Fowkes', n.d. [1950], CAB106/912, TNA; 'Gondar Victor is Only 46', *Daily Express* (London), 29 November 1941.
65. COS(39) 137 (J.P), 28 November 1939, cited in M.O.1 (Records), 'East Africa . . .', n.d., WO106/2337B, TNA.
66. Major-General W. Platt, 'Appreciation of the situation in the Sudan with special reference to a possible war with Italy', September 1939, WO201/252, TNA.
67. Gillan, 'The Importance of the Sudan', *The Listener*, 28 November 1940.
68. 'For Consideration by Joint Planning Staff – Operations against Italy in Libya and I.E.A.', 13 October 1939, WO201/246, TNA.
69. 'Obituary: General Sir William Platt', *The Times* (London), 29 September 1975; Smart, *Biographical Dictionary of British Generals of the Second World War*, p. 252.
70. Platt, 'Appreciation of the situation in the Sudan . . .', September 1939, WO201/252, TNA.
71. 'Allied Policy in Italian East Africa – Reply to French General Staff', 2 November 1939, WO201/250, TNA.
72. Wavell to Dill, 7 January 1940, Wavell Papers, AW.
73. Bishop to Barton, 3 November 1949, CAB106/910, TNA.
74. Troopers to Kaid Khartoum, 18 August 1939, WO201/248, TNA.
75. Force Nairobi to Mideast Cairo, 14 October 1939, WO201/2675, TNA; ibid., Kaid Khartoum to Troopers, 8 October 1939.
76. Ibid., Group Captain H.E. Wrigglesworth to Brigadier A.F. Smith, 7 August 1939.
77. Ibid., Calder (Colonial Office) to Under Secretary of State for Foreign Affairs, 17 May 1939.
78. Ibid., Wrigglesworth to Smith, 7 August 1939; Smith to Wrigglesworth, 10 August 1939.
79. Ibid., Troopers (London) to Mideast, 29 September 1939.
80. Ibid., Troopers to Nairobi, Kaduna, Accra, Mideast, 21 December 1939.
81. Ibid., 'Move of West African Troops to East Africa', n.d.; 'The Role of British Forces in Africa', Lieutenant-Colonel Jack T. Ennals (3 Nigerian Regiment, Royal West African Frontier Force), Box 3, No. 139, MSS. Afr.s.1734, ODRP.
82. 'North Rhodesian Troops are in East Africa, *Rand Daily Mail* (Johannesburg), 21 December 1939; W.V. Brelsford (ed.), *The Story of the Northern Rhodesia Regiment* (Bromley, Kent: Galago [Second Edition], 1994), p. 76.
83. 'Troops in 2,000-mile bus trek', *Daily Mirror* (London), 5 March 1940.
84. Dickinson, 'East Africa Force Report', 31 December 1939, p. 10, WO106/2335, TNA.
85. 'Empire and the War', November 1939, DO35/99/24/3, TNA; Stewart, 'The British Government and the 1938–1939 South African Neutrality Crisis', pp. 947–972.
86. Minute by Cabinet Office, 15 December 1939; CAB21/883, TNA; ibid., minute by Anthony Eden, 7 December 1939.
87. 'Notes on Lieutenant-Colonel Bishop's Visit to South Africa', 5 January 1940, DO35/1003, TNA.
88. 'The Leadership of Smuts', *The Times* (London) 23 January 1940; Clark to Dominions Office, 7 February 1940, DO35/1003, TNA.
89. 'Diary', Brigadier Dudley Clarke Papers, pp. 55–57, DWC1/4, IWM.
90. Ibid., Bishop to Barton, 3 November 1949.
91. 'Draft Notes on Administrative Aspect – Additions resulting from Brigadier Martin's notes', n.d., CAB106/910, TNA.
92. 'Raids and Border Incidents on the Borders of Kenya', July 1958, p. 24, DC/150/2/5/4, KNADS.
93. Dickinson, 'East Africa Force Report', 31 December 1939, p. 11, WO106/2335, TNA.

94. Glover, *An Improvised War*, p. 16.
95. Ibid., p. 17.
96. Dominions Office (London) to High Commissioner (Pretoria), 27 April 1940, DO35/1008, TNA; ibid., minute by Pritchard, 2 May 1940.
97. 'Italy in Arms', *Time*, 24 June 1940.
98. John Gooch, 'Mussolini's Strategy, 1939–1943', in Ferris and Mawdsley (eds), *The Cambridge History of the Second World War: Vol. I*, pp. 157–158.
99. Marc' Antonio Bragadin, *The Italian Navy in World War II* (Annapolis, MD: Naval Institute Press, 1957), p. 6.
100. Playfair et al., *The Mediterranean and Middle East: Vol. I*, p. 28; J.R.M. Butler, *Grand Strategy – Vol. II, September 1939–June 1941* (London: HMSO, 1957), p. 189.
101. 'Daily Summary No. 255', 15 May 1940, WO106/2139, TNA; ibid., 'Weekly Summary No. 39', 16 May 1940.
102. Ibid., 'Daily Summary, No. 259', 19 May 1940; 'Daily Summary, No. 262', 22 May 1940.
103. 'Conscription in Uganda', *Rand Daily Mail* (Johannesburg), 22 May 1940.

3: War Comes to East Africa

1. 'The Role of British Forces in Africa', Lieutenant-Colonel Jack T. Ennals (3 Nigerian Regiment, Royal West African Frontier Force), Box 3, No.139, MSS. Afr.s.1734, ODRP.
2. Bishop to Barton, 3 November 1949, CAB106/910, TNA.
3. 'The Role of British Forces in Africa', Major Ernest C. Lanning (3 Gold Coast Regiment, Royal West African Frontier Force), Box 7, No. 258, MSS.Afr.s.1734, ODRP.
4. Prior to the war the men had not worn boots, and even with this new piece of equipment it took a while to become accepted. Battalions from the KAR were often seen going on route marches with the troops carrying the boots hung around their necks. Tin helmets were only issued to them later when they went to Burma; 'The Role of British Forces in Africa', Lanning, ODRP.
5. Bishop to Barton, 3 November 1949, CAB106/910, TNA; C.R.A.S. (?), 'Obituary: Sir George Giffard', *The Times* (London), 26 November 1964.
6. 'The Memoirs of Brigadier L.F. Field CB CBE' ('That's The Way It Was'), n.d., pp. 150–151, L.F. Field Papers, 10972, IWM.
7. Victoria Schofield, *Wavell: Soldier and Statesman* (London: John Murray, 2007), pp. 139–140.
8. Clark to Dominions Office, 20 March 1940, DO35/1008, TNA.
9. Wavell to Cunningham, 22 January 1941, Alan Cunningham Papers, 8303–104–7, NAM.
10. Winston S. Churchill, *The Second World War: Vol. II, Their Finest Hour* (London: Cassell & Co., 1949), pp. 755–756.
11. Schofield, *Wavell: Soldier and Statesman*, p. 139; High Commissioner (Pretoria) to Dominions Office, 17 April 1940, DO35/1008, TNA.
12. Brooke-Popham to Air Vice Marshal McKean, 8 May 1940, Robert Brooke-Popham Papers, IV/5/11, LHCMA.
13. Brooke-Popham to Street, 15 May 1940, IV/4/6, LHCMA.
14. 'Italy in Arms', *Time*, 24 June 1940.
15. Crosskill, *The Two Thousand Mile War*, p. 64; A.J. Barker, *Eritrea 1941* (London: Faber and Faber, 1957), p. 19.
16. Alberto Sbacchi, 'Haile Selassie and the Italians 1941–1943', *African Studies Review* (Vol. 22, No. 1, Apr. 1979), p. 26.
17. Cited in Kirk, *The Middle East in the War*, p. 42.
18. Barker, *Eritrea 1941*, p. 206.
19. Woollcombe, *The Campaigns of Wavell 1939–1943*, p. 12.

20. John Connell, *Wavell: Scholar and Solider* (London: Collins, 1964), p. 234.
21. Melland to Friedrichsen, 26 July 1950, CAB146/374, TNA.
22. This constituted just slightly in excess of 3 per cent of the total available manpower, the vast majority of which was at this point gathering for the anticipated defence of Britain; Sadkovich, 'Understanding Defeat: Reappraising Italy's Role in World War II', in Smart (ed.), *The Second World War*, p. 389; 'Strength of Troops (fighting) – British and British Empire', 1 July 1940, Lord Nuffield Papers, G510/18, NC.
23. Captain S.W. Roskill, *The Navy at War 1939–1945* (London: Collins Clear-Type Press, 1960), p. 102.
24. Jackson, *The North African Campaign 1940–43*, pp. 28–29.
25. 'America Begins To Act', *The Times* (London), 12 June 1940.
26. Diary, 23 March 1940, in Malcolm Muggeridge (ed.), *Ciano's Diary, 1939–1943* (London: William Heinemann, 1947), p. 225.
27. D.B.H. Grobbelaar, 'Report on Interview with German Consul to Italian East Africa – Dr Strohm – at Hargeisha – British Somaliland on or about 15 Apr 41', n.d., NAREP EA1, NARS.
28. The rarely consulted but excellent German general 'history' of the Second World War can offer only two dedicated paragraphs across its several volumes which give a difficult-to-recognise view of what actually happened: Gerhard Schreiber et al., *Germany and the Second World War: Vol. III, The Mediterranean, South-East Europe and North Africa, 1939–1941 – From Italy's Declaration of Non-Belligerence to the Entry of the United States into the War* (Oxford: Clarendon Press, 1995), pp. 651, 653.
29. 'Italy in Arms', *Time*, 24 June 1940.
30. 'Directive on the Kenya front – Viceroy to General Gazzera', 27 July 1940, CAB146/374, TNA. Captured Italian documents were translated by Jean Hamilton in May 1950 as part of her work for General Playfair and the British official history; Melland to Friedrichsen, 18 September 1956, CAB146/374, TNA.
31. James Ambrose Brown, *The War of a Hundred Days: Springboks in Somalia and Abyssinia 1940–41* (Johannesburg: Ashanti Publishing, 1990), p. 54.
32. Playfair et al., *The Mediterranean and Middle East: Vol. I*, p. 448.
33. Andrew Stewart, 'The Battle for Britain', *History Today* (Vol. 65, Issue 6, June 2015), pp. 19–26.
34. Diary, Monday 10 June 1940, David Dilks (ed.), *The Diaries of Sir Alexander Cadogan, 1938–1945* (London: Cassell & Co., 1971), p. 296.
35. Glover, *An Improvised War*, p. 1.
36. Major-General H. Rowan-Robinson, 'The Italian Failures', *The Journal of the Royal United Service Institution* (Vol. LXXXVI, No. 542, May 1941), pp. 304–330.
37. Colonel R.H. Beadon, 'Italy as an Ally', *The Journal of the Royal United Service Institution* (Vol. LXXXV, No. 539, Aug. 1940), pp. 491–492.
38. Trench, *Men Who Ruled Kenya*, p. 156.
39. 'An Account of Operations at Moyale', n.d., Conf. 3620, JSCSC.
40. 'Daily Intelligence Summary No. 4', 14 June 1940, Military Intelligence Reports 1940–1941, DC/MBT/3/4/2, KNADS.
41. 'Latest Communiques', *Daily Express*, 14 June 1940.
42. 'East African Force Headquarters, Daily Intelligence Summary No. 7', 18/19 June 1940, Military Intelligence Reports 1940–1941, DC/MBT/3/4/2, KNADS; 'Raids and Border Incidents on the Borders of Kenya', July 1958, p. 24, DC/150/2/5/4, KNADS.
43. Brigadier C.C. Fowkes, '2nd East African Infantry Brigade – Some Notes on Preliminary Operations', 20 June 1940, WO276/490, TNA.
44. 'Daily Summary No. 371', 8 September 1940, WO106/2139, TNA.
45. MEIS 59, 18 July 1940, CAB106/954, TNA; EA 8, 11 July 1940, TNA.
46. 'An Account of Operations at Moyale', n.d., JSCSC.

47. 'Moyale's Union Jack is Still Flying . . .', *Daily Express*, 15 July 1940; 'Crept Past Enemy in Socks', *Daily Mirror*, 3 September 1940.
48. 'Diary, 1KAR (Dobel)', 15 July 1940, CAB106/954, TNA.
49. 'Comments by Major-General C.C. Fowkes – Chapter H', n.d. (1950), CAB106/912, TNA.
50. Ibid.
51. Trench, *Men Who Ruled Kenya*, pp. 154–155.
52. 'British Order of Battle and Locations, 10 June 1940', n.d., CAB106/903, TNA.
53. Ibid., Colonel A.D.G. Orr to Barton, 6 October 1944.
54. Ron Laurie to John Orlebar, 6 March 1984, John Orlebar Papers, 740/9/8-9, DSA.
55. 'Daily Summary No. 309', 8 July 1940, WO106/2139, TNA.
56. Playfair et al., *The Mediterranean and Middle East: Vol. I*, p. 392.
57. 'Daily Summary No. 306', 5 July 1940, WO106/2139, TNA; Sir Arthur Longmore, *From Sea to Sky 1910–1945* (London: Geoffrey Bles, 1946), p. 271; 'Gash Area', n.d., CAB106/903, TNA.
58. Gillan, 'The Importance of the Sudan', *The Listener*, 28 November 1940.
59. Peter Upcher, 'As different as chalk from cheese', n.d., Orlebar Papers, 740/8/50-53, DSA.
60. 'Weekly Commentary No. 47', 11 July 1940, WO106/2139, TNA.
61. Ibid., 'Weekly Commentary No. 48', 18 July 1940.
62. H.B. Kittermaster, 'British Somaliland', *Journal of the Royal African Society* (Vol. 27, No. 108, July 1928), pp. 329–337; John Parkinson, 'Customs in Western British Somaliland', *Journal of the Royal African Society* (Vol. 35, No. 140, July 1936), pp. 241–245; Brock Millman, *British Somaliland: An Administrative History, 1920–1960* (Abingdon: Routledge, 2014), pp. 109–116.
63. Donald Cowie, *War for Britain: The Inner Story of the Empire in Action: First Part, September 1939 to September 1940* (London: Chapman & Hall, 1941), p. 196.
64. Cowie, *War for Britain*, p. 196.
65. Winston Churchill (Home Office) to King Edward VII, 28 April 1910, Chartwell Papers, CHAR12/15/68–69, CAC.
66. Douglas Jardine, *The Mad Mullah of Somaliland* (London: Herbert Jenkins, 1923), pp. 156–196.
67. Charles Lucas, *The Empire at War: Vol. IV, Africa* (London: Oxford University Press, 1926), pp. 565–568.
68. Major-General A.C. Duff, ' "Q" in the East African Campaign, 1941: A Second Episode', *The Royal Engineers Journal* (Vol. LVII, 1943), p. 163.
69. 'Notes for GOC-in-C for his Visit . . .', n.d. (January 1940?), WO201/250, TNA; Captain G.C. Foster, 'British Somaliland', n.d., pp. 66–67, CAB44/160, TNA.
70. Minute by A.J. Dawe, 21 November 1940, CO535/136/24, TNA.
71. 'War Committee, Memorandum by the DCIGS – Defence and Administration of British Somaliland', 30 January 1940, WO201/256, TNA.
72. 'Notes for GOC-in-C for his Visit . . .', n.d. (January 1940?), WO201/250, TNA; Glenday to Smith, 16 January 1940, WO201/256, TNA.
73. Ibid., Lawrence to Secretary of State for the Colonies, 13 October 1938.
74. Ibid.
75. Thurburn to DQMG, 17 June 1940, WO201/263, TNA.
76. 'Proposed Amendment to Secret Supplement to the Somaliland Protectorate Defence Scheme 1939', 5 August 1939, WO201/249, TNA.
77. Lieutenant-Colonel Arthur Chater to Brigadier A.F. Smith, 28 September 1939, WO201/247, TNA.
78. Ibid.
79. 'Notes on the Employment of "B" Company, Somaliland Camel Corps', n.d., CAB106/905, TNA; ibid., Nixon to Barton, 6 November 1946.

80. Chater to Smith, 28 September 1939, WO201/247, TNA.
81. GOC-in-C to DCIGS, 18 November 1939, WO201/250, TNA.
82. Ibid., 'Notes for GOC-in-C for his Visit to British Somaliland and Jibuti', n.d. (January 1940?).
83. 'War Committee, Memorandum by the DCIGS . . .', 30 January 1940, WO201/256, TNA.
84. H.L. d'A. Hopkinson (War Cabinet Offices) to F.O. Lee (Colonial Office), 13 October 1939, CAB21/2605, TNA; 'Conversation with D.M.O.', 28 December 1939, WO201/256, TNA; 'Notes for GOC-in-C for his Visit . . .', n.d. (January 1940?), WO201/250, TNA.
85. 'Minutes of a Meeting held at Sheikh, Somaliland Protectorate, on Tuesday 9th January 1940 to discuss the new defence policy of the protectorate', n.d., WO201/250, TNA; Wavell to Dill, 15 January 1940, WO201/2212, TNA; 'War Committee, Memorandum by the DCIGS . . .', 30 January 1940, WO201/256, TNA; Harold E. Raugh Jr., *Wavell in the Middle East, 1939–1941: A Study in Generalship* (London: Brassey's, 1993), p. 76.
86. 'Somaliland Camel Corps', 25 January 1940, WO201/2268, TNA.
87. 'Note on a conversation with Col. Chater', 24 January 1940, WO201/256, TNA.
88. Ibid., Chater to Smith, 10 March 1940; Chater to Smith, 21 March 1940. A review in April discovered that the ammunition was in fact not designed for the single loader rifles and a query went to the Cairo offices of Imperial Chemical Industries to see if they would be able to produce a replacement; General Headquarters to Imperial Chemical House, 6 April 1940.
89. John Kent, 'Funga Safari', 79/27/1, IWM.
90. Eric Moore Ritchie, 'The Land of Lost Tribes', *The Listener*, 15 August 1940, pp. 221–222.
91. 'Notes of a Tour to British Somaliland and French Somaliland by GOC-in-C Middle East, from 8th to 13th January 1940', 20 January 1940, WO201/250, TNA; Wavell to Legentilhomme, 25 January 1940, WO201/256, TNA.
92. 'Notes of a Tour . . .', 20 January 1940, WO201/250, TNA.
93. Ibid., MEIC to General Headquarters, Middle East, 5 January 1940.
94. 'British Somaliland – A/Q Questions', 4 April 1940, WO201/2212, TNA.
95. Wavell to Major-General F.G. Beaumont-Nesbitt (Director of Military Intelligence), 22 January 1940, WO201/250, TNA.
96. Chater to Smith, 10 March 1940, WO201/256, TNA.
97. 'MEIC – British Somaliland', 10/11 January 1940, WO201/250, TNA.
98. 'Notes for Middle East Liaison Officer – General Wavell's Proposals as to Somaliland', 23 February 1940, WO201/256, TNA.
99. Ibid., Glenday to Colonial Office, 18 March 1940.
100. Ibid., Chater to Arthur Smith, 21 March 1940.
101. Ibid., Chater to Smith, 10 December 1939.
102. 'Extract from report on Visit by Colonel J.K. Edwards to Aden, British and French Somaliland', n.d. (28 May 1940?), WO201/257, TNA. He was subsequently promoted to major-general and retired in 1947.
103. Ibid.
104. Glenday to Secretary of State for the Colonies, 22 May 1940, CAB21/2605, TNA.
105. Legentilhomme to AVM Reid, 31 May 1940, WO201/255, TNA.
106. 'War Cabinet – Plans to Meet a Certain Eventuality: French Colonial Empire and Mandated Territories', WP(4) 207, 15 June 1940, p. 5, CAB66/8, TNA.
107. Crosskill, *The Two Thousand Mile War*, p. 64.
108. Wavell to Chater, 8 July 1940, WO201/257, TNA.
109. 'Notes on Visit of Lieut.-Colonel Price to Somaliland 10–12 July, 1940', 16 July 1940, WO201/259, TNA.
110. 'War Cabinet – Implications of French Hostility', WP(40) 256, 16 July 1940, pp. 3, 12, CAB66/9, TNA.

4: Imperial Defeat: The Surrender of British Somaliland

1. 'Italy's Columns Invade British Somaliland', *The War Illustrated* (London), 16 August 1940.
2. 'Southern Theatre: War Without Water', *Time*, 19 August 1940.
3. Margery Perham, 'The Somaliland Campaign', *The Times* (London), 19 August 1940.
4. 'The British in Somaliland', *Manchester Guardian*, 12 August 1940; Moyse-Bartlett, *The King's African Rifles*, pp. 419–433.
5. Crosskill, *The TwoThousand Mile War*, p. 71.
6. 'Notes on the Employment of "B" Company . . .', n.d., CAB106/905, TNA; ibid., Nixon to Barton, 6 November 1946; '800 Britons Hold Up 10,000 Italian Troops', *Daily Mirror* (London), 28 November 1940; Moyse-Bartlett, *The King's African Rifles*, pp. 494–503.
7. 'Extract from report on Visit by Colonel J.K. Edwards . . .', n.d. (28 May 1940?), WO201/257, TNA.
8. Ibid., Chater to Smith, 1 June 1940.
9. 'Notes on the Employment of "B" Company . . .', n.d., CAB106/905, TNA; ibid., Nixon to Barton, 6 November 1946.
10. 'Notes of a Tour to British Somaliland and French Somaliland . . .', 20 January 1940, WO201/250, TNA.
11. 'Artillery Appreciation on the Defensive Position at Tug Argan Gap', 24 March 1940, WO201/251, TNA.
12. Within this total there were fewer than 200 officers; 'Fighting strength by cable from Somaliland', 5 August 1940, WO201/270, TNA.
13. 'Strength of Troops (fighting) – British and British Empire', 1 July 1940, Nuffield Papers, G510/18, NC.
14. Major John Birkbeck to Barton, 9 June 1947, CAB106/906, TNA.
15. Ibid. Edwards ordered the work to begin at once. He left an experienced engineer with Chater to provide assistance although he also believed that additional skilled men were needed.
16. 'Notes on conversation between Brigadier Chater and Governor British Somaliland', 20 July 1940, WO201/259, TNA.
17. 'The Capture of British Somaliland', May 1950, Enemy Documents Section, p. 26, CAB146/160, TNA.
18. 'Translation – Notes on Italian Conquest of British Somaliland', n.d., CAB106/919, TNA.
19. 'Daily Summary No. 337', 5 August 1940, WO106/2139, TNA.
20. 'Situation Report No. 3776', Somaliforce, 6 August 1940, WO201/270, TNA.
21. 'The Italian Invasion of British Somaliland, August 1940', 23 September 1940, WO106/2336, TNA.
22. Ibid.; 'Italian Advance in Somaliland', *The Times* (London), 8 August 1940.
23. 'Obstacles before the Italians', *Manchester Guardian*, 7 August 1940; 'Invasion of British Somaliland', *Manchester Guardian*, 7 August 1940; 'Italy Invades British Somaliland', *The Times* (London), 7 August 1940.
24. 'African War Zones – The Somaliland Scene', *The Times* (London), 8 August 1940; Brigadier-General John Charteris, 'Difficult Campaigning Conditions', *Manchester Guardian*, 8 August 1940.
25. 'The Red Sea Approaches', *Manchester Guardian*, 9 August 1940.
26. 'Situation Report No. 58', Somaliforce, 7 August 1940, WO201/270, TNA.
27. Ibid., Air HQ Aden to Air Ministry London, 5 August 1940.
28. Ibid., Air Headquarters, Aden to Air Ministry, London, 9 August 1940.
29. Ibid., 'Situation Report No. 3852', Somaliforce, 8 August 1940.
30. Ibid., 'Situation Report, No. 3878', Somalilforce, 10 August 1940; Somaliforce to Mideast, No. 3960, 13 August 1940.
31. Ibid., Somaliforce to Mideast, No. 3983, 14 August 1940.

32. Playfair et al., *The Mediterranean and Middle East: Vol. I*, p. 178.
33. HMAS *Hobart* to SNO Red Sea, 8 August 1940, MP1185/8, 1810/2/234, NAA.
34. 'Italians Move On Again', *Manchester Guardian*, 10 August 1940; 'Italians Advance in Somaliland', *The Times* (London), 10 August 1940.
35. Glenday to Godwin-Austin, 15 August 1940, Godwin-Austen 5, LHCMA.
36. 'Notes on the Employment of "B" Company . . .', n.d., CAB106/905, TNA; ibid., Nixon to Barton, 6 November 1946.
37. Mideast to AHQ Aden, 9 August 1940, WO201/270, TNA; ibid., 'Situation Report, No. 3906', Somaliforce, 10 August 1940.
38. Colonel Reggie Price to Barton, 25 March 1947, CAB106/906, TNA.
39. Mideast to Troopers, 10 August 1940, WO201/270, TNA; ibid., Troopers to Mideast, 13 August 1940; ibid., Mideast to Troopers, 13 August 1940.
40. Ibid., 'Situation Report, No. 3906', Somaliforce, 10 August 1940.
41. 'Notes on the Employment of "B" Company . . .', n.d., CAB106/905, TNA; ibid., Nixon to Barton, 6 November 1946; HMAS *Hobart* to SNO Red Sea, 9 August 1940, MP1185/8, 1810/2/234, NAA; 'A "Minor Episode" during World War II', *Hindsight* (Sea Power Centre – Australia) (Issue XX, Aug. 2010); 'Australians' Gallantry in Somaliland', *The Times* (London), 24 August 1940; 'Somaliland Battle, R.A.N, Gunners in Land Action, Posted Missing', *Sydney Morning Herald*, 23 August 1940. Following the evacuation the three naval ratings were initially listed as 'missing believed killed' but they were eventually liberated in April 1941 from an Eritrean prisoner of war camp.
42. Mideast to AHQ Aden, 12 August 1940, WO201/270, TNA.
43. 'Obituary: Lieutenant-Colonel Eric Wilson, VC: Camel Corps Officer', *The Times* (London), 30 December 2008.
44. 'Rector's "Timid" Son Becomes V.C. Hero', *Courier-Mail* (Brisbane), 29 March 1941'; 'Obituary: Lieutenant-Colonel Eric Wilson, VC', *Daily Telegraph*, 29 December 2008.
45. Connell, *Wavell: Soldier and Scholar*, pp. 254–255; Ronald Lewin, *The Chief: Field Marshal Lord Wavell, Commander-in-Chief and Viceroy, 1939–1947* (London: Hutchinson & Co., 1980), pp. 23–26; Raugh, *Wavell in the Middle East*, pp. 94–95.
46. Schofield, *Wavell: Soldier and Statesman*, p. 143.
47. Diary, 30 July 1940, Richard Dewing Papers, LHCMA.
48. Mideast to Troopers, 9 August 1940, WO201/270, TNA.
49. Ibid., Mideast to C. in C. Mediterranean, 14 August 1940.
50. Wavell to Chater, 8 July 1940, WO201/257, TNA.
51. 'Decisions of a "Q" Conference held at GHQ Middle East on 9th August, 1940', n.d., CAB106/919, TNA; ibid., 'Instruction to Base Commandant, Berbera for Layout and Maintenance of Base', 9 August 1940.
52. ACM Longmore to Deputy Chief General Staff, 9 August 1940, WO201/270, TNA.
53. 'Obituary: General Sir Reade Godwin-Austen', *The Times* (London), 21 March 1963.
54. Troopers to Mideast, No. 78569, 10 August 1940, WO201/270, TNA; ibid., Troopers to Mideast, No. 78566, 9 August 1940; Lieutenant-General Sir Arthur Smith, 'Obituary: General Sir Reade Godwin-Austen', *The Times* (London), 30 March 1963.
55. Major-General Arthur Smith, 'Instructions to Major-General Godwin Austen', 10 August 1940, Reade Godwin-Austin Papers, Godwin-Austen 1, LHCMA.
56. Somaliforce to Mideast, No. 3985, 14 August 1940, WO201/270, TNA.
57. Ibid., Somaliforce to Mideast, No. 3989, 14 August 1940.
58. Lieutenant-Colonel W. Robertson, 'Note of an interview with Major-General A.R. Godwin Austin on the 23rd September, 1943', 25 September 1943, WO106/2353A, TNA.
59. Somaliforce to Mideast, No. 155, 15 August 1940, WO201/270, TNA.

60. Ibid., Somaliforce to Mideast, No. 155, 15 August 1940.
61. Field-Marshal Lord Wilson, *Eight Years Overseas 1939–1947* (London: Hutchinson & Co., 1950), p. 41.
62. Ibid., p. 42.
63. Troopers to Mideast, No. 79047, 15 August 1940, WO201/270, TNA.
64. 'Notes on a Visit by Major R.G. Thurburn to Aden and Jibuti etc.', 17 July 1940, WO201/263, TNA.
65. Wavell to War Office, 1 September 1940, WO106/2336, TNA.
66. Only later was it confirmed to the Chiefs of Staff in London that those men from the Camel Corps who had been rescued had been formed into an armoured car unit which retained their title and was still serving in the region; Colonel Hollis to Eastwood (C.O.), 28 November 1940, CAB21/2605, TNA.
67. 'Extract from report on Visit by Colonel J.K. Edwards . . .', n.d. (28 May 1940?), WO201/257, TNA.
68. Cited in, 'A "Minor Episode" during World War II'.
69. Ibid.
70. 'Account of Evacuation from British Somaliland', 25 November 1940, MP1185/9, 406/201/71, NAA.
71. Playfair et al., *The Mediterranean and Middle East: Vol. I*, p. 178.
72. Mideast to Somaliforce, 15 August 1940, WO201/270, TNA.
73. Blake to Cunningham, 17 August 1940, Andrew Cunningham Papers, Add. 52569, BL.
74. Ibid., Cunningham to Blake, 29 August 1940.
75. Glenday to Lord Lloyd, Secretary of State for the Colonies, 5 September 1940, CO535/136/24, TNA.
76. Captain G.C. Foster, 'British Somaliland', n.d., pp. 66–67, CAB44/160, TNA.
77. J.L. Garvin, 'The Battle of Empire – Axis and Africa', *Observer* (Manchester), 11 August 1940; 'We Capture Passes Says Italy', *Daily Mirror*, 12 August 1940.
78. 'Bombing the Italians in Somaliland', *Manchester Guardian*, 12 August 1940; 'Italians Repulsed in British Somaliland', *Manchester Guardian*, 14 August 1940.
79. Garvin, 'The Battle of Empire'.
80. 'Italians Advancing along Coast', *The Times* (London), 16 August 1940.
81. 'Evacuation of Somaliland', *Manchester Guardian*, 20 August 1940; 'British Leave Somaliland', *The Times* (London), 20 August 1940.
82. 'The Loss of Somaliland', *The Times* (London), 20 August 1940; 'Withdrawal from Somaliland', *Manchester Guardian*, 20 August 1940.
83. Kenneth Williams, 'The East and Somaliland Evacuation', *Great Britain and the East* (London), 29 August 1940.
84. 'Fortunes of War in Africa', *The Economist* (London), 24 August 1940.
85. 'Retreat from Somaliland', *The National Review* (Vol. CXV, July–Dec. 1940), p. 265.
86. Saturday 10 August 1940, in Paul Addison and Jeremy A. Crang (eds), *Listening to Britain: Home Intelligence Reports on Britain's Finest Hour, May to September 1940* (London: The Bodley Head, 2010), p. 315.
87. Ibid., p. 316.
88. Ibid., Tuesday 20 August 1940, p. 347.
89. Lord Ismay, *The Memoirs of General the Lord Ismay* (London: Heinemann, 1960), pp. 193–194.
90. *The Abyssinian Campaigns*, p. 18; Douglas Porch, *The Path to Victory: The Mediterranean Theater in World War II* (New York: Farrar, Straus and Giroux, 2005), p. 131.
91. Diary, 7 August 1940, p. 227, Lord Halifax Diary, A7/8/5, BIA.
92. Ibid.
93. Weekly War Office Intelligence Commentary No. 56, 12 September 1940, Chartwell Papers, CHAR20/16/18–19, CAC.

94. Troopers to Mideast (Wavell to Wilson), 15 August 1940, WO201/270, TNA.
95. Minute by Churchill to General Ismay for Chiefs of Staff Committee, 19 August 1940, The Prime Minister's Personal Minutes (August 1940), Chartwell Papers, CHAR20/13/5, CAC.
96. Mideast to Armindia, 20 August 1940, WO201/270, TNA.
97. General Sir Archibald P. Wavell, 'Operations in the Somaliland Protectorate, 1939–1940', *The London Gazette* (1946), p. 2719.
98. Churchill, *Their Finest Hour*, p. 383.
99. Desmond Morton to R.W. Thomson, 21 August 1961, R.W. Thomson Papers, Thomson 1/2, LHCMA; Carlo D'Este, *Warlord: A Life of Winston Churchill at War, 1874–1945* (New York: HarperCollins, 2008), pp. 490–491.
100. Ashley Jackson, *The British Empire and the Second World War* (London: Hambledon Continuum, 2006), p. 211; Churchill to Eden (Secret and Personal), 13 August 1940, cited in Martin Gilbert, *The Churchill War Papers: Vol. II, Never Surrender – May–December 1940* (London: Heinemann, 1994), p. 657; Churchill to Eden, 13 August 1940, Chartwell Papers, CHAR20/2, CAC.
101. Godwin-Austin to Barton, 3 April 1950, CAB106/912, TNA. Cunningham wrote in his obituary of Godwin-Austen's 'absolute reliability, complete integrity – and above all his courage and fortitude', and clearly appreciated the support he had provided; General Sir Alan Cunningham, 'Obituary: General Sir Reade Godwin-Austen', *The Times* (London), 26 March 1963.
102. 'Conversation with the Fuehrer, 29 August 1940', cited in Malcolm Muggeridge (ed.) [trans. Stuart Hood], *Ciano's Diplomatic Papers* (London: Odhams Press, 1948), p. 386.
103. Cowie, *War for Britain*, p. 207.
104. 'Translation – Notes on Italian Conquest of British Somaliland', n.d., CAB106/919, TNA.

5: Preparing for the Counter-offensive

1. General Sir William Platt, *The Campaign against Italian East Africa 1940/41: Lees Knowles Lectures 1951* (Camberley: Army Staff College, 1962), Lecture I, p. 7; David Shirreff, *Bare Feet and Bandoliers: Wingate, Sandford, the Patriots and the Liberation of Ethiopia* (Barnsley: Pen and Sword, 2009), pp. 29–64.
2. M.R.D. Foot, *SOE: The Special Operations Executive 1940–1946* (London: Pimlico, 1999), p. 252; Kirk, *The Middle East in the War*, p. 45; 'An Epic of Abyssinia', *Great Britain and the East*, 20 February 1941.
3. Barton (with handwritten notes by Fabin) . . ., 11 July 1945, CAB106/904, TNA.
4. Schofield, *Wavell: Soldier and Statesman*, p. 173.
5. *The Abyssinian Campaigns*, p. 57; Duncan McNab, *Mission 101: The Untold Story of the SOE and the Second World War in Ethiopia* (Stroud: The History Press, 2012), p. 88; Fort, *Archibald Wavell*, pp. 135–136.
6. Barton (with handwritten notes by Fabin) . . ., 11 July 1945, CAB106/904, TNA.
7. Ibid.
8. Ibid.; 'Selassie Ready to Pounce', *Daily Mirror*, 4 November 1940.
9. Barton (with handwritten notes by Fabin) . . ., 11 July 1945, CAB106/904, TNA.
10. Lieutenant-Colonel A.G. Simonds to Barton, 1 July 1947, CAB106/906, TNA.
11. Blewitt to his father, 30 April 1941, Blewitt Papers, 08/88/3, IWM; 'Haile Selassie is Back Again in the Country', *The War Illustrated*, 7 February 1941.
12. Foot, *SOE*, p. 252.
13. 'Southern Theatre: Revolt in the Desert', *Time*, 22 July 1940.
14. 'War Cabinet – Future Strategy', WP(40)362, 4 September 1940, CAB66/11/42, TNA.
15. Badoglio to Aosta, 1 August 1940, CAB146/374, TNA.

16. Captain Sir James Duncan, House of Commons Debate, 'War Situation', 20 August 1940, *Hansard*, Vol. 364, c 1203.
17. 'The Role of British Forces in Africa', George Young (11th African Division), Box 19, No. 309, MSS. Afr.s.1715, ODRP.
18. Colonel D. Fabin to Barton, 14 September 1944, CAB106/903, TNA.
19. Badoglio to Aosta, 13 August 1940, CAB146/374, TNA.
20. 'The Role of British Forces in Africa', Young, ODRP.
21. Badoglio to Aosta, 13 August 1940, CAB146/374, TNA.
22. Ibid., Badoglio to Aosta, 26 August 1940.
23. 'Daily Summary No. 314', 13 July 1940, WO106/2139, TNA; Major D. Fabin, 'Review of Events (1st to 10th August, 1940)', 14 August 1940, WO106/2341, TNA.
24. GOC East Africa to War Office, 15 August 1940, WO201/270, TNA.
25. 'Precis of Reports by Colonel W.A. Ebsworth to General Headquarters, Middle East, 22 August to 17 October 1940', WO201/2084, TNA.
26. 'War Cabinet – Future Strategy', WP(40)362, 4 September 1940, CAB66/11/42, TNA.
27. 'Order of Battle', n.d., J.E. Barton Papers, 7203–33–2, NAM.
28. Kenneth Williams, 'Wardens of the Empire's Marches – Prospects of East African Campaign', *Great Britain and the East*, 30 January 1941.
29. Crosskill, *The Two Thousand Mile War*, p. 79.
30. Eden to Churchill, 24 September 1940, Wavell Papers, AW.
31. Churchill, *The Gathering Storm*, p. 64.
32. Prime Minister's Personal Minute to Eden and Dill, 22 November 1940, M.330, Wavell Papers, AW.
33. Haining to Dill, 8 October 1940, Wavell Papers, AW.
34. War Office to C. in C. Middle East, 26 November 1940, Wavell Papers, AW.
35. Schofield, *Wavell: Soldier and Statesman*, p. 150.
36. 'Turtle in the Desert', *Time*, 7 October 1940.
37. Major George Fielding Eliot, 'The War Moves into Africa – Continent Waits to be Carved', *Life*, 7 October 1940.
38. Amery to Cranborne, 29 November 1940, Leo Amery Papers, AMEL2/1/31, CAC.
39. John Agar-Hamilton to Liddell Hart, 14 February 1959, Liddell Hart Papers, LH 4/39, LHCMA.
40. Andre Wessels, 'The First Two Years of War: The Development of the Union Defence Forces (UDF), September 1939 to September 1941', *Scientia Militaria – Military History Journal* (Vol. 11, No. 5, June 2000); Ian van der Waag, *A Military History of Modern South Africa* (Cape Town and Johannesburg: Jonathan Ball Publishers, 2015), p. 198.
41. General Kenneth van der Spuy, 'Briton and Boer in the Battle for Freedom', *The Listener*, 8 August 1940.
42. Ian van der Waag, 'The Union Defence Force Between the Two World Wars, 1919–1939', *Scientia Militaria – South African Journal of Military Studies* (Vol. 30, No. 2, 2000), p. 218.
43. Suzanne van den Bergh, 'Ouma Se Stories', *South African Military History Society*, April 2006, pp. 44–47. At its peak in January 1941, approximately 100 vehicles were arriving each day and by May of that same year more than 13,000 had reached East Africa.
44. 'Notes on Conference Held at Khartoum at 0900 hours 29th October 1940', n.d., WO106/2340, TNA.
45. C. in C. East Indies to Admiralty, 18 November 1940, WO106/2339, TNA.
46. Badoglio to Aosta, 7 September 1940, CAB146/374, TNA; Mideast N.L. East Indies to C. in C. East Indies, 31 December 1940, WO106/2339, TNA.
47. Birkby, *It's a Long Way to Addis*, pp. 99–101.
48. Joe Garner, *The Commonwealth Office* (London: Heinemann, 1978), p. 203; John Colville, *Winston Churchill and His Inner Circle* (New York: Wyndham, 1981), pp. 173–174.
49. Lord Moran, *Winston Churchill: The Struggle for Survival* (London: Constable, 1966), p. 53.

50. 'Comments by Major L.F. Turner (Union War Histories)', n.d. (1950), CAB106/912, TNA.
51. Ibid., 'Comments by Major-General C.C. Fowkes – Chapter H', n.d. (1950).
52. Wavell to Dill, 29 October 1940, Wavell Papers, AW; Smart, *Biographical Dictionary of British Generals of the Second World War*, p. 84. Dickinson, in fact, struggled to find another meaningful job and was eventually appointed as the major-general in charge of Western Command's administration before retiring from the army in 1944.
53. Nosworthy led a corps again in Tunisia and finished the war as Commander-in-Chief of West Africa Command but this incident led Dewing to note it had 'impressed on me how great a part chance plays in the careers of soldiers'; Diary, 9 October 1940, Dewing Papers, LHCMA.
54. Michael Craster, 'Cunningham, Ritchie and Leese', in Keegan (ed.), *Churchill's Generals*, p. 203.
55. Diary, 27 August 1940, Alex Danchev and Daniel Todman (eds), *War Diaries 1939–1945: Field Marshal Lord Alanbrooke* (London: Weidenfeld and Nicolson, 2001), p. 102; Andrew Stewart, '"Necessarily of an Experimental Character": The Inter-War Period and the Imperial Defence College', in Doug Delaney and Robert Engen (eds), *Military Education and Empire* (Vancouver: University of British Columbia Press, 2017 [forthcoming]).
56. Lloyd to Moore, 29 October 1940, CO967/159, TNA.
57. Ibid., Moore to Lloyd, 3 December 1940.
58. Ibid., Lloyd to Moore, 29 October 1940.
59. Blewitt to Mama, 22 December 1940, James Blewitt Papers, 08/88/3, IWM.
60. General Sir Archibald P. Wavell, 'Operations in East Africa, November 1940 to July 1941', *The London Gazette* (1946), p. 3528.
61. 'Comments by General Cunningham – Chapter K', 24 February 1950, CAB106/911, TNA.
62. Ibid., 'Comments by General Cunningham – Chapter H', 24 February 1950. When the advance finally began there was still a shortage of drivers and a number of Africans were used despite only having had a fifteen-day basic course of instruction.
63. Wavell, *Generals and Generalship*, p. 14.
64. Van den Bergh, 'Ouma Se Stories', p. 46. Throughout the course of the war they provided 360 water tankers, 120 water purification trucks and 2,200 water-tank trailers.
65. Van der Spuy, 'Briton and Boer in the Battle for Freedom', *The Listener*, 8 August 1940; van der Waag, *A Military History of Modern South Africa*, pp. 196–197.
66. '22nd East African Infantry Brigade, Intelligence Summary No. 30', 25 October 1940, Military Intelligence Reports 1940–1941, DC/MBT/3/4/2, KNADS.
67. 'Daily Summary No. 552', 11 March 1941, WO106/2139, TNA.
68. 'Force Headquarters Intelligence Summary No. 5 – Disposition of Troops', 25 October 1939, Military Intelligence Report and Survey 1938–1939, DC/LDW/2/18/4, KNADS.
69. United Kingdom High Commissioner in the Union of South Africa to Dominions Office, Most Secret and Personal, 5 November 1940, DO35/1008, TNA.
70. 'Notes on interview with Lieutenant-General Sir Alan Cunningham, 7th November 1945', CAB106/904, TNA.
71. War Office to C. in C. Middle East, 26 November 1940, Wavell Papers, AW.
72. Wavell to Dill (Private), 2 December 1940, WO106/2340, TNA.
73. John Bierman and Colin Smith, *Fire in the Night: Wingate of Burma, Ethiopia and Zion* (New York: Random House, 1999), pp. 175–176.
74. Jackson, *The British Empire and the Second World War*, p. 191; Porch, *The Path to Victory*, p. 133; F.H. Hinsley et al., *British Intelligence in the Second World War: Vol. 1* (London: HMSO, 1979), p. 380.
75. Terraine, *The Right of the Line*, p. 320.
76. M.O.1 (Records), 'East Africa . . .', n.d., WO106/2337B, TNA.

77. Gillan, 'The Importance of the Sudan', *The Listener*, 28 November 1940.
78. Ronald Scobie to Barton, 20 January 1947, CAB106/906, TNA.
79. 'An eye-witness account of the battle of Gallabat, Sudan, 6 November 1940', n.d., Conf. 3620, JSCSC.
80. Captain B.H. Liddell Hart, *The Tanks: The History of the Royal Tank Regiment, 1914–1945: Vol. II, 1939–1945* (London: Cassell & Co., 1959), p. 293.
81. Duncan Anderson, 'Slim', in Keegan (ed.), *Churchill's Generals*, pp. 304–305. The general had apparently acquired the nickname when he was a schoolboy at Wellington College.
82. Fort, *Archibald Wavell*, p. 182; Anthony Clayton, *The British Officer: Leading the Army from 1660 to the Present* (Harlow: Pearson Education, 2007), p. 221.
83. 'Daily Summary No. 441', 17 November 1940, WO106/2139, TNA. An analysis of available intelligence the week after the battle concluded that this was the first time the Italians had used white regular troops during the campaign.
84. Platt, *The Campaign against Italian East Africa 1940/41*, Lecture II, p. 10.
85. M.O.1 (Records), 'East Africa . . .', n.d., WO106/2337B, TNA; Glover, *An Improvised War*, p. 62.
86. M.O.1 (Records), 'East Africa . . .', n.d., WO106/2337B, TNA.
87. War Office to C. in C. Middle East, 26 November 1940, WO193/880, TNA.
88. O.A.G to Secretary of State for Colonies, 9 November 1940, CAB21/2605, TNA.
89. Anthony Mockler, *Haile Selassie's War: The Italian–Ethiopian Campaign, 1935–1941* (Oxford: Oxford University Press, 1984), pp. 310–311.
90. Eastwood to Hollis, 4 December 1940, CAB21/2605, TNA.
91. Wavell to Dill, 17 December 1940, WO106/5127, TNA.
92. Wavell to Cunningham, 28 December 1940, Alan Cunningham Papers, 8303–104–7, NAM.
93. Wavell, 'Camilla', 15 December 1940, WO106/5127, TNA.
94. Mannie Centner, 'The 1st South African Light Tank Company: Personal reminiscences of the campaign in East Africa', *Military History Journal* (Vol. 10, No. 3, June 1996); H.E. Sir Arnold W. Hodson, 'An Account of the Part Played by the Gold Coast Brigade in the East African Campaign, August, 1940 to May, 1941: Part I, The Defence of Kenya', *Journal of the Royal African Society* (Vol. XL, Oct. 1941), pp. 306–308.
95. Pitt, 'Adui Mbele (Enemy in Front)', pp. 17–19, 89/1/1, IWM; Emile Coetzee, 'El Wak or Bust', *The South African Military History Society*, 14 October 2010; Birkby, *It's a Long Way to Addis*, pp. 121–127.
96. 'First Stories of Battle of El Wak', *Evening Standard* (Nairobi), 25 December 1940; Deputy-Director Medical Services, East Africa, 'Some Medical Aspects of the Campaign in Somaliland and Ethiopia, 1941', n.d., WO222/24, TNA.
97. Wavell to Cunningham, 19 December 1940, Alan Cunningham Papers, 8303–104–7, NAM.
98. 'Comments by Major L.F. Turner (Union War Histories)', n.d. (1950), CAB106/912, TNA.
99. Cunningham to Wavell, 4 January 1941, Alan Cunningham Papers, 8303–104–7, NAM.
100. 'Abridged report on Operations at El Wak, 14–18 December 1940', NAREP–EA6, NARS; Carel Birkby, *Springbok Victory* (Johannesburg: Libertas Publications, 1941), pp. 95–103; Gandar Dower, *Abyssinian Patchwork*, pp. 86–91; Gustav Bentz, 'Fighting Springboks – C Company, Royal Natal Carbineers: From Premier Mine to Po Valley, 1939–1945' (unpublished thesis, Stellenbosch University, September 2013), pp. 44–48.
101. Wavell to Dill, 28 January 1941, WO106/2340, TNA.
102. Cunningham to Wavell, 4 January 1941, Alan Cunningham Papers, 8303–104–7, NAM.
103. Playfair et al., *The Mediterranean and Middle East: Vol. I*, p. 394.

104. Viceroy's Report, 16 December 1940, CAB146/374, TNA; ibid., Viceroy's Report, 5 January 1941.
105. Lewin, *The Chief*, p. 52.
106. Donald Cowie, *The Campaigns of Wavell: The Inside Story of the Empire in Action* (London: Chapman & Hall, 1942), p. 84.
107. Viceroy's Report, 5 January 1941, CAB146/374, TNA.

6: The Advance from Kenya

1. Blewitt to Mama, 27 January 1941, Blewitt Papers, 08/88/3, IWM.
2. Ibid., Blewitt to Buttons (his cousin, David Budworth), 22 December 1940.
3. 'Maughamesque', *Time*, 23 March 1941; Judith Woods, 'Revealed: The White Mischief Murdered', *Daily Telegraph*, 11 May 2007.
4. Lieutenant-Colonel H. Moyse-Bartlett, 'The King's African Rifles', *The Army Quarterly* (Vol. LXXI, Oct. 1955), p. 73.
5. Cunningham to Wavell, 25 January 1941, Alan Cunningham Papers, 8303–107–4, NAM.
6. 'Notes on interview with . . . Cunningham, 7th November 1945', CAB106/904, TNA.
7. Major-General A.C. Duff, '"Q" in the East African Campaign, 1941: An Episode', *The Royal Engineers Journal* (Vol. LVI, 1942), p. 269.
8. Correlli Barnett, *The Desert Generals* (London: Cassell, 2001), p. 85; David Williamson, *A Most Diplomatic General: The Life of General Lord Robertson of Oakridge* (Trowbridge: Brassey's, 1996), p. 37.
9. Jon Sutherland and Diane Canwell, *Air War East Africa 1940–1941: The RAF versus the Italian Air Force* (Barnsley: Pen and Sword Books, 2009), p. 93.
10. Crosskill, *The Two Thousand Mile War*, p. 100.
11. Playfair et al., *The Mediterranean and Middle East: Vol. I*, p. 393.
12. Pitt, 'Adui Mbele (Enemy in Front)', p. 21, 89/1/1, IWM.
13. 'The Role of British Forces in Africa', Lanning, Box 7, No. 258, MSS. Afr.s.1734, ODRP.
14. Barton to Brigadier C.E.M. Richards, 21 August 1950, CAB106/912, TNA.
15. Williamson, *Diplomatic General*, p. 35.
16. 'The Memoirs of Brigadier L.F. Field CB CBE', pp. 150–151, n.d., 10972, IWM.
17. Ibid.
18. M.O.1 (Records), 'East Africa . . .', n.d., WO106/2337B, TNA; Duff, '"Q" in the East African Campaign 1941: An Episode', p. 270.
19. Barnett, *Desert Generals*, p. 85.
20. David Killingray, 'The Idea of a British Imperial African Army', *Journal of African History* (Vol. 20, No. 3, 1979), p. 422.
21. 'The Role of British Forces in Africa', Ennals, ODRP.
22. Lieutenant-Colonel John Filmer-Bennett (3 Nigerian Regiment, Royal West African Frontier Force), Box 3, No. 139, MSS.Afr.s.1734, ODRP.
23. 'The Role of British Forces in Africa', Ennals, ODRP.
24. Wavell to Dill, 2 February 1941, WO106/2340, TNA.
25. Wavell to Cunningham, 10 January 1941, Alan Cunningham Papers, 8303–104–7, NAM.
26. 'Comments by General Cunningham – Chapter J', 24 February 1950, CAB106/911, TNA. Despite the previous written letter, Cunningham later claimed that it was only now at this late stage that he was also told about the pressure being placed on the commander-in-chief by the leadership in London.
27. Wavell to Cunningham, 10 January 1941, Alan Cunningham Papers, 8303–104–7, NAM.
28. Inter Service X by Cable, 8 February 1941, CAB121/540, TNA.

29. Cunningham to Barton, 24 February 1950, CAB106/911, TNA.
30. Cunningham to Wavell, 17 February 1941, Alan Cunningham Papers, 8303-104-7, NAM.
31. Pitt, 'Adui Mbele (Enemy in Front)', pp. 22–25, 89/1/1, IWM.
32. Brown, *The War of a Hundred Days*, p. 132.
33. Deputy-Director Medical Services, East Africa, 'Some Medical Aspects of the Campaign in Somaliland and Ethiopia, 1941', n.d., WO222/24, TNA.
34. M.O.1 (Records), 'East Africa . . .', n.d., WO106/2337B, TNA.
35. Playfair et al., *The Mediterranean and Middle East: Vol. I*, p. 395.
36. 'Annexure to The Fortnightly Review of the Military Situation, No. 16 – Review of Destruction of Enemy Forces in Italian Somaliland and Abyssinia by the East African Forces (from 15th January 1941 – 3rd July 1941)', n.d., WO201/2683, TNA.
37. Ibid., 'Review of the East African Campaign . . .', n.d.
38. *The Abyssinian Campaigns*, p. 71.
39. Crosskill, *The Two Thousand Mile War*, p. 99; Glover, *An Improvised War*, pp. 100–104.
40. 'Review of the East African Campaign . . .', n.d., WO201/2683, TNA.
41. Eric S. Packham, *Africa in War and Peace* (New York: Nova Science Publishers, 2004), p. 9; 'The Role of British Forces in Africa', Lanning, Box 7, No. 258, MSS. Afr.s.1734, ODRP.
42. Richards to Barton, 18 August 1950, CAB106/912, TNA; Cunningham to Wavell, 17 February 1941, Alan Cunningham Papers, 8303-104-7.
43. Colonel A. Haywood, and Brigadier F.A.S. Clarke, *The History of the Royal West African Frontier Force* (Aldershot: Gale and Polden, 1964), pp. 335–336.
44. H.E. Sir Arnold W. Hodson, 'An Account of the Part Played by the Gold Coast Brigade in the East African Campaign, August, 1940 to May, 1941: Part II, The Invasion of Italian Somaliland', *Journal of the Royal African Society* (Vol. XLI, Jan. 1942), pp. 14–16.
45. Brown, *The War of a Hundred Days*, pp. 135–140; Neil Orpen, *East African and Abyssinian Campaigns* (South African Forces World War II – Vol. I) (Cape Town: Purnell and Sons, 1968), pp. 192–198.
46. Glover, *An Improvised War*, p. 104.
47. Barnett, *The Desert Generals*, p. 83; 'Notes on interview with . . . Cunningham, 7th November 1945', CAB106/904, TNA.
48. Cunningham to Wavell, 25 January 1941, Alan Cunningham Papers, 8303-104-7, NAM.
49. Gandar Dower, *Abyssinian Patchwork*, pp. 110–112.
50. 'The Role of British Forces in Africa', Young, ODRP; 'Review of the East African Campaign . . .', n.d., WO201/2683, TNA.
51. C. in C. East Indies to Admiralty, 24 February 1941, WO106/2340, TNA.
52. SO1 Kilindini to Admiralty, 22 February 1941, ADM223/681, TNA; Gandar Dower, *Abyssinian Patchwork*, pp. 111–114.
53. Van den Bergh, 'Ouma Se Stories'.
54. Glover, *An Improvised War*, pp. 72–73; 'Stirring Story of Fall of Mega to Rand Men', *The Star* (Johannesburg), 28 February 1941.
55. Blewitt to Mama, 13 February 1941, Blewitt Papers, 08/88/3, IWM.
56. Ibid., Blewitt to Buttons, 13 April 1941.
57. Pitt, 'Adui Mbele (Enemy in Front)', pp. 26–27, 89/1/1, IWM.
58. 'The Role of British Forces in Africa', Ennals, Box 3, No. 139, MSS. Afr.s.1734, ODRP.
59. Moyse-Bartlett to Acheson, 3 September 1954, CAB106/916, TNA.
60. 'The Role of British Forces in Africa', Major John H. Davis (1 Nigeria Regiment, Royal West African Frontier Force), Box 2, No. 118, MSS. Afr.s.1734, ODRP; Hennessy, 'The Nigerian Advance from Mogadiscio to Harrar', pp. 65–66.
61. Blewitt to family, 11 March 1941, Blewitt Papers, 08/88/3, IWM; ibid., Blewitt to Buttons, 13 April 1941.
62. 'King's African Rifles', *The Oxfordshire and Buckinghamshire Light Infantry Chronicle* (Vol. LI, Jan.–Dec. 1949), p. 195.

63. 'The Role of British Forces in Africa', Filmer-Bennett, ODRP.
64. Duff, '"Q" in the East African Campaign, 1941: An Episode', pp. 269–270.
65. Ibid., p. 270.
66. 'Mopping up!', *Illustrated* (London), 10 May 1941.
67. Churchill to Ismay, 15 February 1941, CHAR20/36/2, CAC; Chiefs of Staff Committee, COS(41) 56, 15 February 1941, CAB121/540, TNA.
68. Churchill to Ismay, 15 February 1941, CHAR20/36/2, CAC.
69. Ibid., War Office to C-in-C Middle East, 16 February 1941.
70. Ibid., Ismay to Captain Nicholl, 20 February 1941.
71. Chiefs of Staff Committee Meeting, COS(41) 116, 20 February 1941, CAB121/540, TNA; M.O.1 (Records), 'East Africa ...', n.d., WO106/2337B, TNA; Wavell to Cunningham, 22 January 1941, Alan Cunningham Papers, 8303–104–7, NAM.
72. 'The Role of British Forces in Africa', Filmer-Bennett, ODRP.
73. 'Comments by General Cunningham – Chapter K', 24 February 1950, CAB106/911, TNA; Sutherland and Canwell, *Air War East Africa 1940–1941*, p. 127.
74. Ibid., p. 100.
75. 'The Role of British Forces in Africa', Young, ODRP.
76. Alan Moorehead, 'Speed! Broke the Italians', *Daily Express*, 17 April 1941.
77. Major M.N. Hennessy, 'The Nigerian Advance from Mogadiscio to Harrar', *The Army Quarterly* (Vol. LVII, No. 1, Oct. 1948), p. 65.
78. 'Notes on interview with ... Cunningham, 7th November 1945', CAB106/904, TNA.
79. Blewitt to Buttons, 13 April 1941, Blewitt Papers, 08/88/3, IWM; 'The Role of British Forces in Africa', Davis, ODRP; Glover, *An Improvised War*, p. 128.
80. Lieutenant-Colonel A.C. Martin, *The Durban Light Infantry: Vol. II, 1935 to 1960* (Durban: The Headquarter Board of the Durban Light Infantry in co-operation with the Regimental Association, 1969), p. 20.
81. 'Notes on interview with ... Cunningham, 7th November 1945', CAB106/904, TNA.
82. Wavell to Dill, 2 February 1941, WO106/2340, TNA.
83. Report No. 605, February 1941, CAB146/374, TNA.
84. Captain H. Hickling, 'Capture of Berbera – Operation "Appearance"', 17 March 1941, DEFE2/857, TNA.
85. D.J.E. Collins, *The Royal Indian Navy, 1935–45: Vol. I* (Bombay: Orient Longman, 1964), p. 385.
86. Vice Admiral Harold Hickling, *Sailor at Sea* (London: William Kimber, 1965), pp. 152–173.
87. 'War Diary – Aden Striking Force', February/April 1941, WO169/3235, TNA.
88. Ibid., 'Translation of an Italian document marked "secret"... dated 2 March 1941'.
89. 'War Diary – Aden Striking Force', February/April 1941, WO169/3235, TNA.
90. 'Report on Operation Appearance', 26 March 1941, WO201/289, TNA; Second Lieutenant J.A. Hollands, 'Intelligence Summary No.1', 18 March 1941, WO169/3235, TNA.
91. Commander M.L. Vernon, 'Berbera, 16 March 1941', 29 March 1941, DEFE2/857, TNA; Air Vice Marshal Reid to Wavell, 2 April 1941, WO201/289, TNA.
92. 'R.A.F. Report on Operation Appearance', 29 March 1941, WO201/289, TNA.
93. 'War Diary – Aden Striking Force', February/April 1941, WO169/3235, TNA.
94. Glover, *An Improvised War*, pp. 128–129.
95. 'Report on Interview with General C. de Simone', n.d., WO201/289, TNA.
96. 'Berbera Retaken', *The Economist*, 22 March 1941.
97. Haywood and Clarke, *The History of the Royal West African Frontier Force*, pp. 341–346.
98. 'The Role of British Forces in Africa', Filmer-Bennett, ODRP; Glover, *An Improvised War*, pp. 129–131; Keith Ford, *From Addis to the Aosta Valley: A South African in the North African and Italian Campaigns 1940–1945* (Solihull: Helion & Co., 2012), pp. 54–55.

99. Hennessy, 'The Nigerian Advance from Mogadiscio to Harrar', pp. 67–69.
100. Gandar Dower, *Abyssinian Patchwork*, pp. 128–132.
101. 'Notes on interview with . . . Cunningham, 7th November 1945', CAB106/904, TNA.
102. Hennessy, 'The Nigerian Advance from Mogadiscio to Harrar', pp. 69–70.
103. Minute by Cockram (High Commission, Pretoria), 1 September 1941, WO106/2351, TNA. Although described as the 'West African Rifles', the officer who provided the account, a Captain Greenspan, was almost certainly from the KAR.
104. 'Italians Evacuate Rail City in Africa', *New York Times*, 31 March 1941; ibid., 'British Pushing on for Addis Ababa', 4 April 1941.
105. 'Notes on interview with . . . Cunningham, 7th November 1945', CAB106/904, TNA.
106. 'Review of the East African Campaign . . .', n.d., WO201/2683, TNA.
107. Wavell, 'Operations in East Africa, November 1940 to July 1941', p. 3529.
108. 'Obituary: General Sir Alan Cunningham', *The Times* (London), 1 February 1983.
109. Crosskill, *The Two Thousand Mile War*, p. 131.
110. Wavell to Cunningham, 10 January 1941, Alan Cunningham Papers, 8303–104–7, NAM.
111. 'Obituary: General Sir Alan Cunningham', *The Times* (London), 1 February 1983.
112. J.S., 'The Rise and Fall of the Italian African Empire', 21 January 1943, CAB106/404, TNA.
113. Blewitt to family, 21 March 1941, Blewitt Papers, 08/88/3, IWM.
114. Ibid., Blewitt to family, 2 April 1941; Koos Hamman to General (?), 30 March 1941, EA1/68–71, NARS.
115. 'Review of the East African Campaign . . .', n.d., WO201/2683, TNA.
116. Blewitt to Buttons, 13 April 1941, Blewitt Papers, 08/88/3, IWM.
117. Ibid., Blewitt to family, 6 April 1941.
118. Ibid., Blewitt to family, 24 March 1941.
119. 'Report on Interview with General C. de Simone', n.d., WO201/289, TNA.
120. 'Review of the East African Campaign . . .', n.d., WO201/2683, TNA.
121. 'Report on Interview with General C. de Simone', n.d., WO201/289, TNA.
122. 'Review of the East African Campaign . . .', n.d., WO201/2683, TNA.
123. Brigadier H. Charrington, 'Notes on the Operations in Eritrea and Northern Abyssinia, Jan–Mar. 1941', 10 June 1941, Harold Charrington Papers, 3/7, LHCMA.
124. 'Daily Summary No. 554', 3 March 1941, WO106/2139, TNA.
125. Blewitt to family, 24 March 1941, Blewitt Papers, 08/88/3, IWM.

7: Second Front: Striking from the Sudan

1. Barker, *Eritrea 1941*, p. 73.
2. Scobie to Barton, 20 January 1947, CAB106/906, TNA.
3. Colonel B.C. Fletcher, 'Lecture on Eritrean Campaign', n.d., CAB106/921, TNA.
4. Antony Brett-James, *Ball of Fire: The Fifth Indian Division in the Second World War* (Aldershot: Gale and Polden, 1951), pp. 74, 76.
5. Steven Morewood, *The British Defence of Egypt, 1935–1940: Conflict and Crisis in the Eastern Mediterranean* (London: Frank Cass, 2005), pp. 198–199. In May 1940 Captain Lorenzo Muiesan personally supervised the loading of the SS *Umbria* in the ports of Genoa, Leghorn and Naples with 360,000 bombs, 60 boxes of detonators and other stores totalling 8,600 tons. On 3 June 1940 the boat arrived at Port Said bound for Massawa. Although expected to enter the war any day, Italy was still technically neutral and the War Cabinet in London overruled the local authorities in Cairo who wanted to halt its movement. Having been allowed to continue, the *Umbria* was shadowed by HMS *Grimsby* and, on 9 June, when close to Port Sudan, it was finally forced to anchor close inshore. The following morning, despite a party of Royal Navy seamen being onboard, Captain Muiesan heard via his radio that war had been declared and succeeded in scuttling his ship.

6. Barker, *Eritrea 1941*, p. 117.
7. Platt, *The Campaign against Italian East Africa 1940/41*, Lecture II, p. 16.
8. Ibid.
9. Ibid.
10. 'Administrative Account and Lessons of the Eritrean Campaign, June 1940–May 1941' (Brigadier C. Surtees and Lieutenant-Colonel G. Staymer), n.d., NAREP EA3, NARS.
11. General Sir Mosley Mayne to Barton, 4 April 1945, CAB106/903, TNA; Mayne to Colonel H.B. Latham, 8 February 1946, CAB106/905, TNA.
12. Playfair et al., *The Mediterranean and Middle East: Vol. I*, p. 171; Platt, *The Campaign against Italian East Africa 1940/41*, Lecture II, p. 4.
13. Brett-James, *Ball of Fire*, pp. 18–19; Henry Maule, *Spearhead General: The Epic Story of General Sir Frank Messervy and his Men in Eritrea, North Africa and Burma* (London: Odhams Press, 1961), pp. 30–45.
14. 'The East African Campaign', comments by Frank Messervy, n.d. (1950), CAB106/912, TNA.
15. Upcher, 'The Advance from Kassala to Keren with Gazelle Force', n.d., Orlebar Papers, 740/7/18, DSA.
16. Lieutenant-General Sir Geoffrey Evans, *The Desert and the Jungle* (London: William Kimber, 1959), p. 43.
17. Raugh, *Wavell in the Middle East*, p. 172.
18. Brigadier W.E.H. Condon (ed.), *The Frontier Force Regiment* (Aldershot: Gale and Polden, 1962), pp. 234–237; 'Terror in Italians' Town', *Daily Mirror*, 27 December 1940.
19. Glover, *An Improvised War*, p. 177.
20. 'The East African Campaign', comments by Frank Messervy, n.d. (1950), CAB106/912, TNA.
21. He has subsequently been questionably criticised for a decision that has been portrayed as having 'delayed a conclusive British victory in Libya'; Sadkovich, 'Understanding Defeat', p. 39.
22. Lieutenant-Colonel G.R. Stevens, *Fourth Indian Division* (Toronto: McLaren and Son, 1948), pp. 29–30.
23. Barnett, *The Desert Generals*, p. 33; Smart, *Biographical Dictionary of British Generals of the Second World War*, p. 30; 'Obituary: Lieutenant-General Sir Noel Beresford-Peirse', *The Times* (London), 16 January 1953.
24. Barker, *Eritrea 1941*, pp. 44–45; Maule, *Spearhead General*, p. 21; 'Obituary: Lieutenant-General Sir Lewis Heath', *The Times* (London), 12 January 1954.
25. 'Weekly Summary No. 73', 9 January 1941, WO106/2139, TNA.
26. 'Comments by Lt-General Sir N. Beresford-Peirse, KBE, CB, DSO, Late Commander, 4th Indian Division', 8 January 1946, CAB106/940, TNA.
27. Ibid.
28. 'Obituary: Gen. Sir Frank Messervy', *The Times* (London), 4 February 1974.
29. 'Daily Summary No. 510', 26 January 1941, WO106/2139, TNA; ibid., 'Daily Summary No. 512', 28 January 1941.
30. Fletcher, 'Lecture on Eritrean Campaign', n.d., CAB106/921, TNA.
31. Ibid.
32. Interview with Air Vice Marshal Graham Magill, 23 March 1992, IWM Oral History, Reel 2, IWM.
33. Colonel D. Fabin to Barton, 14 September 1944, CAB106/903, TNA.
34. Lieutenant-Colonel E.W.C. Sandes, *From Pyramid to Pagoda: The Story of the West Yorkshire Regiment (The Prince of Wales's Own) in The War 1939–45 and afterwards* (London: F.J. Parsons, 1951), p. 94; Brett-James, *Ball of Fire*, pp. 18–19; Fletcher, 'Lecture on Eritrean Campaign', n.d., CAB106/921, TNA.
35. Brigadier H. Charrington, 'Notes on the Operations in Eritrea and Northern Abyssinia – Jan–May 1941', n.d., CAB106/947, TNA.

36. Barker, *Eritrea 1941*, p. 84; Amedeo Guillet to Platt, 19 August 1974, Orlebar Papers, 740/8/33, SDA. Amedeo Guillet was widely reported to have commanded the cavalry unit, and he survived the encounter and the subsequent campaign and went on to become Italian ambassador in India before eventually dying at the age of 101 at his home in Ireland; 'Obituary: Amedeo Guillet', *Daily Telegraph* (London), 1 July 2010; 'Obituary: Amedeo Guillet', *The Times* (London), 7 July 2010. According to another account, the commander in charge of the cavalry squadron was actually a Captain Santasila who was posthumously awarded the Gold Medal, the Italian version of the Victoria Cross; Ben Coutts, *A Scotsman's War* (Edinburgh: The Mercat Press, 1995), p. 31.
37. Upcher, 'The Advance from Kassala to Keren with Gazelle Force', n.d., Orlebar Papers, 740/7/22, SDA.
38. Lieutenant-Colonel T.B. Davis, *The Surrey and Sussex Yeomanry in the Second World War* (Hassocks: Ditchling Press, 1980), pp. 218–219; Maule, *Spearhead General*, pp. 48–49.
39. Reginald Savory, 'Action on Mount Cochen – 28–31 January 1941', n.d. (1941?), CAB106/903, TNA.
40. Savory to Elliott, 27 March 1974, Reginald Savory Papers, 7603–93–46E, NAM.
41. 'East African Campaign – Comments by Colonel Fabin', 23 May 1945, CAB106/903, TNA.
42. Liddell Hart, *The Tanks*, p. 293.
43. Mohammed Ibrahim Qureshi, *History of the First Punjab Regiment, 1759–1956* (Aldershot: Gale and Polden, 1958), pp. 346–347.
44. 'Daily Summary No. 553', 12 March 1941, WO106/2139, TNA.
45. Charrington, 'Notes on the Operations . . .', n.d., CAB106/947, TNA.
46. 'Account by J.A.A. Blaikie of the capture of Barentu from the Italians, 2 February 1941', Orlebar Papers, 740/7/16–17, SDA.
47. Lieutenant-Colonel Lord Birdwood, *The Worcestershire Regiment 1922–1950* (Aldershot: Gale and Polden, 1952), p. 22; Richard Gale, *The Worcestershire Regiment* (London: Leo Cooper, 1970), pp. 99–100; Lieutenant-Colonel Sir Geoffrey Betham and Major H.V.R. Geary, *The Golden Galley – The Story of the Second Punjab Regiment, 1761–1947* (Oxford: The University Press, 1956), pp. 187–188.
48. 'War Diary – 1st Battalion, The Royal Fusiliers', 3 February 1941, RFA; 'The Royal Fusiliers in the Middle East – Events Leading up to the Capture of Agordat', *The Royal Fusiliers Chronicle*, December 1941.
49. 'Report by J.A.A. Blaikie on the looting of Barentu between 1–3 February 1941', 8 February 1941, Orlebar Papers, 740/7/11–15, SDA.
50. Bisheshwar Prasad (ed.), *Official History of the Indian Armed Forces in the Second World War 1939–1945: East African Campaign 1940–41* (Bombay: Combined Inter-Services Historical Section (India and Pakistan), 1963), pp. 48–49.
51. Major Graham, 'East African Campaign', 12 July 1941, p. 4, CAB106/390, TNA.
52. 'The East African Campaign', comments by Frank Messervy, n.d. (1950), CAB106/912, TNA.
53. Wavell to Cunningham, 12 February 1941, Alan Cunningham Papers, 8303–104–7.
54. Mockler, *Haile Selassie's War*, p. 333; Playfair et al., *The Mediterranean and Middle East: Vol. I*, p. 440.
55. Savory to T. Cosgrove, 19 December 1973, Savory Papers, 7603–93–46E, NAM.

8: Triumph in the Mountains: The Battle of Keren

1. 'Weekly Summary No. 80', 27 February 1941, WO106/2139, TNA.
2. Stevens, *Fourth Indian Division*, p. 46.
3. Barker, *Eritrea 1941*, p. 91.
4. Ibid., p. 118.

5. Stevens, *Fourth Indian Division*, p. 27.
6. Barker, *Eritrea 1941*, p. 109.
7. Raugh, *Wavell in the Middle East*, p. 180.
8. Stevens, *Fourth Indian Division*, p. 39.
9. Mockler, *Haile Selassie's War*, p. 337.
10. Savory to Elliott, 27 March 1974, Savory Papers, 7603–93–46E, NAM.
11. Ibid.
12. Compton Mackenzie, *Eastern Epic: Vol. I, September 1939–March 1943 – Defence* (London: Chatto and Windus, 1951), p. 64.
13. Peter Cochrane, *Charlie Company: In Service with C Company 2nd Queen's Own Cameron Highlanders 1940–1944* (Stroud: Spellmount [Second Edition], 2007), pp. 53–60.
14. During another attack on the same position four days later, his right foot was blown off and he eventually succumbed to his wounds.
15. Stevens, *Fourth Indian Division*, pp. 41–42.
16. Platt, *The Campaign against Italian East Africa 1940/41*, Lecture II, p. 18.
17. Louis Scully, '1st Battalion, The Worcestershire Regiment in Eritrea', n.d., *The History of the Regiment 1694–1970*, The Worcestershire Regiment Museum, Worcester.
18. Savory to Elliott, 27 March 1974, Savory Papers, 7603–93-46E, NAM.
19. Birdwood, *The Worcestershire Regiment 1922–1950*, p. 26.
20. Cochrane, *Charlie Company*, p. 66.
21. Evans, *The Desert and the Jungle*, p. 39.
22. Cited in 'Fool's Day of 1941 in Asmara: The Brits Enter, the Italians Exit', *The Eritrean Newsletter* (Issue 34, April 1979).
23. Report by Colonel Fletcher, 'Keren – The Breakthrough', CAB106/924, TNA.
24. 'Comments by Major-General T.W. Rees on Chapter C – The Battle of Keren', n.d., CAB106/912, TNA.
25. Ibid.
26. Platt, *The Campaign against Italian East Africa 1940/41*, Lecture III, p. 13.
27. Steer, *Sealed and Delivered*, p. 134.
28. Ibid., pp. 133–134.
29. Ibid., p. 100; Wavell, 'Operations in East Africa, November 1940 to July 1941', p. 3573; Captain G.L. Steer, 'Reform of British Wartime Propaganda (Organisation)', 5 July 1941, FO898/309, TNA.
30. Nicholas Rankin, *Telegram from Guernica* (London: Faber and Faber, 2003), pp. 1–6.
31. Steer, *Sealed and Delivered*, p. 165.
32. Lieutenant-Colonel A.E. Cocksedge to Barton, 22 January 1947, CAB106/906, TNA.
33. Barker, *Eritrea 1941*, p. 138.
34. Ibid., p. 142.
35. Platt, *The Campaign against Italian East Africa 1940/41*, Lecture III, p. 20.
36. 'The Battle for Keren – How We Began It', *Manchester Guardian*, 20 March 1941.
37. *The Abyssinian Campaigns*, pp. 44–46; Cochrane, *Charlie Company*, p. 70.
38. Interview with Reginald Collis, 1 August 1993, Reel 2, 13292, IWM.
39. Condon (ed.), *The Frontier Force Regiment*, pp. 240–249.
40. Maule, *Spearhead General*, p. 90.
41. Birdwood, *The Worcestershire Regiment 1922–1950*, p. 26.
42. 'The East African Campaign – Comments by Frank Messervy', n.d. (1950), CAB106/912, TNA.
43. Major A.E. Cocksedge, 'The Left Flank at Keren', n.d. (1941?), Savory Papers, 7603–93–46C, NAM.
44. 'The Battle for Keren – How We Began It', *Manchester Guardian*, 20 March 1941.
45. Barker, *Eritrea 1941*, p. 155.

46. A.J. Barker, *The West Yorkshire Regiment* (London: Leo Cooper, 1974), pp. 60–61; Sandes, *From Pyramid to Pagoda*, pp. 102–107; Betham and Geary, *The Golden Galley*, pp. 188–189.
47. Interview with Reginald Collis, 1 August 1993, IWM Oral History, Reel 2, 13292, IWM.
48. Qureshi, *History of the First Punjab Regiment*, pp. 347–352.
49. 'Our Grip on Keren', *Manchester Guardian*, 27 March 1941; 'Italian Counter-Attacks Fail at Keren', *Manchester Guardian*, 19 March 1941.
50. Platt, *The Campaign against Italian East Africa 1940/41*, Lecture III, p. 4.
51. The Royal Fusiliers, 'War Diary – 1st Battalion, 16 March 1941', RFA.
52. Captain Philip Searight, 'Sudan and Eritrea, January–April 1941', RFA.
53. 'R.A.F.'s Big Part at Keren', *Manchester Guardian*, 29 March 1941.
54. Philip Guedalla, *Middle East 1940–1942: A Study in Air Power* (London: Hodder and Stoughton, 1944), p. 109.
55. Ibid., p. 87.
56. *The Abyssinian Campaigns*, p. 35.
57. Brett-James, *Ball of Fire*, p. 224.
58. Raugh, *Wavell in the Middle East*, p. 180; 'Last Act in East Africa', *Time*, 7 April 1941.
59. Shirreff, *Bare Feet and Bandoliers*, p. 285.
60. Playfair et al., *The Mediterranean and Middle East: Vol. I*, p. 440.
61. 'Part taken by the Free French forces in the Eritrean campaign, 1941', prepared by Barton, 1 November 1946, CAB106/905, TNA; Jean-Noël Vincent, *Les Forces françaises dans la lutte contre l'Axe en Afrique: Les Forces françaises libres en Afrique 1940–1943* (Paris: Ministère de la Défense, 1983), pp. 68–92. The French commander was actually Raoul Magrin-Vernerey who had commanded two battalions of legionnaires at the Battle of Narvik but who now employed a pseudonym to protect his family back in France.
62. G.D. Martineau, *A History of the Royal Sussex Regiment* (Chichester: Moore and Tillyer, 1955), pp. 240–241.
63. Barker, *Eritrea 1941*, p. 163.
64. 'General Wavell's Keren Visit', *Manchester Guardian*, 29 March 1941.
65. M.O.1 (Records), 'East Africa . . .', n.d., WO106/2337B, TNA.
66. Glover, *An Improvised War*, p. 120.
67. Sandes, *From Pyramid to Pagoda*, p. 107.
68. Liddell Hart, *The Tanks*, p. 294.
69. Fletcher to Barton, 9 July 1946, CAB106/905, TNA.
70. 'Keren – The Breakthrough', n.d., CAB106/904, TNA.
71. Charrington, 'Notes on the Operations . . .', 10 June 1941, Charrington Papers, 3/7, LHCMA.
72. Connell, *Wavell: Scholar and Soldier*, p. 376.
73. Barker, *The West Yorkshire Regiment*, p. 61; Betham and Geary, *The Golden Galley*, p. 191.
74. *Regimental History of the 6th Royal Battalion (Scinde), 13th Frontier Force Rifles 1934–1947* (Aldershot: Gale and Polden, 1951), pp. 31–32.
75. 'The East African Campaign', comments by Frank Messervy, n.d. (1950), CAB106/912, TNA. Gazelle was finally disbanded on 14 February 1941 after three months of service, during which time it had achieved a great deal, and Messervy was given command of this brigade. He was eventually promoted to major-general and took charge of 7th Armoured Division in the battle fought in the Western Desert.
76. 'Keren – The Breakthrough', n.d., CAB106/904, TNA.
77. Sir Arthur Longmore, *From Sea to Sky 1910–1945* (London: Geoffrey Bles, 1946), p. 272.
78. Rees to Barton, 25 May 1946, CAB106/905, TNA.

79. 'Comments by Major-General D. Russell on Chapter "D" – The Advance to Masawa (sic)', n.d., CAB106/925, TNA.
80. Ibid., 'Chapter "E" – Note on Administrative Aspect', n.d., CAB106/925, TNA.
81. Lieutenant-Colonel J.P. Lawford and Major W.E. Catto (eds), *Solah Punjab: The History of the 16th Punjab Regiment* (Aldershot: Gale and Polden, 1967), pp. 137–141.
82. 'Food Shortage in Eritrea', *Sydney Morning Herald*, 26 October 1940.
83. *The Abyssinian Campaigns*, p. 50.
84. Ibid., pp. 49–50.
85. Charrington, 'Notes on the Operations . . .', n.d., CAB106/947, TNA; SO1 Kilindini to Admiralty, 22 February 1941, ADM223/681, TNA.
86. Barrie Pitt, *The Crucible of War: Vol. I, Wavell's Command* (London: Cassell, 2001), pp. 209–210.
87. 'Massawa', April 1941, Lieutenant-General Sir Lewis Heath Papers, LMH3, IWM.
88. Vincent, *Les Forces françaises dans la lutte contre l'Axe en Afrique*, p. 98.
89. 'Part taken by the Free French forces in the Eritrean campaign, 1941', prepared by Barton, 1 November 1946, CAB106/905, TNA; Ray Ward, *With the Argylls: A Soldier's Memoir* (Edinburgh: Birlinn [Electronic Edition], 2014), Chapter 3.
90. *The Abyssinian Campaigns*, pp. 50–51.
91. 'Massawa', April 1941, Heath Papers, LMH3, IWM.
92. Major Graham, 'East African Campaign', 12 July 1941, pp. 5–6, CAB106/390, TNA.
93. Charrington, 'Notes on the Operations . . .', n.d., CAB106/947, TNA; Brett-James, *Ball of Fire*, p. 99.
94. Roskill, *The Navy at War 1939–1945*, p. 152.
95. Crosskill, *The Two Thousand Mile War*, p. 141; Prasad, *East African Campaign 1940–41*, p. 131.
96. Raugh, *Wavell in the Middle East*, p. 183.
97. Crosskill, *The Two Thousand Mile War*, p. 136.
98. Heath to Barton, 24 August 1946, CAB106/905, TNA.
99. Barker, *Eritrea 1941*, p. 174.
100. Mockler, *Haile Selassie's War*, p. 333.
101. Glover, *An Improvised War*, p. 178; Barker, *Eritrea 1941*, p. 102; Playfair et al., *The Mediterranean and Middle East: Vol. I*, p. 440.
102. Barker, *Eritrea 1941*, p. 162.
103. Ibid., p. 122.
104. Evans, *The Desert and the Jungle*, p. 74.
105. 'Comments by Maj. Gen, D.R. Bateman on the Draft Chapter "C" – The Battle of Keren', 26 January 1946, CAB106/925, TNA.
106. Raugh, *Wavell in the Middle East*, p. 181.
107. Platt, *The Campaign against Italian East Africa 1940/41*, Lecture II, p. 19.
108. Mackenzie, *Eastern Epic*, p. 64.
109. W.G. Hingston, *The Tiger Strikes* (Calcutta: J.F. Parr, 1942), p. 92.
110. Charrington, 'Notes on the Operations . . .', n.d., CAB106/947, TNA.
111. 'East African Campaigns', House of Lords Debate, 28 May 1941, *Hansard*, Vol. 119, cc 297–311.
112. 'The Final Assault on Keren', *Manchester Guardian*, 28 March 1941.
113. Mockler, *Haile Selassie's War*, p. 335.

9: A Third Front: The Patriots

1. Porch, *The Path to Victory*, p. 136; Foot, *SOE*, pp. 251–264.
2. Raugh, 'General Wavell and the Italian East African Campaign', p. 57.
3. The British scholar Simon Anglim has spent much of his career studying Wingate and produced a series of books and articles that examine the controversial British military

officer. For a more detailed discussion, the relevant section in his most important work should be studied; Simon Anglim, *Orde Wingate and the British Army, 1933–1944* (London: Pickering and Chatto, 2010), pp. 101–144.
4. Douglas Dodds-Parker, *Setting Europe Ablaze: Some Account of Ungentlemanly Warfare* (London: Springwood Books, 1984), pp. 59–73; Shirreff, *Bare Feet and Bandoliers*, p. 65; Allen, *Guerrilla War in Abyssinia*, p. 63.
5. Desmond White, 'A Trying Chindit', *British Medical Journal* (Vol. 285, 18–25 Dec. 1982), p. 1779.
6. Talk with Major Anthony Irwin, 13 January 1945, Liddell Hart Papers, LH11/1945/9, LHCMA.
7. Trevor Royle, *Orde Wingate: Irregular Soldier* (London: Weidenfeld and Nicolson, 1995), pp. 186–187; Wilfred Thesiger, *The Life of My Choice* (London: Collins, 1987), p. 321.
8. Foot, *SOE*, pp. 255–256; Christopher Sykes, *Orde Wingate* (London: Collins, 1959), p. 248.
9. Dodds-Parker, *Setting Europe Ablaze*, p. 57.
10. Glover, *An Improvised War*, p. 150; Foot, *SOE*, p. 255.
11. 'An Epic of Abyssinia', *Great Britain and the East*, 20 February 1941.
12. Foot, *SOE*, p. 256.
13. Interview with Reginald Collis, 1 August 1993, IWM Oral History, Reel 2, IWM.
14. M.O.1 (Records), 'East Africa . . .', n.d., WO106/2337B, TNA.
15. Platt, *The Campaign Against Italian East Africa 1940/41*, Lecture I, pp. 8–9; Glover, *An Improvised War*, p. 62.
16. Sbacchi, 'Haile Selassie and the Italians 1941–1943', p. 28.
17. Platt, *The Campaign Against Italian East Africa 1940/41*, Lecture I, p. 14.
18. Churchill, *The Grand Alliance*, p. 81; Mockler, *Haile Selassie's War*, p. 312.
19. M.R.D. Foot, 'Obituary: Lt-Col. Tony Simonds', *Independent* (London), 26 January 1999.
20. Foot, *SOE*, p. 258; Angelo Del Boca [trans. Antony Shugaar], *The Negus: The Life and Death of the Last King of Kings* (Addis Ababa: Arada Books, 2012), p. 202.
21. Del Boca, *The Negus*, p. 205.
22. Foot, *SOE*, pp. 260–262.
23. Jeff Pearce, *Prevail: The Inspiring Story of Ethiopia's Victory over Mussolini's Invasion, 1935–1941* (New York: Skyhorse Publishing [Electronic Edition], 2014), Chapter 23.
24. Royle, *Orde Wingate: Irregular Soldier*, p. 180.
25. Boca, *The Negus*, pp. 206–207; *The Abyssinian Campaigns*, p. 63.
26. Trevor Royle, *Orde Wingate: A Man of Genius, 1903–1944* (Barnsley: Pen and Sword, 2010), p. 317; Playfair et al., *The Mediterranean and Middle East: Vol. I*, pp. 425–428.
27. Report No. 605, February 1941, CAB146/374, TNA.
28. Mackenzie, *Eastern Epic*, pp. 69–70.
29. This brief meeting with Wingate, who was sitting on a white horse near the Awash River, still remained clear to him sixty years later; interview with Jim Brown, 13 January 2001, IWM Oral History, Reels 1 and 2, IWM.
30. Shirreff, *Bare Feet and Bandoliers*, p. 286; Dawn M. Miller, ' "Raising the Tribes": British Policy in Italian East Africa, 1938–41', *Journal of Strategic Studies* (Vol. 22, No. 1, Mar. 1999), p. 115; David Rooney, *Wingate and the Chindits* (London: Cassell & Co., 1994), pp. 52–56.
31. Playfair et al., *The Mediterranean and Middle East: Vol. I*, p. 427; Bierman and Smith, *Fire in the Night*, p. 166; Shirreff, *Bare Feet and Bandoliers*, p. 219; Miller, *Raising the Tribes*, p. 98.
32. *The Abyssinian Campaigns*, p. 13. This was written by George Steer, a correspondent for *The Times* based in Addis Ababa during the Italian invasion and himself an intelligence officer in the campaign, and an entire chapter is devoted to 'Mission 101', pp. 56–67.
33. Barker, *Eritrea 1941*, p. 47.

34. Playfair et al., *The Mediterranean and Middle East: Vol. I*, p. 427.
35. Ibid., p. 428.
36. Miller, *Raising the Tribes*, p. 117.
37. R.J. Collins, *Lord Wavell 1883–1941* (London: Hodder and Stoughton, 1947), pp. 278–279.
38. Platt, *The Campaign Against Italian East Africa 1940/41*, Lecture I, pp. 12–13.
39. Ibid., Lecture III, p. 15.
40. Royle, *Orde Wingate: Irregular Soldier*, p. 187; Thesiger, *The Life of My Choice*, p. 320.
41. Unknown to Barton, 20 February 1948, CAB106/908, TNA.
42. Mockler, *Haile Selassie's War*, pp. 310–313.
43. Wavell to Cunningham, 19 December 1940, Alan Cunningham Papers, 8303–104–7, NAM; ibid., Cunningham to Wavell, 4 January 1941; 'East Africa, Vol. IV – Miscellaneous', handwritten comments, n.d., Wavell Papers, AW.
44. Wavell to Cunningham, 10 January 1941, Alan Cunningham Papers, 8303–104–7, NAM; 'East Africa, Vol. IV – Miscellaneous', handwritten comments, n.d., Wavell Papers, AW.
45. 'Notes on interview with . . . Cunningham, 7th November 1945', CAB106/904, TNA.
46. Typical of such accounts is that by the *Daily Express* correspondent who followed Wingate in Burma; W.G. Burchett, *Wingate's Phantom Army* (Bombay: Thacker & Co., 1944), pp. 60–67. The best wartime account is undoubtedly W.E.D. Allen, *Guerrilla War in Abyssinia* (London: Penguin Books, 1943).
47. Foot, *SOE*, p. 252.
48. Brooke to Amery, 21 July 1942, Amery Papers, AMEL2/1/34, CAC.
49. Rooney, *Wingate and the Chindits*, p. 53; Royle, *Orde Wingate: Irregular Soldier*, pp. 204, 206.
50. Wavell, 'Operations in East Africa, November 1940–July 1941', p. 3528; Sykes, *Orde Wingate*, pp. 236–320.
51. 'The Role of British Forces in Africa', Lanning, ODRP.
52. Foot, *SOE*, p. 253.
53. Barton, 'Notes on Meeting with Field-Marshal Slim', January 1953, f.355, CAB106/206, TNA.
54. Platt, *The Campaign against Italian East Africa 1940/41*, Lecture III, p. 12.
55. Andrew Railton to Barton, 20 April 1948, CAB106/908, TNA.
56. Rooney, *Wingate and the Chindits*, pp. 52–53.
57. Winston Churchill, 'War Situation', House of Commons Debate, 2 August 1944, *Hansard*, Vol. 402, c 1459.
58. Talk with Major Anthony Irwin, 13 January 1945, Liddell Hart Papers, LH11/1945/9, LHCMA.

10: Winning the War, Worrying about the Peace

1. Orpen, *East African and Abyssinian Campaigns*, p. 94.
2. Wavell, cited in Barker, *Eritrea 1941*, p. 171.
3. Sykes, *Orde Wingate*, p. 295; Sutherland and Canwell, *Air War East Africa*, p. 100.
4. Birkby, *It's a Long Way to Addis*, p. 246.
5. Raugh, *Wavell in the Middle East*, p. 168.
6. Major G.P. Wallace, 'Abyssinia', 17 October 1941, DO35/1001, TNA.
7. 'Operations of 22nd E.A. Infantry Brigade', Part II, *Askari* (formerly *The Journal of the King's African Rifles*), January 1964, p. 11.
8. Viceroy to Mussolini, 4 April 1941, CAB146/374, TNA.
9. 'Notes of the Week', *Great Britain and the East*, 3 April 1941.
10. 'The Role of British Forces in Africa', Ennals, ODRP.
11. Pitt, 'Adui Mbele (Enemy in Front)', pp. 30–32, 89/1/1, IWM.

12. Stephen Bell, 'The Liberation of Addis Ababa', *After the Battle* (No. 71, 1991), p. 39.
13. 'The Role of British Forces in Africa', Young, ODRP; Brown, *The War of a Hundred Days*, p. 197.
14. 'The Role of British Forces in Africa', Captain C.W. Catt (22nd East African Infantry Brigade), Box 3, No. 39, MSS. Afr.s.1715, ODRP.
15. Blewitt to Buttons, 13 April 1941, Blewitt Papers, 08/88/3, IWM.
16. Birkby, *It's a Long Way to Addis*, pp. 232–234.
17. Pitt, 'Adui Mbele (Enemy in Front)', pp. 30–32, 89/1/1, IWM. They also captured the wine cellars and their contents, which were later distributed throughout the brigade units.
18. Churchill, *The Grand Alliance*, p. 76.
19. Cunningham to Barton, 30 September 1942, Alan Cunningham Papers, 8303–104–22, NAM.
20. Blewitt to family, 8 April 1941, Blewitt Papers, 08/88/3, IWM.
21. Blewitt to Buttons, 13 April 1941, Blewitt Papers, 08/88/3, IWM.
22. 'The Role of British Forces in Africa', Filmer-Bennett, ODRP. This was quickly converted into a British officers' club and dances were later held, with Italian and Hungarian hostesses as partners.
23. 'The Role of British Forces in Africa', Davis, ODRP.
24. Blewitt to Miss Annie Blewitt, 17 April 1941, Blewitt Papers, 08/88/3, IWM.
25. Wavell, 'Operations in East Africa, November 1940 to July 1941', p. 3589.
26. Blewitt to family, 6 April 1941, Blewitt Papers, 08/88/3, IWM.
27. 'Keren – The Breakthrough', n.d., CAB106/904, TNA.
28. Fletcher to Barton, 25 June 1946, CAB106/905, TNA.
29. Major Graham, 'East African Campaign', 12 July 1941, p. 3, CAB106/390, TNA.
30. 'A Troop Sudan Artillery, War Diary', 16 May 1941, 80/27/1, IWM.
31. Birdwood, *The Worcestershire Regiment 1922–1950*, pp. 28–29.
32. Crosskill, *The Two Thousand Mile War*, p. 199.
33. Blewitt (Jakes) to family, 30 June 1941, Blewitt Papers, 08/88/3, IWM.
34. General Mayne, 'Extract from Liaison Letter No. 9', 28 May 1941, CAB106/925, TNA.
35. Smart, *Biographical Dictionary of British Generals of the Second World War*, pp. 214–215; 'Obituary: General Sir Mosley Mayne', *The Times* (London), 20 December 1955.
36. Birkby, *Springbok Victory*, pp. 244–246.
37. General Mayne, 'Extract from Liaison Letter No. 9', 28 May 1941, CAB106/925, TNA.
38. Ibid., 'Chapter "E" – Note on Administrative Aspect', n.d.
39. Birdwood, *The Worcestershire Regiment 1922–1950*, p. 28.
40. George Munn to Barton, 27 April 1948, CAB106/908, TNA.
41. Condon (ed.), *The Frontier Force Regiment*, pp. 251–253.
42. Major Graham, 'East African Campaign', 12 July 1941, p. 3, CAB106/390, TNA.
43. Ibid.
44. 'Notes on Operations in East Africa 11th February 1941–3rd July 1941' (Army Staff College), n.d., p. 39, JSCSC.
45. Orpen, *East African and Abyssinian Campaigns*, pp. 256–272.
46. Brown, *The War of a Hundred Days*, pp. 212–232.
47. General Mayne, 'Extract from Liaison Letter No. 9', 28 May 1941, CAB106/925, TNA.
48. Captain Shaukat Hyat, 'The Battle of Ambar Alagi or The Fall of an Empire', *The Journal of the United Service Institution of India* (Vol. LXXII, No. 306, Jan. 1942), p. 90.
49. 'Review of the East African Campaign Based on Captured Documents and the Interrogation of Senior Italian Officers', n.d., WO201/2683, TNA.
50. Letter from Major J.D. de C. Guille (Skinner's Horse) to his parents, July 1941, CAB106/907, TNA.
51. Major Graham, 'East African Campaign', 12 July 1941, p. 10, CAB106/390, TNA.
52. 'A Troop Sudan Artillery, War Diary', 16 May 1941, 80/27/1, IWM.

53. 'Review of the East African Campaign . . .', n.d., WO201/2683, TNA.
54. 'A Troop Sudan Artillery, War Diary', 16 May 1941, 80/27/1, IWM.
55. Lieutenant-Colonel J. Gifford, 'Fighting in Abyssinia: Being an Account of the Part Played by the Composite Infantry Battalion of the Eastern Arab Corps', *The Army Quarterly* (Vol. XLIV, No. 2, Aug. 1942), pp. 59–64.
56. Scully, '1st Battalion, The Worcestershire Regiment in Eritrea', n.d., The Worcestershire Regiment Museum; Birkby, *It's a Long Way to Addis*, p. 296.
57. Mackenzie, *Eastern Epic*, pp. 67–70.
58. Mayne to Colonel H.B. Latham, 28 January 1946, CAB106/905, TNA.
59. 'Duke of Aosta's Funeral', *The Times* (London), 9 March 1942.
60. M.O.1 (Records), 'East Africa . . .', n.d., WO106/2337B.
61. Playfair et al., *The Mediterranean and Middle East: Vol. I*, p. 396.
62. Blewitt to family, 23 April 1941, Blewitt Papers, 08/88/3, IWM.
63. Ibid., Blewitt to family, 6 April 1941.
64. Ibid., Blewitt to family, 18 May 1941.
65. 'The Role of British Forces in Africa', Ennals, ODRP.
66. Cunningham to Wavell, 6 June 1941, Alan Cunningham Papers, 8303–104–7, NAM.
67. Haywood and Clarke, *The History of the Royal West African Frontier Force*, pp. 358–359; Brigadier M.W. Biggs, 'The End of Mussolini's East African Empire', *Royal Engineers Journal* (1994), p. 147.
68. Cunningham to Wavell, 6 June 1941, Alan Cunningham Papers, 8303–104–7, NAM; Blewitt to family, 8 June 1941, Blewitt Papers, 08/88/3, IWM.
69. Ibid., Blewitt to family, 29 May 1941; Birkby, *Springbok Victory*, pp. 259–262.
70. Wavell to Cunningham, 15 May 1941, Alan Cunningham Papers, 8303–104–7, NAM.
71. Blewitt (Jakes) to family, 30 June 1941, Blewitt Papers, 08/88/3, IWM.
72. Ibid., Blewitt to family, 10 June 1941; Cunningham to Selassie, 25 June 1941, Alan Cunningham Papers, 8303–104–6, NAM.
73. Letter to Barton, 11 March 1948, CAB106/908, TNA.
74. 'La Campagne des troupes Coloniales Belges en Abyssinie', CAB106/573, TNA. They fought seven engagements between March and July during which a total of 10 Europeans were killed or injured along with more than 600 local troops.
75. Blewitt (Jakes) to family, 14 July 1941, Blewitt Papers, 08/88/3, IWM; ibid., Blewitt (Jakes) to family, 14 July 1941.
76. Ibid., Blewitt (Jakes) to family, 12 June 1941; Blewitt (Jakes) to Family, 18 June 1941.
77. Ibid., Blewitt (Jakes) to family, 30 June 1941.
78. 'East African Intelligence Summary', Nairobi, 15 April 1941, WO208/34, TNA.
79. Ibid.
80. Moore to Lord Moyne, 14 June 1941, CO967/62, TNA.
81. Frederick Cocks MP, House of Commons Debate, 'War Situation', 20 August 1940, *Hansard*, Vol. 364, cc 1198–1199.
82. M.O.1 (Records), 'East Africa . . .', n.d., WO106/2337B, TNA; 'Operations of East Africa Command, From 12th July 1941 to 8th January 1943', 31 March 1943, pp. 9–11, DEFE2/712, TNA; Kenneth Williams, 'An Empire That Fights for Principle – Sincerity Put to Test in Ethiopia', *Great Britain and the East*, 10 April 1941.
83. 'In East Africa', Great Britain and the East, 20 February 1941.
84. Del Boca, The Negus, p. 204.
85. Amery to Cranborne, 24 January 1941, Amery Papers, AMEL2/1/32, CAC.
86. Ibid., Cranborne to Amery, 24 January 1941.
87. Ibid., Eden to Amery, 28 January 1941.
88. 'New Regime in Africa – Sir P. Mitchell's Post', The Times (London), 5 March 1941.
89. Blewitt (Jakes) to family, 30 June 1941, Blewitt Papers, 08/88/3, IWM.
90. Eden to Amery, 28 January 1941, Amery Papers, AMEL2/1/32, CAC; Barton (with handwritten notes by Fabin) . . ., 11 July 1945, CAB106/904, TNA.

91. Blewitt to his father, 30 April 1941, Blewitt Papers, 08/88/3, IWM.
92. Sandford to Barton, 12 October 1950, CAB106/911, TNA.
93. Ibid., Cunningham to Barton, 24 February 1950.
94. War Office to Wavell, 10 April 1941, CAB120/471, TNA.
95. Churchill to Eden and Dill, 10 May 1941, WO106/5905, TNA.
96. 'The Strange Case of – Haile Selassie', *Life*, 21 July 1941.
97. Moore to Sir Cosmo Parkinson, 1 May 1941, CO967/55, TNA.
98. Blewitt (Jakes) to family, 30 June 1941, Blewitt Papers, 08/88/3, IWM.
99. Ibid., Blewitt to family, 11 April 1941.
100. Ibid., Blewitt to Colin, 2 August 1941.
101. Wavell to Cunningham, 15 May 1941, Alan Cunningham Papers, 8303–104–7, NAM.
102. Blewitt (Jakes) to family, 14 July 1941, Blewitt Papers, 08/88/3, IWM; Churchill to Selassie, 22 September 1941, Chartwell Papers, CHAR 20/43/7, CAC.
103. Major G.P. Wallace, 'Abyssinia', 17 October 1941, DO35/1001, TNA.
104. Amery to Eden, 31 October 1941, Amery Papers, AMEL2/1/32, CAC.
105. Ibid., Eden to Amery, 4 November 1941.
106. Churchill to Selassie, 11 October 1941, Chartwell Papers, CHAR 20/43/120, CAC; Selassie to Churchill, 25 October 1941, CHAR 20/44/79, CAC; *British Military Administration of Occupied Territories in Africa during the Years 1941–43* (London: HMSO, 1945), pp. 8–11; *The First to Be Freed: The Record of British Military Administration in Eritrea and Somalia, 1941–1943* (London: HMSO, 1944), pp. 49–71. Two years later Mitchell was appointed Governor of Kenya.
107. Saul Kelly, 'Desert Conquests: Early British Planning on the Future of the Italian Colonies, June 1940–September 1943', *Middle Eastern Studies* (Vol. 50, No. 6, 2014), p. 1012.
108. Jackson, *The British Empire and the Second World War*, p. 194.
109. Cunningham to Wavell, 4 January 1941, Alan Cunningham Papers, 8303–104-7, NAM.
110. M.O.1 (Records), 'East Africa . . .', n.d., WO106/2337B, TNA.
111. Blewitt to his father, 30 April 1941, Blewitt Papers, 08/88/3, IWM.
112. Major G.P. Wallace, 'Abyssinia', 17 October 1941, DO35/1001, TNA.
113. Minute by Brigadier M.S. Lush (Deputy Chief Political Officer), 22 April 1941, Alan Cunningham Papers, 8303–104–6, NAM.
114. M.O.1 (Records), 'East Africa . . .', n.d., WO106/2337B, TNA; 'Operations of East Africa Command . . .', 31 March 1943, pp. 7–9, DEFE2/712, TNA.
115. 'Report on Operation Marie', 5 December 1940, WO106/2357A, TNA.
116. Mideast to Somaliforce, 21 July 1941, CAB106/919, TNA.
117. Blewitt (Jakes) to family, 12 June 1941, Blewitt Papers, 08/88/3, IWM.
118. Ismay, *The Memoirs of General the Lord Ismay*, p. 210.
119. Basil Liddell Hart, *The Rommel Papers* (London: Collins, 1953), p. 78.
120. Diary, 12 August 1941, Lady Moore Papers, MSS Brit Emp s466/2, File 5, Bodleian Library, Oxford.
121. Blewitt (Jakes) to family, 30 June 1941, Blewitt Papers, 08/88/3, IWM.
122. Letter to Cunningham, 10 September 1941, Alan Cunningham Papers, 8303–104–18, NAM.
123. Rosenthal, *The Fall of Italian East Africa*, pp. 87–88.
124. 'Surrender of Gondar', *The Times* (London), 29 November 1941.
125. George Weller [ed. Anthony Weller], *Weller's War: A Legendary Foreign Correspondent's Saga of World War II on Five Continents* (New York: Three Rivers Press, 2009), pp. 153–159.
126. 'Enemy Intelligence in Gondar Area', 4 December 1941, WO106/2352, TNA.
127. Ibid., 'Security Notes on Occupation of Gondar – Enemy Communications with Other Parts of Eritrea', 11 November 1941.
128. 'Security Report 269 F.S. Section', 30 November 1941, WO106/2352, TNA.

129. War Office to GOC East Africa, 2 December 1941, CAB121/540, TNA.
130. 'Operations of East Africa Command . . .', 31 March 1943, pp. 4–7, DEFE2/712, TNA.
131. Lieutenant-Colonel G.J. Pine to Barton, 4 March 1947, CAB106/906, TNA.
132. Bell, 'The Liberation of Addis Ababa', p. 39.

Conclusion: The British Empire's First Victory

1. Prasad, *East African Campaign 1940–41*, p. 154.
2. Birkby, *It's a Long Way to Addis*, p. 131; Crosskill, *The Two Thousand Mile War*, p. 212.
3. Blewitt to family, 6 April 1941, Blewitt Papers, 08/88/3, IWM.
4. 'East African Campaigns', House of Lords Debate, 28 May 1941, *Hansard*, Vol. 119, cc 297–311.
5. Ibid.
6. Wavell, 'Operations in East Africa, November 1940–July 1941', p. 3529.
7. 'East African Campaigns', House of Lords Debate, 28 May 1941.
8. Stewart, 'The Battle for Britain', pp. 19–26.
9. Platt, *The Campaign Against Italian East Africa 1940/41*, Lecture II, p. 7.
10. Orpen, *East African and Abyssinian Campaigns*, pp. 346–351.
11. Minute by Cockram (High Commission, Pretoria), 1 September 1941, WO106/2351, TNA.
12. Blewitt (Jakes) to family, 12 June 1941, Blewitt Papers, 08/88/3, IWM.
13. Wessels, 'The First Two Years of War'.
14. 'Comments on Chapters A, B, C, & D by Lt-General Sir L.M. Heath . . .', n.d., CAB106/941, TNA; Heath to Barton, 24 August 1946, CAB106/905, TNA.
15. Barnett, *The Desert Generals*, pp. 29–30.
16. Crosskill, *The Two Thousand Mile War*, p. 79.
17. Mackenzie, *Eastern Epic*, p. 62.
18. *The Abyssinian Campaigns*, p. 9.
19. 'The War: Resolution of Thanks', House of Lords Debate, 9 April 1941, *Hansard*, Vol. 118, cc 1032–47.
20. A.P. Wavell, *Generals and Generalship* (London: The Times, 1941), p. 27.
21. Glover, *An Improvised War*, pp. 38, 75.
22. Churchill, *The Grand Alliance*, p. 75.
23. Cunningham to Playfair, 8 June 1952, CAB106/926, TNA.
24. Schofield, *Wavell: Soldier and Statesman*, p. 150.
25. John Connell to Ismay, 6 September 1961, Lord Ismay Papers, ISMAY4/9/38, LHCMA.
26. Ismay to Connell, 13 September 1961, Lord Ismay Papers, ISMAY4/9/39, LHCMA.
27. Churchill, *Their Finest Hour*, p. 383.
28. 'Notes', n.d., Chartwell Papers, CHUR4/196A–C, CAC.
29. 'Note on C-in-C Middle East's Despatch on Operations in the Somaliland Protectorate, 1939/40', 5 October 1940, WO106/2354B, TNA.
30. 'Somaliland Campaign', *The Times* (London), 6 June 1946; Wavell, 'Operations in the Somaliland Protectorate, 1939–1940', p. 2719.
31. Jackson, *The British Empire and the Second World War*, p. 211.
32. Morton to Thomson, 21 August 1961, Thomson Papers, Thomson 1/2, LHCMA.
33. 'Italian East Africa – A Swift Campaign', *The Times* (London), 11 July 1946.
34. Wavell, 'Operations in East Africa, November 1940–July 1941', p. 3530; 'East Africa – Vol. I, Kenya', handwritten comment, n.d., Wavell Papers, AW.
35. Woollcombe, *The Campaigns of Wavell 1939–1943*, p. 42.
36. Ibid.
37. Kenneth Williams, 'Cordon Closing in on East Africa', *Great Britain and the East*, 13 February 1941, p. 126.

38. Barnett, The Desert Generals, p. 83.
39. Cunningham to Barton and 'Comments by General Cunningham – Chapter I', 25 July 1950, CAB106/912, TNA.
40. Blewitt to family, 29 May 1941, Blewitt Papers, 08/88/3, IWM.
41. Harold Raugh, 'General Wavell and the Italian East African Campaign', *Military Review* (July 1998), p. 63.
42. Cunningham to Wavell, 6 June 1941, Alan Cunningham Papers, 8303–104-7, NAM.
43. Barnett, *The Desert Generals*, p. 83; Andrew Stewart, *A Very British Experience: Coalition, Defence and Strategy in the Second World War* (Eastbourne: Sussex Academic Press, 2012), pp. 65–81.
44. 'Talk with Major-General Hobart', 28 November 1942, Liddell Hart Papers, LH 11/1942/102, LHCMA; L.F. Turner to Liddell Hart, 20 August 1954, LH 4/39, LHCMA.
45. Secretary of State for the Colonies to Palestine (OAG), 8 November 1945, CO967/94, TNA.
46. Montgomery to Hall, 6 August 1945, CO967/100, TNA.
47. Platt, *The Campaign against Italian East Africa 1940/41*, Lecture III, p. 20.
48. Heath to Barton, 24 August 1946, CAB106/905, TNA.
49. 'Notes by General Cunningham', n.d. (for Neil Orpen, 1967?), Alan Cunningham Papers, 8303–104–18, NAM.
50. 'Obituary: General Sir William Platt', *The Times* (London), 29 September 1975.
51. Ibid.
52. J.S., 'The Rise and Fall of the Italian African Empire', 21 January 1943, CAB106/404, TNA.
53. Sbacchi, 'Haile Selassie and the Italians 1941–1943', p. 26.
54. Hyat, 'The Battle of Ambar Alagi', pp. 92–94.
55. 'The Role of British Forces in Africa', Young, ODRP.
56. Barker, *Eritrea 1941*, p. 24.
57. Bragadin, *The Italian Navy in World War II*, p. 3.
58. Prasad, *East African Campaign 1940–41*, p. 9.
59. Terraine, *The Right of the Line*, p. 302.
60. Brown, *The War of a Hundred Days*, p. 181.
61. 'Starvation in Greece: Insults for Italians', *The Times* (London), 15 July 1941.
62. 'East African Campaigns', House of Lords Debate, 28 May 1941, *Hansard*, Vol. 119, cc 297–311.
63. Ibid.
64. Blewitt to family, 6 April 1941, Blewitt Papers, 08/88/3, IWM; ibid., Blewitt to family, 23 April 1941.
65. Ball, 'The Mediterranean and North Africa, 1940–1944', p. 383.
66. D.B.H. Grobbelaar, 'Report on Interview with German Consul to Italian East Africa – Dr Strohm – at Hargeisha – British Somaliland on or about 15 Apr 41', n.d., NAREP EA1, NARS.
67. Crosskill, *The Two Thousand Mile War*, pp. 13–14.
68. Weerd, *Great Soldiers of the Second World War*, p. 66.
69. 'East African Campaigns', House of Lords Debate, 28 May 1941, *Hansard*, Vol. 119, cc 297–311.
70. Ibid.
71. David Fraser, *And We Shall Shock Them: The British Army in the Second World War* (London: Hodder and Stoughton, 1983), p. 130.

BIBLIOGRAPHY

ARCHIVES/SELECTED PAPERS

Bodleian Library, Oxford Development Records Project – ODRP
Borthwick Institute for Archives, University of York (York) – BIA
    Lord Halifax Diary
British Library (London) – BL
    Andrew Cunningham Papers
Churchill Archives Centre, Churchill College (Cambridge) – CAC
    Chartwell Papers
    Leo Amery Papers
Imperial War Museum (London) – IWM
    James Blewitt Papers
    L.F. Field Papers
    John Pitt Papers
Joint Services Command and Staff College Library (Shrivenham) – JSCSC
Kenya National Archives and Documentation Service (Nairobi) – KNADS
Liddell Hart Centre for Military Archives, King's College London (London) – LHCMA
    Robert Brooke-Popham Papers
    Harold Charrington Papers
    Richard Dewing Papers
    Reade Godwin-Austin Papers
    Lord Ismay Papers
    Basil Liddell Hart Papers
    R.W. Thomson Papers
National Archives of Australia (Canberra) – NAA
National Army Museum (London) – NAM
    J.E.B. Barton Papers
    Alan Cunningham Papers
    Reginald Savory Papers
Nuffield College (Oxford) – NC
    Lord Nuffield Papers
South African National Records and Archives Service (Pretoria) – NARS

BIBLIOGRAPHY

Sudan Archive, Durham University (Durham) – DSA
   John Orlebar Papers
The National Archives, Kew (London) – TNA
The Royal Fusiliers Archives, Tower of London (London) – RFA
Field Marshal Lord Wavell Papers (privately held) – AW

OFFICIAL PUBLICATIONS

Air Historical Branch, *R.A.F. Narrative: Middle East, Vol. V (First Draft): The East African Campaigns 1940–1941* (London: Air Historical Branch, Air Ministry, n.d.)

British Military Administration of Occupied Territories in Africa during the Years 1941–43 (London: HMSO, 1945)

Butler, J.R.M., *Grand Strategy: Vol. II, September 1939–June 1941* [History of the Second World War – United Kingdom Military Series] (London: HMSO, 1957)

Butler, J.R.M., *Grand Strategy: Vol. III, Part II, June 1941–August 1942* [History of the Second World War – United Kingdom Military Series] (London: HMSO, 1964)

Gibbs, N.H., *Grand Strategy: Vol. I, Rearmament Policy* [History of the Second World War – United Kingdom Military Series] (London: HMSO, 1976)

La Guerra in Africa Orientale: Giugno 1940 – Novembre 1941 (Roma: Ministero della difesa, Stato maggiore dell'esercito, Ufficio storico, 1952)

Hansard

Hingston, W.G., *The Tiger Strikes* (Calcutta: J.F. Parr, 1942)

Hinsley, F.H., et al., *British Intelligence in the Second World War: Vol. I* (London: HMSO, 1979)

Hordern, Lieutenant-Colonel Charles [from a draft by Major Henry FitzMaurice Stacke], *History of the Great War, Military Operations: East Africa, Vol. 1, August 1914–September 1916* (London: Historical Section of the Committee of Imperial Defence, 1941)

Kenya Colony and Protectorate, 1936 (London: HMSO, 1937)

Platt, Lieutenant-General Sir William, 'Operations of East Africa Command, 12 July 1941 to 8 January 1943', *The London Gazette* (1946)

Platt, General Sir William, *The Campaign against Italian East Africa 1940/41: Lees Knowles Lectures 1951* (Camberley: Army Staff College, 1962)

Playfair, Major-General I.S.O., et al., *The Mediterranean and Middle East: Vol. I, The Early Successes against Italy (to May 1941)* [History of the Second World War – United Kingdom Military Series] (London: HMSO, 1954)

Playfair, Major-General I.S.O., et al., *The Mediterranean and Middle East: Vol. II, The Germans Come to the Help of their Ally (1941)* [History of the Second World War – United Kingdom Military Series] (London: HMSO, 1956)

Playfair, Major-General I.S.O., et al., *The Mediterranean and Middle East: Vol. III, British Fortunes Reach their Lowest Ebb (September 1941 to September 1942)* [History of the Second World War – United Kingdom Military Series] (London: HMSO, 1960)

Prasad, Bisheshwar (ed.), *Official History of the Indian Armed Forces in the Second World War 1939–1945: East African Campaign 1940–41* (Bombay: Combined Inter-Services Historical Section [India and Pakistan], 1963)

Richards, Denise, *Royal Air Force 1939–1945: Vol. I* (London: HMSO, 1974)

Roskill, S.W., *The Navy at War 1939–1945* (London: Collins Clear-Type Press, 1960)

Roskill, S.W., *The War at Sea: Vol. I, The Defensive* (London: HMSO, 1954)

The Abyssinian Campaigns: The Official Story of the Conquest of Italian East Africa (London: HMSO, 1942)

The First to Be Freed: The Record of British Military Administration in Eritrea and Somalia, 1941–1943 (London: HMSO, 1944)

The Tiger Strikes (HMSO, Government of India, 1942)

Wavell, General Sir Archibald P., 'Operations in East Africa, November 1940 to July 1941', *The London Gazette* (1946)

BIBLIOGRAPHY

Wavell, General Sir Archibald P., 'Operations in the Somaliland Protectorate, 1939–1940', *The London Gazette* (1946)

UNIT HISTORIES

Barker, A.J., *The West Yorkshire Regiment* (London: Leo Cooper, 1974)

Betham, Lieutenant-Colonel Sir Geoffrey and Geary, Major H.V.R., *The Golden Galley: The Story of the Second Punjab Regiment, 1761–1947* (Oxford: The University Press, 1956)

Birdwood, Lieutenant-Colonel Lord, *The Worcestershire Regiment 1922–1950* (Aldershot: Gale & Polden, 1952)

Brelsford, W.V. (ed.), *The Story of the Northern Rhodesia Regiment* (Bromley: Galago [Second Edition], 1994)

Brett-James, Antony, *Ball of Fire: The Fifth Indian Division in the Second World War* (Aldershot: Gale and Polden, 1951)

Cochrane, Peter, *Charlie Company: In Service with C Company 2nd Queen's Own Cameron Highlanders 1940–1944* (Stroud: Spellmount [Second Edition], 2007)

Collins, D.J.E., *The Royal Indian Navy, 1935–45: Vol. I* (Bombay: Orient Longman, 1964)

Condon, W.E.H. (ed.), *The Frontier Force Regiment* (Aldershot: Gale and Polden, 1962)

Davis, Lieutenant-Colonel T.B., *The Surrey and Sussex Yeomanry in the Second World War* (Hassocks: Ditchling Press, 1980)

Draffan, W.D. and Lewin, T.C.C., *A War Journal of the Fifth (Kenya) Battalion* (Uckfield: The Naval and Military Press, 2007)

Fendall, Brigadier-General C.P., *The East African Field Force 1915–1919* (London: H.F. and G. Witherby, 1921)

Gale, Richard, *The Worcestershire Regiment* (London: Leo Cooper, 1970)

Haywood, Colonel A. and Clarke, Brigadier F.A.S., *The History of the Royal West African Frontier Force* (Aldershot: Gale and Polden, 1964)

Lawford, Lieutenant-Colonel J.P. and Catto, Major W.E. (eds), *Solah Punjab: The History of the 16th Punjab Regiment* (Aldershot: Gale and Polden, 1967)

Liddell Hart, Captain B.H., *The Tanks: The History of the Royal Tank Regiment, 1914–1945: Vol. II, 1939–1945* (London: Cassell & Co., 1959)

Macdonald, J.F., *Lion with Tusk Guardant* (Salisbury, Southern Rhodesia: The Rhodesian Printing and Publishing Co., 1945)

Mangilli-Climpson, Massimo, *Larkhill's Wartime Locators: The History of Twelve Artillery Survey Regiments (RA and IA) in the Second World War* (Barnsley: Pen and Sword, 2007)

Martin, Lieutenant-Colonel A.C., *The Durban Light Infantry: Vol. II, 1935 to 1960* (Durban: The Headquarter Board of the Durban Light Infantry in co-operation with the Regimental Association, 1969)

Martin, T.A., *The Essex Regiment, 1929–1950* (Brentwood: The Essex Regiment Association, 1952)

Martineau, G.D., *A History of the Royal Sussex Regiment* (Chichester: Moore and Tillyer, 1955)

Moyse-Bartlett, Lieutenant-Colonel H., *The King's African Rifles: A Study in the Military History of East and Central Africa, 1890–1945* (Aldershot: Gale and Polden, 1956)

Qureshi, Mohammed Ibrahim, *History of the First Punjab Regiment, 1759–1956* (Aldershot: Gale and Polden, 1958)

Regimental History of the 6th Royal Battalion (Scinde), 13th Frontier Force Rifles 1934–1947 (Aldershot: Gale and Polden, 1951)

Sandes, Lieutenant-Colonel E.W.C., *From Pyramid to Pagoda: The Story of the West Yorkshire Regiment (The Prince of Wales's Own) in The War 1939–45 and afterwards* (London: F.J. Parsons, 1951)

Schoeman, Michael, *Springbok Fighter Victory: SAAF Fighter Operations 1939–1945: East Africa, Vol. I, 1940–1941* (Nelspruit: Freeworld Publications, 2002)

BIBLIOGRAPHY

Stevens, G.R., *Fourth Indian Division* (Toronto: McLaren and Son, 1948)
Vincent, Jean-Noël, *Les Forces françaises dans la lutte contre L'Axe en Afrique: Les Forces françaises libres en Afrique 1940–1943* (Paris: Ministère de la Défense, 1983)

GENERAL SECONDARY SOURCES

Abbink, J., Brujin, M.D. and Walraven, K. (eds), *Rethinking Resistance: Revolt and Violence in African History* (Netherlands: Koninklije, 2003)
Abulafia, David, *The Great Sea: A Human History of the Mediterranean* (Oxford: Oxford University Press, 2011)
Addison, Paul and Crang, Jeremy A. (eds), *Listening to Britain: Home Intelligence Reports on Britain's Finest Hour, May to September 1940* (London: The Bodley Head, 2010)
Alfieri, Dino, *Dictators Face to Face* (London: Elek Books, 1954)
Allen, W.E.D., *Guerrilla War in Abyssinia* (London: Penguin Books, 1943)
Anglim, Simon, *Orde Wingate and the British Army, 1933–1944* (London: Pickering and Chatto, 2010)
Anderson, Ross, *The Forgotten War 1914–18: The East African Campaign* (Stroud: Tempus Publishing, 2007)
Armellini, Quirino, *Diario di Guerra* (Milan: Garzanti, 1946)
Asprey, Robert, *War in the Shadows: The Guerrilla in History* (London: Little, Brown, 1994)
Badoglio, Pietro, *Italy in the Second World War: Memories and Documents* (London: Oxford University Press, 1948)
Barker, A.J., *Eritrea 1941* (London: Faber and Faber, 1957)
Barker, A.J., *The Civilizing Mission* (London: Cassell & Co., 1968)
Barnett, Correlli, *The Collapse of British Power* (London: Eyre Methuen, 1972)
Barnett, Correlli, *The Desert Generals* (London: Cassell, 2001)
Best, Geoffrey, *Churchill and War* (London: Hambledon and London, 2005)
Bierman, John and Smith, Colin, *Fire in the Night: Wingate of Burma, Ethiopia and Zion* (New York: Random House, 1999)
Birkby, Carel, *It's a Long Way to Addis* (London: Frederick Muller, 1942)
Birkby, Carel, *Springbok Victory* (Johannesburg: Libertas Publications, 1941)
Blinkhorn, Martin, *Mussolini and Fascist Italy* (London: Routledge, 2006)
Boca, Angelo Del [trans. P. D. Cummins], *The Ethiopian War 1935–1941* (Chicago: University of Chicago Press, 1969)
Boca, Angelo Del [trans. Antony Shugaar], *The Negus: The Life and Death of the Last King of Kings* (Addis Ababa: Arada Books, 2012)
Boustead, Hugh, *The Winds of Morning* (London: Chatto and Windus, 1971)
Bragadin, Marc' Antonio, *The Italian Navy in World War II* (Annapolis, MD: Naval Institute Press, 1957)
Brown, James Ambrose, *The War of a Hundred Days: Springboks in Somalia and Abyssinia 1940–41* (Johannesburg: Ashanti Publishing, 1990)
Brown, Judith and Louis, William Roger (eds), *The Oxford History of the British Empire: Vol. IV, The Twentieth Century* (Oxford: Oxford University Press, 1999)
Bullock, Alan, *Hitler: A Study in Tyranny* (London: Penguin Books, 1962)
Burchett, W.G., *Wingate's Phantom Army* (Bombay: Thacker & Co., 1944)
Burley, Kevin, *British Shipping and Australia 1920–1939* (Cambridge: Cambridge University Press, 1968)
Cervi, Mario, *The Hollow Legions: Mussolini's Blunder in Greece 1940–41* (London: Chatto and Windus, 1972)
Churchill, Winston S., *The Second World War: Vol. I, The Gathering Storm* (London: Cassell & Co., 1948)
Churchill, Winston S., *The Second World War: Vol. II, Their Finest Hour* (London: Cassell & Co., 1949)

BIBLIOGRAPHY

Churchill, Winston S., *The Second World War: Vol. III, The Grand Alliance* (London: Cassell & Co., 1950)
Clark, Martin, *Mussolini: Profiles in Power* (Harlow: Pearson Education, 2005)
Coffey, Thomas M., *Lion by the Tail: The Story of the Italian–Ethiopian War* (London: Hamish Hamilton, 1974)
Collins, R.J., *Lord Wavell 1883–1941* (London: Hodder and Stoughton, 1947)
Colville, John, *Winston Churchill and His Inner Circle* (New York: Wyndham, 1981)
Connell, John, *Wavell: Scholar and Soldier* (London: Collins, 1964)
Corvaja, Santi, *Hitler and Mussolini: The Secret Meetings* (New York: Enigma Books, 2001)
Costi, Robinio, *Mussolini: L'ultima illusione* (Roma: Datanews, 2011)
Coutts, Ben, *A Scotsman's War* (Edinburgh: The Mercat Press, 1995)
Cowie, Donald, *The Campaigns of Wavell: The Inner Story of the Empire in Action; Second Part, September 1940 to September 1941* (London: Chapman and Hall, 1942)
Cowie, Donald, *War for Britain: The Inner Story of the Empire in Action: First Part, September 1939 to September 1940* (London: Chapman and Hall, 1941)
Crosskill, W.E., *The Two Thousand Mile War* (London: Robert Hale, 1980)
Curle, Sandy [ed. Christian Curle], *Letters from the Horn of Africa, 1923–1942: Soldier and Diplomat Extraordinary* (Barnsley: Pen and Sword, 2008)
Danchev, Alex and Todman, Daniel (eds), *War Diaries 1939–1945: Field Marshal Lord Alanbrooke* (London: Weidenfeld and Nicolson, 2001)
Deakin, F., *The Brutal Friendship: Mussolini, Hitler and the Fall of Italian Fascism* (London: Weidenfeld and Nicolson, 1962)
D'Este, Carlo, *Warlord: A Life of Winston Churchill at War, 1874–1945* (New York: Harper Collins, 2008)
Dilks, David (ed.), *The Diaries of Sir Alexander Cadogan, 1938–1945* (London: Cassell & Co., 1971)
Dodds-Parker, Douglas, *Setting Europe Ablaze: Some Account of Ungentlemanly Warfare* (London: Springwood Books, 1984)
Eliot, Sir Charles, *The East Africa Protectorate* (London: Edward Arnold, 1905)
Evans, Lieutenant-General Sir Geoffrey, *The Desert and the Jungle* (London: William Kimber, 1959)
Ferris, John and Mawdsley, Evan (eds), *The Cambridge History of the Second World War: Vol. I, Fighting the War* (Cambridge: Cambridge University Press, 2015)
Fielding, Xan, *One Man in His Time* (London: Macmillan, 1990)
Flower, Desmond and Reeves, James, *The End of the Italian Empire* (London: Cassell & Co., 1960)
Foot, M.R.D., *SOE: The Special Operations Executive 1940–1946* (London: Pimlico, 1999)
Ford, Keith, *From Addis to the Aosta Valley: A South African in the North African and Italian Campaigns 1940–1945* (Solihull: Helion & Co., 2012)
Fort, Adrian, *Archibald Wavell: The Life and Times of an Imperial Servant* (London: Jonathan Cape, 2009)
Fraser, David, *And We Shall Shock Them: The British Army in the Second World War* (London: Hodder and Stoughton, 1983)
Gandar Dower, Kenneth, *Abyssinian Patchwork* (London: Frederick Muller, 1949)
Garner, Joe, *The Commonwealth Office* (London: Heinemann, 1978)
Gathorne-Hardy, G.M., *A Short History of International Affairs 1920–1939* (London: Oxford University Press, 1950)
Gilbert, Martin, *Finest Hour: Winston S. Churchill, 1939–1941* (London: William Heinemann, 1983)
Gilbert, Martin, *The Churchill War Papers: Vol. I, At the Admiralty, September 1939–May 1940* (London: William Heinemann, 1993)
Gilbert, Martin, *The Churchill War Papers: Vol. II, Never Surrender, May–December 1940* (London: William Heinemann, 1994)

BIBLIOGRAPHY

Glover, Michael, *An Improvised War: The Abyssinian Campaign of 1940–1941* (London: Leo Cooper, 1987)
Guedalla, Philip, *Middle East 1940–1942: A Study in Air Power* (London: Hodder and Stoughton, 1944)
Halck, Jørgen [trans. Estrid Bannister], *Strictly Confidential* (London: Jonathan Cape, 1961)
Hastings, Max, *Finest Years: Churchill as Warlord 1940–45* (London: Harper Press, 2009)
Hickling, Harold, *Sailor at Sea* (London: William Kimber, 1965)
Holmes, Richard, *In the Footsteps of Churchill* (London: BBC Books, 2005)
Ismay, Lord, *The Memoirs of General the Lord Ismay* (London: Heinemann, 1960)
Jackson, Andrew, *The Battle for North Africa* (New York: Mason/Charter Publishing, 1975)
Jackson, Ashley, *The British Empire and the Second World War* (London: Hambledon Continuum, 2006)
Jackson, William, *The North African Campaign 1940–43* (London: Batsford, 1975)
Jardine, Douglas, *The Mad Mullah of Somaliland* (London: Herbert Jenkins, 1923)
Keegan, John (ed.), *Churchill's Generals* (London: Weidenfeld and Nicolson, 1991)
Keegan, John, *The Second World War* (London: Hutchinson, 1989)
Khan, Yasmin, *The Raj At War: A People's History of India's Second World War* (London: Bodley Head, 2015)
Kiernan, R.H., *Wavell* (London: George G. Harrap, 1945)
Killingray, David, *Fighting for Britain: African Soldiers in the Second World War* (Martlesham: Boydell and Brewer, 2010)
Killingray, David and Rathbone, Richard (eds), *Africa and the Second World War* (Basingstoke: Macmillan Press, 1986)
Kirk, George, *The Middle East in the War* [Survey of International Affairs 1939–1946] (London: Oxford University Press, 1952)
Kirkpatrick, Ivone, *Mussolini: A Study of a Demagogue* (London: Odhams Books, 1964)
Knight, Patricia, *Mussolini and Fascism* (London: Routledge, 2003)
Knox, MacGregor, *Common Destiny: Dictatorship, Foreign Policy, and War in Fascist Italy and Nazi Germany* (Cambridge: Cambridge University Press, 2000)
Knox, MacGregor, *Hitler's Italian Allies: Royal Armed Forces, Fascist Regime, and the War of 1940–1943* (Cambridge: Cambridge University Press, 2000)
Knox, MacGregor, *Mussolini Unleashed 1939–1941* (Cambridge: Cambridge University Press, 1999)
Lamb, Richard, *Churchill as War Leader: Right or Wrong?* (London: Bloomsbury, 1993)
Lettow-Vorbeck, General Paul von, *My Reminiscences of East Africa: The Campaign for German East Africa in World War One* (London: Hurst and Blackett, 1920)
Lewin, Ronald, *The Chief: Field Marshal Lord Wavell, Commander-in-Chief and Viceroy, 1939–1947* (London: Hutchinson & Co., 1980)
Liddell Hart, Captain B.H., *The Rommel Papers* (London: Collins, 1953)
Longmore, Sir Arthur, *From Sea to Sky 1910–1945* (London: Geoffrey Bles, 1946)
Lucas, Charles, *The Empire at War: Vol. IV, Africa* (London: Oxford University Press, 1926)
Macdonald, J.F., *Abyssinian Adventure* (London: Cassell & Co., 1957)
Macdonald, J.F., *The War History of Southern Rhodesia*, 2 vols (Bulawayo, Southern Rhodesia: Books of Rhodesia Publishing Co., 1976)
Mackenzie, Compton, *Eastern Epic: Vol. I, September 1939–March 1943 – Defence* (London: Chatto and Windus, 1951)
Mack Smith, Denis *Mussolini* (London: Phoenix Press, 2001)
McNab, Duncan, *Mission 101: The Untold Story of the SOE and the Second World War in Ethiopia* (Stroud: The History Press, 2012)
Mallett, Robert, *Mussolini and the Origins of the Second World War, 1933–1940* (Basingstoke: Palgrave Macmillan, 2003)
Marcus, Harold, *A History of Ethiopia* (Los Angeles: University of California Press, 1996)

BIBLIOGRAPHY

Maule, Henry, *Spearhead General: The Epic Story of General Sir Frank Messervy and his Men in Eritrea, North Africa and Burma* (London: Odhams Press, 1961)

Maxon, Robert M., *Struggle for Kenya: The Loss and Reassertion of Imperial Initiative, 1912–1923* (London: Associated University Presses, 1993)

Mead, Richard, *Churchill's Lions: A Biographical Guide to the Key British Generals of World War II* (Stroud: Spellmount, 2007)

Millett, Allan R. and Murray, Williamson (eds), *Military Effectiveness: Vol. III, The Second World War* (Cambridge: Cambridge University Press, 2010)

Millman, Brock, *British Somaliland: An Administrative History, 1920–1960* (Abingdon: Routledge, 2014)

Mockler, Anthony, *Haile Selassie's War: The Italian–Ethiopian Campaign, 1935–1941* (Oxford: Oxford University Press, 1984)

Molinari, Andrea, *La conquista dell'Impero: La guerra in Africa Orientale, 1935–1941* (Bresso: Hobby and Work Publishing, 2007)

Moorehead, Alan, *The Desert War: The Classic Trilogy on the North African Campaign 1940–43* (London: Aurum Press, 2009)

Moran, Lord, *Winston Churchill: The Struggle for Survival* (London: Constable, 1966)

Morewood, Steven, *The British Defence of Egypt, 1935–1940: Conflict and Crisis in the Eastern Mediterranean* (London: Frank Cass, 2005)

Mosley, Leonard, *Gideon Goes to War* (London: A. Barker, 1956)

Muggeridge, Malcolm (ed.), *Ciano's Diary, 1939–1943* (London: William Heinemann, 1947)

Muggeridge, Malcolm (ed.) [trans. Stuart Hood], *Ciano's Diplomatic Papers* (London: Odhams Press, 1948)

Neville, Peter, *Mussolini* (London: Routledge, 2003)

Nicholls, Christine Stephanie, *Red Strangers: The White Tribe of Kenya* (London: Timewell Press, 2005)

Oliver, Roland and Atmore, Anthony, *Africa Since 1800* (Cambridge: Cambridge University Press [Fifth Edition], 2005)

Orpen, Neil, *East African and Abyssinian Campaigns: South African Forces World War II, Vol. I* (Cape Town: Purnell and Sons, 1968)

Packham, Eric S., *Africa in War and Peace* (New York: Nova Science Publishers, 2004)

Paice, Edward, *Tip and Run: The Untold Tragedy of the Great War in Africa* (London: Weidenfeld and Nicolson, 2007)

Palla, Marco, *Mussolini and Fascism* (New York: Interlink Books, 2000)

Pearce, Jeff, *Prevail: The Inspiring Story of Ethiopia's Victory over Mussolini's Invasion, 1935–1941* (New York: Skyhorse Publishing, 2014)

Pitt, Barrie, *The Crucible of War: Vol. I, Wavell's Command* (London: Cassell, 2001)

Porch, Douglas, *The Path to Victory: The Mediterranean Theater in World War II* (New York: Farrar, Straus and Giroux, 2005)

Prithvi, Colonel Nath, *Wingate: His Relevancy to Contemporary Warfare* (London: Sterling, 1990)

Pugliiese, Stanislao, *Fascism, Antifascism and the Resistance in Italy* (Oxford: Rowman and Littlefield, 2004)

Raugh, Harold E., Jr., *Wavell in the Middle East, 1939–1941: A Study in Generalship* (London: Brassey's, 1993)

Reynolds, David, *Britannia Overruled: British Policy and World Power in the Twentieth Century* (London: Longman, 2000)

Roberts, Andrew, *The Storm of War: A New History of the Second World War* (London: Penguin, 2010)

Rochat, Giorgio, *Le guerre italiane 1935–1943: Dall'impero d'Etiopia alla disfatta* (Torino: Einaudi, 2005)

BIBLIOGRAPHY

Rooney, David, *Wingate and the Chindits* (London: Cassell & Co., 1994)
Rosenthal, Eric, *The Fall of Italian East Africa* (London: Hutchinson, 1941)
Rossetto, Luigi, *Major-General Orde Charles Wingate and the Development of Long-Range Penetration* (Manhattan: AH/HA Publishing, 1982)
Royle, Trevor, *Orde Wingate: A Man of Genius, 1903–1944* (Barnsley: Pen and Sword, 2010)
Royle, Trevor, *Orde Wingate: Irregular Soldier* (London: Weidenfeld and Nicolson, 1995)
Sandford, Christine, *Ethiopia Under Haile Selassie* (London: Dent, 1946)
Sandford, Christine, *The Lion of Judah Hath Prevailed* (London: J.M. Dent & Sons, 1955)
Schofield, Victoria, *Wavell: Soldier and Statesman* (London: John Murray, 2007)
Schreiber, Gerhard et al., *Germany and the Second World War: Vol. III, The Mediterranean, South-East Europe and North Africa, 1939–1941 – From Italy's Declaration of Non-Belligerence to the Entry of the United States into the War* (Oxford: Clarendon Press, 1995)
Selassie, Haile [ed. Edward Ullendorff], *My Life and Ethiopia's Progress: Vol. II* (East Lansing: Michigan State University Press, 1994)
Shirreff, David, *Bare Feet and Bandoliers: Wingate, Sandford, the Patriots and the Liberation of Ethiopia* (Barnsley: Pen and Sword, 2009)
Shores, Christopher, *Dust Clouds in the Middle East: The Air War for East Africa, Iraq, Syria, Iran and Madagascar, 1940–42* (London: Grub Street, 1996)
Slim, William, *Unofficial History* (London: Cassell & Co., 1959)
Smart, Nick, *Biographical Dictionary of British Generals of the Second World War* (Barnsley: Pen and Sword, 2005)
Smart, Nick (ed.), *The Second World War* (Aldershot: Ashgate Publishing, 2006)
Steer, G.L., *Sealed and Delivered: A Book on the Abyssinian Campaign* (London: Faber and Faber, 2009)
Stewart, Andrew, *Empire Lost: Britain, the Dominions and the Second World War* (London: Continuum, 2008)
Stewart, Andrew, *A Very British Experience: Coalition, Defence and Strategy in the Second World War* (Eastbourne: Sussex Academic Press, 2012)
Strawson, John, *The Battle for North Africa* (Barnsley: Pen and Sword, 2004)
Sutherland, Jon and Canwell, Diane, *Air War in East Africa 1940–41: The RAF versus the Italian Air Force* (Barnsley: Pen and Sword, 2009)
Sykes, Christopher, *Orde Wingate* (London: Collins, 1959)
Terraine, John, *The Right of the Line: The Royal Air Force in the European War 1939–1945* (Suffolk: St Edmundsbury Press, 1985)
Thesiger, Wilfred, *The Life of My Choices* (London: Collins, 1987)
Thornhill, Christopher J., *Taking Tanganyika: Experiences of an Intelligence Officer, 1914–1918* (London: Stanley Paul & Co., 1937)
Trench, Charles Chevenix, *Men Who Ruled Kenya: The Kenya Administration, 1892–1963* (London: The Radcliffe Press, 1993)
van der Waag, Ian, *A Military History of Modern South Africa* (Cape Town and Johannesburg: Jonathan Ball Publishers, 2015)
Ward, Ray, *With the Argylls: A Soldier's Memoir* (Edinburgh: Birlinn, 2014)
Wavell, A.P., *Generals and Generalship* (London: The Times, 1941)
Weerd, Major H.A. De, *Great Soldiers of the Second World War* (London: Robert Hale, 1946)
Weinberg, Gerhard L., *A World at Arms: A Global History of World War II* (Cambridge: Cambridge University Press, 1994)
Weir, William, *Guerrilla Warfare: Irregular Warfare in the Twentieth Century* (Mechanicsburg, PA: Stackpole Books, 2008)
Weller, George [ed. Anthony Weller], *Weller's War: A Legendary Foreign Correspondent's Saga of World War II on Five Continents* (New York: Three Rivers Press, 2009)
Williamson, David, *A Most Diplomatic General: The Life of General Lord Robertson of Oakridge* (Trowbridge: Brassey's, 1996)

BIBLIOGRAPHY

Wilson, Field-Marshal Lord, *Eight Years Overseas 1939–1947* (London: Hutchinson, 1950)
Winter, Jay (ed.), *The Cambridge History of the First World War: Vol. I, Global War* (Cambridge: Cambridge University Press, 2014)
Wiskemann, Elizabeth, *The Rome–Berlin Axis* (London: Oxford University Press, 1949)
Woollcombe, Robert, *The Campaigns of Wavell 1939–1943* (London: Cassell & Co., 1959)
Young, Francis Brett, *Marching on Tanga: With General Smuts in East Africa* (New York: E.P. Dutton, 1917)

INDEX

Army Formations (or Units)
Armies
　Eighth Army 241
　Fourteenth Army 113
Corps
　I Corps 40
　IV Corps 107
Divisions
　2nd African Division 85
　12th African Division 206
　4th Indian Division 153, 155, 159, 160, 164, 205
　5th Indian Division 112, 153, 160, 161, 215
　1st South African Division 110
Brigades
　1st East African Infantry Brigade 34
　22nd East African Infantry Brigade 132, 205
　26th East African Brigade 229
　3rd Gold Coast Brigade 130
　24th Gold Coast Brigade 130
　7th Indian Infantry Brigade 153, 184, 186
　9th Indian Infantry Brigade 183, 212
　10th Indian Infantry Brigade 113, 157, 184
　11th Indian Infantry Brigade 158, 159–60, 164, 166
　29th Indian Infantry Brigade 175, 210
　29th Infantry Brigade 160
　23rd Nigerian Brigade 133
　1st South African Infantry Brigade 117, 129
Regiments
　Essex Regiment
　　1st Battalion 58, 114
　144th Field Regiment 157
　King's African Rifles *see also* KAR
　　1st Battalion 125
　　3rd Battalion 4, 10
　　5th Battalion 35
　　6th Battalion 208
　5th Mahratta Light Infantry
　　2nd Battalion 168
　　3rd Battalion 174
　Nigerian Regiment
　　1st Battalion 57, 209
　　3rd Battalion 125
　North Rhodesian Regiment
　　1st Battalion 42, 72
　1st Punjab Regiment
　　3rd Battalion 176
　2nd Punjab Regiment
　　3rd Battalion 161
　Rajputana Rifles
　　6th Battalion 169–70
　Royal Sussex Regiment
　　1st Battalion 83
　4th Royal Tank Regiment 153
　6th Royal Tank Regiment 113

INDEX

The Argyll and Sutherland Highlanders
   1st Battalion 231
The Camerons 166
   2nd Battalion 168
West Yorkshire Regiment
   2nd Battalion 174
Worcestershire Regiment
   1st Battalion 160

Other Units

1st East African Light Battery 81
22nd Indian Mountain Battery 142
51 (Middle East) Commando 212

Air Formations (or Units)

No. 1 Squadron South African Air Force 177
No. 1 Squadron, Southern Rhodesia Air Force 42

Italian Army Formations (or Units)

2nd Colonial Brigade 158
27th Colonial Battalion 115
101st Division 131, 145

Abyssinia xv–xvi, 11, 12, 28 *see also* Ethiopia
Ad Teclesan 182, 183
Adardeb 60
Addis Ababa 205–10
   1936 capture of 13
   advance on 128, 142, 232–4, 248
   Aosta's problems 45
   capture of xi, 236
   Cunningham's Star of Solomon 222
   fall of 198
   German consul 246
   Italian fear of reprisals against 53
   last major objective 205
   Longmore aims to attack 84
   sale of documents xiii
   Savoia Grenadiers from 168, 182, 199
   Selassie kept away from 221
   three-day massacre in 15
Aden
   aircraft and ships 79, 243
   attack on Massawa 25
   becomes part of Wavell's command area 23
   British and French officers convene 17–18
   control of sea communications 16–17
   Godwin-Austen's instructions 85
   Gulf of 16, 138, 187
   Military Mission No. 106 116
   naval forces back up 6
   resources and facilities 138
Adi Ugri 210, 216
Adowa 210
Adowa, Battle of 12–13, 14, 220
Afmadu 44, 128, 130, 146
African Colonial Forces 7–8
African Divisions 136 *see also* named divisions (at head of index)
Afrika Korps 173, 227
Agibar 198
Agidrat 210
Agordat 158–63
   3rd Battalion, 1st Punjab Regiment 176
   airfield 180
   Indian brigade 166
   rail line cleared 184
   routes to 155, 172
Aicota 156–7
Akaki 207
Albania 128
Alexandria 7
Allen, Bill 193
Allenby, General 28
Alsace-Lorraine 13
Amba, Mount 162
Amba Alagi 187, 210–14, 217, 227, 242
Amba Gorgias 227
Americans 52, 104, 142, 187, 189
   see also United States
Amery, Leo 105, 220–1, 223
Amhara people 15, 97, 220, 223
Amharic language 250 n17
Ancona, Duke of 216
Anglim, Simon 277 n3
Anglo-Iranian oilfield 6
Angola 101
Aosta, Duke of (Prince Amedeo of Savoy-Aosta)
   101st Division acquired 145
   background 26
   British in the Gojjam 198
   British intelligence read wireless traffic 112
   death 216
   defensive campaign of 244
   fixes on course of action 91
   headquarters for final battle 217
   Jibuti 74
   mental defeat of 120
   Mussolini and 42, 52–3, 128
   Operation 'Camilla' 106, 117
   praise for 246

294

INDEX

strategic understanding of 99–100
surrender 93, 205–6, 215
understands necessity of commanding the sea 45
warns of attack on Sudan 119
Aqiq 151
Arabs 28, 60, 212
Arbegnoch 29
Argyll and Sutherland Highlanders, The 231
Armacheho 97
artillery 102
Asfa Wossen, Crown Prince 195
askaris 3, 55, 133–4, 143
Asmara
  aiming to cut off 178
  battalions left in 212
  captured 184–5
  daytime temperatures 184
  main road 59, 216
  rumours of infantry company 100
  surrender of 183
  transfer of prisoners to 187
  Wavell orders advance 165
Asmara, Bishop of 183
Asmara road 181
Assab 15
Assab, Bay of 11
Atbara 38, 39, 58, 60, 99
Atbara, River 149
Auchinleck, General Claude 227, 241
Australia 6, 52, 81, 205
Austria 98
Awash, River 142, 143, 205, 277 n29

Babile Gap 141
Badoglio, Marshal Pietro
  Aosta and 52, 100
  concern over Haile Selassie 98–9
  first Governor-General 14
  pre-eminent positions held 46
  time taken on march 143
Bagemdir 97
bande 55, 129, 146
Bangalore torpedoes 128
Bardera 129, 145
Barentu 158, 161, 172
Barracouta, HMS 2
Barton, Lieutenant-Colonel J.E.B. xv
Barton, Lady Mary 223
battalions, British 58, 102 *see also individual battalions (at head of index)*
battalions, Commonwealth 103 *see also individual battalions (at head of index)*

Battle of Britain 49, 90, 93, 99
Begemder Force 195
Belfield, Sir Henry 1
Belgian Congo 100
Belgians xi, 163, 218–19, 280 n74
Benghazi 144, 229
Bentinck, Major Count A.W.D. 98
Berbera
  defence of 65, 68, 82, 86
  defenders fall back on 82
  Italian objective 75
  main population centre (British Somaliland) 61
  police force 66
  political and military differences 74
  port facilities 83, 243
  recovered 138–40
  reinforcements arrive 72
  shelling of 87
  short postings 62
  temporary landing strips 78
Beresford-Peirse, Major-General 153, 155, 169
Berlin 50
Berlin Conference 1884 1–2
Bertoldi, Lieutenant-General Sisto 77
Biggs, Major Michael 231
Bir, River 195
Birdwood, Lord 233
Birkby, Carel xiii
Bishop, Alec 31, 33, 43, 255 n45
Bisidimo Pass 141
Biyad 75
Blackshirt militia 39, 75, 79, 142, 207
Black Watch 22, 83, 113
Blake, Vice Admiral Sir Geoffrey 88
Blenheim aircraft 75
Bletchley Park 112
Blewitt, Major James
  Ethiopia and Selassie 222
  ever-present aide, an 232
  Gimma surrender 218
  letters home xv, 121
  on Africa 235
  on Italian capabilities 217
  on Italian colonial towns 209
  speed of British advance 144
  'us against the Bosch' 246
Blue Nile 97
Boers 104
Bombay 52, 69
Bon Voisinage agreement 28
Bonetti, Rear-Admiral Mario 185, 187

295

INDEX

Boustead, Colonel Hugh 97
Brig's Peak 162, 168, 169, 174–6
Briggs, Brigadier Rawdon 178, 180, 186
Briggs Force 178
British
   25 pounders 166
   aircraft 150 *see also* Royal Air Force
   battalions available 58, 102, 103
   Berlin Conference 1–2
   British infantrymen 28
   Churchill's interventions 237
   colonies and First World War 5
   Commonwealth forces 103
   Defence Force ordinance 10
   Dunkirk and its effects 53
   fastest and longest advance of? 232–3
   food available for troops 124
   garrison force for administered and occupied territories 226
   Golis targets 77
   greatest issue facing commanders 122–3
   language skills required 34
   local police and 4
   military capabilities 16
   Military Cross awards 56
   multinational force of xi, 233
   naval force 245 *see also* Royal Navy
   oil supply 245
   outflanking manoeuvres 164
   press reporting x
   primary area objective 17
   Reserved Areas (Ethiopia) 224
   Selassie's plight and 220
   signals intercept stations 152
   smallest force in field 202
   South Africa and 18–19
   vital commodities from Empire 6
British Empire
   East Africa's strategic importance 5, 6
   first loss of territory xii
   first offensive 113, 158
   general lack of foresight 20
   huge morale boost, a 247
   paucity of military resources 32
   position in East Africa unclear 21
   threat to East African territories 38
   war's first invasion of 4
British-Ethiopian Boundary Commission 13, 35
British Somaliland 61–70, 90–4
   at beginning of Second World War 71
   Black Watch evacuate 113
   Colonial Office responsibility 62

   effect of loss 93
   establishment of 2
   Ethiopian refugees 97
   Galla and 220
   Italian East Africa and 14
   Italian operations against 84
   media response 88
   prison camp 210
   reconquest 137
   troop movements 46
   troop numbers in 24, 51
   views after the event 90–4
   Wavell's command includes 23
   'wretched tract' 61, 78
British South Africa Company 250 n6
Brocklehurst, Henry 201
Brocklehurst Mission 200–1
Broken Hill 42, 106
Brooke-Popham, Sir Robert 31, 49
buglers 141
Bulhar 77
Bulo Merere 131
Buna 54, 57
Burao 65, 66
Burma 113, 168, 192, 242
Buro Erillo 130
Burye 195, 197
Butana Bridge 58

Cabinet Office xiii
Cadogan, Sir Alexander 53–4
Cairo 7, 111
Camberley 194, 211, 241
Camel Corps
   depleted garrison 50
   'excellent and capable' 77
   headquarters and personnel 66
   holding up the Italians 75
   machine gun company of 73
   return to their homes 87
   senior officer 63
   strengthened 72
Camel Saddle Hill 140
Cameron Ridge 162, 168–71, 172, 176
Camerons 166, 176
Cape of Good Hope 17, 52
Caproni bombers 54
Carnimeo, General Nicolangelo 166, 172, 188
Castle Hill 73
Cavagnari, Admiral Domenico 46
Central India Horse 102
Chad 178

INDEX

Chalbi desert 132
Chamberlain, Neville 82
Channel Islands 90
Chater, Lieutenant-Colonel Arthur
   background 63–4
   complains about conflicting information 67–8
   co-operating with the French 64–5
   Glenday and 74
   proposals for reinforcements 66
   recommended for promotion 72
   replaced 85
   Wavell's communications with 69–70
Cheeseman, Robert 96
Chiefs of Staff 17, 20, 101, 103, 134
Chindits 201
Churchill, Winston
   considers himself superior 103–4
   Haile Selassie intervention 194, 223
   Ismay as adviser 135
   message of thanks to Cunningham 208
   message to Fowkes 231
   Mogadishu 134
   on Aosta 26
   on Mussolini 12–13
   reduction in military expenditure 7
   Smuts and 108, 111, 119, 235
   Wavell and 82–3, 91–3, 128, 134, 226, 238–9
   whims and interventions 237–8
   Wingate, an opinion 203
Ciano, Gian Galeazzo 50
Coastal Belt 32
Cochen, Mount 158–9
Collis, Flight Lieutenant Reginald 193
Colonial Division 37
Colonial Office
   British Somaliland and 62–3
   confirms start of First World War 1
   correspondence with 219
   Inspector General responsible to 21
   limited term of service with 4
   unsure of actual threat from Italy 68
Combined Middle East Bureau 112
Combolcia Pass 214
Committee of Imperial Defence 4
Commonwealth 42, 103, 226, 233
Connell, John 238
Copperbelt 101
Crete xi, 237, 248
Croft, Lord 247
Crosskill, Ted xiii
Cub Cub 180

Cunningham, General Sir Alan 115–18, 216–27
   Addis Ababa 204, 208, 216
   Amba Alagi 211
   appointment of and background 108
   assessment of 240
   captured Italians, arrangements for 140
   Churchill's message of thanks 208
   deception campaign 128
   fuel concerns 124
   Happy Valley tensions 121–2
   importance of supplies to 109, 122–3, 137, 144
   irregular warfare, attitude to 200
   Kismayu 130, 132
   mobile capabilities 136
   multinational force of 233
   Operation 'Canvas' 111
   remarkable advance, a 143
   return to England on medical grounds 241
   Star of Solomon awarded 222
   Wingate, an opinion 201
Cunningham, Admiral Sir Andrew 22, 51, 88, 107
Cyprus 23, 170
Cyrenaica 208

Daily Express x, xii
Daily Mirror x
Dalflecha Ridge 230
Dangila 97
Dar es Salaam 4
Darfur 60
D-Day 139
Debra Marcos 195
de Fabritus, Fausto 206
Defence Committee, London 221
de Gaulle, General Charles 225
   captured and interviewed 145, 146
   evacuation and panic 132
   Juba section command 129
   laments withdrawal 140
   main objectives 75
   Nasi and 77
Delville Wood Day 105
Dendi 227
desertion 173
De Simone, Lieutenant-General Carlo
Dessie 195, 214, 228, 246
Deuxième Bureau 27
Dickinson, Major-General Douglas 30–8
   doubts over abilities 107

INDEX

lack of preparation 109
Lord Haw-Haw's broadcasts 50
Moyale garrison 54
reinforcements for 49
remarkable achievement of 45
struggles to find another job 266 n52
values Giffard's achievements 40
Wavell and Smuts meet 106–7
Wavell's HQ takes over 44
Diego Suarez 242
Dif 55
Dill, John
  I Corps command 40
  Cunningham approved of by 108
  informed of Kismayu attack 125–6
  on Italian morale 104
  stresses time factor to Wavell 135
  urges defence of Somaliland 239
Dimoline, Brigadier William 230
Dinder River 195
Dingaan's Day 117
Diredawa 140, 142
Djibouti *see* Jibuti
Dobel 57
Dobo 65, 67
Dologorodoc 162, 174, 176, 188
Dongolaas Gorge 163
Douanle 225
Dower, Kenneth Gander xiii
Dunkirk 53

Eagle, HMS 51, 185
East Africa 1–3, 5
East African Command 231, 242
East African Force 231
East African Protectorate 1, 2
Eastern Arab Corps 60
Ebsworth, Colonel Wilfrid 101
Economist, The 140
Eden, Anthony
  Amery's concerns re Selassie 223
  discussing Wavell over lunch 91
  Khartoum meeting 106
  planning recommendations submitted to 101
  topics for discussion with PM 103
  welcomes restoration of Selassie 220–1
Egypt
  British prestige in 40
  concerns about Italy 25
  end of military occupation 6–7
  Italian threat to 19, 235

Mussolini's focus 20
securing lines of communication 17
separate military command 21
threat of invasion from Libya 49
Wavell's main effort 24
El Alamein xvi
El Dima Hills 9
El Wak 55, 117, 118
Elghena 180
Enemy Document Section (Cabinet Office) xiii
Enghiahat, Mount 184
Engibara 195
Entoto Hills 205
Equatorial Corps 103
equipment 48, 66, 102, 170, 180
Eritrea
  banda 55
  British advance through 17
  Italian manpower available in 165
  Italians work well with 39, 166
  Libya and 13
  Mussolini's East African empire 14
  rainy season 110
  refugees 97
  River Gash 59
  troops desert 190
Erskine, Esme 201
Essex Regiment 58, 60, 114
Ethiopia 11–14
  Abyssinia and, nomenclature xv–xvi
  banda 55
  Boundary Commission 13, 35
  Britain's debt to? 54
  British offensive 17
  ceded to Italy 11–12
  defending against invasion 243
  Eden commits to 221
  Eritreans and 39
  Haile Selassie recognised 98, 197
  increasingly pro-British attitude 37
  Italian units in south 36
  Italy's campaign to conquer 19
  possibility of invasion from 9
  problems in west of 28
  refugees 97
  Reserved Areas 224
  restoration of Selassie party 29
  size of 205
  Somalis and 209
  Thesiger's attachment to 192
Ethiopian Bureau 96

INDEX

Falaga Pass 213–14
Fascists (Italian) 12
First World War 1, 2–3, 5, 19, 62, 164
Fleet Air Arm 186
Fleet Street xi
Fletcher Force 213
food rations 123–4, 171
Ford motors 105
Foreign Legion 178
Foreign Office 62, 68
Formidable, HMS 186
Fort Capuzzo 99
Fort Dologorodoc 162, 174, 176, 188
Fort Hall 99
Fort Laquetat 158
Fort Victor Emanuele 186
'Fourth Australian Division' 129
Fowkes, Charles 'Fluffy'
   arrives in Nairobi 37
   fuel reserves 206
   Gondar 228–9, 231
   little confidence in Dickinson 107
   Moyale 57
Fraser, David 247
French
   British co-operation with 20, 29, 40, 64–5, 67
   collapse of 50, 89, 99
   defeated and bitter 234
   fighting in British regiments xi
   Franco-British conversations 16, 17
   Free French 163, 178, 186, 225–6
   further meeting in Aden 17
   Menelik seeks assistance from 12
   Vichy France 61, 69, 225
French Equatorial Africa 100
French Mint 98
French Somaliland *see* Jibuti
'friction of war' 215
Frusci, Luigi
   2nd Colonial Brigade and 158
   concern about British armour 153, 159
   delaying actions 162
   Keren 164, 188
   Platt and 149–50
   pulls back forces 172
fuel supplies 124, 212
Fuse 101 95

Galla 53, 220
Galla-Sidamo 217, 227
Galla people 12, 201, 223
Gallabat 112–15

attempted commando raid 151
British Empire first 158
moving out of 163
old fort 58–9
Slim at 156
Gallipoli 25, 63, 87
Galmagalla 123
Garibaldi Pass 206
Garissa 32, 44, 125, 128
Gash, River 59, 149, 156
Gaulle, General Charles de 225
Gazelle Force 151–2, 155, 157, 163, 213, 275 n75
Gazi 4
Gazzera, General Pietro 53, 218
Gedaref 228
Gelib 44, 128, 131, 144–5
General Headquarters India 33
General Headquarters Middle East Forces (Cairo) 95, 101, 227
Geneva 13
George V, King 1, 9
George VI, King 222, 242
Germain, General 69
German East Africa 4, 5
German South West Africa 4
Germans
   advance on Mombasa 4
   an African empire for 19
   anticipated invasion of Britain 83
   Berlin Conference, 1884 2
   Britain and, post-Dunkirk 53
   effects of 1918 11
   First World War begins 1
   France and Low Countries attacked 46, 49
   Greece invaded 208
   guarantees to Poland against 16
   Italians and 32, 54, 126, 216
   power of blitzkrieg 233
   Russian invasion 227
   South Africa and the Nazis 42
   territory controlled in Africa 3
Gibraltar 22
Gideon Force 192, 197, 199, 201–3
Giffard, Major-General Sir George
   Alec Bishop and 31
   asks for modern equipment 48
   character and background 7–8
   Kenya Regiment and 9–10
   pre-war organisation by 40
   transfer and replacement 30
Gimma 217, 218

Gladiator aircraft 75
Glasgow, HMS 138
Glenday, Vincent 53, 68, 74, 79, 91
Gloucester, HMS 33
Gocti 139
Godwin-Austen, Major-General Reade
  background 85
  his advice accepted 86
  loss of British Somaliland 93
  obituary 264 n101
  Tug Argan 92
Gojjam plateau
  clearing operations 97, 202
  controlling insurgency 27
  focus for British resources 28, 95
  irregular forces control 15
  Robert Cheeseman 96
  Wingate advances across 195, 197
  Wingate's hazardous flight 193
Gold Coast Regiment 130, 131, 202, 227
Golis mountains 77
Gondar
  artillery from 182
  Bentinck heads for 98
  described 228–9
  El Alamein and xvi
  Fowkes charged with capture of 228
  Italian battalions advance from 114
  Italian garrison 155, 162
  Italian manpower at 187
  Italians' finest hour 231
  Ringrose near 203
  surrender of x–xi
Graziani, Marshal Rodolfo 15, 99, 100
Great Lakes 3
Greece
  Badoglio resigns over 52–3
  defeat of xi, 237, 245, 248
  forces diverted to 204
  Germans invade 208
  in need of equipment 117
  Italians attack 128
Guala goldmine 159
Guillet, Amadeo 273 n36
Gulf of Aden 16, 138, 187 *see also* Aden

Hagadera 123, 134
Haifa 6
Haile Selassie, Emperor *see* Selassie, Emperor Haile
Haining, General Sir Robert 104
Halifax, Lord 91
Hamilton, Jean 258 n30

Hamilton's Mission 116
Happy Valley 121–2
Hargeisa 64, 75, 78, 139
Harrar 116, 135, 139–40, 142, 146
Harrar Division 75
Hassan, Mohammed Abdullah 62
Haw-Haw, Lord (William Joyce) 50
Hay, Josslyn, 22nd Earl of Errol 122
Heath, Major-General Lewis 114, 153,
  186, 188, 212
Herero revolt 4
Highland Light Infantry 156–7, 176, 186
Hitler, Adolf 50, 89, 93
Hobart, HMAS 79, 81, 87
Holland 49
Horn of Africa 6
Hotchkiss guns 81, 98
House of Commons 98, 203, 220
House of Lords 190, 233, 247
Howden, Captain H.L. 79
Hurricane aircraft 144

ICI (Imperial Chemical Industries) 260
  n88
Illaloes, the 70
Imperial Defence College 144
Indian Ocean 2, 3, 5, 134
Indians *see also individual regiments
  (at head of index)*
  builders fixing defences 72
  cavalry units 102
  commander of division 114
  Egypt and 6
  engineers 160
  first Victoria Cross 163
  forces arrive 87
  General Headquarters 33, 152
  high morale of 159
  mountain battery from 34
  trading ships from 6
  Triangle attack 214
  troops landing reverse 4
  two divisions 172
  Wavell makes divisions available 153
  Wavell posted to 226
Inspector Generals 21
Iran 23
Iraq 6, 245
Ironside, General Sir Edmund 21
Isiolo 42
Islam 59, 66
Ismay, General Hastings 'Pug' 89–90,
  134–5, 226, 238

INDEX

Italian Somaliland
  advance into 123, 125
  Brocklehurst Mission 201
  importance of Kismayu 106
  Kenya border 36
  map 127
  protectorate, a 14
  rainfall 110
Italians 10–17, 243–7
  Addis Ababa population of 224
  airpower 97, 102, 114, 150, 157
  Anglo-Italian agreement, 1938 16
  Aosta 26 *see also* Aosta, Duke of
  army formations and units *see head of index*
  attacks Greece 128
  brigades and divisions 129
  ciphers broken 112, 117
  civilian population 142
  Colonial Cavalry 157
  Colonial Office attitude 68
  Daily Express on defeat of xii
  De Simone's retreat 132
  deterioration of morale 104
  dividing up the Middle East 50
  Eritreans and 39
  Ethiopian evacuation announced 224–5
  evacuation and repatriation 224
  first significant attack by 56
  focusing on Africa 10–11
  friendly relations with 36
  Germans and 32, 54, 126, 216
  High Command 91, 111, 126
  humiliation of Adowa 12
  indiscriminate killing of Ethiopians 13, 14–15, 27
  insurgent atrocities against 198
  intelligence services' incompetence 150–1
  interrogation of their prisoners 111–12
  invasion of British Somaliland 76
  Kassala 60
  Keren in retrospect 246
  lack of control of sea 45
  land in Sudan ceded to 93
  main advance 67
  manpower in the field xi, 37, 51
  Moorehead on 136
  mules, use of 74
  Northern Frontier District and 31
  reasons for failure 243–7
  Red Sea Flotilla 15, 51, 244–5
  resources available to counter 73
  shifta units 55
  Smuts on Italy in Africa 19
  state of war 25
  strategy of avoidance 54
  surrender 206–8, 215–16, 218–19
  The Times on 89
  travel ban 47
  tribal objections to 194
  Tug Argan 80
  Wavell disrupts 29
  weaponry 74

Japan
  1931 Manchurian invasion 13
  report of German–Italian disagreement 126
  Singapore 114
  supplies for Italians 106
  threat posed by 135, 242
Jews 212
Jibuti
  Aosta wishes to attack 74
  British withdrawal plans 65
  Chater and the French 72
  collapse of France and 78
  focus for action 27
  Free French plan to capture 225
  French hold position 64
  French Somaliland, as 17
  Hamilton's Mission 116
  possibility of combined Italian attack on 69
  refugees in 97
  vital railway link 224
Jijiga 137, 144
Jinja 34
Jirreh 65, 67
Joint Planning Staff 29, 37
Joyce, William 50
Juba River
  Aosta's resistance 145
  De Simone's command 129
  early demonstration of Cunningham's ability 240
  importance of crossing 136
  natural defensive barrier of 130
  South Africans cross 132
  Tana River and water problems 32, 122
Jubaland 99
Junkers 52 aircraft 144

Kalam 44
Kampala 34
Kandahar, HMS 138

301

INDEX

KAR (King's African Rifles)
  1st Battalion 125
  3rd Battalion 4, 10
  5th Battalion 35
  6th Battalion 208
  Awash crossing 142
  Giffard serves with 8
  infantry units 102
  initial deployment 3
  Inspector General for 21
  main pre-war role 34
  martial law 1
  Northern Brigade 30
  popularity with Africans 219
  pre-war activity 4
  reserves 10
  troops advance 44
  Wavell requests 66
Karora 58, 180
Kassala 59–61
  intelligence network 152
  one of two planned operations 97
  Platt's key target 148–9
  rail link 38
  recaptured 115
Kavirondo people 8
Kennedy, Sir Donald Mackenzie 31
Kenton College 30
Kenya 31–8
  Axis forces plan attack 52–3
  Dickinson in 107
  fragility of tenure 8–9
  Happy Valley 121–2
  Italian East Africa and 14
  map 127
  Mussolini and 19
  priorities 103
  produce proposed for Britain 219
  Smuts offers brigade 43
  Wavell's African troops 24
Kenya Defence Force 10
Kenya highlands 32, 34, 42, 44
Kenya Regiment 10, 30, 33–4, 102, 107
Keren 162–82
  a battle of world importance 189
  an arduous battle 171
  decisive blow to Italians 187
  desert sores 177
  first two phases 176
  future planning for 235
  House of Lords debate 190, 246
  Italians' many military mistakes 172
  maps 167, 179

  peak defences 166
  pivotal campaign point 188
  Platt the victor of 242
  precautions taken against Patriots 199
  Regia Aeronautica destroyed 178
  soldiers' battle, a 189
  strategic importance of 165
  temperatures 173
  Wavell's title 189
  withdrawal to 160
Keru 156–7
Kharif 62
Khartoum xiii, 18, 38–41, 96, 186
Kikuyu people 8–9
King's African Rifles *see* KAR
Kingston, HMS 138
Kirkuk 6
Kismayu 109–11
  Afmadu and 128
  approval for attack on 126
  capture of 132, 134–6
  importance of 130
  Italian assessments 119
  Mogadishu and 106
  one of two planned operations 97
  Smuts's emphasis on 124
  Wavell's initial intentions 115
Knobbly Hill 73, 82
Kut 25

La Croce del Sud 183
Lakes 217
Lakes, Battle of the 218
Lawrence, Sir Arthur 63
Lawrence, T.E. 28, 200, 203
League of Nations 7, 13
Legentilhomme, Brigadier-General Paul 64, 65, 69
Lettow-Vorbeck, Lieutenant-Colonel Paul von 4, 5
Libya xiv, 12–13, 15, 49, 59, 99
Life magazine 105
Listener, The 18, 66
'Little Ghebbi' 207–8
Lloyd, Lord 108
Lokitaung 32
Lone Tree Ridge 56
Longmore, Air Chief Marshal Sir Arthur 22, 84
Lorenzini, Brigadier-General Orlando 188
Lorraine Squadron 186

Mabungo 131
Maclean, 'Billy' 193

INDEX

Madagascar 242
Magrin-Vernerey, Raoul 275 n61
Mahdi, the 11, 18
Mahratta Ridge 171
Maidenhead 217
Maldiba 230
Mambrini, General Renzo 206
Manchester Guardian 89
Manchuria 13
Mandera 32
Maraventano, Colonel Saverio 198
Marda Pass 140, 141
Maria Theresa of Austria 98
Marsa Taclai 178
Marsabit 9, 110, 117
Marshall, Lieutenant-Colonel H. 125
Masai people 8
Massawa
    Briggs Force advance 178
    geography of 184–5
    Italian Red Sea flotilla 15
    key Red Sea port 165
    Platt's losses 187
    pressing on towards 152
    rail links to 184
    road to 27, 214
    strategic possibility, a 245
    surrender 186–7
    Wavell wants to bomb 25
Matilda tanks 153, 159, 181
Maychew, Battle of 197
Mayne, Major-General Mosley 212–16
media coverage 88–90
Mediterranean 5, 17–18, 107, 235, 245
Mega 133, 146
Menelik II, Emperor 11–12, 205
Mescelit Pass 180
Messervy, Colonel Frank 151, 152, 155, 183, 275–6 n75
Metemma 113, 115, 151
MI6 116
Middle East Command 25
Military Administration 221
Military Cross 56, 228
Military Intelligence, Cairo 152
Mill Hill 73, 81, 82
Ministry of Defence 93
Ministry of Information 90
'Mission 101' 95, 97, 193, 195, 199, 278 n32
Mitchell, Major-General Philip 221, 223
Modun 145

Mogadishu 15, 53, 106, 130, 133–7, 144–6
Mombasa
    evacuations to 69
    German focus on 52
    HMS *Barracouta* visits 2
    Indian troops sail for 4
    likely enemy advance 32
    petrol storage 124
    railway links 3
    reinforcements arrive 132
    spared bombing 53
    troops from West Africa 48
Monclar, Colonel Ralph 178, 186
Monte Cassino 171
Montgomery, Field Marshal 241
Moore, Sir Henry Monck-Mason 31, 108, 219, 222
Moorehead, Alan 136
Moroto, River 45
mountains 162
Moyale
    East African infantry 34–5
    evacuations 32
    first significant Italian attack 56
    Fowkes tries to relieve 57
    garrison enlarged 44–5
    garrison reduced 54
    harassing the Italians from 44
    Italian reinforcements 47
    old camel tracks 9
    recovered 133
    subsidiary operations 27
Mulberry harbours 139
mules 74, 170
Munich agreement 63
Mussolini, Benito
    ambitions 12–13
    Aosta and 45, 52–3, 120, 128
    consequences of defeat 247
    declares East African Empire 14
    focus on Egypt 20
    German aims and 19, 100
    giving up without a struggle 140
    invests in settlements for surplus population 36
    lack of military strategy 46
    Nazis' view of 54
    potential frailties of empire 15
    revises strategy 244

Nairobi
    3rd Battalion KAR in 10
    doubt over Giffard's proposals 8

INDEX

in 1903 3
Monck-Mason Moore in 31
officer in charge 30, 34
planning campaigns 118
railway workshops 74
shooting in 122
Nanyuki 34, 44, 57
Napoleon Bonaparte 241
Nasi, General Guglielmo 75, 77, 197, 228, 230–1
Natale, Colonel Leopoldo 197, 198
naval ships 51 see also Royal Navy
Nazis 42, 54, 212 see also Germans
Negelli 27
Nepau 45
New Zealand 6
Nigerian Regiment 30, 57, 125, 209, 217
Nigerians
 approaching Mogadishu 133
 boarding troopships 41
 British-led forces 72
 defence of Tana 125
 occupying key positions 73
 reaching Mombasa 48
 vacating 227
 well suited for fighting Italians 134
Nile, River 18
No. 1 Operations Centre 195
Normandy 139
North Africa
 balancing the units 102
 defeats xi
 East Africa alleged to be distraction from xiv
 multinational forces involved 233–4
 South Africans and 122
 troops moved from 180
 Wavell's view as prerequisite to victory 26, 236
North-West Frontier 190
Northern Brigade, KAR 30 see also KAR (King's African Rifles)
Northern Frontier District xii, 9, 31, 35
Northern Rhodesia 7, 34, 67, 103, 250 n6
Northern Rhodesia Regiment 42, 72, 73, 75, 81
Nosworthy, General Francis 107–8, 266 n53
Nyasaland 7, 31, 34, 250 n6

Observation Hill 73, 82
Odweina 75
Offensive Propaganda 172
oil 6, 245
Omdurman, Battle of 18
Omo River 217
Operational Centres 192
Operations
 'Appearance' 139
 'Battleaxe' 226
 'Camilla' 116–17
 'Canvas' 111, 143
 'Compass' 119, 236, 245
 'Crusader' x, 241
 'Marie' 225
 'Torch' 225
Oran 69
Ottomans 186

Palestine
 British battalions withdrawn from 83
 Giffard moved to 30
 reinforcements from 17
 Wavell's command area 23
 Wavell's troop numbers in 24
 Wavell's unorthodox tactics in 28
Palestine–Trans-Jordan 21
Patriots 193–203
 captured Italians and 175
 control territory around Italians 214, 218
 doubts re reliability 202
 Italian precaution against 199
 looter warning 230
 main role of 203
 map of advance 196
 Nasi tries to cut off 197
 Platt's opinion of 194, 200
 various fighters with 193
 vengefulness of 198
 weaponry of 193
 Wingate on 201
Pemba 2
Percival, Arthur 108
Perham, Margery 71
petrol supplies 124, 212
Philips' School Atlases 33
Pienaar, Brigadier Dan 117, 131, 207, 214, 216
Platt, Major-General William 38–40
 a positive outcome 114–15
 Aosta's death 216
 capturing Massawa 165
 Cheeseman's appointment 96
 control of the air 177
 dedicated mobile column 151
 discussions with Dickinson 30

304

INDEX

does everything asked of him 204
East African Command 231
focuses on Kassala 148
fostering insurrection 200
Gallabat offensive 112
Indian divisions 153, 155, 164, 233
Massawa casualties 187
multinational force, a 163
Patriots, his opinion of 194
road from Asmara, the 59
scuttling of Italian ships 185
sums up achievements 241–2
unsustainable losses 169
use of deception 150
Wavell and Smuts meet 106
Wingate and 202
Poland 16
Ponte Mussolini 163
Port Said 81
Port Sudan 38, 39, 50, 185, 214
Portuguese 231
Premindra Singh Bat 163
Pretoria 106
Pricolo, General Francesco 46
Public Works Department 33
Punch 227
Punjabis 138, 161, 176, 182

railways 3, 115, 184, 224
Railways Workshops 33, 44, 74
rainfall 110
Rajputana Rifles 168, 169
Ras Hailu 197
rations 32
'red bombs' 174–5
'Red Oath' 43
Red Sea
  attractions of to Italians 148
  danger from Italy 16
  Italian Flotilla 15, 51, 244–5
  lines of communication 236
  Massawa 165
  opening of Suez Canal and 11
  safeguarding access to 6, 17
  Umbria detained 149
  Wavell understands importance of 25, 38, 182
Regia Aeronautica 150, 178
Regia Marina Italiana 51
Reserved Areas 224
Rhodes, Cecil 2
Ringrose, Basil 193, 203
Robertson, Colonel Brian 123–4

Rommel, General Erwin 173, 205, 226, 227, 244
Roosevelt, President Franklin D. 187
Royal Air Force
  achieving air superiority 211
  aerial photography and reconnaissance 112, 139
  available resources 41
  identifying Italian artillery 181
  Keren 178
  little support from 25
  Tug Argan 78
Royal Artillery 72, 96
Royal Engineers 9, 102, 123, 131
Royal Fusiliers 161, 177
Royal Mint 98
Royal Natal Carbineers 116
Royal Navy
  air support required 25
  attack on French ships 69
  representative of 22
  ships available 51
  transport of supplies 124, 138
  Volunteer Supplementary Reserve 34
Royal Palace, Addis Ababa 205
Royal Sussex Regiment 83
Royal Tank Regiment 153
Royal United Services Institute 28
Ruanda-Urundi 3
Rudolf, Lake 9, 32, 44, 45, 106

Sabderat 156
Sanchil, Mount 162, 168, 176–7, 181, 188
Sandford, Daniel 95–8, 191–5, 200–2
Santoro, General Giuseppe 53
Savoia Grenadiers
  Keren 165, 168, 182
  last remaining battalions 211
  machine gun battalion 113, 142
  protecting Addis Ababa 199
Savory, Brigadier Sir Reginald 158–9, 164, 166, 168, 170
Schnee, Heinrich 1
Schutztruppe 4
'Scramble for Africa' 1
Selassie, Emperor Haile 95–8, 220–3
  Churchill's intervention 194
  Crown Prince 195
  Ethiopians in favour of 29
  forced to flee 13–14
  George Steer 173
  liberates regional capital 197
  rebel movement awaits return 27

INDEX

Royal Palace 205
   Wingate and 192, 198–9
Senegal 178, 225
Sheikh Pass 74, 75
shifta 55, 56
shipping routes, importance of 51–2
Sidamo 53
Sidi Barrani 99, 153, 158–9
Signal Hill 185, 186
Sikhs 72, 213
Simonds, Major Tony 194–5
Singapore 108, 114
Skinner's Horse 102, 151, 213
Slatter, Air Commodore Leonard 177
Slim, Brigadier William 103, 113–14, 156–7, 202
Smallwood, Brigadier Gerald 207
Smith, Brigadier Arthur 22, 85
Smith, Reginald 116
Smuts, Lieutenant-General Jan
   Addis Ababa decision 206, 207
   additional division offered 118
   appointed commander-in-chief 5
   becomes prime minister 42
   Churchill and 108, 111, 118–19, 235
   domestic tensions 119, 122
   greater responsibility for 105
   increasingly forceful opinions of 106
   international control of East Africa 220
   Kismayu 130
   senior politician, a 19
   united Africa, ideas for 235
   Whitehall turns down offer 43, 49
Soddu 217
Somaliland Camel Corps 50 *see* Camel Corps
Somalis *see also* British Somaliland; Italian Somaliland
   characteristics of 66
   KAR operations against rebels 4
   nomadic population 61
   refugees in Aden 115–16
   trouble with Ethiopians 209
South Africans
   acknowledgement of role 234
   Addis Ababa 206
   aircraft 144
   Air Force (SAAF) 125, 128, 177, 211
   British relationship with 19
   Chalbi desert advance 132
   decisive contribution 214
   field guns 140, 141
   first major military action 117
   forces arrive 49
   loss of unit 137
   political instability 101
   settlers from in East Africa 3
   Smuts put in command 5, 42–3,
   support from requested 37
   tanks 103
   water, provision for 109–10, 123
   Wavell on understrength battalions 119
Southern Rhodesia 33, 71, 103, 133, 250 n6
Southern Rhodesia Air Force 42, 44
Staff College, Camberley 194, 211, 241
Star of Solomon 222
Steer, Captain George xiii, 172, 278 n32
Strada Imperiale 137
Strada Royale 137
Strohm, Dr 246
Subadar Richpal Ram 168
Sudan
   aircraft based in 6, 84
   Churchill's priority 103
   conditions xii
   insufficient garrison 17
   Mahdist threat 11
   mode of governing 18
   rainy season 110
   separate military commands 21
   threat of Italian expansion 19
   Wavell's command area 23
   Wavell's troop numbers 24
Sudan Defence Force (SDF) 38–9, 58, 103, 113–15, 152, 161
Suez Canal
   1869 opening 11
   continued British presence required 7, 69
   Italian threat 19, 20, 37
   one point of access guaranteed 148
   shortens delivery times 5
Sussex Regiment 180
Swahili (language) 219
Symes, Sir Stewart 96
Syria 233

Tana, Lake 195, 228
Tana, River 32, 122, 125, 130
Tanga 4
Tanganyika 3, 7, 19, 43, 47, 100
'Tempest' (code word) 41
Tessenei 59, 156, 169
Tessitore, General Vincenzo 99, 187
Thesiger, Wilfred 192
Times, The x, 89, 173, 239, 245
Tobruk x

INDEX

Toselli, Major 210
Toselli Pass 210, 215
Transjordan 21, 23
Transvaal Scottish 215
Triangle 214
Tripoli (Syria) 6
Tug Argan gap 77–81
  Aosta and 93
  Chater surmises 70
  Churchill questions 91
  difficulties in holding 73
  main defensive effort at 72
Turkana, Lake *see* Rudolf, Lake
Turks 28, 233

Uaso Nyiro, River 32
Ucciali, Treaty of 11
Uganda
  conscription introduced 47
  Germans plan Kenya invasion as far as 52
  Italian East Africa and 14, 19
  mobilisation 1
  population statistics 3
  protectorate established 2
  Railway Workshops 33
Umbria, SS 149, 271–2 n5
Um Idla 195
United States 148, 234, 245 *see also* Americans

van Ryneveld, General Pierre 108
Via Imperiale 210
Vichy France 61, 69, 225 *see also* France
Victoria, Lake 2, 3, 34
Victoria Cross xii, 163, 168, 210
Victoria Nyanza Sailing Club 33
Volpini, General 215

Wadi Halfa 96
Wajir 32, 34, 35, 44–5, 58, 129
Wal Wal 13
Walker, Colonel H.A. 9
Wandagaz 97
War Cabinet 69, 91, 101, 128, 220, 224
War Office, London
  authorises troop sailings 41
  becomes convinced of Mussolini's intentions 15
  Brocklehurst Mission 200
  censorship 71
  Churchill and Wavell 83
  defends itself against Wavell 239
  fails to consult Wavell 135

Mission 101 and Gideon Force 199
  prevalent views within 29
  use of Somalis 116
  Wavell advises on force required in occupied territories 226
water (for drinking) 109–10, 118, 122–3
Wavell, Lieutenant-General Sir Archibald 22–30, 235–40
  4th Indian Division moved from Western Desert 153
  advises on force required for occupied territories 226
  approves attack on Kismayu 125–6
  arrangements with French 64, 65
  Asmara via Keren 165
  Brocklehurst Mission and 201
  Chater complains 68
  chooses Keren title when ennobled 189
  Churchill and 82–3, 91–3, 128, 134, 226, 238–9
  complains of lack of directives 40
  Dickinson and 44
  East Africa and the Western Desert 204–5
  forces and equipment available to 102–3
  given administrative control 66
  modest approach of 233
  objectives for Platt 148
  plan of intimidation 151–2
  pre-war lectures 109, 237
  reads Italian communications 112
  recognised by most as deserving major credit 235
  Red Sea concerns 38
  removed from post 226
  requirements of a good general 237
  Sandford and 95
  Smuts and 106
  South African troops and 119
  strategy of necessity 247
  strengths of 120
  troops from North Africa 180
  use of irregulars 191
  visits Keren 180
  War Cabinet pressure 128
  War Office and 135
  Wingate backed 192, 202
West African Field Force 40–1
West Yorkshire Regiment 58, 174, 182
Western, Lieutenant-Colonel 'Tank' 130
Western Desert
  4th Indian Division moved 153
  11th Indian Infantry Brigade 158–9
  Italians face defeat 129

INDEX

Operation 'Camilla' 116
reversal of fortune 204
Rommel arrives 173
siege of Tobruk x
Smuts's role and 105, 235
Wavell's intended operations in 25, 49, 115, 119
Wetherall, Major-General Henry 207, 227
wildlife 125
Wilson, Acting Captain Eric 82, 210
Wilson, General Maitland 'Jumbo' 86
Wilson Airways 33, 42
Wingate, Major Orde 192–203
    character of 192
    Churchill on 203
    Cunningham and 201–2
    death 201
    first major victory 197
    Haile Selassie and 192, 199
    high opinion of his own contribution 235
    on a white horse 277 n29
    Platt and 200
    presents strategy to Wavell 193–4
    Simon Anglim's work on 277 n3
    smallest British force 202
Wolchefit 203, 228, 229
Worcestershire Regiment 58, 60, 160, 161, 169
Wuchale, Treaty of 11

Yemen 229
Yonte 131
Young, George 244
Yugoslavia 208

Zambezi River 231
Zanzibar 2
Zeilah 70, 77, 78, 79
Zulus 117